The Not-for-Profit CEO

How to Attain and Retain the Corner Office

The Not-for-Profit CEO

How to Attain and Retain the Corner Office

WALTER P. PIDGEON JR.

WILEY

John Wiley & Sons, Inc.

For general information on our other products and services, or technical support, please contact our Customer Care Department within the United States at 800-762-2974, outside the United States at 317-572-3993 or fax 317-572-4002.

Wiley also publishes its books in a variety of electronic formats. Some content that appears in print may not be available in electronic books.

For more information about Wiley products, visit our Web site at *www.wiley.com*.

ISBN: 0-471-64875-2

Printed in the United States of America

10 9 8 7 6 5 4 3 2 1

Dedication

In thinking about who would be the ideal person to dedicate this publication to, several individuals came to mind. Should it be those who came before us, who started a whole new sector to serve humankind? They certainly deserve to be thanked. Should I thank those who understood the need to introduce the first paid, full-time employees to serve not-for-profit organizations? After all, without them, where would we be? I began to wonder if I should dedicate the book to those who transformed mere employees into trained managers of highly successful not-for-profit institutions in the last century. If it were not for those dedicated individuals, the role of the chief executive officers would not exist and they would not have become key players in our not-for-profit institutions today.

What about the current array of quality professionals who are playing a greater leadership role rather than just a pure management role? By doing so, they are helping to move the organizations they serve and the overall CEO role to a higher level than ever. They really need to be thanked as well.

I began to ponder what could happen in the future. Who is going to advance the full-time leadership role in not-for-profits to the level that it richly deserves; namely, a profession? Who are those individuals? Are they conducting research, or will they be conducting research in the future? Will they publish a work that profoundly affects our field, or will they speak out for elevating our career choice to a profession as recognized by people both within and outside of our sector?

So it is that a difficult choice became a little easier when I realized that everyone of these individuals are truly deserving of special recognition.

Therefore, it is my honor and pleasure to dedicate this book to those individuals in the past, present, and future who have spent or will spend their careers with distinction as professional leaders in the not-for-profit sector.

August 2004 WALTER P. PIDGEON JR.

Meet ASAE

The American Society of Association Executives (ASAE), known as the association for associations, is the advocate for the nonprofit sector. Founded in 1920 as the American Trade Association Executives, the society is dedicated to advancing the value of voluntary associations to society and supporting the professionalism of the individuals that lead them. In July 2004, an historic merger (GWSAE, ASAE, the ASAE Foundation, and The Center for Association Leadership) brought together ASAE and The Center for Association Leadership. Within these merged organizations, ASAE is the principal membership organization servicing a market of 295,000 association professionals and business partnerships nationwide, including 75,000 just in the Washington, D.C. metro area. The Center is the primary learning and knowledge source for the association community. It provides education programs, future-focused research and learning communities and identifies and showcases new ideas, thought-leaders and knowledge relevant to association management and leadership.

ASAE AND THE CENTER FOR ASSOCIATION LEADERSHIP: OUR BRAND PROMISE

- The principal resource for ideas, models and learning that advance associations, association professionals, and association business partners.

- A vibrant, stimulating and welcoming community of professionals that inspires those who interact with us to become actively engaged.

- The recognized leader in advancing, promoting and supporting the value of voluntary organizations worldwide.

- The leading model of organizational excellence and execution within the association profession.

Types of Members

There are two types of ASAE members: association executives and business partners. All members join professional-interest sections that relate to their job responsibilities. Sections include:

- Association management company
- Component relations
- Communication
- Executive management
- Finance and administration
- Government relations
- International
- Legal
- Marketing
- Meetings and expositions
- Membership
- Professional development
- Technology

For More Information

Contact ASAE by phone at 202-626-2723; by fax at 202-371-8315; by e-mail at *service@asaenet.org;* or visit *www.asaenet.org* for more information on programs and services available from ASAE. Contact The Center for Association Leadership at *www.centeronline.org* or 202-326-9550.

About the Author

Walter (Bud) Pidgeon Jr. is a recognized authority on how not-for-profit organizations function. He conducts research on the subject and is credited with the first empirical research published on the benefits that volunteering provides to volunteers. He is a published author and consultant in the areas of government relations, volunteering, fundraising, strategic planning, and membership enhancement. Dr. Pidgeon is responsible for the development of a doctorate degree program in association management through a partnership with the Union Institute & University and the American Society of Association Executives.

His previous books include *The Universal Benefits of Volunteering: A Practical Workbook for Nonprofit Organizations, Volunteers, and Corporations* (1998) and *The Legislative Labyrinth: A Map for Not-For-Profits* (2001), both published by John Wiley & Sons, Inc.

Dr. Pidgeon has had a distinguished career as a not-for-profit leader. He has held positions that require expertise in government relations, finance, membership development, program enhancement, fund raising, meeting planning, education and administration. Dr. Pidgeon is currently president and chief executive officer of the United States Sportsmen's Alliance, a 501(c)4 organization, and the United States Sportsmen's Alliance Foundation, a 501(c)3 organization. These organizations represent more than 1.5 million outdoor sports enthusiasts and wildlife management officials at both the federal and state levels. These organizations are headquartered in Columbus, Ohio, and their federal affairs office is located in Washington, D.C.

Dr. Pidgeon earned his bachelor's degree in human relations and nonprofit administration at Salem International University, Salem, West Virginia. His major was an American Humanics, Inc., sponsored program. Dr. Pidgeon earned his doctorate in philanthropy, leadership, and voluntary studies at the Union Institute & University, Cincinnati, Ohio.

Dr. Pidgeon is certified by the American Society of Association Executives as a Certified Association Executive (CAE). He is also certified by CFRE International as a Certified Fund Raising Executive (CFRE).

Dr. Pidgeon is an active civic leader and a volunteer in a number of professional, business, and social service organizations.

Contents

Chief Executive Officers Who Participated in the National Study of Not-For-Profit CEOs

Thank you for providing your advice and insight on how to attain and retain the corner office.

Name	Not-for-Profit Organization
Joseph G. Acker	Synthetic Organic Chemical Manufacturers Association
Jack Advent	Ohio Veterinary Medical Association
John Alfano	Association of OH Philanthropic Home, Housing & Services for the Aging
Andrea W. Aughenbaugh, CAE	New Jersey State Nurses Association
William M. Babcock	Wisconsin Society of Architects
Mark Barford, CAE	Appalachian Hardwood Manufacturers, Inc.
Alvin M. Bargas	Associated Builders and Contractors Association Pelican Chapter
Ann-Marie Bartels, AAP	Mid-America Payment Exchange
Andrew R. Behrman	Florida Association of Community Health Centers
Barbara Belmont, CAE	American School Food Service Association
Edwin W. Benson, Jr.	Country Music Association
William G. Bishop, III	Institute of Internal Auditors
John O. Boyd, III	Business Professionals of America, Inc.
Betsy Browne	National Council of Examiners for Engineering and Surveying

Anne L. Bryant, Ed.D., CAE	National School Boards Association
Dr. Thomas J. Burkgren	American Association of Swine Veterinarians
James R. Castle	Ohio Hospital Association
Dr. Elizabeth J. Clark	National Association of Social Workers
Bill Connors	National Business Travel Association, Inc.
Ann R. Cox, CAE	American Association of Occupational Health Nurses, Inc.
Alan B. Davis	National Association for Campus Activities
Arthur T. Dean	Community Anti-Drug Coalitions of America (CADCA)
Alice DeForest, CAE	American Academy of Periodontology
Garis F. Distelhorst	Marble Institute of America
Andrew E. Doehrel	Ohio Chamber of Commerce
Karen Dreyer	Ohio Petroleum Marketers & C-Store Association
Mike Duffin	Precision Machined Products Association
Kay C. Durnett	Arkansas State Employees Association
Dr. Glenda Earwood-Smith	National Alpha Lambda Delta
Barry S. Eisenberg, CAE	American College of Occupational and Environmental Medicine
Douglas S. Evans	Ohio Library Council
Marie M. Fallon	National Association of Local Boards of Health
Dr. Alan E. Farstrup	International Reading Association
David W. Field, CAE	Accent on Management
Katherine Mandusic Finley, CAE, CFRE, CMP	Association for Research on Nonprofit Organizations & Voluntary Action
Brian Fitzgerald	Easter Seal New Jersey
Richard L. Forman	Associated General Contractors of New Jersey
Donald L. Frendberg	Heating, Airconditioning & Refrigeration Distributors International
William F. Fulginiti	New Mexico Municipal League
Bill Gaskin	Precision Metalforming Association
Roger R. Geiger	NFIB-Ohio
William A. Good, CAE	National Roofing Contractors Association
Robert K. Goodwin	Points of Light Foundation
John H. Graham, IV	American Society of Association Executives
Owen Graham	Alaska Forest Association
Albert C. Gray, Ph.D., PE, CAE	National Society of Professional Engineers
Ann Guiberson, PRP, CAE	Pinellas Suncoast Association of Realtors, Inc.
Phillip A. Gutt, CAE	Association Managers, Inc.
Glenn F. Harvey	The American Ceramic Society

Ruth D. Henning	Firelands Association of Realtors, Inc.
Wayne N. Holliday	American Society for Nondestructive Testing
Alberta E. Hultman, CAE	USFN—America's Mortgage Banking Attorneys
Thomas S. Jackson, CAE	Ohio Grocers Association
Allen James, CAE	Responsible Industry for a Sound Environment
Jady Johnson	Reading Recovery Council of North America
Rob Keck	The National Wild Turkey Federation, Inc.
John H. Klesch	Vermont Retail Association
Anne H. LeClair, CAE	San Mateo County Convention and Visitors Bureau
Larry L. Long	County Commissioners Association of Ohio
Mac MacArthur	Alabama State Employees Association
Paulette V. Maehara, CFRE, CAE	Association of Fundraising Professionals
Anna Marie Mason	Society for Computer Applications in Radiology
Kevin McCray, CAE	National Ground Water Association
Dr. Anne W. Miller	Association of School Business Officials International
D. Alex Mills	Texas Alliance of Energy Producers
Brent Mulpren	Ohio State Medical Association
Allen E. Murfin, CAE	Southwest Hardware & Implement Association
Algie Hill Neill	Alabama State Chiropractic Association
James L. Nell	Rental Housing Association of Puget Sound
Joann Ort	Ohio State Health Network
Jerry S. Panz, RCE, CAE	Wilmington Regional Association of Realtors
Phillip L. Parker, CAE, CCE	Dayton Area Chamber of Commerce
Alexander D. Perwich, II	Golden Key International Honour Society
Rodney K. Pierini	California Automotive Wholesalers Association
C. Allen Powell	National Technical Honor Society
Suanne M. Powell	Ohio Fire Chiefs' Association
Alan T. Rains, Jr.	Family Career and Community Leaders of America, Inc.
Michael O. Ranney	Ohio Psychological Association
Alan H. Richardson	American Public Power Association
Beth Risinger	International Executive Housekeepers Association
Carla Roehl, JD, CAE, RCE, CMP	Cleveland Area Board of Realtors
Amy Rohling	Ohio Association of Free Clinics
Roy Rushing	Ohio Gas Association
Anthony Schopp	Savannah Area Convention and Visitors Bureau
Gary J. Schwarzmueller	Association of College and University Housing Officers

John P. Shumate	American Foreign Service Protective Association
Ann M. Spicer	Ohio Academy of Family Physicians
Mary R. Tebeau, CAE	Associated Builders & Contractors, Inc.
Laura L. Tiberi	Ohio Chapter, American College of Emergency Physicians
Albert E. Trexler III, CAE	Pennsylvania Institute of Certified Public Accountants
Ann T. Turner, Ph.D., CAE	American Association for Laboratory Animal Science
Kelly M. Wettengel	American Board of Bariatric Medicine
Jon F. Wills	Ohio Osteopathic Association
Jeannine Windbigler	Office Business Center Association International
Susan F. Wooley	American School Health Association
Katherine Williams Wright, CAE	The Ohio College Association, Inc.
Roy L. Williams	Boy Scouts of America
Sandra L. Yost, MBA	American Academy of Disability Evaluating Physicians

Foreword

The Chief Executive Officer (CEO) plays two pivotal roles in a not-for-profit organization—one as the chief advisor and counsel for the volunteer board of directors and the other as the leader of the organization's staff. The skills required for these roles have changed dramatically over the years.

CEOs and CEO candidates must achieve higher recognized credentials and have more significant and diverse work experiences than their counterparts did just a decade ago. To meet this unprecedented demand, the not-for-profit field must work together to provide the support and resources necessary to elevate our career choice to a professional status.

The Not-for-Profit CEO: How to Attain and Retain the Corner Office is one of these resources. This publication provides both the incumbent CEO and the seasoned CEO with a reference guide and a workbook on attaining and retaining this sought-after position. The Not-for-Profit CEO traces the historical origins of the not-for-profit community and provides practical advice for obtaining and securing the CEO position.

The publication's contents are based on research conducted by its author, Dr. Walter (Bud) Pidgeon Jr., CAE, CFRE, president and chief executive officer of the U.S. Sportsmen's Alliance. Bud sought advice from hundreds of CEOs, with more than100 CEOs contributing directly to his research. This book is a remarkable contribution to our field.

I highly recommend this publication for students and professionals in the field who aspire to become CEOs someday, as well as to current CEOs who want to bolster their positions or seek new leadership opportunities. *The Not-for-Profit CEO* should be a part of every association executive's library.

President and Chief Executive Officer JOHN H. GRAHAM IV
American Society of Association Executives CAE
Washington, D.C.

Preface

The chief executive officer (CEO) of a not-for-profit organization is one of the most exciting positions to hold if you really want to make a difference. CEOs of not-for-profit organizations hold various titles, including executive director, executive vice president, president, chief staff officer, and chief executive officer. I am personally fond of the title of chief executive officer. It is a term that everyone understands, and it also properly describes the level of responsibility that the number-one professional in a not-for-profit wields.

There is a growing need to encourage qualified professionals to seek the role of CEO in our not-for-profits. Current not-for-profit leaders face increased challenges in finding quality people and the financial resources to fulfill their missions. Staff and volunteers are at a premium, and the increased competition for this limited pool of resources is becoming more challenging.

To react to these challenges, individuals who are employed within the not-for-profit community need to be working toward elevating the role that they play to a full professional status. To accomplish this goal, the quality and breadth of research and credentialing needs to be significantly increased. Research needs to be conducted to discover more innovative ways to meet organizations' needs, and credentialing needs to be increased to properly equip our best professional leaders to make sure that those needs are met.

These dramatic shifts can only happen through acts of leadership. The not-for-profit profession has leaders in its ranks, but not nearly enough of them. To encourage leadership enhancement in the not-for-profit community we must do the following:

- Attract a new generation of quality people to assume leadership roles.
- Provide these candidates with methods and avenues to attain these roles.
- Show them how to retain and flourish in these roles.
- Encourage them to seek even greater leadership responsibilities.

THE GOAL OF THIS BOOK

The Not-for-Profit CEO: How to Attain and Retain the Corner Office is designed for those who aspire to and wish to make a long-term career investment in a significant leadership role in the not-for-profit community.

The book is a product of historical research, two studies in which more than 100 not-for-profit CEOs participated, and the author's professional background. The end result is a text that is both a reference guide and a practical workbook—a rare combination.

Those who can benefit from this publication include the following:

- Individuals who aspire to become a chief executive officer of a not-for-profit someday, including
  ○ Students
  ○ Seasoned not-for-profit professionals
  ○ For-profit executives who wish to change careers
- Current chief executive officers of not-for-profits who wish to gain insight on how to
  ○ Retain their positions
  ○ Open doors to even greater leadership roles

The book spans the life cycle of a professional leader and acts as a core reference on how to make a significant difference in the not-for-profit world, and how to be properly positioned to become a key leader in the not-for-profit community.

HOW THE BOOK IS ORGANIZED

Chapter 1, "The Evolution of the Not-for-Profit CEO Position," provides a historical overview of the not-for-profit community and the changes that have occurred in the CEO role. The purpose of this chapter is to lay the groundwork on how the professional leader position became so vital to the success of a not-for-profit and to provide a sense of history and significance concerning the position.

Chapter 2, "How Not-for-Profit CEOs Attain Their Positions," provides an overview based on practical applications and research concerning how others attained their leadership positions. A companion chapter, Chapter 5, "Suggested Methods of Attaining a CEO Position," provides several practical ideas about attaining a CEO position.

Chapter 3, "How Not-for-Profit CEOs Retain Their Positions," reviews the many challenges and opportunities of retaining a CEO position and being highly successful in that position. Chapter 6, "The CEO's Survival Kit," is a companion chapter that provides a variety of ways to help the CEO maintain the Corner Office.

Chapter 4, "Case Studies of Successful Not-for-Profit CEOs," summarizes the interviews that the author had with 12 CEOs that represented trade, professional, and philanthropic organizations. These interviews cover each CEO's personal road to becoming a CEO as well as their insights on how individuals can attain and retain the Corner Office.

Chapter 7, "Positioning Yourself to Attain a Higher-Level CEO Position," helps the reader to determine if a move is wise from a personal and professional standpoint. It provides a number of ways to find new opportunities, to properly cultivate key individuals, and to secure a new CEO position.

Chapter 8, "Summary of the National Study of Not-For-Profit CEOs," provides an overview of part of the research for the book that involved a study of more than 100 not-for-profit CEOs. The not-for-profit organizations that these CEOs lead are located throughout the country and represent a good mix of missions and IRS classifications. The most exciting finding of the study revealed that participants understood and cherished the CEO role as a vehicle of making a real difference.

The Epilogue, "A Message to Not-for-Profit Volunteer Leaders," provides a reflection by the author concerning the role of the volunteer leadership of not-for-profit organizations in choosing the proper candidate for the CEO position. The author encourages volunteer leaders to more fully understand the unique and vital role that the professional CEO of a not-for-profit organization plays and to strive to attract and maintain quality people in the CEO position.

In this fast moving, technology-driven world, we must still rely on the wisdom and dedication of our leaders. This is particularly true for the professional leader of a not-for-profit organization, the chief executive officer.

If we intend to continue to make history, we need more history makers. To do that, we need to encourage prospective leaders to take the risk to be out front, we need to provide them with the tools to be successful, and we need to reward them for their efforts. *The Not-for-Profit CEO: How to Attain and Retain the Corner Office*, I hope, helps to further these worthy goals.

WALTER P. PIDGEON JR.
PHD, CAE, CFRE

Acknowledgments

$\mathbb{A}$ publication of this kind is not created by one person. From the beginning, I relied on a number of people to make this book a reality.

First of all, I would like to thank everyone at John Wiley & Sons, particularly Susan McDermott, editor, and Jennifer Hanley, senior production editor, for the support they provided—from believing in the project to helping me to produce this book.

I would also like to thank the leadership of the American Society of Association Executives (ASAE) for their support. Greta Kotler, CAE, vice president, Professional Development & Credentialing, supported me in conducting the National Study of Not-For-Profit CEOs. John Graham IV, CAE, president and CEO, believed enough in this project to provide the foreword to the book and helped to make this publication available through ASAE.

I would like to thank Michael Faulkner, senior vice president, Direct Marketing Association, and Jimelle Rumberg, executive director, West Virginia Psychological Association. I had the privilege to serve on both of their doctorate committees, and both of these individuals have provided key information and access to make this publication complete.

I would also like to thank the U.S. Sportsmen's Alliance staff, which supported this effort as well, including Connie Myers, executive secretary; Ginne Beightler, administrative assistant; Christy Harvey, fundraising coordinator; and a special thank you to Patty Leffler, marketing coordinator, for the graphics work.

One of the major reasons that I am able to continue to work on research and publishing projects like this is the love and support that my family provides through encouragement and direct help. A special thank you to my oldest son, Walter (BJ) Pidgeon III, for providing editing support; your expertise really made a difference. To my youngest son, Spencer W. Pidgeon, thank you for your support, and to my wife, Susan W. Pidgeon, thank you for your constant encouragement and devotion.

Finally, I would like to thank every not-for-profit CEO who participated in the two formal studies and the hundreds of other CEOs from whom I received advice and encouragement during the two-and-a-half years this project took. I hope that you are satisfied with the results.

CHAPTER 1

The Evolution of the Not-for-Profit CEO

Lives of great men all remind us we can make our lives sublime, and departing, leave behind us footprints in the sand of time.

Henry Wadsworth Longfellow

INTRODUCTION

To attain and then successfully retain a CEO position in a not-for-profit, an individual needs to understand the role that the CEO plays from an historical perspective. Those who know this historical path are more likely to obtain the Corner Office. The information in this book will be useful for people from a number of different walks in life and career paths, including the following:

- Students who aspire to become a CEO someday
- Not-for-profit professionals who seek advice on what to do to attain a CEO position
- Individuals who wish to enter the not-for-profit community from the for-profit arena
- Not-for-profit CEOs who want to retain their positions
- CEOs who wish to attain even greater leadership positions

All of these individuals need to fully understand the origins of the not-for-profit community. Volunteer boards of directors are charged with the responsibility of securing quality leadership for their not-for-profits, and they have a fiduciary duty to take the utmost care in this process.

Throughout history, humans have grouped together and leaders have emerged. They grouped together for protection and for social reasons, and the pattern has not really changed all that much. While some of us have had the privilege of being leaders from time to time, most of us play the follower role.

Each role, either leader or follower, is equally important if the group is to be successful. The professional leader or CEO of a not-for-profit organization is generally chosen because the governing body of the group, or at least the majority of the group, feels that he or she has the capacity to lead the organization. How this is determined and how one prepares for becoming a CEO will be detailed in later chapters.

It is impossible to place in a single chapter the entire evolution of group activity as it relates to the development of the not-for-profit sector. The purpose of this chapter is to document the origins of the not-for-profit organization, as well as documenting the leadership role that famous and ordinary people played in achieving one of the major social changes of humankind. One of the most exciting parts of this history is the realization that this evolution was one of the underpinnings of a new kind of government that would someday be emulated throughout the world.

Group selection was not generally the practice for humans during the early origins of societies. The group leader was often self-appointed, based on who had the most strength and power. This phenomena can still be observed in a number of species of wildlife today. In fact, the "king of the mountain" methodology still exists in our human culture as exemplified by neighborhood bullies or mighty nations clanging their swords. Although humans have made significant progress, basic social instincts continue to play a crucial role in the selection and retention of CEOs by not-for-profit boards.

To better understand the underlying process and the human factors that determine who will serve as a CEO of a not-for-profit, one needs to look beyond the leadership opportunity and the not-for-profit itself. The truly successful not-for-profit CEO builds his or her success on the overall historical aspects that made this position available in the first place.

THE PROCESS BEGAN MUCH EARLIER THAN YOU THINK

The link to present-day not-for-profits can be traced to the beginning of humankind. Groups or associations fulfill a fundamental function that is as natural as life itself. Organizations bring individuals together for a common purpose. Not-for-profits provide a safe haven, including strength in numbers, and provide a natural outlet for imagination and innovation to flourish.

From the very beginning, humans gathered together into tribes for protection and survival. Yet, ample evidence also reveals that humans found other, more deeply rooted needs to form groups, including socialization factors and the need to help each other. Although little is known about early humans, ample evidence reveals that every group had a leader. Through this group process and the leadership of individual, humans began the process of becoming the dominant species on earth.

The First Recorded Messages

James L. Fisher and Gary H. Quehl noted in their book *The President and Fund Raising* that the first recorded message of people helping others can be found during the Egyptian Civilization within the *Book of the Dead,* which dates to around 4000 B.C. Passages can be found that praised those who gave bread for the hungry and water for the thirsty. Ancient Egyptian artifacts even show evidence of organized trade groups. China, Japan, and India had trade groups as well.

Records were found in the Egyptian tombs of Harkhuf and Pepi-Naknt that encouraged giving and doing good to improve an individual's after life. These tombs date to the sixth dynasty around 2500 B.C. Although these recorded messages are based on individual thought rather than group action, they were some of the core resources for thought, influencing future cultural developments that would emerge in the western world.

It is in the ancient Greek and Roman Empires that the first clear record of charity emerges. "They gave for the benefit of any worthy citizen or for the state, rather than out of pity for the needy." "In Roman terms, people owed it to themselves and to society to establish a sound economic base for their lives and, subsequently, to fulfill their duties as citizens." The Roman Empire also had trade groups that served regulatory protective functions and trained apprentices. More than 2,000 years ago, Phoenician merchants worked together to protect their vessels from pirates.

The Jewish faith fosters sharing what we have with the poor and doing good deeds. Jesus taught that the spirit of the givers is more important than the size of the gift. From ancient Egypt through early Christianity, there was a movement toward religion as a way to influence individuals to help each other. The convergence of religion during these times greatly influenced all behavior.

The Evolution to Nonreligious Groups

In the late Middle Ages when the power of religion began to decrease, a new order started to emerge. Individuals with wealth assisted the growth of the secular state. Those of like interest formed groups, called *guilds,* based on the type of work or trade they performed. Medieval guilds had many reasons for existence similar to not-for-profits today. They were organized for mutual interest. Guilds, however, became rigid and were used to maintain social status and self-interest. They tended to protect the interest of a few at the expense of the craft they represented. Guilds became quite powerful, often taking control of local governments. They began to die, however, in the eighteenth century with the tide of inventions and rise of factories and mass production.

The European Influence

A major benchmark, according to Fisher and Quehl, in the development of the group process occurred in England, during Queen Elizabeth's reign, when "An Act to

Redresse the Misemployment of Lendes, Goodes, and Stockes of Money Heretofore Given to Charitable Uses" became law in 1601. This law is more commonly known as "The Statute of Charitable Uses." This statute marked the first time that a government assumed responsibility for what had been deemed at the time a *charity*.

"The English poor laws marked the watershed between medieval and modern philanthropy." Modern philanthropy and the essence of what we know today as a not-for-profit organization would come much later, however.

The American system of benevolence, both public and private, originated in Europe before colonization began. American immigrants brought their culture with them— a culture that included charity. In fact, American institutions sought and received support from aboard for centuries, and early institutions in America reflected the European models.

"The real founders of American Philanthropy," as Robert H. Brenner noted in *American Philanthropy,* "were men and women who crossed the Atlantic to establish communities that would be better than, instead of like or different from the ones they had known at home."

Thus it was and still is the individual action within a group, either positive or negative, that can strengthen or weaken the cause. Some choose to lead while others choose to follow, but all make the decision to participate, and that is what makes the difference.

Professional societies have their roots in the late Renaissance. The Academia Secretorum Naturae of Naples was organized in 1560 to collect and disseminate knowledge. Several other societies were organized during that period to perform similar functions.

The New World—New Order

The Puritan John Winthrop (1588–1649) came to the New World to create a community for the common good. While European influences helped to shape the new order, the role of freedom cannot be overlooked as a key component of adapting these traditions to better serve everyone in the group.

Susan J. Ellis and Katherine H. Noyes's book, *By the People,* provides a rich history of the volunteer experience in America. The authors noted that the Pilgrims who founded Jamestown, Virginia, in 1607 instituted the Social Compact of 1620 that affirmed the necessity for a government based on the consent of the governed. This document served as a governing force for all of the activities of the Massachusetts Bay Colony. Although the chief reason to come to America was to flee from religious persecution in Europe, the main concern upon arrival was to survive in a land where most of the familiar organizational structures were missing. The Social Compact helped provide some of the organizational structure, but new and different methods were needed to perform tasks for the common good.

The first formal institutions that the Pilgrims formed tended to focus on the reason why they had come to America in the first place, namely religious freedom. By forming their government based on the consent of the governed, the Pilgrims joined in a covenant that bound them strictly to care for each other's goods and for everyone as well. They also accepted the advice and cooperation of Native Americans, who taught the Pilgrims how to live off the land through hunting, fishing and trapping techniques.

From the start, the settlers understood the need to come together for the common cause. Although the early objectives of the pioneers were to survive, they soon used these same principals in every aspect of life. This process has been refined in America for nearly four centuries and is the basis of everything we do including the operation of a not-for-profit.

While America cannot claim to have invented the not-for-profit concept, it can be said that America has refined the process to its greatest height. How did this happen? It wasn't really designed as a grand plan. It occurred mostly out of necessity. There was simply no other way to get things done. Those who settled in the Americas came from countries that had social order, but it was often one sided in favor of a few. The opportunity to challenge and replace this reality existed in the new country. Just as important, those who settled in the New World wanted to create a new order—one that all people could share.

Most things start small, then grow. The not-for-profit evolution in America did as well. At first it was simply neighbors helping neighbors; everything from helping harvest crops to barn raising. Everyone knew that survival depended on helping each other.

One of the first government structures adopted in New England was based on channeling individual thought through a group process—the town meeting. This forum provided an open opportunity to discuss the town's current activities and to achieve a consensus on issues.

In other parts of the country, due to distances between settlements, the family unit became the primary way of tending to needs such as work, education, caring for the sick, and ensuring that each member of the family was a good citizen. In the south, for example, each plantation was self-contained and self-governed. Local parishes maintained a self-help system for other citizens. These early group activities depended on citizens who were willing to volunteer.

Religion played a strong part in early group activity in America. Whatever church was dominant in the community would often direct the social welfare of citizens. For example, William Penn, founder of the Quaker Colony, emphasized religion, charity, and philanthropy. The Quakers felt that there was no conflict between the efforts to live together in the world and the endeavors to improve it. The Quaker meeting, for example, served both a religious and a governmental function.

Social welfare during those early days in America depended largely on individual volunteer participation. Before long, however, clubs, societies, and fraternal orders began to appear. The Scots Charitable Society of Boston, founded in 1657, and St. Andrew's Society of Charleston, South Carolina, established in 1730, are examples.

Private legacies also became common. For example, in 1716, Matthew Godfrey of Virginia bequeathed to Norfolk County his slaves and the income of his 100-acre estate for assistance to the poor. Many of the early colonists were clearly caring and charitable people.

In 1749, the Weekly Society of Gentlemen in New York was formed to seek higher medical standards. The society would evolve into the Medical Society of the State of New York in 1794. Other medical societies formed to more fully address medical concerns, including New Jersey Medical Society established in 1766 and the Philadelphia Medical Society founded in 1765. By 1770, the Philadelphia Medical Society became the American Medical Society. Associations that existed in the colonies were local in scope due to transportation limitations. Carryovers from the guilds in the old country would continue among craftsmen.

Caring for the sick was done on an individual basis. Caring during epidemics often occurred in *pesthouses*. These places were designed to quarantine the sick more than to treat them. Hospitals as permanent facilities were unknown until 1751, when the Philadelphia Hospital was formed as a voluntary philanthropic enterprise.

The first schools were founded and supported by religious groups. Many of the first teachers were clergy. From the beginning, colonists believed that public schools would advance the general welfare of the community. Funding for schools came from fees paid by parents or from wealthy individuals who would endow the schools. The poor were allowed to attend for free. Volunteers would often teach needy children to read and write.

Upon his death, James Logan of Philadelphia left his collection of scientific works to be used as a library. Such donations occurred throughout America dating back to 1656. Ben Franklin organized the Library Company of Philadelphia in 1731 by pooling individual resources to establish a subscription library.

In 1636, Massachusetts clergy founded the first American college. The school was made possible through the generosity of John Harvard and it was named Harvard College. In 1700, Connecticut clergy established an institution that would become Yale College. American colleges differed from their English counterparts in that they were governed by lay boards rather than by clergy. It was the community that organized, funded and controlled them.

Clubs, fraternal orders, and societies had grown considerably by the early 1700s. Philadelphia had a Masonic Lodge as early as 1715. By 1770, Masonic Lodges could be found in most of America's seacoast towns. Other clubs were formed to exchange knowledge or for social reasons. Sportsmen formed jockey clubs in the south and middle colonies.

The group approach was used by religious dissenters in England to offset ineffective efforts from established institutions such as the church or government. In America, this concept was utilized for more practical matters. By 1775, the voluntary organization had become the standard way to deal with any civic problem that the government refused to face.

Lotteries became popular to fund needed services from lighthouses to schools. More than 158 lotteries were conducted before 1776; over 130 of them were for civic or state purposes.

Commercial banking did not exist in America until after the Revolutionary War. Ben Franklin started one of the first savings banks. He also organized the first volunteer fire company in 1736—a concept that soon spread to every major city. He founded the American Philosophical Society in 1743. This is the oldest society still in existence. The American Academy of Arts and Sciences had its start in Boston in 1780.

From 1740 to 1780, American magazines were produced by club-like associations and had a very limited circulation. While the magazine clubs were designed to make money, most contributors had other jobs. Authors and editors usually volunteered their time and received no money for their contribution. By 1820, private-subscription magazines had disappeared. What survived as the main communication vehicles were the newspapers and pamphlets that had advocated the revolution.

In 1764, The Society for the Promotion of Arts, Agriculture and Economy was formed in New York to foster local manufacturing of linens and woolens.

Independence from Old Group Structures

The Committees of Correspondence became the chief network for the American colonists. This was an effective way to react to hostile British activities. In 1772, the Massachusetts Committees of Correspondence was formed and Virginia took similar action in 1773. The committee process gave structure to the growing protest and mobilized volunteer activity across the colonies. The committees became an important symbol of unity and demonstrated democracy at its best. In 1774, the British closed Boston as punishment for the Boston Tea Party. Due to the new unity of the colonies, other colonies responded with generous aid.

Risking charges of treason, the writing and signing of the Declaration of Independence in the heat of the summer of 1776 is one of the best examples of what group activity can produce for the common good. Individuals representing thirteen diverse colonies united together to start a new country and a new way of life. In many ways, the American Revolution was an act of good works by individuals who volunteered to form groups to protest, to defend, and to establish a new type of government that would allow organizations to represent citizens' interests.

THE RISE OF VOLUNTEER-DRIVEN ORGANIZATIONS

The end of the Revolutionary War brought new problems for Americans. The need to self-govern and the methods of accomplishing this task created a great deal of discussion, and it seemed painful at the time. The process they created has stood the test of time, however.

In the early days after the Revolutionary War, most of the social welfare, education, arts, and other functions were handled by individuals. As the country began to grow in population and area, individualized methods gave way to more collective concepts.

Communication became an important issue. The postal service was improved. Samuel Morse worked for more than 10 years without pay to develop the telegraph. Newspapers were gaining a following, and their editors were looked upon as community leaders. The editors sought authors to write stories on a variety of topics. Most of the authors were not paid but they were provided with the opportunity to express their opinion. In the early nineteenth century, well-known American writers formed the Copyright League, which helped to establish international copyright laws to protect writers.

In 1787, the Philadelphia Society for Alleviating the Miseries of Public Prisons was formed and it still exists today as the Pennsylvania Prison Society. The society advocates the humane treatment of prisoners.

The Abington Horse Association was formed in 1847. This organization and others like it were formed as vigilante groups and mutual insurance institutions. Members would patrol other members' pastures and, if a horse was stolen, the association would reimburse the owner out of the association's treasury. These organizations were common until the invention of the automobile.

In St. Louis, The Travelers Aid Society was formed in 1851 to aid travelers. This volunteer-driven group was so successful that other cities formed similar groups.

The Revolutionary War opened a new chapter for American farmers as well. They began to establish business ties with European countries. During this period of organizing for political and social reasons, a number of agricultural societies were formed. The Society for the Promotion of Agriculture, established in 1785, and the Patriotic Society in Virginia, formed in 1886, are examples.

Due to the dominant role that farming played during this time, many business and trade associations did not develop as early; most formed after 1850. However, a few early examples are the New York Chamber of Commerce established in 1768 and the New York Stock Exchange formed in 1792.

American banking had volunteer roots as well. In 1780, a committee of Philadelphia citizens found ways to provide supplies to the Revolutionary army. This produced the first bank in the United States, the Bank of North America. Many of these organizations that began as volunteer citizen groups have evolved over the years into thriving commercial enterprises. Many others, however, remain as not-for-profit organizations. (We briefly discuss their history here, roughly categorizing them for easier review.)

Charitable Organizations

Philanthropy has always been a part of the American scene, although it was traditionally done on an individual basis. Prior to 1850, philanthropy remained a private affair in America. Both the rich and not-so-rich volunteered their time to various groups and provided funding for them. The rich generally left part of their wealth to charitable organizations. The first American Charity Organization Society began in Buffalo in 1877. By 1893, nearly 100 similar organizations were established throughout the country. The New York Charity Organization Society trained workers who became the first paid employees of a charity. In 1887, the first federated fundraising effort began in Denver as the Charity Organization Society. This format would act as the model for the United Way of America.

Charitable organizations were formed in response to the war of 1812. The war was fought with a combination of both regular and voluntary militia. The war also produced the first peace movement. The New York Peace Society was the first organization of its kind not affiliated with a religious movement. By 1828, the group had grown so much that it was renamed the American Peace Society.

The first efforts to coordinate charity and a social welfare plan began to appear in the early nineteenth century. The Pennsylvania Society for the Promotion of Public Economy and the Prevention of Pauperism in the City of New York, established in 1817, are examples that were managed by volunteers. Outbreaks of yellow fever and cholera between 1790 and 1835 lead to the formation of secular orphan asylums. Dorothea Lynde Dix was a notable advocate against the harsh treatment of the mentally ill during the 1840s. She traveled the entire country gathering facts on the subject and reported her findings to Congress. Although governmental action did not result from her efforts, her work helped to motivate voluntary action.

The National Association of the Deaf was founded in 1880 but it would not have professional assistance until 1949. The Volunteers of America was founded in 1896 by Ballington and Maud Booth. They received support in launching the organization from the leaders of the day, including Theodore Roosevelt, John Wanamaker, Bishop Manning and Rabbi Stephen Wise.

A number of organizations were created to address various social problems. Others began to refine previous missions to address social needs. The Salvation Army, for example, while still promoting religion to the poor, began to address the overall needs of the needy.

Educational Societies

Increased interest in adult education occurred in the early 1800s. The concept of the day focused on spreading knowledge to all classes of people. The Mechanics Institute, established in 1826, the Society for the Diffusion of Useful Knowledge, established in 1829, the Lowell Institute, formed in 1836, and the New York City Cooper Union, started in 1859, were among the many organizations formed.

Nationwide, associations were formed in all branches of science and health. The Philadelphia Academy of Natural Sciences, established in 1812, was founded to support scientific study as an avocation. The American Chemical Society was formed in 1876, and the American Psychological Association was established in 1892.

In 1876, librarians founded the American Library Association in Philadelphia to promote the establishment of free libraries. By 1900, more than 9,000 libraries had been built throughout the country.

Health Organizations

Local boards of health began to be founded as early 1797. Concern about public health grew quickly. In 1802, New York established a Vaccination Institute; the next year Boston did the same. Volunteer doctors staffed these group efforts. In 1839, the Nurses Society of Philadelphia was formed. The purpose of the society was to train women to care for ailing poor and to ensure that they were paid for their services. Other medical areas soon began to be addressed. The Asylum for the Deaf and Dumb, established in 1827, the New York Institution for the Blind, founded in 1831, and the New York Ophthalmic Hospital, formed in 1852, were all started by New York citizens.

Health became a major issue in the 1860s. The relationship of health and sanitation became a political issue. In 1866, the Metropolitan Board of Health was formed, which later became the American Public Health Association. The members of this organization were both doctors and lay people. In 1881, Clara Barton helped to organize the American National Red Cross. In 1892, Lawrence Flick founded the Pennsylvania Society for the Prevention of Tuberculosis—the first organization that was devoted exclusively to conquering an individual disease.

Religious Organizations

Religion continued to be a major factor in the lives of early Americans. Therefore, many of the institutions of this time reflected this influence. In 1815, the American Bible Society was founded. Within five years, it had established more than 200 local chapters. The Jewish Independent Order of B'nai B'rith, established in 1843, and the Catholic Society of Saint Vincent de Paul, founded in 1845, were formed to help children and to promote religious beliefs.

In 1851, Thomas V. Sullivan established the first Young Men's Christian Association (YMCA). The purpose of this group was to serve boys who came from rural areas or who had immigrated to America by providing them with a home and good moral base. Protestant volunteers were responsible for carrying out all the activities. The Young Women's Christian Association (YWCA) soon followed.

In New York, the Union Temperance Society of Moreau and Northumberland was formed to stop the use of alcohol in 1808. By the end of 1829, more than 1,000 such societies had been formed. The importing of spirits into the United States fell from $5 million in 1824 to $1 million in 1830. More than 50 distilleries were closed. In 1836, Canadian and United States societies joined to form the American Temperance Union.

Civil Rights Organizations

Early in America's history, free blacks organized self-help groups. Richard Allen and Absalom Jones led the formation of the Free African Society in 1787 in Philadelphia. In Baltimore alone, more than 35 societies existed by 1835.

The time before the Civil War marked a time of major citizen involvement in the concerns of that period. The women's rights movement began with the Seneca Falls Convention in 1848. A proslavery group called the Know Nothings, or American Party, became a strong force beginning in 1854. Movements of the day often tended to be rooted in secret societies such as the Blue Lodge, The Social Band, and Sons of the South. Some of the groups supported illegal acts in order to attain political victories.

Women's suffrage became a major issue. The American Women's Equal Rights Association favored the Fourteenth Amendment. Elizabeth Cady Stanton and Sojourner Truth spoke against the passage of this Amendment due to the fact that it only allowed men to vote. When the amendment passed in 1870, two new feminist groups were established. Stanton broke off and established the National Woman's Suffrage Association to work on women's rights at all costs. The American Women's Suffrage Association took a more conservative direction. By 1890, the groups merged to once again provide a united front for women's suffrage. The new group was called the National American Women's Suffrage Association.

Susan B. Anthony urged the formation of independent unions for women, which led to the Working Women's Association and Protective Association for Women. In 1903, the National Women's Trade Union League was formed by working women, women's clubs, and social workers.

Immigrant groups began to form in the latter part of the nineteenth century. In 1894, the Alianza Hispano Americana was formed to aid Mexican Americans. In 1878, Six Companies was formed to aid Chinese immigrants in representing members to both the U.S. government and to the Emperor of China.

Leisure Organizations and Social Clubs

Early Americans had little time for leisure activities. In fact, there was a widespread disapproval of using free time for fun. As the nineteenth century progressed, however, some holidays began to emerge, and each one was celebrated eagerly. Picnics and other outings became a tradition for families and friends to celebrate a common American holiday such as the Fourth of July.

In 1842, a group of New York business and professional men began to play a sport called town-ball at Elysian Fields in Hoboken, New Jersey. They formed the Knickerbocker Club and adopted a code of rules in 1845. By 1858, the National Association of Base Ball Players had 25 charter club members. The National Rifle Association was incorporated in 1871 to promote recreational gun use and safety.

Secret fraternities began to increase in the late part of the nineteenth century. The Odd Fellows, The Freemasons, The Knights of Pythias, and the Ancient Order of United Workmen were among the largest groups. These groups were open to men only.

Women, however, had a number of groups as well, including The New England Woman's Club of Boston, the National Council of Women, and the Woman's Christian Temperance Union. Many of these organizations joined the General Federation of Women's Clubs in 1889. By 1914, more than one million women were represented by the General Federation of Women's Clubs.

Youth-related organizations began to emerge. By 1906, 50 boys' clubs formed the Boys' Clubs of America and the YMCA helped to establish the League of American Wheelmen to promote bicycle riding. The Big Brothers Association was formed in 1903 in Cincinnati and the Big Sisters Association was established in 1908. Volunteers initially dominated both but paid staff became the dominant force due to the need of having full-time experts.

The Boy Scouts of America was founded in 1910 based on a British model and it soon became the preeminent boys' organization in America. The Camp Fire Girls started in 1910 and the Girl Scouts of America began in 1912. Both became significant girls' institutions.

Conservation of our natural woodlands and wildlife became hot issues at the end of the nineteenth century. The American Forestry Association pressured Congress and state legislatures to protect woodlands. In 1896, the National Forest Commission was formed and aided financially by Congress for a public education campaign. Various outdoor and sportsmen's clubs and associations became directly involved with the conservation of wildlife. They are still the key leaders today.

Trade Associations

The first labor organizations were formed to provide benefits to workers. In the early 1800s more than 20 were formed in New York alone.

The early 1800s also gave rise to professional societies, including the American Statistical Association, established in 1839, and The American Psychiatric Association, founded in 1844. The American Institute of Marine Underwriters was formed in 1820 to support marine underwriters who appraised risk to determine an insurance premium and to collect information so claims could be paid.

In 1847, the American Medical Association was formed. Trade associations began to boom in the years from 1865 to 1877 due to the industrial expansion in America.

More than 100 were formed between those years. The earliest recorded model trade association was the American Brass Association, established in 1853 for the purpose of sharing raw materials and customers.

The majority of trade associations were volunteer driven. In 1868, a federation of local chambers of commerce formed the National Board of Trade to represent member businesses, both nationally and internationally. The American Bankers Association was formed in 1875 to assist its member banks with various aspects of the business as well as for providing social functions for its members.

In 1887, the American Association of Public Accountants developed a code of ethics for accountants. They also helped to open an accounting college and obtained legal recognition for the Certified Public Accountant status (CPA). In 1890, the National Association of Life Underwriters was formed and adopted standards for its industry. In 1895, the National Fire Protection Association was formed by insurance and industry representatives to enact standards, rules, and regulations that would result in lower fire hazards in factories.

In 1854, the American and Foreign Emigrant Protection and Employment Society was formed through philanthropic means to assist in finding jobs for immigrants. Social welfare continued to be a concern for many. The Association for Improving the Condition of the Poor led housing reform. The Working Men's Home Association was formed to build model tenements.

One unusual example of religious groups helping in the industrialization of America happened in the late 1860s. Mormon volunteers constructed 37 miles of railroads between Salt Lake City and Ogden, Utah. The railroad workers began to organize by forming protection associations in 1855, many of which were short in duration.

The Brotherhood of Locomotive Firemen was established in 1873 to help the widows of workers killed in train accidents.

Incidents of strikes began in the early 1870s. The American Federation of Labor was established in 1881 and Samuel Gompers' "Doctrine of Voluntarism" emerged as an influential force.

The Grange was founded as the Patrons of Husbandry in 1867. It was the most popular farm association in the Midwest and the South and it was headquartered in Washington, DC. It was supported by the Department of Agriculture. The Grange attracted mostly small farmers. By 1878, however, the Grange was replaced by various alliances including the National Farmers' Alliance and the Industrial Union.

Several mergers and name changes occurred in the groups that represented farmers. For example, the Wheel and National Alliance became the Laborers' Union of America and became better known as the Southern Alliance starting in 1889. A Northern Alliance was formed in 1880. These alliances all merged becoming known as the People's Party and, eventually, the Populists.

In 1890, the first election the Populists participated in, they managed to gather 21 electoral votes and they elected 5 senators, 10 congressmen, 50 state officials, and more than 1,500 country officials. By 1896, the Populist Party had disbanded, but it had made its point that farming issues were important to the future of the country. The impact of the Grange and other farming organizations that would follow made a lasting impact throughout the country, even in urban areas. Other unions began to form and emulated them. In 1873, for example, the Wyoming Stock-Growers' Association was established, and some say it became as powerful as the Wyoming territorial government.

By the 1890s, trade associations were entrenched as business institutions maintaining offices, electing officials, and holding regular meetings. They served mainly for social functions at the time, but they also lobbied in Congress and state legislatures and developed programs in areas such as standardization and quality inspections. Some trade associations, however, attempted to create unfair market conditions through the use of monopolies and price fixing. Congress passed the Sherman Antitrust Act in 1890 to curb this abuse. Consumers also formed groups to protect their interests. The National Consumers League was formed in 1899 and led a number of fights to improve working conditions and rally for minimum wage laws.

TRANSITION FROM A FRONTIER NATION TO AN INDUSTRIAL NATION

America was changing from a frontier nation to an industrialized nation. Not-for-profits and their leaders, mostly volunteers, played a key role in that transition.

The Niagara Movement called for the end of discrimination. This group lasted only five years, but it lead to the formation of the National Association for the Advancement of Colored People (NAACP) in 1909. The National League on Urban Conditions Among Negroes was formed from a conference held in New York City in 1910. This group would later be known as the National Urban League. The League and NAACP brought the issue of racial prejudice to the public's attention.

The National Federation of Women's Clubs approached Congress in 1908 to request the establishment of a Department of Education. They also asked that their director be a member of the president's cabinet.

Health-related associations began to be formed in the first part of the twentieth century. This was due to a number of factors including new medical discoveries and urbanization issues. A sampling of these organizations include The American Social Hygiene Association, established in 1905, the American Child Health Association, founded in 1909, the American Society for the Control of Cancer, formed in 1913, the Association for the Prevention and Relief of Heart Disease of New York, begun in 1915, the Ohio Society for Crippled Children, started in 1919, and the National Tuberculosis Association, formed in 1904.

The Modern Health Crusade was a national campaign to encourage proper hygiene among youth. Tuberculosis Association volunteers established Modern Health Crusade

Chapters in schools and, by 1920, more than 7 million children had pledged to lead a healthier lifestyle. The Modern Health Crusade was so successful that most schools adopted its principles and the program was discontinued.

In 1907, Emily Bissell created the Christmas Seal program to secure funds for the Delaware Anti-Tuberculosis Society. The seals were so successful they were used nationwide.

The Rockefeller Foundation was formed in 1913 through the leadership of John D. Rockefeller and Frederick T. Gates, a Baptist minister. The group was established to assist a number of educational and medical projects. The foundation became a model for how businesses can support good works.

Throughout this period, trade associations continued to be run by volunteers. New associations were also being formed to answer unmet needs that the more generalized existing associations did not fully address. The number of trade associations grew from around 100 in 1900 to more than 1,000 by 1920. By the 1950s, the number had jumped to around 2000. Trade associations eventually became more professional, hiring full-time staff and forming their own professional society in 1920, the American Trade Association Executives. This group currently operates as the American Society of Association Executives.

The American Hotel Association was formed in 1910; although its mission at the time was a little different than its mission today: "apprehension and punishment to the fullest extent of the law, of professional deadbeats, check forgers, dishonest and undesirable employees and crooks of all descriptions." This is a great example of how a not-for-profit's mission needs to be updated regularly.

The Association of Iron and Steel Electrical Engineers was the driving force for the first Congress of the National Council for Industrial Safety. This group became the National Safety Council in 1914. The council tackled all aspects of industrial, home and street safety. The American Association of Public Accountants voluntarily established a written exam for accountants in every state.

Civic clubs began to appear and became national movements. Their mission was to directly help the community by providing good will and a networking for their members. The Rotary Clubs, established as early as 1910, the Kiwanis Clubs, formed as early as 1916, and the Lions Clubs, started as early as 1916, were among these new entities. Civic clubs like the Kiwanis Club began to focus on youth support at the high school and college level. Kiwanis Key Clubs and Circle K Clubs offered career and community services.

The YMCA helped to form yet another organization called the Toastmasters Clubs in 1924. The program helped members to develop effective speaking habits.

Alcohol became a leading topic during first part of the twentieth century. In 1920, America ushered in Prohibition though the Volstead Act. This was due to the decades of work on behalf of the temperance movement and its leaders. By 1933, the amendment had been repealed through the effort of unions and several associations like the Women's Committee for Modification of the Volstead Act, which later became the Women's Organization for National Prohibition Reform. Alcoholics Anonymous began as a support group in 1934.

War became a major concern by the end of the 1930s. As the United States entered World War II, associations took on major supportive roles. The Association of American Railroads, for example, helped to transport 600,000 troops during the first few months of the war. The Council of Machine Tool and Equipment Services inventoried and cross-indexed 250,000 pieces of production equipment and machinery in more than 450 plants.

POSTWAR EXPANSION

After World War II, not-for-profits began to play an even greater role in America. Some of the war-directed organizations were kept. In 1946, the Civil Air Patrol was reorganized and chartered by Congress. The USO was actually terminated for a brief time, and then reactivated. The War Advertising Council became the Advertising Council.

In the 1950s the American Automobile Association's School Safety Patrol became a common sight in schools.

Voluntary health agencies continued to grow. In 1946, the National Heart Association changed from a group of medical professionals to a lay group. The National Association for Mental Health was organized in 1950, the Multiple Sclerosis Society was established in 1946, and the Muscular Dystrophy Association of America was formed in 1950.

The conservation movement continued to grow with the aid of the Department of the Interior and local, regional and national associations. The American Forestry Association held three conferences from 1946 to 1963 to promote forest protection. The United States Forest Service and the network of national forests would not have been possible without volunteer support and the action of conservation and sportsmen's associations.

During the 1950s and 1960s, a number of organizations continued to advocate their original mission while other not-for-profits refined or expanded their missions to better serve their constituents. There were a number of new organizations that were formed to address a variety of issues from civil rights to the Vietnam War. The American Friends Service Committee maintained its historic mission while protesting the Vietnam War. The National Welfare Rights Organization was formed in 1966 to address public policy relating to poor families.

Government-directed programs became popular during this era. These groups included the Peace Corps, established in 1961, the Volunteers in Service to America (VISTA), and the Serve and Enrich Retirement by Volunteer Experience (SERVE). These programs had varying degrees of success.

The National Alliance of Businessmen (NAB), through the leadership of Henry Ford II, addressed the challenge of unemployment through a highly organized approach that involved thousands of businesses that pledged to hire the hard-core unemployed. The concept was quite successful.

John Gardner created a not-for-profit called Common Cause to encourage America to help rebuild the nation during the Vietnam era of the late 1960s. The organization became a watchdog for legislative issues by motivating volunteers to monitor local government activities. Gardner was also responsible for starting the Independent Sector, which is still an important think tank for not-for-profit issues.

The rise of the use of political action committees (PACs) occurred during the 1970s and 1980s. By the late 1980s, more than 4,000 PACs were registered with the Federal Election Commission. PACs have become a powerful force in informing government officials of the concerns of special interest groups.

The formation of new organizations continued to increase. An organization formed to address the older population in America, the American Association of Retired People (AARP), was founded in the 1960s. AARP became a major power with over 25 million members. The World Federation of Friends of Museums was founded in 1975, and the U.S. Association of Museum Volunteers began in 1979 to address American museum issues.

In Columbus, Ohio, a major grass-roots voter initiative to ban trapping in the state was successfully stopped in 1977 and sportsmen from other states began to ask for assistance on similar issues. As a result, The Wildlife Legislative Fund of America was formed to provide both national and grassroots representation for sportsmen. It is currently named the United States Sportsmen's Alliance. This organization would become the leading advocate group for sportsmen at both the federal and state level.

Habitat for Humanity was established in 1976 to provide housing for the poor, and Mothers Against Drunk Driving (MADD) was formed in 1980 to stop drunk driving. Local and regional organizations continued to be created to address the issues of the day. The Aliveness Project in Minneapolis promoted AIDS awareness. The Points of Light Initiative proposed by President George H. W. Bush encouraged more volunteering and, eventually, gave rise to the Points of Light Foundation which is the leading not-for-profit advocate of volunteering today.

From the latter part of the twentieth century to today, thousands of new not-for-profits were formed, others have merged to better serve their constituents, and still others have ceased to operate at all. In all, the process has worked well. The key for successful not-for-profits has been the quality service they provided through their volunteer and professional talent.

What is so interesting to see is the number of worthwhile organizations that came into existence for a particular purpose and, when the purpose was fulfilled, ceased to exist. We often think that not-for-profits organizations should last forever. The truth is that this is not the case at all. Most of the not-for-profits that were around a hundred years ago are no longer in existence.

The most interesting part of the development of the not-for-profit sector and its leaders has not been told yet. The evolution is still underway. Some of the most powerful organizations of today may be gone in a generation, while the small struggling associations of today may become the giants of the future. Mergers, name changes, refinement of missions and many other factors will play a role in this process.

Just think—at this moment, someone or a small group of like-minded people are probably gathering together to start a new not-for-profit. While the chances of that organization surviving may be low, those organizations who do survive may have a profound influence on our way of life in less than a generation. That is why it is so exciting to have a leadership role in this process.

In my previous book, *The Legislative Labyrinth: A Guide For Not-For-Profits,* I encouraged all not-for-profit leaders to make sure that their organizations are fully represented through an active government-affairs program at the appropriate level, based on the mission of the association. The longevity of any organization is based on worth. If an association can demonstrate true value through various means, then people will join or contribute. Strong mission, good visibility, creative programs, and a sound government affairs program are essential.

Government-affairs programs need to be a key strategic factor for all not-for-profits. This includes 501(c)3 organizations that are able, with certain limitations, to represent their constituents in this fashion. Thousands of not-for-profits do not take advantage of this fundamental right and forgo what our founding fathers meant by a representative government.

DEFINING THE NOT-FOR-PROFIT

The not-for-profit sector is immense. According to the Independent Sector's most recent report on the status of the not-for-profit sector, *The New Nonprofit Almanac in Brief,* 1.2 million not-for-profit organizations exist in the United States with IRS designations of 501(c)3 and 501(c)4. They employ 10.6 million workers and have revenues of over $664.8 billion. They employ 7.1 percent of the work force and represent 6.1 percent of the national income. In addition, 44 percent of the population, or 89 million adults, volunteer. This is the equivalent of more than 9 million full-time employees at a value of $239 billion. More than 89 percent of households donate to not-for-profits; the average annual contribution is $1,620.

The Independent Sector's report did not include 501(c)6 organizations, however. The North American Industrial Classification System 2001 Report estimates that over 100,000 additional civic and social organizations and professional and trade associations exist in America. The bottom line is that the not-for-profit sector is a major factor in the social and economical success of the United States.

Just like the for-profit sector, the not-for-profit community cannot function without leaders who understand how best to serve their market. Not-for-profits come in a number of packages including their IRS classification, but almost all of the not-for-profits in America fall into the 501(c)3, 501(c)4, 501(c)6 categories. Although these groups represent different missions and different constituents, and come in various sizes, each not-for-profit has similar challenges.

It is easy to dwell on the differences between not-for-profits, but successful CEOs focus on the similarities. These similarities provide a base to build a standard in which to measure the effectiveness of the not-for-profit, as well as providing an opportunity to study the qualities that are needed to successfully lead these organizations.

The Volunteer's Role

Volunteering is one of the core functions of a not-for-profit organization. In many cases, thousands of volunteers make it possible for a not-for-profit to dramatically expand its capacity to better serve its constituents. Volunteering is one of the most exciting parts of the process.

Some not-for-profit professionals consider volunteers more of a nuisance than an asset, and they rely on full-time employees to do most of the work of the organization. These professionals are not students of the not-for-profit process, nor do they understand the historical origins of the sector. If they did, they would understand that almost all not-for-profits were started by volunteers. They would also recognize that volunteers and members are the true owners of the organization and, most importantly, that much more can be accomplished if volunteers are used efficiently in conjunction with the staff.

However, the volunteer role is increasingly threatened due to a number of factors, including the lack of time individuals have to volunteer, individual and collective financial concerns, and how new generations view the volunteering process. Today's successful not-for-profit CEO understands the key role that volunteers play. They also strive to discover new ways to attract and retain quality volunteers.

Introduction of the Professional Leader

Paid staff and leaders in not-for-profits can be found in the United States as early as the late nineteenth century. Although their job description differed greatly from today's CEO, the implied role of overseer of the organization was in place. Ultimately, the role of the professional leader emerged when volunteers began to understand that the mission of their organizations could not be maintained without full-time assistance.

The original roles of paid individuals often related to the mission of the organization rather than administrative issues. For example, a health group might have hired nurses to tend to the sick or an advocacy group might have hired lawyers to represent them in court.

Eventually, as the not-for-profit grew, they may have appointed an individual to oversee the administration of the organization. In many cases, the individual was given the title of secretary. This title was still in use as late as the mid-twentieth century to identify the top professional in a not-for-profit. Clearly, the volunteer leaders had absolute power in these organizations.

Today's CEO

Today's not-for-profit CEO role blends the traditions of the past with many of the characteristics of the for-profit CEO. This blend reflects the increased role that CEOs play in a not-for-profit. Today, CEOs need to focus on achieving a core mission, as well as making sure that the fiscal integrity of the organization is maintained. These duties may include the following:

- Supervising large staffs that support thousands of volunteers
- Developing hundreds of programs, including activities that benefit individual members on up-to-full-scale government-affairs functions for the benefit of the group as a whole
- Raising millions of dollars annually to support these activities

The relationship of the CEO with the volunteer leadership has been transformed into a partnership relationship. The leadership, both volunteer and professional, of successful not-for-profits understands the administrative balance that is needed to get things done. Although this relationship is based on a for-profit model, the bonds between the board of directors and the CEO are much more cooperative. In fact, the for-profit sector could learn a few things from the not-for-profit community in the area of governance.

Just like the for-profit community, the not-for-profit community has had its share of scandals. As a result, boards of directors of not-for-profits are requiring more checks and balances. Successful CEOs welcome these changes. They understand the need for them and have the vision to see the opportunities that they bring in attracting quality volunteer leaders and long-term members and donors.

The Future Role of the Not-for-Profit CEO

One of the questions that every CEO of a not-for-profit needs to ask is: Will my association exist in the future? Do not assume that the most visible and successful not-for-profits will be around in 50 years. This is true for a number of reasons. Exhibit 1.1 provides an opportunity to measure how well your not-for-profit organization will adapt to the future.

Every not-for-profit is formed to fill a void. They are designed to achieve a mission that cannot be accomplished by individuals, other groups, government, or for-profit

EXHIBIT 1.1   THE NOT-FOR-PROFIT SURVIVAL TEST

1. *Do you think that your not-for-profit's core mission will be needed in the future?*	Yes ☐	No ☐
Now ask yourself, on what empirical study did you base your answer? If none, it is time to conduct a study.		
2. *Is the average age of your members above the current average age in America?*	Yes ☐	No ☐
If so, your organization needs to focus on younger members.		
3. *Has the quality of your volunteer leadership improved or declined in the last five years?*	Improved ☐	Declined ☐
Less interest in volunteering may be due to a number of factors including less interest in your mission.		
4. *Have you increased your members/donors by an average of 5 percent or more per year in the last five years?*	Yes ☐	No ☐
If you are not increasing your membership/donor base, discover if your competitor is or if your entire field is on the decrease.		
5. *Is your member/donor base diverse enough?*	Yes ☐	No ☐
If your organization has not begun to address how to attract a more diverse participation base, you may find a large drop in numbers in the next decade.		
6. *Could your association survive three or more years if your income was cut by 50 percent?*	Yes ☐	No ☐
The methods not-for-profits use to raise funds is changing; is your organization staying ahead of the curve?		
7. *Is your competition gaining on you?*	Yes ☐	No ☐
Your competition may be another not-for-profit, a government agency, or even a for-profit that you have never considered a threat before. You should widen your focus to determine who may be aiming to take your customers.		
8. *Has public opinion toward your mission increased or decreased in your favor?*	Increased ☐	Decreased ☐
For many not-for-profits, favorable public opinion helps to fulfill the mission and to raise the funds needed to exist. A not-for-profit's survival will depend on identifying both the positive and the negative signs, and through that process, creating a strategic effort to enhance the positive aspects while finding solutions to turn the negative aspects around.		

entities. What would happen if your not-for-profit's mission was being fulfilled by some other means? Could you compete, or even survive? Students of the history of not-for-profits know that thousands of not-for-profits are founded each year while thousands fail, merge, or just fade away.

The entire playing field is changing for not-for-profits as well as every other kind of entity. For example, access to information used to be the major reason why individuals joined associations. Now, individuals can find any information they want with a simple Internet search; they no longer need to get their information through an association membership. Ironically, they are probably finding the information they desire for free on your association's Web site.

Other kinds of organizations are feeling the heat as well and many are expanding their missions into areas traditionally filled by not-for-profits. For-profits are competing for a share of the not-for-profit market in ways that were previously unthinkable. Many for-profits are holding major conferences or, even, conducting extensive fundraising campaigns for the not-for-profit groups that they have formed. While their "mission" is to gain a greater customer base or to create positive community relations, the result is that they are often competing for the same members or funding base as the traditional not-for-profit community. Future CEOs need to understand this trend as well as having the ability to find viable ways to compete with this changing environment.

Diversity and generational issues continue to be major factors as well. Who do you want to be your members or donors in the future? My association's foundation recently conducted a study to determine that question based on current and future interests. We concluded that the current trends over the next decade seem to indicate growth in our field as well as growth for the organization in terms of both members and donors.

While the short-term prospects were good, the long-term outlook was not as positive. The trends showed that the fastest growing populations of minority groups, urban dwellers and individuals under 35 considered our field and our organization's mission to be of a moderate or low level of concern to them. The study, however, recommended ways to reverse these trends over the long term.

Every not-for-profit needs to know how outside trends may affect the organization's stability. More importantly, these studies need to be designed to identify specific challenges as well as to explore practical solutions for strategically reconfiguring the organization to meet the future head on.

Technology is one of the major challenges that CEOs face both now and in the future. For many associations, the difference between success and failure can be categorized by these factors:

- The level of information that they collect
- The ways that they distill that information

- The speed and methods that they use to distribute it to their members and beyond

The shelf life of the average computer system is around three years. This presents a challenge for associations from both an economic and a learning standpoint. Not-for-profits that find ways to overcome these challenges will be the winners in the future.

CEOs that correctly determine the true values and needs of current and potential members will be very successful. A major transitional change is underway, and only those who fully understand it will survive, but lessons from the past can be used to determine how to proceed. Many groups were formed hundreds of years ago to meet various needs. Some survived; most did not. The organizations that did not survive ceased to be relevant to their constituents. CEOs need to determine the following:

- Does your organization have a sound mission for the future?
- If not, can the mission be updated?
- Can the organization survive on its own?
- Should the association merge with another organization?
- If not, should it go out of business?

SUMMARY

The opportunity for individuals to work together for the common good through a collective process within the not-for-profit organization has become the standard way in which we get things done. Although this process evolved as a stopgap measure to fill a void that the community or the government could not perform, it has become the preferred method of operation.

The not-for-profit model is based on an individual's fundamental need to form groups for increased security, socialization and freedom. These early forms of group activity provided the base for the current not-for-profit model.

In the United States, expressing individual thought through the group process became one of the key ingredients in the formation of a new form of government that would become the envy of the world. Immigrants who came to America wanted a form of government that promoted individual freedom and they wanted to be part of the process. The new form of government encouraged citizens to meet in groups and, through the collective process, to persuade elected representatives to advocate their opinions. This process has been successful in promoting both majority and minority opinions for more than 225 years.

The thought of becoming the chief executive officer of a not-for-profit organization may seem like a far-fetched dream. For some it is. Others determine that it is not worth the time or effort and some never really figure out how to attain it. The

Corner Office is not for everyone, but it should not be lost due to a lack of knowledge of how to get there.

Successful CEOs begin their journey to the top position by first obtaining a basic understanding of the origins of the not-for-profit community. Once you understand the historical context in which not-for-profits exist, you will begin to understand the unique role played by those who lead them.

Providing leadership in the not-for-profit community is not just a way of making a living. Instead, it is a profession that is important to the people who you represent, and it is fundamental to the continued advancement of individual freedom and our way of life. Successful not-for-profit professionals, both CEOs and others, understand that careers in this sector are not only rewarding, they are privilege to hold.

The role of the not-for-profit CEO has come a long way. CEOs are no longer playing the secretary's role. They are key players acting as both the chief professional and as a key partner with the volunteer leadership of the association. The CEO is a highly trained and experienced professional who has the educational and professional background to serve her or his constituents well.

CHAPTER 2

How Not-for-Profit CEOs Attain Their Positions

When one door closes, another opens; but we often look so long so regretfully upon the closed door that we do not see the one which has opened for us.

Alexander Graham Bell

INTRODUCTION

It was a cold winter day in Valley Forge, Pennsylvania, several years ago, and I had just arrived at the office. At the time, I was the president of a small, local start-up not-for-profit organization. I had held this position for the past three years.

To say the least, this project had been an incredible challenge. I often wondered if I had made a wise decision leaving the secure middle-management position I held before I accepted this job. I had been with a large organization at which I could have stayed for my entire career.

As I arrived at the office, my secretary told me that I had received a call from one of my professional friends. When I returned the call, my friend immediately told me about a position that had just opened up at a small national organization in his hometown. He thought I would be perfect fit for the position, and he told me that he could arrange an interview prior to the public announcement that the position was open, if I was interested.

Within a week, my friend called and told me that the leadership of the organization would like to meet me. He had arranged for the organization's leadership to meet me for dinner. At dinner, I met with the organization's volunteer officers, who spent most of the night reviewing the association's history and mission and discussing several of the challenges that they faced. I provided a few suggestions on how they might turn the challenges into opportunities.

To my surprise, the next day the chief volunteer leader called me and offered me the position. As I thought about the process, I began to wonder if this opportunity was a matter of luck or something else. In some respects, of course, it was luck, but I had also set into motion a plan that I wasn't even aware of. Over the years, I had networked with this friend to exchange ideas because he held a similar position.

In the process of networking, we had become friends, and I told him about my career goal of becoming a CEO of a national organization. As soon as he heard about the position opening in his area, he thought of me. My friend not only helped me make a strategic career move, he showed me how key positions are often secured through the networking process. The lesson I learned was, it is often who you know and what they know about you that opens the door to future opportunities.

The not-for-profit community is a close-knit group of people in many ways. Individuals who make an effort to network properly can use the process to maximum advantage. CEOs, in particular, can benefit from networking.

The not-for-profit (NFP) CEO holds an important and, in many cases, a powerful position in our society. You can catch not-for-profit CEOs representing certain points of view on the evening news or on shows like *60 Minutes* or *20/20*. Not-for-profit CEOs are visible in a variety of settings at the community level as well. For the most part, these CEOs and thousands of others like them are representing a body of constituents who have chosen him or her to lead. Not-for-profit CEOs represent just about everyone in America in one way or the other. The CEO position of a not-for-profit is not for everyone, but a select number of individuals may envision the not-for-profit CEO's role as a way of fulfilling their lifetime goals:

- Students from all walks of life may want to enter the professional ranks of the not-for-profit field with the hopes of becoming a CEO someday.
- Individuals who hold professional positions in a variety of not-for-profits from social-serving groups to trade associations may begin to eye the Corner Office.
- A business executive from the for-profit sector may wish to switch to the not-for-profit sector to seek a CEO position.

The question they and others like them may have is, how can it be done? The answer to this question is like a lot of things in life—it all depends:

- Are you suited for such a position?
- Is your educational background suited for such a position?
- What are your personal characteristics?
- How timely are you?
- Do you like to deal with people?
- A myriad of other factors are both within and outside of your control.

Most of all, it depends on if you are committed to putting the time and energy into preparing for that opportunity. If you are willing to pay your dues, then the next step is to know the steps and, more importantly, how you can take full advantage of the process.

Yes, some CEOs rise to the top seemingly overnight due to some kind of mysterious clout they or someone else they know may have. Although some beat the system, there is not a thing you can do about it but to find ways to emulate and learn from them in the future. Clout, of course, is something you want to acquire, but most individuals beginning their careers will have to earn it.

This chapter is not for the very few who make it to the top early in their careers. They will be better off skipping this chapter and going to Chapter 3 to discover ways of keeping the job they have attained. This chapter is for those who wish to begin or enhance the process of designing a personal strategic plan to attain a CEO position.

Historical Overview of Attaining CEO Positions

From your review of Chapter 1 you may have acquired a few ideas on how pioneering not-for-profit CEOs attained their positions. Some of them were the founders of an organization. They were the ones who believed in a particular cause and started an organization to fulfill the vision they had. Others attained their positions by being hired to run the office operation only. These individuals usually had little say in the overall process of the group. As the not-for-profit sector began to take hold the process of hiring the number-one professional was refined and the role of that individual began to grow.

Today, the general method of attaining a new career position seems, for some, to be a choice of two alternatives:

1. Stay with one entity and advance through the ranks.
2. Check the want ads in the trades and send a resume for that position.

These two models are used by the majority of those looking for positions in most fields today. Yet, the really good positions are seldom attained this way.

The National Study of Not-For-Profit Chief Executive Officers offers a more creative response to this question (see Exhibit 2.2). The summary of the total survey findings can be found in Chapter 8, and more in-depth interviews with 12 CEOs are found in Chapter 4. Both of these studies provide interesting details on how more than 100 CEOs obtained their current positions. I encourage you to take the time to review the findings to obtain a keener prospective on the subject. While some CEOs still found their positions in the want ads, the greater majority found their positions through various methods of networking and hard work.

Exhibit 2.1 overwhelmingly reveals that nothing beats past experiences. Paying your dues through past experiences far outranked any other category for the chief reason why CEOs gained their positions. As you review both the national study and the individual case studies, note that while some attained their positions by going through the ranks at one organization, most attained their current CEO position by gaining experiences in a variety of positions in more than one organization. While there is no right or wrong way to get to the top, the odds show that advancing through the ranks of one organization may not be the preferred option of gaining a CEO position.

Advancing through the ranks of one organization can place a number of obstacles in your way. Here are some of the important questions that you need to consider:

- Will I be willing to wait longer to attain the position?
- Will current and possible future staff members be seen as better candidates?
- Will a future board reward my loyalty?
- Will the board look for someone outside the organization?

The question of time is always a factor. Climbing through the ranks of one organization often takes longer than advancing your career by assuming greater responsibility at another not-for-profit. It may be that your CEO is retiring soon and you have positioned yourself well to be considered as the replacement. In that case, it may be logical for you to stay for a while. However, if the timeline is several years, it may not be a good idea.

Competition is always a factor. You need to be honest with yourself in evaluating your chances for the top spot among others within your organization. If you are clearly positioned as the number-two person, you may be in good shape. If not, your chances are lower.

EXHIBIT 2.1   THE CHIEF REASONS WHY CEOS WERE ABLE TO ATTAIN THEIR POSITIONS

	First Choice	Second Choice	Third Choice
Formal education	10.89	23.76	21.78
Certifications	1.98	5.94	8.91
Past experiences	69.30	13.86	0.99
Networking	11.88	17.83	20.79
Ongoing training	1.98	2.97	9.90
Other	3.94	7.92	3.96

The not-for-profit board is always the key factor. It is the board that chooses the new CEO. Later in this chapter and also in Chapter 5, I will review the important role that boards play. Keep in mind, the board that is currently in place may not be the board that determines who will be the next CEO in your organization. Will you be able to maintain a high profile with the members of that board in the future? This is probably a question you cannot answer. The real question, however, is, is it worth the risk of staying at one organization to find out?

Boards often do not recognize current staff members as CEO material, even though they should. They often want to bring in someone who can provide a fresh approach to the association, and sometimes they are correct in doing so. In any case, if you are waiting to be selected by your board because you have been loyal and you feel you are qualified, it may not be enough.

Staying with one organization for an entire career and hoping to attain the CEO position is certainly possible, and it might be the best thing to do if you have an especially strong belief in the mission of the association. It is important to recognize, however, that you may not have the same level of opportunity to gain the Corner Office.

If you choose to attain a CEO position at another organization you will need to develop a much more aggressive plan of action. Chapter 5 is designed to get you started. Attaining a CEO position in a not-for-profit, for the most part, is not as simple as answering an advertisement in the trades.

If an ad is placed for a CEO position, which occasionally happens, your resume will be competing with the resumes of several hundred others who have applied. In that case, your future may be determined by someone who is sorting resumes based on predetermined criteria that the volunteer board thinks it needs in the new CEO. This method may not highlight your strong points, which could be the very strengths that the leadership of the organization in question should really be seeking in their next CEO. In the case of the applicant, the selection process depends a great deal on who is sorting the resumes and, frankly, on a lot of luck. Although applying to ads can and should be a part of the process, it should not be the major thrust of the CEO position search.

Test Yourself

Before you begin to gain a better understanding of how the participating CEOs attained their positions, I invite you to do two things:

1. Review and respond to the survey questions that the participating CEOs completed in the National Study of Not-For-Profit Chief Executive Officers (see Exhibit 2.2).

EXHIBIT 2.2   THE NATIONAL STUDY OF NOT-FOR-PROFIT
CEOS SURVEY DOCUMENT

The National Study
of
Not-For-Profit
Chief Executive Officers

In Cooperation with the

*Thank you for helping our profession
by taking the time to complete this important survey*

<u>**A Special Recognition**</u>

We would like to recognize you for your advice and your leadership involvement with this study by

listing your name, title, organization, and city in both the survey findings and in the workbook to be

published by John Wiley & Sons. Please sign here to give us permission.

_____   _____

SIGNATURE   DATE

<u>**Please provide the following information**</u>

_____
NAME
_____
TITLE
_____
ORGANIZATION
_____
STREET ADDRESS
_____   _____   _____
CITY   STATE   ZIP
_____   _____
PHONE   FAX
_____
EMAIL

Please Complete the Following Career Profile

a) Your highest education degree _____, your major _____

b) What certifications have you earned: _____

c) How many years have you worked for: Not-for-Profits _____ [YEARS] and/or for profit Business _____ [YEARS]?

d) Please provide an overview of your current organization: Serve: ☐Local, ☐State, ☐National, ☐International

   My current organization's budget is $_____

   Number of full-time staff in my organization is _____. Do you have local chapters? ☐Yes ☐No
                                               [NUMBER]
   If yes, how many _____ [NUMBER]

   Please indicate, by IRS designation, the number of incorporated entities that make up your organization:

IRS DESIGNATION INCORPORATED	NUMBER OF ENTITIES
501(c)3	_____
501(c)4	_____
501(c)6	_____
For profit	_____
Other [please explain] _____	

e) Please list past employment starting with your first professional position:

POSITION	EMPLOYER	CITY/STATE	BUDGET	STAFF SIZE	YEAR

f) Do you currently have a contract? ☐Yes ☐No. What do you feel are the advantages and/or disadvantages of a contract? _____
   _____

Please Provide Your Advice and Insight on the Following Questions

1 Please rank the chief reasons why you were able to <u>attain your current CEO position</u> (1 BEING THE HIGHEST):
   ___ Formal education   ___ Past experience   ___ On-going training
   ___ Certifications   ___ Networking
   ___ Other, please explain _____

2 What are the major personal skills that have helped you to <u>retain your current CEO position</u>? Please rank in order of importance (1 BEING THE HIGHEST)
   ___ Producer - making goals   ___ Volunteer management   ___ Member relations
   ___ Fiscal control   ___ Planning   ___ Keeping on the cutting edge
   ___ Government relations   ___ Networking
   ___ Other, please explain _____
   _____

(continues)

EXHIBIT 2.2   THE NATIONAL STUDY OF NOT-FOR-PROFIT CEOS SURVEY DOCUMENT *(continued)*

3 What kind of career experiences would you recommend to aspiring CEO's to prepare them for the top position. Please rank (1 BEING THE MOST DESIRED).

___ Program related   ___ Finance   ___ Volunteer management
___ Fund Raising   ___ Membership development   ___ Government affairs
___ Other, please explain _____
_____

4 Do you network with other not-for-profit CEOs? ☐Yes ☐No ~ If yes, why? _____
_____

5 What qualities, in your opinion, do not-for-profit boards seek in their CEOs? Please rank the following (1 BEING THE HIGHEST).

___ Integrity, trust   ___ Leadership traits   ___ Education credentials
___ Staff management skills   ___ Ability to raise funds   ___ Gvmt. affairs experience
___ Volunteer management skills   ___ Successful admin. & fiscal mgmt.
___ Ability to articulate & write a message
___ Other, please explain _____

6 How did you become aware of your current CEO position?
___ Were you a member of the organzation?
___ Did you know someone who was a member or in a leadership position of the organization?
___ Through networking
___ Did you answer an ad
___ Other, please explain _____

7 What were the major factors that helped you to successfully win your current CEO position? Please rank (1 BEING THE HIGHEST).
___ My negotiating skills
___ A well prepared resume and cover letter
___ How I prepared & executed the interview meeting process
___ Understanding what the organization sought in the new CEO
___ Ability to connect with the key volunteer leadership
___ Other, please explain _____

8 What kind of preparation did you do prior to the interview? Please rank (1 BEING THE HIGHEST):
___ Obtained information about the organization via the Internet, etc.
___ Prepared questions to ask and anticipated questions to answer
___ Brought examples of my work
___ Rehearsed
___ Other, please explain _____

9 What were the major three reasons you were selected for your current position?
a. _____   b. _____
c. _____

10 What did you do during the first six-months as a new CEO to cement your relationships? Please rank (1 BEING THE HIGHEST).

___ Met key leadership   ___ Did an overall evaluation of the organization
___ Created a personal plan of action   ___ Insured that proper fiscal controls were in place
___ Evaluated staff   ___ Evaluated volunteer leadership
___ Made significant changes & or refinements
___ Prepared a status report for member leaders
___ Made sure program functions were in order
___ Other, please explain _____

11 What measures have you taken to continue to strengthen your position at your current organization? Please rank (1 BEING THE HIGHEST).

___ Maintain a high level of interaction with key leadership
___ Keep myself as visible as possible with members
___ Keep my organization fiscally sound
___ Raise more income
___ Keep on the cutting edge through training
___ Make sure that a clearly defined strategic plan is in place
___ Insist upon an annual review based on mutually agreed upon goals
___ Find opportunities to speak and write
___ Develop a relationship with the media or trade press
___ Make sure that I am linked to the highest priority issues
___ Maintain a key role in the government affairs function
___ Increase staff effectiveness
___ Other, please explain _____

12 How have you or would you prepare to attain another CEO position? Please rank (1 BEING THE HIGHEST).

___ Check want ads
___ Increase my visibility with the volunteer leadership of the targeted organization(s)
___ Maintain a network that would alert me to possible positions
___ Keep on the cutting-edge through training
___ Become a volunteer at the prospective organization
___ Donate to the prospective organization
___ Other, please explain _____

13 In your opinion, what are the major three changes in the not-for-profit CEO role in the last decade?

a. _____   b. _____
c. _____

14 What do you feel are the major three challenges that not-for-profit CEOs face in the next decade?

a. _____   b. _____
c. _____

15 We would welcome any additional information or advice that you would like to provide that would help to prepare an individual to attain and retain a CEO position in a not-for-profit organization.

_____
_____
_____

Thank You

For taking the time to complete this survey. Your comments will help both current and future not-for-profit CEOs to be more successful and therefore better able to serve the missions and members of their respective organizations.

Please place the completed survey in the envelope provided and foward it to:

The National Study of Not-For-Profit CEOs
c/o Walter P. Pidgeon, Jr.
801 Kingsmill Parkway
Columbus, OH 43229-1137

2. Answer the following questions to determine if you are CEO material:

- What is your highest academic degree earned?

- How many hours a week do you prefer to work?

- How would you gauge your main career objective (e.g., to provide income for my needs, something I enjoy doing, a way to make a difference, etc.)?

- Do you understand the fundamental principles of accounting and finance?

- Do you volunteer? Have you ever managed volunteers?

- Have you ever been in a leadership position? Did you enjoy those experiences?

- Do you have an understanding of a representative form of government? Have you ever participated in any election or cause-related campaign that involved a local, state, or the federal government? If so, did you enjoy the experience?

- Do you enjoy dealing with a diverse group of people?

- Have you ever raised funds for a charity? If so, did you enjoy doing it?

- How many times have you spoken before a group? If you have spoken before a group, how did you feel about these experiences?

As you answer the questions, be honest with yourself. The exercise is designed to reveal the areas that you may need to work on before you enter the hunt for your future Corner Office. Compare your responses to the participating CEO responses as we examine various parts of the survey throughout the book.

Just Who Is CEO Material, Anyway?

A further review of data obtained from Question 1: Please rank the chief reasons why you were able to attain your current CEO position, from The National Study of Not-For-Profit Chief Executive Officers, reveals the basic first step or consideration that every aspiring CEO must ask: Do I have the skills and abilities needed to be a CEO, or can I acquire them? If you have most of them, you are well on your way. If not, they can be acquired over time. The participating CEOs were asked to rank the chief reasons they obtained their current CEO position. The following responses are based on the first three responses of each CEO:

- Past experience
- Formal education
- Networking
- Other (several comments)
- Ongoing training
- Certifications

Note that in Exhibit 2.1 networking came in second for the first response but third when comparing the first three responses. Note also that "Past experiences" was a huge winner with 69.3 percent of the participating CEOs making it their first choice. This finding sends a powerful message to aspiring CEOs to be prepared to pay your dues. Today's not-for-profit boards seek a CEO who can manage the day-to-day operations as well as providing the leadership necessary to fulfill the collective vision of the organization. Board leadership of successful organizations understands that a CEO must have appropriate past experience in the areas of operating a not-for-profit to be successful.

Formal education continues to be a factor in choosing the not-for-profit CEO. While formal education is important, the exact degree level or particular field of study may or may not be important; it all depends on the organization that you wish to lead. For example, educational associations continue to hold a high regard to the level of education that the CEO possesses; a doctorate degree often provides an edge for a candidate. Other associations may want the CEO to have a business-related degree such as an MBA. Technical organizations or professional societies may want a degree that pertains to their mission. A law degree is often sought by various trade association boards, for example. The bottom line is that the formal education credential is often an aid to the candidate.

Networking is one of the most powerful tools that you can use to attain and retain your CEO position. First of all, CEO position openings may not even be made public. Networking brings you closer to the game and often provides you with a number of new opportunities to seek. We will discuss this area of attaining and retaining a CEO position in greater detail throughout the book.

The "Other" response came in fourth out of six answers. It is always interesting when this occurs; 25 responses were recorded. The complete list can be found in Chapter 8, but here are a few of the more interesting responses:

- *"Respect among volunteer leaders."* This is clearly a reply from a CEO who attained his position by advancing through the ranks.
- *"Inside knowledge of the association as a former member."* Obviously, networking played a key factor here.
- *"My referrals."* Having the right people to impress the search committee and board always helps.
- *"Ability to build trust and unity."* All boards are looking for this—the challenge is to convince a board that you have these qualities.
- *"Success in a similar position."* Boards are looking for a good fit.

"Certifications" and "Ongoing training" came in fifth and sixth, respectively. Both are similar in nature to the extent that boards are looking for a CEO that stays on the cutting edge through continual training. However, as the finding indicates, it is not the top reason why boards select candidates to be CEOs. That, of course, does not mean that it is not an important part of the package that aspiring CEOs need to present when applying for a position.

How Should I Prepare to Become a CEO?

Detailed preparation is the key factor. Very few not-for-profit CEOs have ascended to their positions without a lot of planning, positioning, and hard work. It was evident from the participating CEOs that preparation included both formal training and practical experiences. Positioning was also evident. They networked with those who could provide them future access to the career positions that they sought. Hard work was evident as well. They knew that they needed to gain the experience and pay their dues.

What was most interesting was a clear sensation from both the CEOs who participated in the study and 12 CEOs that I interviewed personally that they considered their position as a calling or profession rather than just a mere job. They conveyed a sense that they are doing vital work for either a special group of people or for their country. I encourage you to study the findings of The National Study of Not-For-Profit Chief Executive Officers found in Chapter 8 and the personal interviews of 12 national not-for-profit CEOs found in Chapter 4.

Question 3 on the survey asked, "What kind of career experiences would you recommend to aspiring CEOs to prepare them for the top position?" The results of this question provided a more evenly spread response. I have condensed the responses to the top three responses and placed them in Exhibit 2.3.

Note that "Finance" received the highest response both as the first choice at 22.77 percent and for the top three choices combined at 67.23 percent. "Program related"

| EXHIBIT 2.3 | CAREER EXPERIENCES RECOMMENDED TO ASPIRING CEOS TO PREPARE THEM FOR THE TOP POSITION |

	First Choice	Second Choice	Third Choice
Program related	16.83	6.93	14.85
Fundraising	1.98	5.94	2.97
Finance	22.77	30.60	13.86
Membership development	10.89	8.91	21.78
Volunteer management	16.83	18.81	9.90
Government relations	14.85	7.92	14.85
Other	9.90	1.98	1.98

and "Volunteer management" were tied at 16.83 percent, but by adding the top three responses together, "Volunteer management" received a total of 45.54 percent compared to "Program related" at 38.61 percent. "Government relations" came in fourth as a first choice at 14.85 percent and, for the top three choices, came in fifth place at 37.62 percent. "Membership development" came in fifth place, at 10.8 percent as the number one choice but in fourth place, at 41.58 percent, when comparing the top three choices. The "Other" category came in sixth place as both first choice, at 9.90 percent and top three choices at 13.86 percent. "Fundraising" was dead last at 1.98 percent for first choice and 10.89 percent for the top three choices.

The participating CEOs sent a strong message that finance was by far the most important background skill needed to be a successful not-for-profit CEO. Chief executive officers need to be fully engaged in the fiscal integrity of the organization that they serve. Being fully engaged, however, does not mean that you need to be constantly looking over the shoulder of the individual or department that performs the accounting services and manages the budget.

Successful CEOs need to understand what procedures or safeguards need to be in place to ensure that these functions are performed at the highest standard. The process will depend on the size of the association, but the CEO needs to be vigilant in this area. I meet with my manager of finance and support on a nearly daily basis so I can stay informed. She appreciates that I do not like surprises, so I am kept informed of any changes that may occur. I have a number of checks and balances that I have learned over the years, some the hard way, that help me keep fully abreast of the financial condition of my association on a day-to-day basis. One of the most important members of the CEOs executive team is a good finance person. I am fortunate to have one of the best.

The participating CEOs' choice of "Volunteer management" as the second most important career experience goes back to one of the core elements of how a not-for-profit organization should function. As Chapter 1 detailed, the not-for-profit sector historically has been and still should be volunteer driven.

ACTION STEPS

➤ **Students** who aspire to become not-for-profit CEOs should take courses in accounting and budgeting while they are still in school, and they should find ways to gain practical experience in applying these core principles in a business setting.

➤ **Professionals** in the field should gain practical experience. This can be obtained though offering to help the association with part of the budgeting process or by managing a project that requires fiscal accountability.

➤ **For-profit executives** often have a business background that is a real asset. They will need to adapt these skills to the not-for-profit world.

The role of the professional staff is to support that function. In order to do this successfully, the culture of the not-for-profit has to reflect the proper role that both volunteers and staff play. The successful CEO knows how to create the best blend of volunteer and professional leadership taking into account the purpose of the organization.

Anyone who is planning a career in the not-for-profit sector, particularly anyone who aspires to become a CEO, needs to perfect his or her skills as a volunteer manager. There are techniques that can be learned, but it is really more of an acquired skill. The best solution is to volunteer early and often while you are in school and continue to do so as you enter professional life. If you are currently employed by a not-for-profit, ask if you can gain experience working with volunteers and ask other professionals about how they manage volunteers.

Volunteering provides other opportunities for you as well. In my book *The Universal Benefits of Volunteering,* I conducted empirical research on the volunteer process and created a practical plan of action to attract quality individuals to volunteer. The research documented that everyone who volunteers receives "return value," or various skills enhancements that have lifetime value. The *return value* principle is not only a value for not-for-profit leaders to utilize in their volunteer management programs; it is also a valuable tool for the aspiring CEO to take advantage of by volunteering to gain desirable attributes or skills including leadership traits.

ACTION STEPS

➤ **Students** need to begin to understand the valuable role volunteering plays in not-for-profit-organizations. Volunteer on campus or in a nearby community. Observe the process in action; sit down and discuss what you have observed with a professional in the field.

➤ **Professionals** in the field need to gain experience as a volunteer manager. If your current position does not offer this opportunity, ask your supervisor if you can gain some volunteer management experience.

➤ **For-profit executives** should strive to gain volunteer management experience by volunteering to manage a project at a not-for-profit that includes supervising other volunteers.

"Membership development" came in a strong third place. It is a core skill that not-for-profit CEOs need to know. The core of most not-for-profit organizations is the strength of its membership base. Membership levels vary in associations; they can be as high as 40 million or as low as 10 people. It all depends on the constituency that is served. In most cases, the best way to judge the strength of the membership base is to determine the size of the market and the share that the organization serves in that market.

Membership development is more important than ever as a core skill of a CEO. While she may not be the person whose primary role it is to attract members, the CEO will always be accountable in this area. A good rule of thumb—and one that I preach in my association—is that everyone, whether volunteer or professional, is charged with attracting and retaining members.

Member relations is the number-one priority at my shop. Consequently, we have over a 90-percent retention level and we have increased our member base by over 400 percent in the last six years. Once again, membership development is an acquired skill but certain course work including marketing, communications, and sales can provide a good base.

ACTION STEPS

➤ **Students** should become an active member of two to three organizations and discover how they can serve their members.

➤ **Professionals** in the field need to find ways to gain membership development experience.

➤ **For-profit executives** need to equate membership development with how customers are acquired and, then, distinguish the fine differences.

"Program related" came in fourth as a career experience that participating CEOs felt that aspiring CEOs should possess. The assumption here is that a successful CEO knows that people join organizations to gain something in return. The program that is provided must fulfill these expectations.

Certain core services are in place for most organizations, including the ability to tap into the knowledge base of the organization. Each organization also has unique

ACTION STEPS

➤ **Students** can prepare for this by being up to date on technology and changing cultural patterns including generational and diversity issues.

➤ **Professionals** in the field need to be keenly aware of which programs still make sense, which need refinement and which need to be dropped. Most importantly, they should be aware of what new programs need to be added. New program development, either revamping existing programs or developing new ones, will need to happen at a much quicker pace if an association wishes to remain relevant.

➤ **For-profit executives** need to realize that the not-for-profit program is one of the most important elements of success. It is the product that attracts and retains members.

programs that often set them apart from other groups. The CEO needs to fully under-stand the wants and desires of the members of the organization that he serves. These wants and desires often change, however. They have changed, particularly in the last decade, and they will continue to shift in the coming decades at a much quicker pace. CEOs have to understand how to keep abreast of these changes and to position their associations to meet new needs.

"Government affairs" came in fifth as the career experience recommended by the participating CEOs. Government affairs continues to be an important skill require-ment for not-for-profit CEOs. The successful CEO understands that almost every not-for-profit, no matter what the IRS classification, should have in place some type of government affairs program.

In my book *The Legislative Labyrinth: A Map For Not-For-Profits,* I assembled a number of government affairs experts who provided ample evidence that not-for-profits need to offer their members proper representation. Aspiring not-for-profit CEOs need to understand the fundamentals of how the government works and why not-for-profits have both a role and a duty to lobby for their constituency.

ACTION STEPS

➤ **Students** should take political science courses and get involved in the political process as a volunteer.

➤ **Professionals** in the field should seek on-the-job experience if possible and, if not, they should volunteer with another organization.

➤ **For-profit executives** should gain insight on the subtle difference between corporate and not-for-profit government affairs programs.

When "Other" comes in higher on a survey than one or more of the suggested responses, it is cause to take notice. Here are some of the responses:

ACTION STEPS

➤ **Students**
  ❑ Gain skills and knowledge working with people
  ❑ Look within to strengthen your personal management skills
  ❑ Develop your communication skills
  ❑ Know the skills of goal setting
  ❑ Understand and refine skills to work successfully with groups
➤ **Professionals in the field**
  ❑ Obtain a diverse and different work experience

❑ Gain people management and organizational development skills
❑ Try to attain any position that requires some management skills
❑ Obtain a high level of association management skills
❑ Investigate the various ways to gain training
❑ Find ways to work with volunteer boards as both a professional and a volunteer
❑ Make it a point to be skilled in government affairs
❑ Know how to increase revenue streams
❑ Find opportunities early in a career to manage an entire area in all respects
❑ Become a strategic planner and a visionary
❑ Increase your skills in managing your time and show others to do the same
❑ Always keep promises
❑ Never stop furthering your education
❑ Acquire business management skills
❑ Become as well rounded as possible; do not specialize
❑ Keep in touch with industry and member needs

➤ **For-profit executives**
❑ Develop a broad set of transferable skills
❑ Active participation in the profession represented by the organization is sometimes a plus.
❑ Become aware of the importance of an organization's mission and how not-for-profits run
❑ Volunteer to be on not-for-profit boards to better understand their role

The last career experience that participating CEOs recommended was "Fundraising." Only 1.98 percent ranked this in first place, and only 10.89 percent ranked it in the top three categories. As one who has raised funds for all of the organizations that I have led, including the one that I lead now, I was surprised at this low response.

In looking at the overall responses to this question, 46.53 percent of the participating CEOs listed it between one and seven in importance. The responses peaked at the fourth and fifth response, 11.88 percent and 12.87 percent respectively. In my evaluation, I came to the conclusion that the participating CEOs either felt that finance covered both fiscal and fundraising functions or that many felt that they did not raise funds that much since their association's income was generated mainly from memberships and program related activities.

Whether it takes the form of asking for an outright gift or securing funding through providing value through membership or services, fundraising is vital to the stability of a not-for-profit organization. If you are heading a 501(c)3 organization, you better know how to raise funds. CEOs of these organizations often play a key role in identifying and securing major gifts. If you are a CEO of a 501(c)6 organization, either a professional society or a trade association, raising funds comes into play when you have a foundation, 501(c)3 organization or, even, a political action committee (PAC). In both cases, your personal success is usually measured, at least to some degree, by the level of income secured by these entities.

ACTION STEPS

➤ **Students** should get involved in fundraising opportunities in not-for-profits. Go online and discover the ample literature available on the subject.

➤ **Professionals** in the field need to get some practical background in this area, either at your current organization or by volunteering at another organization.

➤ **For-profit executives** need to understand the importance of fundraising for the average not-for-profit and how fundraising plays a role even in a trade association game plan.

THE ROAD LESS TRAVELED

As noted before, I conducted individual case studies with 12 not-for-profit CEOs. These individuals represent leading national associations with widely varying missions, sizes, and other dynamics. Although the responses of the CEOs were very similar at a quick glance, they all reflect the unique outlooks and thoughts of the respondents. I found this part of the research process to be very rewarding.

To illustrate the diversity of these CEOs, consider the following:

• They have academic backgrounds ranging from bachelor degrees to doctorate degrees with an extremely wide range of majors.

• Their career tenure in not-for-profits range from 8 years to 33 years, while their for-profit tenure ranges from 4 years to 30 years.

• The budgets of their current organizations range from $750,000 to $700 million.

• The number of members in their organization range from 1,300 to 5,950,000.

• The number of employees in their associations range from 4 to 1,100.

• The number of individual or local chapters in their organization ranges from none to 2,200.

Each of the 12 CEOs completed the survey, as well as responding to additional questions on an individual basis. The responses to both the interview questions and the survey for each of the 12 CEOs can be found in Chapter 4. This makes for fascinating reading when you compare the 12 CEOs with each other.

The following questions pertained to how the 12 CEOs attained their current position.

Were there unique circumstances in your past that may have helped you to attain your current position?

Goal   To discover if the 12 CEOs shared common paths to the CEO position or, instead, if they arrived on different paths.

Collective Response   A number of the 12 CEOs noted that either their academic or their association experience helped a great deal in attaining their current position. Some came from a particular industry or professional background while a few had experience as a teacher and one was a minister.

The common thread seemed to be that all of these professions helped them refine the art of dealing with people and focused their energy on getting things done.

Two of the CEOs attained their positions as a result of being involved as a member or being on the board of the association that they now lead. Other CEOs felt that knowledge or working in the field was the key.

The common area for all seemed to be a burning desire to lead a not-for-profit organization. Of the 12 CEOs, 8 had experience as the CEO of another organization before assuming their present position. Two of the four CEOs had only one CEO experience yet they have been at their positions for 25 years and 12 years, respectively Both of the organizations that these individuals lead have grown substantially under their leadership and neither CEO has any desire to search for another position.

Conclusion   Several common traits emerged:

- All had a desire to lead.
- All seemed to look for ways to prepare themselves for the CEO position.
- None of the CEOs were afraid of hard work.
- All had a personal vision.
- None of the CEOs let anyone or anything stop them from attaining their goal.

A few unique circumstances were evident as well:

- Each of the CEOs arrived at the same goal using different paths.
- Some of the CEOs made it to a CEO position early in their careers.
- Some of the CEOs have stayed at one organization for most of their careers.
- Some of the CEOs had experience as CEOs of other smaller not-for-profits and used these experiences to attain their current position.

- A few of the CEOs built their current not-for-profit from a relatively small organization into a very large institution.

If you knew that you would become a CEO of a not-for-profit organization someday, would you have taken different steps to prepare?

Goal   To discover if the 12 CEOs knew where they were going and if they prepared for it. If so, were there common or unique circumstances between the respondents? The question was also designed to reveal experiences that the CEOs may have wished they had.

Collective Response   Most of the CEOs would not have taken different steps in their careers. Several offered advice to aspiring CEOs by outlining the steps that they took, as well as the steps they wish they had taken. The following is a summary of their advice and comments:

Students:

- Take a variety of courses to discover your strengths and weaknesses.
- I spent three years in the military, which taught me a few things.
- I would have taken more business courses like finance and accounting.
- I should have sought an MBA.
- My liberal arts education made a great deal of difference in my success. It provided a good background to learn the art of dealing with people.

Professionals in the field:

- Surround yourself with those who can strengthen your weaknesses.
- I still participate in training courses to keep myself relevant.
- My multimanagement firm experience provided me with a wonderful background to lead an association.
- I sought on-the-job experiences that helped me gain an overall prospective.
- I became a Certified Association Executive (CAE) through the American Society of Association Executives.
- I took graduate courses that helped to strengthen my weaknesses.
- I was lucky that my first professional position was with the Boy Scouts of America; they were very good at showing me the value of organization, volunteer management and fundraising.
- The value of continual education is so important; in fact, I am currently attaining a doctorate degree in Association Management through the Union Institute & University, which is made possible through a partnership agreement with the American Society of Association Executives.

For-profit executives:

- I spent several years in the business that my association now serves.

- I made sure that I understood the differences between a for-profit and a not-for-profit.

- I had an extensive volunteering background; in fact, I created and chaired a not-for-profit for several years.

Conclusion   These CEOs demonstrated that they saw the need for preparation to enter the not-for-profit profession as well as recognizing the need of continuing to keep ahead of the curve through training. For most of the participating leaders, preparation for the CEO position started in college and continued in the various positions that they held throughout their career.

What formal educational courses do you feel that every not-for-profit CEO should have taken?

Goal   To discover the educational background that is best suited for aspiring CEOs.

Collective Response

- Success for not-for-profit CEOs depends on how you deal with people, advanced courses in marketing, negotiations, and use of the media would help.

- Gain more legal and political training, including knowing how Congress really works.

- A law school background may serve a CEO well.

- A good business background

- Students should take course work in organizational behavior, human resources, planning and practical courses in finance.

- Basic courses in finance, accounting and other management areas

- Suggest that young not-for-profit professionals take the organizational development program offered by the Chamber of Commerce

- Keep your choice of courses as broad as possible. CEOs have to know everything.

- Find educational programs or on-the-job training that teach operational system functions.

- Take course work on time management and planning. A CEO has to how to make things happen.

- Financial management seems to be a weakness for most CEOs.

- Expressing yourself through speaking and writing is a must. Try to take courses that provide the opportunity to do both.

- Find a way to take a course on community service or volunteering. It is critical that CEOs understand volunteer management.

- CEOs should take course work in human relations, public speaking, and communications.

- CEOs need to have taken a course that deals with human resource management, particularly the legal aspects of the employee relationship.

Conclusion   CEOs of not-for-profit organizations need the fundamental course work that relates to the business side of the operation. When you review the twelve profiles, the interviews and the survey responses found in Chapter 4, you will discover that most of the CEOs did not have such a background and that they had to gain this knowledge along the way. They did advocate, however, that aspiring CEOs who are still in school would be well served to take core business courses.

Note that the participating CEOs looked beyond the core business courses of finance, accounting and other business administration. They suggested that aspiring CEOs should take courses such as marketing, negotiations, the use of media, law and political science, organizational behavior, human resources management, planning, public speaking, writing, community service and volunteering, human relations, and communications. Knowledge of all of these areas and more are used everyday by successful not-for-profit CEOs.

Students may not be able to find courses available that would cover all of these areas even if they did have the time to take them all. What students need to do is to take core courses that begin this process:

- Basic business courses:
    - Accounting
    - Business management
    - Business writing
- Public speaking
- Community service

All of these courses should be available at any educational institution, with the possible exception of community service. If a community service course is not offered, choose a not-for-profit nearby and volunteer.

Professionals in the field who aspire to become CEOs will obviously have an educational background already, but they may still need additional course work. If so, look into local educational institutions and, perhaps, online programs. Some of the core courses should be taken in-person as much as possible.

I was one of the individuals who needed more course work even though my undergraduate major dealt with not-for-profit organizational work. When I attended college, they did not include courses in various business disciplines so I spent a year attending night school. Part of that course work provided the base for receiving my doctorate degree several years later.

For-profit executives may have already completed impressive business-related course work. However, they may not have had some of the courses specializing in areas dealing with the not-for-profit world. Keep in mind that leading a not-for-profit is different than leading a for-profit. The mission goes way beyond the bottom line and, to accomplish it all, you must motivate volunteers.

What advice would you provide an individual who has set a career goal to become a CEO of a not-for-profit organization?

Goal   To peer into the minds of current CEOs and gain a few insights into attaining the CEO position.

Collective Response   I have divided the responses into three groups: students, professionals in the field, and for–profit executives:

Students:

- Understand what the term not-for-profit really means. It does not mean, for example, that we do not raise the funds needed to fulfill the mission.
- Find opportunities to play leadership roles through sports, student government, clubs, etc.
- Gain a good understanding of government relations from both the federal and state perspective.
- Learn how to prepare a budget and read a balance sheet.
- Have an understanding of the legal aspects of an entity.
- Embrace technology; you will always need to be up to speed.
- Get as broad of an exposure to a number of disciplines as possible.
- Find course work or other situations to obtain a better understanding of what motivates people.
- Take a course in ethics. CEOs need to be ethical to the core, and sometimes it is the most challenging thing you do.
- Take the course work that you really like and excel in it.
- Take the time to learn the fundamentals of finance.
- Become an intern at a not-for-profit to see if a career in the field is for you.

Professionals in the field:

- Understand that building a team effort, including both staff and volunteers, is essential.

- CEOs must have passion in their work; it is not just a job.
- Know how to get the organization's mission accomplished through others. You will not be able to do it all yourself.
- Become aware of the management side of the not-for-profit operation.
- Try many experiences, and learn to stretch yourself.
- Talk with leaders in the field both within your organization and outside to acquire insight on the path you need to take to the top.
- Never stop learning.
- Keep asking for assignments outside your field of interest and solve problems.
- Become a better decision maker and planner.
- Begin to understand the best timing to move to new opportunities.
- Take the time to volunteer yourself, it is not only rewarding but it will help you to better understand how to motivate volunteers.
- Having good ideas is not enough; you have to know how to move your idea from the vision stage to practical application.

For-profit executives:

- Remember that the mission and the stakeholders are the bottom line in a not-for-profit.
- More people skills are needed in not-for-profits.
- You work for the members and you report to volunteers, which is a bit different than the for-profit arrangement.
- While the traditional bottom line is still important, selling the vision to your members is often the key to your success.
- A number of for-profit skills will be an asset.
- Not-for-profit leaders can make a difference within an industry through discovering how their association can provide the value needed to orchestrate effective change.
- From personal experience, it takes some adjusting to come from a for-profit to a not-for-profit environment.
- You need to treat a CEO position in a not-for-profit as more than a job or you will fail.
- Watch the political pitfalls that can occur within a volunteer board.
- Have an open mind and be passionate about the role that you play.

Conclusion   The participating leaders provided some sound advice to those who aspire to become a CEO of a not-for-profit organization. At the core is the passion that you must have to inspire others to share your vision and to work with you to turn your vision into reality. Education is needed in the basic areas as well as the area that one CEO called the "art of dealing with people." The role of a CEO is one of motivating others including staff and volunteers.

Did you have mentors?

Goal   To discover if others influenced the CEO's decision of becoming a CEO of a not-for-profit organization.

Collective Response   Most of the participating CEOs had mentors, and many of them have become mentors to others. When the respondents discussed their mentors, it was obvious that they were very special people in their lives. The details of these mentors can be found in Chapter 4.

Mentors are a very special breed. They give their time to help someone be more successful in life. Some of the CEOs noted that they could tell their mentor things that they could not tell their spouses. If you are an aspiring CEO, chances are that you had or presently have mentors in your life that have gotten you to this point. Don't assume that you can make it to the top without a mentor. While some do, most leaders have one or more mentors in their hip pocket.

As with several of the participating CEOs, my parents were mentors to me. They went far beyond the role of a good parent, and I will be always grateful for their help. One CEO noted that his parents taught him that a simple "thank you" could make a world of difference. How often is this forgotten, both in our personal and professional lives? Volunteers and staff need to be thanked several times a year for the work that they do. It is a simple thing and it is so often forgotten.

Conclusion   Mentoring should be a vital part of anyone's career game plan. Mentoring usually involves someone who has had vast experience in the field that you are pursuing. As Sheila Wellington noted in her book *Be Your Own Mentor,* mentoring can take both a formal and an informal approach. Developing networks can be a substitute for some mentoring functions and should be part of everyone's strategy.

Wellington states, "The single most important reason why, among equal talents, men tend to rise higher than women is that men have mentors and most women do not." The need for mentors for both women and men is obvious.

Students:

If you are still in school, no matter what career you pursue, a mentor will make you more successful. If you have started the process and you have one or more mentors, congratulations. You may need more, however. If you don't have any mentors, get to work—you are going to need them.

So, how do you find a mentor? I had four mentors in college. I knew that I wanted to become a CEO of a not-for-profit when I was in college. My mentors were individuals who wanted me to reach my goal. They ranged from a college professor to individuals in the not-for-profit field. Throughout my life I have had mentors and even now, at my age, I still have a network of associates that act as sounding boards for ideas or help by providing fresh perspectives to problems.

Professionals in the field:

Not-for-profit professionals are busy people; particularly the successful ones. There is a tendency to put off thinking about long-term career goals. Mentors bring you right back to the core questions:

- Where are you heading?
- Is it the direction you want to go?
- If not, what are you going to do about it?

Mentors ask a lot of very hard questions that we sometimes don't want to answer. They are a vital part of your success package.

If you don't have a mentor, look around and discover who can help you achieve your career goal. In Chapter 5, you will find a suggested plan to secure a mentor, called "Find a Mentor." This plan will help you get started.

For-profit executives:

One of the CEOs in the study told me that he had a mentor at his company that made a world of difference in his career. I suggest that those who are entering the not-for-profit world from the for-profit sector should seek mentors in the not-for-profit field to guide them.

Take the Comprehensive Approach

Now that you have all of this advice you may still wonder, how do I put these ideas into practice? Sending out resumes to advertised positions may still be part of the plan. This, of course, depends on a number of factors including how urgently you need a new position. What about search firms? Letting the proper search firms know that you are thinking of putting your papers out is fine, but it should not be your main strategic approach.

Securing a CEO position is quite different than applying for the other positions you may have held. Your future boss is no longer a full-time professional; instead, it is a group of volunteer leaders. These leaders may be dedicated to the mission of the organization but they only have a small view of the operational aspects and needs of the association.

Each member of the board relates to the association differently; therefore, they have individual visions of the role of the CEO in their organization. Most of the time, not-for-profit boards appoint a search committee made up of key leaders to find the new CEO. They may even hire a search firm to assist with this process. If they do, it may make it that much more difficult to get your message to the board.

If you need a position right away, applying for a CEO position is probably not the right thing to do unless you can find other employment in between.

If you are a student or currently employed in either a not-for-profit or for-profit business, then a comprehensive plan makes more sense. Chapter 5 provides a process to get started.

The CEOs who participated in The National Study of Not-For-Profit Chief Executive Officers have provided a wealth of information as well. Their combined comments can be found in Chapter 8. In addition, make sure to read the comments made by the 12 CEOs selected for more in-depth interviews. They can be found in Chapter 4.

THE REALITY CHECK

The not-for-profit CEO position is not for everyone. If you think you would like to be a leader, then take the necessary steps to achieve your goal. The first step is to make sure that you are ready to assume the level of work and commitment that it will take to be successful. If you are not ready, don't attempt it. You will be miserable and it will have an adverse effect on a large number of people, including the staff, volunteers, members, and those served by a not-for-profit institution.

SUMMARY

Take one step at a time. The road to the Corner Office can be traveled in many different ways. It will ultimately be up to each person who aspires to become a CEO to figure out the direction that they must take. However, there are various common areas to explore, and there are ways to emulate or, even borrow, wonderful ideas that you can adapt to fit into your plan. The plan will depend on several variables; the most obvious is the time in your life that you begin the process:

- Some will discover they want to be a CEO of a not-for-profit when they are still in school.
- Some will want to attain a CEO position when they are well into their career as a not-for-profit professional.
- Others will want to cross over from the for-profit sector to attain the CEO position.

Whatever the stage of your life or reason for your desire, the ability of attaining a not-for-profit CEO position is there for those who have the drive and enthusiasm to grab the brass ring.

Is the CEO position of a not-for-profit association attainable by anyone? Of course not. Only a few make it to the Corner Office. From the study and the research, however, those who have made it have followed both a common and yet somehow unique journey to attain their positions. On the one hand, these individuals seem to possess certain leadership traits. They seek education and training throughout their lives and have the skills to get others to work toward fulfilling their vision. On the other hand, successful CEOs all seem to have a unique side, and they have found ways to personalize their career path. They look and act just a bit differently than others, they seem to get noticed as they enter a room, and they are not afraid to work hard to achieve their goals.

These not-for profit CEOs are strong advocates of their organizations' missions. It is the cause, therefore, above all other things, that is their concern.

Those who wish to become a CEO of a not-for-profit organization and to carry on the work that these and other CEOs have performed before them must understand that, like joining any club, you have to pay your dues.

CHAPTER 3

How Not-for-Profit CEOs Retain Their Positions

Leadership is such a gripping subject that once it is given center stage it draws attention away from everything else.

John W. Gardner

INTRODUCTION

It was 11:30 A.M. on the second day of a national convention in the heat of discussion with the board of delegates numbering about 300 that an association CEO received a hand-written message from his chairman. The chairman's note asked the CEO to meet him at his suite at noon. When the CEO came into the suite, the entire executive committee greeted him. Within 10 minutes the meeting was over, and so was the CEO.

The CEO had no idea what had happened. The association was doing fine. Funding and memberships were up, the annual conference had record attendance, and the government–affairs activities were stronger than ever. So, what happened? For now, I will leave that up to your imagination. The important thing is to understand that similar incidents happen all the time, and the reasons for them are not always obvious.

There are many reasons why CEOs of not-for-profits fail. A few are listed in Exhibit 3.1. It would be easy to say that the CEO in the previous example was incompetent or, maybe, cooked the books, or simply didn't make the organization's goals. These are not the reasons that most CEOs lose their positions, however.

Most CEOs lose their positions due to the relationships they have or don't have with the key players in the organization. A relationship problem can be overcome sometimes but, in many cases, the bottom line is that the CEO was not the right fit for the culture of the organization.

EXHIBIT 3.1	WHY NOT-FOR-PROFIT CEOS DO NOT SUCCEED

- They do not pay attention to the bottom line.
- They do not maintain a close relationship with key volunteers.
- They do not relate well with the staff.
- They do not bother to associate with members or donors.
- They keep to themselves.
- They do not seem to care about the mission.

What can a CEO do from day one to avoid the call to the chairman's suite? The *National Study of Not-For-Profit Chief Executive Officers* explores a number of ways that this problem may have been avoided. Please note the details of the study contained in Chapter 8.

The first step in the process starts when you're a candidate for the CEO position. Aspiring CEOs need to be honest with themselves when they interview for a position. They need to ask key questions:

- Is the position a good fit for me?
- Am I the right person to serve this constituent group?
- Can I relate well to the organization's leadership?
- Is the culture of the organization something that I can live with?
- Do I think I can function as the CEO under the organization's governance structure?

What the study discovered was an interesting pattern among CEOs who have successfully retained their positions. The key to retaining the CEO position is less dependent on the technical skills or achievement of organizational goals than it is on the close relationships that the CEOs form with the key volunteer leaders in the organization.

I knew a CEO who maintained close relationships with key volunteer leaders in his association for over a decade. When the CEO announced that he was leaving the organization to assume a CEO position in another organization, the leadership decided to merge the association with another organization. It seems that, due to the respect that they had for the CEO, they would not have taken this action if he had stayed on. That is a great example of the art of human relations.

Although forming close relationships with the organization's volunteer leadership sounds like a common-sense approach, it is not easy to actually achieve. Several factors might cloud this process, including the current culture of an organization, fractionalization of the membership, a poor governance structure, and a disorganized staff. The solution lies partly in three factors:

1. Is the new CEO entering the position for the right reasons?
2. Does the new CEO have the capabilities to manage this type of organization?
3. Does the new CEO have the capacity to lead?

Although it is important that all three of these factors are part of the new CEO's makeup, the capacity to lead will be the prime factor that will help the new CEO to achieve greatness and to win the "hearts and minds" of the key players in the organization. Some say, "Leadership is the process of setting the direction of fulfilling the mission." That is partly true. What that statement overlooks is that someone has to set the direction and someone has to attract others to help move the organization successfully in the intended direction.

Every organization needs to know where it is going. The chief role of the CEO is to help the organization's volunteer leadership to establish clearly defined goals that everyone involved with the association understands and, more importantly, buys into. Bruce Butterfield, president and CEO of the Forbes Group, noted recently, "These are perilous times for associations. Fundamental assumptions about function, form, and funding are under assault by sweeping changes in technology and demographics, and association managers are beginning to wonder whether they and their organizations will survive the onslaught. New association competitors are emerging, such as Microsoft and AOL Time-Warner, that understand that money isn't in the technology, it's in the content." Competition is a newly considered factor for many not-for-profits, although, in reality, they have been in competition for the time and financial resources of their constituents for decades.

CEOs of 501(c)6 associations need to understand that change has always been a factor, but these days it is faster and more interesting. CEOs of 501(c)3 organizations are facing a lot of the same challenges as CEOs of professional and trade associations. In addition, they are faced with increased numbers of not-for-profits that are competing for the same pool of donations. One CEO noted that a local United Way chapter used to serve 25 to 30 organizations. Now the same United Way chapter may serve as many as 1,000 not-for-profits, even though the general funding pool has not grown that much in recent years.

A recent article in the Money section of *USA Today* noted, "Rules change after you take charge." The article was referring to how for-profit CEOs encountered a whole different world in the Corner Office than they knew in the positions they had getting to the top. Not-for-profit CEOs have also expressed the same feelings of isolation, running into mine fields everywhere and needing a completely different skill set.

Bill George noted in a recent article in *Fortune* that, "Today's CEOs are being swayed by every voice—except their own." The title of his article says it all: "Why It's

Hard to Do What's Right." Ethics has become a huge issue in for-profit leadership. It also has and will remain a fundamental issue for the not-for-profit community as well.

CEOs have a rare opportunity to do profound things, both for their constituents and for the general public. But, they can also do detrimental things. It is a choice that every leader must make, and most make the right decision.

Governance can become a major issue in the not-for-profit world. The participating CEOs provided some insight in the role that the CEO, the volunteer leaders and the staff should play. The participating CEOs also knew that governance is not an exact science. Each not-for-profit has its own culture that plays a major role in how the governance functions. The role of the CEO will vary differently due to this phenomenon. I have been the CEO of both staff-driven and volunteer-driven organizations. Neither extreme is beneficial to the volunteers or the staff. A proper blend of volunteers and staff produce the team effect that makes a good organization run smoothly.

The chief goal of a CEO of a not-for-profit is to find the best way to be most effective. If the CEO can achieve this, the organization will use its resources in the best possible way to fulfill its mission. In today's world, this is not an easy task to fulfill. The pressures of the moment always seems to get in the way of taking the time to think about the "what-ifs." Effective CEOs look beyond the moment to visualize what could be changed, modified, or created that could move the organization to a new level of service.

Tom Peters, the management guru of the 1960s, noted in a recent interview, "Wouldn't you like to think that a quiet leader will lead you to the Promised Land? I think its total utter bull, because I consider this to be a time of chaos." Peters referenced his recent book, *Re-imagines,* where he discusses the new realities of business including:

- Destroy to create.
- Women roar.
- It's an XF (Cross-Functional) world.
- Power dreaming
- Think weird.
- Design is the ultimate edge.

Peters feels that you may have to destroy and remake an entire company or face irrelevance. Not-for-profits face similar issues and should heed his advice that strategic change may be the only way to survive.

His reference to "women roar" is due to the power he feels they have in the economy, both from a buyers' role and from a wealth-base standpoint. Not-for-profit leaders need to better understand that diversity roars. The changing demographics of both members and donors are becoming more evident each year and, if organizations do not recognize this, they will fade away.

Peters' reference to the "XF world" refers to his belief that honest and open communications between decision makers is essential. Demolishing red tape and moving on to the greater objective of change is the only way that a company or a not-for-profit will be able to compete.

Peters mentions *power dreaming* in reference to successful companies that sell a lifestyle or an image rather than a largely tangible product. Not-for-profits need to get back to selling their core mission instead of focusing on a benefits package for their mentors.

"Think weird" is Peters' suggestion of attracting gifted people to join your cause to effect true transformation in the workplace. Encourage these people to pursue their ideas and projects and then get them to help you to support your own revolutionary change ideas.

Not-for-profit CEOs need to think a bit weird as well. It may take new and, in some cases, innovative ideas to orchestrate the changes needed for not-for-profits to survive on the new playing field.

In referring to "design, the ultimate edge," Peters feels that companies that ignore the power of elegant and functional design will lose. Not-for-profits that don't design an elegant and functional message and operational structure will also lose. Not-for-profits can no longer get away with simply presenting worn-out ideas.

The role of the not-for-profit CEO is both an exciting and challenging experience. To be successful and to retain your position, as a leader you need to be effective at molding the organization into a brilliant machine that is capable of fulfilling the mission in the most proficient and efficient manner possible.

DEMONSTRATE PERSONAL SKILLS

Once you have accepted the CEO position, you will be eager to show that you are capable of leading the organization. Both your board and your staff will be looking for some sign that you are now in charge. This is a crucial time for the new leader. The first few steps you take will set the tone of your tenure at the organization.

Your personal skills will be tested and, for the CEOs who are ready, it will be what they have been waiting to do for a long time. Examine what the CEOs who participated in the study said (see Exhibit 3.2). Show the volunteer leadership and the staff that you mean business. Show them that you are going to be a major producer and that you are going to achieve and exceed your goals.

Take control of the fiscal operation of the organization right away to make sure that is up to standard. If it is not, immediately implement the necessary procedures and measures to bring it up to the proper standard.

Member relations is an important role, and you should begin that role as soon as you can. A number of members will contact you when you first come on board—make sure that you follow up with them. The time you spend talking and meeting

EXHIBIT 3.2   MAJOR PERSONAL SKILLS THAT HELPED
RETAIN A NOT-FOR-PROFIT CEO POSITION

| | Top Three Responses | | |
Top Five Categories	1	2	3
1. Producer—Making goals	36.64	10.89	12.87
2. Fiscal control	14.85	20.79	16.83
3. Member relations	11.88	14.85	9.90
4. Government relations	8.91	9.90	9.90
5. Volunteer management	8.91	7.92	7.82

with members during this period will be invaluable in establishing yourself in your role and in getting to know the thoughts of the members.

Government relations came in fourth as a priority for the CEOs who participated in the survey. This is an area that a number of not-for-profits do not take full advantage of and it can be an opportunity for a new CEO to open a whole new area of support for their membership. My last book, *The Legislative Labyrinth: A Map for Not-For-Profits,* provides the background and a suggested plan of action to create and refine a government affairs program for any not-for-profit.

Volunteer management was the fifth priority for our participating CEOs. In many ways, it is the foundation for the retention of a quality CEO. Attracting and retaining quality volunteers should be a major goal for a not-for-profit CEO. It is often the key to success or failure.

The CEOs who participated in the study also provided additional advice to leaders who want to be successful. They urged CEOs to do the following:

- Refine people skills. Be able to work well with diverse individuals and groups.
- Improve speaking abilities.
- Find ways to motivate staff to do great things.
- Think strategically.
- Understand and execute the team approach with volunteers and staff.
- Expand your ability to be multitask oriented.
- Refine your management skills.
- Refine leadership role in relation to the major issues that affect the organization, its constituents, or industry.

One of the realizations that new CEOs or, for that matter, seasoned CEOs should determine is that they cannot go it alone. The CEO position can feel very isolated at times. Although it sometimes seems like there is no one to consult with, that is not true at all. The CEO has many people to turn to:

- The network that helped you get the position in the first place
- The volunteer leadership of the organization that you are now leading
- The staff of the new organization, particularly the senior staff
- The growing number of other CEOs that you are getting to know
- Other people who can provide outside advice

Every seasoned CEO in both the not-for-profit and for-profit arena should continually seek advice from outside sources. Business publications from the *Wall Street Journal* to *Fortune* are filled with stories of business leaders advising other leaders. Seeking advice is not unique in the business world, and it shouldn't be unique in the not-for-profit world.

THE FIRST SIX MONTHS IS CRITICAL

Once you know where the stapler is, and after you have rearranged your office and adjusted your chair, it is time to get your administration moving. You are the next generation leader who, in many respects, was elected to your post by the majority of stockholders in your organization, the board of directors. These volunteer leaders saw something in you, and they are waiting for you to set the stage to move the organization to the next level.

In order to do this, a short-term plan of action should be implemented. Each time that I start as the new CEO, I implement a six-month plan to completely review the organization. At the end of the review, I create a report of my findings and present it to the volunteer leadership. The process has a number of benefits for both the CEO and organization.

The process helps the CEO to:

- Understand the entire organization in a short amount of time
- Document the organization's condition at that moment in time
- Discover new opportunities that may be hidden under the surface
- Begin to determine what goals should be undertaken in the future

The six-month review provides a rare opportunity during the honeymoon to get on top of the game. It is a way to begin to "walk the walk," to better understand the values of this particular organization and to begin to embrace these values as your own. Chapter 6 features "The Six Month Plan for a New Not-for-Profit CEO." The plan offers a suggested step-by-step approach that can be easily adapted for anyone's use.

The purpose of the six-month review is to determine if the organization is moving in the right direction. Keep in mind as you undertake your review that the organization may be generally well thought of, it may be increasing its revenue each year, and it may be producing a wealth of programs and activities. At the same time, it might not be fulfilling its core mission.

Not-for-profit organizations go through a number of growth patterns. On occasion, they change direction. The direction might only change slightly at first but, after a period of time, just like being a degree or two off a compass reading, the organization has suddenly veered far off the path of its core mission.

The classic example of this is often when a not-for-profit accepts a new source of funding that has certain strings attached. These strings may call for the organization to alter its program or to be not as aggressive in its issues management activities. The strings don't seem to affect the organization at first, but the bottom line is that the organization has literally walked away from its core mission and no longer fully represents its members.

I know of a large, well respected not-for-profit that determined that its core member base had peaked out. It determined that, if the organization was ever to secure additional revenue, it would have to find it elsewhere. So, by using its brand name, it partnered with for-profit firms to produce goods, magazines, and TV shows that provided both visibility and funds to expand its operations.

As the organization broadened its appeal, however, it suddenly found that it could not represent its original constituency with the same zeal and passion as it once did because it ran the risk of offending the consumers of its products and the readers of its magazines. As a result, the organization began to take a more middle-of-the-road approach or just didn't bother to take a stand at all. While this organization is still well respected by a number of the individuals it serves, it has lost its soul.

So, what is the measurement of a successful organization, and how can a CEO guide the organization to that zenith? First and foremost, the level of revenue that is generated by a not-for-profit organization should not measure success. That doesn't mean that CEOs shouldn't be responsible for raising the necessary funds to fulfill the mission of the organization. However, funding or any other variable should not cause a sudden change in the core mission of the organization.

There are, of course, exceptions to this rule, especially in cases where not-for-profits have refined their mission because the original mission was achieved. Several examples of this are detailed in Chapter 1. The CEO should ask the question, "Is this change weakening the purpose of the not-for-profit to simply fulfill some short-term advantage?" The new CEO needs to determine if this has occurred and put safeguards into place so it doesn't happen in the future.

THE INITIAL REVIEW FINDINGS

The initial review findings will be a great asset to the new CEO. The findings can become a rather large document, which should be separated into logical divisions and made available to both the volunteers and staff. The first product from the find-ings should be a brief report that the new CEO will present to the board in person.

Before presenting it to the entire board, however, you should first present it to key leaders on an individual basis. Make sure that you present it to each person as a draft and have him or her help you refine it. Walk them through the document and explain each point. The document is not really a selling tool; it is a fact-finding tool with a few preliminary recommendations.

The objective at this point is to have your board leadership understand the following:

- You are on top of things and that you understand most aspects of the organi-zation.
- Your role and the roles of the volunteer leadership are clearly defined.
- There are areas that need to be addressed.
- The organization needs a more extensive planning process.
- The new CEO is beginning to move the organization in the right direction.

No matter how experienced the new CEO is, the volunteer board wants to see signs that she understands what the organization is all about and has a pretty good idea of how to manage the operation. When you present the review, they will be impressed with your initiative and with what you have found.

By that time, you will know a lot more about the organization than anyone else. The board will have very little idea about the overall operations and your staff will not know the overall picture either. The CEO is the only person who can see all aspects of the organization. Once the board sees that you have attained that overview, they will count on you as the key person to make it work.

The roles that both the board and the new CEO will play will be determined in the first days of the position. While most of the formal roles for both the board and the CEO have been determined, it is the informal roles that lie on the fringes that still need to be determined. These roles often have to do with the micromanagement issues that can hinder the freedom of the CEO to really make a difference. The review process can help the board and the CEO form a mutual working relationship that is beneficial to all.

The review will outline the areas that need to be addressed. This is not the time to give details on how to resolve these issues but, rather, to place them on the table and to come to a mutual understanding that they will need attention.

More extensive planning may or may not be needed; however, you do not need to spend months planning. Yes, spend some time to create a direction and a method of getting there but, more importantly, make sure that you start implementing the plan. In today's fast-paced environment, the plan may be refined on a daily basis and new opportunities may come your way to achieve the goal in a completely different way. Planning has to be flexible and updated constantly if you want to succeed.

One of the overall objectives of this exercise is to send a clear message that you now have the information that you need to begin to move the organization in the right direction. Now that you have obtained this information, you now need to secure the advice and support of the leadership to make it happen. Most board members will like the direction that you are moving in. It will tell them that you are in control and that you are ready to do great things. After all, that is why they chose you and it will make them feel more confident that they made a good choice in hiring you as the new CEO.

Work with Volunteers and the Board

The key to success for the not-for-profit CEO is creating both a working and a personal relationship with volunteers. A lot has been written about this relationship and how both sides need to work equally well with each other to create the proper environment.

The onus of this relationship, however, sits squarely on the shoulders of the CEO. The CEO needs to create the culture that encourages the proper blending of the roles that both the CEO and the volunteers play. This is not always possible, however. I have been the CEO of one or two organizations that never fully got this relationship. The governance structure was so bent in one direction that neither the CEO nor the volunteer leadership benefited. There are two extremes of this phenomenon:

1. A volunteer-driven culture that does not allow the CEO or his staff to do anything without major involvement from the board. This is the classic micromanagement syndrome.

2. A god-like CEO that dictates to the volunteer leadership what needs to be done and how they will do it

Both of these extremes are counterproductive to the health and vitality of a not-for-profit. Several of the CEOs who participated in the study noted that one of the keys to their success was the ability to build a team effort of volunteers and staff working together to fulfill the mission of the organization.

I have been generally blessed over the years to have professional leadership positions in not-for-profits that understand this principle. I have also been professionally involved with organizations that didn't have a clue in this area. The organizations that don't have a clue are usually those that have very poorly developed cultures. This is often the result of too diverse of a constituency that never agrees on anything or weak leadership on the volunteer or professional side.

In the case of a diverse constituency, there is a 50/50 chance that such an organization will ever agree on anything. It you are in that situation, the best solution may be to split the organization or to find a way to run two suborganizations that report to a federated board with limited functions. In the case of weak leadership, the solution is to find the proper leadership to refine the culture and to move the association in a desirable direction.

My current association, U.S. Sportsmen's Alliance, has a unique and very effective governance structure. When the organization was established, its founder and first CEO, James Glass, came from the business community. The culture that was established for this organization, therefore, had more of a for-profit feel than the traditional not-for-profit model.

The board was designed to attract high-level volunteers who would establish policy and help seek funding, but the CEO was given full responsibility for the day-to-day operations. This was important for this particular organization since its core mission was fulfilled through legislative and legal work that required dozens of quick decisions on a daily basis.

One of the unique aspects of my association's governance that I have found builds team effort without affecting power is that the president and the senior vice president, both professional positions, are given voting rights on the board. Traditionally, not-for-profit CEOs are ex-officio or nonvoting members of the board, and no other staff member has a place on the board.

At the U.S. Sportsmen's Alliance, the president sits at the head of table next to the volunteer chair. The senior vice president acts as the secretary to the board. Our board averages roughly 15 members, so the two votes of the staff members could not change any outcome that the volunteer members want to endorse. It does, however, provide the opportunity to nurture the team approach.

One other tradition has remained, as well. When our board of directors meets at our national headquarters, our entire staff attends the meeting from beginning to end. This includes the formal meeting, the receptions, and meal functions. This practice allows the board to get a more in-depth understanding of the current and future activities of the organization.

The staff presence at board meetings helps familiarize the staff with the concerns and priorities of our volunteer board. Overall, the process fosters an integrated team approach. This board and other volunteers are more comfortable and more likely to team up with staff members to open doors to key individuals or brainstorm new ideas to further our mission.

The CEOs who participated in the study knew that the key to retaining their positions was, in large part, due to their ability to work effectively with their volunteer board of directors. To do this, they had to come to the table with certain core skills. Exhibit 3.3 provides a summary of what the participating CEOs felt were the essential qualities of a successful CEO. Note that the top two responses of "integrity, trust," measuring 68.23 percent, and "leadership traits," measuring 56.41 percent, far outscored the three other top qualities.

Volunteer boards seek a CEO who has soundness of character and moral wholeness and honesty. They want someone they can trust. Therefore, one of the major goals of any CEO is to earn the reputation of being trustworthy.

EXHIBIT 3.3   QUALITIES THAT NOT-FOR-PROFIT BOARDS
OF DIRECTORS SEEK IN THE CEO

| | Top Three Responses | | | |
Top Five Categories	1	2	3	Total
1. Integrity, trust	41.5	16.83	9.90	68.23
2. Leadership traits	37.6	9.90	8.91	56.41
3. Successful admininstration and fiscal management	7.92	11.88	24.75	44.55
4. Staff management skills	1.98	8.91	11.88	22.77
5. Articulate and good writing skills	1.98	5.94	12.87	20.79

The participating CEOs selected leadership traits as the second most important quality. This is not a surprise, as a not-for-profit CEO needs to be a leader first and a manager second. Managers are a dime a dozen, but leaders are rare, and every not-for-profit board wants to have one. To be successful, therefore, the CEO needs to possess leadership traits. How one acquires leadership traits can be debated. Certain individuals are born with a desire to lead, but if that quality is not nurtured, it will not blossom.

Not everyone who makes it to the Corner Office is a leader, however. The not-for-profit community certainly has its share of manager CEOs. These individuals may be good administrators and, therefore, they may be able to keep the not-for-profit functioning. However, they do not have the passion to move the organization to a higher level of service.

In my book *The Universal Benefits of Volunteering: A Practical Workbook for Nonprofit Organizations, Volunteers, and Corporations,* I outlined and expanded on my empirical study researching value that volunteers receive from their service. Leadership traits are chief among the numerous benefits that individuals receive from their experiences. Keeping these skills sharp is a major incentive for CEOs to volunteer in different organizations.

Another thing that not-for-profit organizations can learn from the for-profit community is the number of individuals that should sit on a board of directors. Take a look at the following:

- The average for-profit board size is 10.9.
- The largest board has 31 members.
- The smallest board has 3 members.

Think of the largest corporations in America and, then, consider that these multi-billion-dollar conglomerates are being administered by no more than 31 members on their boards of directors.

The not-for-profit community seems to favor large boards. This stems from the thought that a larger board can produce greater volunteer support and funding. I was once the CEO of a not-for-profit organization with a board of directors numbering into the hundreds. It was a zoo every time they met. It took more time than it was worth to prepare and conduct the meetings, and they produced little or no meaningful results.

My suggestion to CEOs who are stuck with large boards is to try to quell the large-board concept through a strategic planning exercise. If this does not work, see if you can change the large board into a board of delegates that meets yearly and assemble a small action-oriented board made up of your best volunteers. That is what I did with the association I just mentioned. In that particular case, we had an executive committee of less than 20 members that we simply converted into the board of directors.

The successful organizations that are light on their feet, are action oriented, and make the most effective difference have small boards that meet a couple times a year. In between those meetings, the members are actually out doing something to further the cause. If you have selected the right people for the board, they will have little time to go to meetings to discuss theory. You need to put them to work where it counts—where the action is. Quality volunteers will thank you for respecting their time.

Recruitment of board members and other volunteers has become a greater challenge in the last decade due to the lack of time that quality prospects have to spend and the competition from other not-for-profits. Recruiting the right people is impossible unless you have a quality product to attract them. Even quality organizations have a tough time finding and persuading the right individuals to volunteer.

Organizations that have a successful ongoing volunteer recruitment program work really hard at it. The idea of spending time doing good works is not good enough to attract people anymore. You need to find out what the volunteer wants out of the experience, and you need to find a way to deliver it with a bright bow on it. In my book, *The Universal Benefits of Volunteering,* I laid out a detailed plan to help not-for-profits accomplish this task.

The best volunteer experiences are those that are enjoyable and those that the volunteer can see are truly helping to fulfill the mission of the organization. I am a great believer that everything we do for volunteers has to have an element of fun and meaningful results. If a volunteer position can't produce both of these qualities, it should be refined or dropped.

But, certainly not every volunteer experience can be fun? Wrong. Whether you are volunteering to help terminal patients or digging a ditch at a youth camp, the not-for-profit organization can make it a fun experience with activities before or after the volunteer act. They can provide the proper recognition for every volunteer; a recognition that tells them how much they are appreciated for their meaningful efforts. The CEO and other not-for-profit professionals need to provide these important parts of the volunteer experience. If volunteers are recruited well, nurtured through the volunteer experience and then recognized for the contribution that they have made, the not-for-profit will retain more volunteers as well as attracting others.

The CEO has a major responsibility to ensure that the volunteer process within the organization is well managed. It should be one of the top priorities of the new CEO to determine the status of the volunteer program and how to enhance it from the board on down.

The chief role of the CEO is to build a board of directors that can help the organization fulfill its mission. Depending on that mission and the method created to elect board members, the CEO needs to find exciting ways to attract the people to serve. It is not always easy, particularly if the board is more of a representative body and those who serve are elected from another entity. In some cases, it might be a few board members who will make the difference. Exhibit 3.4 provides a few suggestions on how to attract, maintain, and recognize board members.

THE LEADER'S RELATIONSHIP WITH THE ORGANIZATION'S STAFF

While the volunteers and the board of directors need to be a major priority for the CEO, it is the staff that helps the professional leader fulfill a number of key functions that will measure his or her success or failure. A recent article in the *Wall Street Journal* by Carol Hymowitz noted:

> There is a simpler way to judge who makes a great leader: The number of people who would follow him or her out the door. I felt that unwavering loyalty at a recent farewell party for a veteran colleague. Amid the toasts and speeches, the stories of triumphant and difficult times shared together over the years; his former employees conveyed how deeply he had touched their lives and made work fun and engaging. They weren't simply going to miss him; they were going to stay in touch. Quite a few indicated they would happily work for him again.

Wouldn't that be a great way to be remembered? Often, administrators feel that they need to put extreme pressure on their employees to get results. In fact, these types of supervisors often do get results for a short period of time. Ultimately, however, people will revolt. The true leaders understand that individuals are motivated by different things; the key is to find out what they are.

Exhibit 3.5 provides a few examples of how a CEO can build a staff team and can motivate them to do great things. If you have been in the work force for an extended time, you have seen both good and bad supervisors. A successful not-for-profit CEO is much more than a good supervisor. In fact, the word *supervisor* is not appropriate at

EXHIBIT 3.4   DEVELOPING A BOARD OF CHAMPIONS

Recruit Well

- Seek only those who believe in your mission.
- Develop a testing system to help you discover the top prospects.
- Attract a diverse group that represents your constituents.

Support Well

- Educate before, during, and after the tenure of the member.
- Make sure that each member is informed about all aspects of the association.
- Meet with each board member individually at least once a year.
- Help each board member discover the area on which they wish to focus.
- Give each board member a meaningful assignment based on his or her focus area.
- Make sure that each board member gives and gets funding.
- Don't ever keep anything from the board members, even the bad news, and always ask for their advice.

Recognize Well

- Always thank board members in person and through the mail.
- Offer recognition that each board member would like to receive.
- Recognize them as a group and individually each time an exciting advance occurs.
- Recognize outgoing board members at a board function.
- Keep in touch with past board members. Drop in to see them, as well. They have a wealth of information, and it is the right thing to do.

EXHIBIT 3.5   THE TEN STEPS TO MOTIVATING A NOT-FOR-PROFIT STAFF

1. Get to know the players.
2. Shake up the structure.
3. Get everyone involved in the decision-making process.
4. Open their minds to new ideas.
5. Listen to what they say.
6. Don't hide anything.
7. Question everything.
8. Delegate, delegate, delegate.
9. Don't allow closed doors.
10. Recognize each and every one of them.

all. The CEO is a motivator of people. Like the previous example, the time spent between paychecks should not feel like work at all—it should be more of a calling. Entire staffs can feel this way, no matter what they earn on their paychecks. It is up to the CEO to set the tone and refine the culture.

Much has been said about the culture of a not-for-profit, both in this book and in other publications. It is true that the incoming CEO should respect the culture of the organization and should refrain from refining any aspects of that culture until it is fully understood and appreciated. Once the CEO of the organization understands the culture and sees the areas that need refinement, the CEO should then begin to work with the staff and the volunteer leadership to begin to make those refinements. This process may take time, but it is worth it.

Get to Know the Players

Getting to know the staff is an ongoing process. People do not stay the same; they are evolving constantly. This is one of the challenges with staff that stays with one organization for a long period of time: What often happens is that the staff members evolve while the "supervisor" remains static. The result is that the staff members are not being coached properly.

One of the CEOs who participated in the study told me that his football experience in college taught him the value of knowing each of the players on his staff. Each one is unique and needs to be approached differently.

Shake Up the Structure

The first rule is to never shake up the structure of your staff until you fully understand the core goals of the organization and what really needs to be done to fulfill the mission. Not-for-profits are just like many entities that function over a period of time—the leaders get busy accomplishing various objectives and, over time, the core goals don't seem to get achieved. This is often due to the organization devoting most of its time to secondary priorities while the top priorities are put on the back burner.

Here are nine steps to shake up the staff structure:

1. Do research to determine the major priorities.
2. Review staff functions to determine how they relate to these priorities.
3. Meet with staff to verify your findings.
4. Develop a new draft staff structure.
5. Meet with each department head to present your new structure and ask for advice.
6. Meet with key staff to present your second draft and ask for advice.

7. Meet with the entire staff to present your third draft and ask for advice.

8. With the assistance of key staff, present the restructuring plan to the staff at your next board meeting, illustrating how the new structure will help to better serve the mission of the organization.

9. Never make the structure static; keep it flexible.

Let Everyone Be Involved in the Decision-Making Process

The restructuring of the staff should involve the entire staff from the very beginning. Don't get into the trap that you are the sole decision maker. The entire staff can provide the CEO with a very powerful advisory group. Every one of them has a hand in the functions that make up the association. Most of them can tell you which programs are successful and which should have been dropped 10 years ago if only someone would have asked them. They have ideas for new programs, too. The successful CEO asks the staff for information and gets them involved in the entire decision-making process.

Open Minds to New Ideas

Once you begin to involve your staff in the decision-making process, a strange thing happens. The staff buys into the direction that you are headed and, better yet, they begin to provide ideas on how to get to the destination.

Dr. Edward Wakin, a professor of communications at Fordham University, noted that you need to create a climate that generates innovative ideas that can make a difference. It may be old ideas used in new ways, new connections between familiar pieces of information or completely new discoveries that work. This is the pure joy of being a leader—seeing the process take off where everyone is contributing to a noble effort.

Listen to What They Say

Your staff is your eyes and ears. I do a lot more listening than talking around my staff. Many who observe me would think that I am not playing a leadership role. I, of course, would disagree. The CEO's role is to grow talent. The staff needs to have the ability to express themselves and to provide solutions to their problems.

The CEO's role is often to hear the staff out and to make a short comment or decision based on the lengthy discussion. Staff meetings at my shop often find me listening to the reports of what has been accomplished and the game plan for the next period. If a staff member is performing well in this environment, then I let that person have the lead. If not, rather than confronting the individual at the staff meeting, we meet afterward to determine what is wrong, and together we determine how to solve the situation. Listening is 80 percent of the leadership process.

Don't Hide Anything

If a bad situation comes up, the staff will find out anyway. If not, they will conjure up a story that is far worse than what actually happened. Do I really tell my staff everything? Just about. Of course, there are always a few things that must be kept confidential, but they are often to protect the staff.

The staff has the right to know how the organization is running, the funds that are being raised, the volunteers that are recruited, the programs that are being developed and so on. A staff that is told everything is more loyal and team driven. They will cross over to other departments, without being asked, to give a hand to make sure the organization succeeds. They will feel that they are the trustees of the organization.

Question Everything

I had a mentor who always told me to "listen with the third ear." What is said is often not as important as how it was said or what is unsaid. Staff reports are traditional times for me to question progress. Most of my staff has gotten used to my questions, and therefore they provide me with what I need to know—but there are always one or two who don't.

Asking questions is one of the most productive things that a CEO can do. You become more aware of what is going on and you also help advance the given project or activity.

Delegate, Delegate, Delegate

One of the greatest challenges for CEOs is understanding that you can no longer do everything. You won the position by being an aggressive player and your rise to the top may have entailed getting deeply involved in a part of the organization. You probably loved that part of not-for-profit work. Even though your organization may still need that function covered, the bottom line is that you are limited as to what you can do as the CEO. Your responsibilities now encompass the entire operation and, if you continue to spend the time needed to successfully fulfill the area you love, the overall operation will fail.

You have to find a way to delegate these functions of the organization to other players. This does not mean that you will never get involved or that you don't provide your expertise to one or more parts of the operation. What it means is that you cannot do both functions full time.

Don't Allow Closed Doors

At my shop, I rarely close my office door. Symbolically, every door in the office needs to be wide open. I want my staff to know that I am available at any time to talk to them. Our staff takes advantage of this. This might seem like a waste of time, and the constant interruptions may seem counterproductive, but it is the best way to feel the pulse of the organization. Any work that requires privacy or quiet thought is usually reserved for after hours.

I am also a wanderer. I don't stay in my office; I am always dropping into my staff members' offices and sitting down with them to discuss everything from the last night's ball game to the organization's goals. I never use this time to point fingers. Rather, it is time for me to get a better understanding of what is happening and for the staff to ask for advice on how to proceed. The open-door policy strengthens the team/coach approach.

Recognize Each and Every One of Them

All of these steps that a CEO employs are really just a way of recognizing the staff for what they do. However, a formal recognition process is needed as well. I am not a big fan of formal annual reviews. I hated them as a staff member because they are usually designed to find fault and to ensure as minimal recognition as possible. While I do have annual meetings with the staff, it is not the only time I meet with them. In some ways, with weekly staff meetings, two retreats per year, and regular one-on-one meetings, we really don't need an annual review.

The annual meeting is designed to celebrate the work that the individual performed during the year. It is also designed to look for ways to help the individual improve in the following year through training or coaching and, of course, it is designed to provide a compensation increment.

Although I believe in motivating the staff throughout the year, nothing beats the ultimate recognition at the end of each year: increased compensation. In our shop, everyone is rewarded with an increase in salary. Why everyone? Because it took everyone to achieve another successful year.

Those who provided more than their share are rewarded a little more. If the organization had a very good year, which happened this past year, the entire staff also receives an equal bonus. The bonus is not given every year; only in years when the collective goals are over-achieved. The bonus, therefore, comes as a surprise, and it acts as one hell of an incentive to kick off the new program year.

Employee recognition is a daily effort that requires constant attention. How you talk with your staff is a form of recognition. Compliment work that is done well and, if work needs improvement, return to your coaching mode to provide your support and guidance.

Even though we try our best to hire individuals who have the necessary skills and who are dedicated to the mission of our organization, not all new hires work out. In my experience, it is the staff that generally puts new employees to the test. If the individual is willing to really make an effort, he or she will be accepted into the team and will be coached and supported by everyone on the staff.

Taking the Strategic Approach

As a CEO of a not-for-profit organization you will have all kinds of duties to perform. In other words, you can keep yourself pretty busy doing a million things that may or may not be worthwhile. The chief job of the CEO is to think strategically. This requires the CEO to look to the past for inspiration, to conduct the business of the day, and to determine where the organization should be in the future.

The wise CEO always looks to the past for inspiration. The past often provides a window for the future in that it can identify patterns, culture, and purpose. Every association has a certain pattern that they have etched in their history that is unique to that association. The CEO needs to know these patterns and to understand if they are still vital or if they can be refined to remain current. The culture of an organization is similar to its patterns in that it has been developed over a period of time, but culture is more people oriented than it is tangible. The purpose or mission of an organization tends to remain fairly steady, but it might become slightly altered over time. The association's past can tell a lot about its character and where it may want to go in the future.

Of course, the business of the day is always important and pressing. Although it might seem to be the most important thing to do at the moment, it really may not be. CEOs need to determine if they are really meeting the mission of the organization. If not, the CEO needs to determine how to change the course of the organization and get it headed in the right direction again.

The future is where the CEO needs to be focused most of the time. This is the most challenging part of the position. The CEO needs to assist the organization's volunteer leadership in determining where the association will be in 3, 5, or 10 years. Once this is determined, it is the CEO who will be charged with moving the association to these destinations. Although a number of people need to be involved with the planning process, including the board of directors, the staff and other key volunteers, it is the CEO who will lead the day-to-day charge.

Measures to Strengthen a CEO's Position

In order to lead this dynamic undertaking, the volunteer leadership needs to have full confidence in its CEO. The CEO, therefore, needs to take every measure possible to strengthen his or her position as the professional leader. Exhibit 3.6 summarizes responses from the CEOs who participated in the study on strengthening the CEO's position. Note that the percentage total at the end of each response reflects the percentage of CEOs who selected that category for their first, second, or third choice.

Maintaining a high level of interaction with key leaders seems like a common-sense approach, but it is amazing how many CEOs do not follow this simple rule. The participating CEOs, however, knew this lesson well, and made it their overwhelming top choice.

Successful CEOs make it a point to contact key volunteer leadership on an ongoing basis. If the volunteers are active players, this task is easy, but the few semi-active volunteers still need to be in the loop. This may involve regular telephone calls, one-on-one side meetings, and visits to their home cities. If you are a national organization, it may mean a side meeting from another activity when you happen to be nearby, or a special trip just for them. This is a very important part of the job. I like to visit them in their hometown to see where they work and, possibly, where they live. It reveals a lot about the person, and it helps to form a closer bond with them.

Keeping your organization fiscally sound is another obvious way to strengthen your position. One of the first things I do when I start at a new position is assess the fiscal integrity of the organization. Knowing where the funds come from, how they are being spent, if the organization owes money, if it has a reserve or an endowment, and how it invests its funds is vitally important. Ask questions like, "How can we improve one or more areas immediately?" or "What should be done over the next year to five years to dramatically improve the fiscal health of the organization?"

Make sure that you have a clearly defined strategic plan. As you enter the organization as the new CEO, you need to ask what kind of planning process is in place. Then you should request a copy of the strategic plan, if it exists. If a written plan does not exist or if the plan is hopelessly outdated or incomplete, you don't need to

| EXHIBIT 3.6 | THE SIX MAJOR WAYS TO STRENGTHEN A CEO'S POSITION |

Responses	Top Three Choice
1. Maintain a high level of interaction with key leaders.	63.36%
2. Keep the organization fiscally sound.	45.54%
3. Make sure that a clearly defined strategic plan is in place.	29.70%
4. Make sure that you are linked to the highest-priority issues.	24.75%
5. Keep as visible as possible with members.	22.77%
6. Increase staff effectiveness.	21.78%

worry. Often, this can provide an opportunity to help the organization's volunteer leadership create a new or better plan.

Making sure you are linked to the highest-priority issues is a good way to show the volunteer leadership, members, and donors that you have deep feelings about the issues that affect the association. This does not mean that you need to do everything for every issue, but you should be kept abreast of the issues and you should refer to them in your conversations. After all, these issues are the foundation of what the organization is all about, and you should be on top of all of them.

Keeping yourself as visible as possible with members is important. The CEO should take the time to meet with as many members or donors as possible. This can be done in a number of ways, from being visible at key meetings to making visits to members or donors. A CEO cannot meet with everyone; however, a CEO *can* maintain an open dialog with the members through a number of in-person opportunities.

Increased staff effectiveness is one of the key goals that any successful CEO should strive to attain. There are various ways to measure effectiveness and a ton of books to help with this process. The important thing is the realization that effectiveness is deeper than pure production; it is how the individuals apply themselves to the role that they are playing. Many times, the staff can significantly increase their effectiveness through a simple restructuring. It is a matter of direction and focus.

The CEOs who participated in the study provided a few gems that are worthy of noting. One CEO made it clear that he had both strengths and weaknesses. His success therefore, depended on applying his strengths to the things he liked to do and finding the best talent possible to cover his weaknesses and to perform the things he did not like to do. Another executive noted that she strived to make her association the prime source of knowledge and information with regard to their issue. Both of these examples illustrate how differently CEOs think about how they do their jobs. It is not simply a process of performing a function—it is much deeper than that. It deals with the human equation and the positioning of the entity that you are leading. It is an exciting place to be, but it is not a status quo position.

Instituting Change

One of the major roles that a CEO plays is instituting change. In order to do this successfully, the CEO needs to know which changes are outside of her control and which are within her sphere of influence. For example, you cannot control the weather for a certain event, but you can protect your members from the elements with a temporary or permanent structure. Many fear change. As a CEO, you need to be aware of those who embrace change and those who fear change.

Change is a natural process. Not-for-profit organizations that do not have an active change policy will not survive. For-profits also are in constant change. They have their ups and downs, and the stock market reflects these changes, measuring the health of thousands of companies. A recent *Wall Street Journal* article titled, "Success Stories: Companies Around the Globe are Finding Ways to Buck the Economic Downturn" noted that, "while some companies have battened down the hatches or have disappeared altogether, other companies have opened their wallets, pouring money into innovation, research and development, marketing acquisitions and new products, achieving record sales along the way."

Taking advantage of up and down cycles in business or within the not-for-profit community is an art. The not-for-profit CEO needs to understand these cycles and how to take full advantage of them. The *Wall Street Journal* article notes that there are two basic philosophies to addressing change: (1) do nothing, or (2) welcome change as an opportunity.

When the economy is down, the CEOs who do nothing are eager to let everyone know that the not-for-profit sector is in big trouble. Luckily, the sector is not filled with such people.

CEOs who are constantly examining the normal cycles of their individual organization, the not-for-profit sector, and the world in general understand that flexibility is the key. It is like a farmer who nurtures his crop during the good times and sells it for maximum profit. During the bad times, he may not even plant a crop but finds other ways to make a living. Not-for-profits need to think the same way.

Organizations often find a winning cycle in raising the funds they need and delivering the activities they feel are appropriate to their constituents. After a period of time, these functions do not produce the same results. This is perfectly normal. In bad economic times, for example, traditional ways of raising money may not be as productive. This is perfectly normal as well. Sometimes these cycles are predictable and sometimes they are not; however, the CEO needs to have contingency plans in place for these occasions.

Like other organizations, our shop began to experience a slowdown of funds coming from our direct-mail program during a recent slowdown in the economy. Our traditional mailing level is a little over one million pieces per year. Direct mail is expensive, and we knew we needed to at least break even to continue the program. With the trends that we were seeing, we decided to cut the direct-mail program by two-thirds.

If we had made only that move, however, we would have been in deep trouble. Instead, at the same time, we instituted an aggressive major gift program that emphasized multiyear gifts averaging five years. The major gift program was very successful and more than made up for the direct-mail shortfall. The new form of fundraising proved to be more economical to support and it provided other additional benefits, including an increased level of volunteer prospects. While the move was a reaction to a recession, the solution provided a long-term way of stabilizing the organization.

Like the business community, successful not-for-profits need to use downtime to gear up for the future. This is particularly true for upgrading your support system.

This includes training volunteers and staff, as well as testing new programs and refining existing activities.

Not-for-profit organizations come in all sizes and, therefore, need to approach the cycles of ups and downs differently. If you are in an association with a budget under $500,000, each dollar coming in is very important. CEOs of $30 million organizations have a similar problem, only much larger. Controls and innovation can generally be implemented more quickly with smaller associations, but not always. It depends on the culture of the organization and how the CEO anticipates change.

The key to instituting change is to have the entire team on board. It may take awhile for some board members and staff to understand what you are doing, but when they see the results, they will know that it is the logical thing to do. Instituting change brings the entire not-for-profit process alive. Everything is up for grabs.

The process should result in new programs being introduced after testing, refining existing activities and dropping dated and nonproductive programs, even though they may have been the mainstay of the organization at one time. Thinking this way becomes a habit to which everyone in the organization will readily adapt. It introduces an excitement to the process and a feeling that everyone can and should contribute.

LESSONS OF THE PAST

The CEOs who participated in the study were asked to list the three major changes in the role of the not-for-profit CEO in the last decade. Exhibit 3.7 lists the top three major reasons that more than 100 not-for-profit CEOs offered. The entire list of changes, more than 60 in total, can be found in Chapter 8 under Question 13: "In Your Opinion, What Are the Three Major Changes in the Not-For-Profit CEO's Role in the Last Decade?" The number-one major change that the participating CEOs listed was the ability to acquire and use technology to the fullest. Amen to that! Technology provides a major competitive advantage to those who embrace it. Recently, a research team came to our shop to interview the staff for a study that compared how not-for-profit organizations operate. The first thing the researchers noticed was that our organization was the first not-for-profit they had encountered with flat-screen monitors for its staff. Since they seemed to have an interest in our

EXHIBIT 3.7   MAJOR CHANGES IN THE NOT-FOR-PROFIT CEO'S ROLE IN THE LAST DECADE

- The ability to acquire and use technology to the fullest
- The increased need to find new ways to raise revenue
- The call for greater accountability

technology, we gave them a tour and showed them that every member of the staff, from the interns to the CEO, had state-of-the-art computers linked to a server with more capacity than needed. They were amazed.

I reviewed our entire technology philosophy and showed them other hardware and software currently in use. I also told them that we consider all of our technology to have short shelf life, and we have already scheduled to replace every item before it has outlived its usefulness. We are also in a constant search for new technology to add.

Not-for-profits have very few products to sell, namely their mission or cause, their reputation, and their ability to effectively serve their constituents. Technology helps a great deal in supporting not-for-profits since they are primarily knowledge-based entities. Technology can get things done quicker, it can help store more valuable information, and it can produce greater products that we could dream of just a decade ago.

To compete, not-for-profits have to keep up with technology. This has not really changed over the decades. Not-for-profits that spend the time and funds to stay on the cutting edge get a return value of many times their investment. It is just good business. At our shop, our annual budget appropriates funds for continual technology upgrades.

One other important aspect of updating technology is making sure that the staff keeps up with the changes as well. This requires ongoing training that may include internal and external course work. Even after extensive training at my organization, we still don't use our technology to its fullest. There is a constant push to improve and refine the operations.

The increased need to find new ways to raise revenue is becoming a real challenge these days. This is particularly true for meeting-based associations that depend on major revenue streams from events. Not-for-profit members are changing the ways in which they wish to acquire the knowledge they seek. They no longer need to go to meetings to gain knowledge.

The Internet can provide all or more than we need. Not-for-profits need to reinvent themselves, and reducing the number of meetings or reemphasizing the core reason to attend meetings is one way of doing that. The bottom line is, why continue with a meeting or any other activity if it is not fulfilling a need anymore?

The challenge is to find new ways to communicate with current and potential members while continuing to produce enough revenue to operate. This might mean that many not-for-profits will need to merge to cut costs, or they might even decide to go out of business. As discussed in Chapter 1, not-for-profits have always faced this problem. Many of the most productive organizations of the past no longer exist simply because they outlived their usefulness.

There are a multitude of ways to raise revenue. A not-for-profit needs to look beyond the traditional methods of raising funds to find new sources of income. This can include establishing a 501(c)3 foundation or even a for-profit subsidiary. If the mission of the organization is still needed, there is a way to tap into a revenue stream.

The third major change in the not-for-profit CEO's role in the last decade is the call for greater accountability. This is a high profile issue for both the for-profit and the not-for-profit community. People want to know how their money is being used, particularly when it is donated. Of course, they are absolutely right in this expectation. Any organization that solicits funds from memberships or donations has a responsibility to provide a full explanation of how their gift is going to be used and as well as providing an overview of how the organization operates as a whole.

Ethical CEOs who want to make a difference welcome this new scrutiny. In my organization, our books are open to anyone who wants to see them, including staff, members, and outside people. We painstakingly maintain our fiscal integrity and we make sure that the donor intent is honored to the fullest.

Full accountability procedures provide the association with a great way to sell themselves to possible donors. This past year, our organization developed an endowment program. One of the key selling points was full accountability and no wavering on donor intent.

Over the years, I have seen a number of prestigious organizations that did not honor donor intent. They used restricted funds for unauthorized expenditures, often for causes that would have been the last thing that the donor would have wanted. This is particularly sad when it is a donor who is deceased. CEOs should never fall into this trap. When a gift is made, the CEO should determine what the donor intent is and then develop a process to ensure that the funds will be used for that purpose.

ANTICIPATED CHALLENGES FOR THE FUTURE

The CEOs who participated in the study were asked to list the top three major challenges that not-for-profit CEOs face in the next decade. Exhibit 3.8 lists the top three responses from the participating CEOs. The CEOs also provided an additional 58 responses that can be found in Chapter 8.

Note that two out of the three perceived challenges are quite similar to the top major changes of the CEO's role in the last decade. This is not unusual as people tend to think that the events of the day will be the challenges of the future.

The leading response deals with technology, but note the emphasis on how technology needs to be used to save and serve. This is an important statement of the participating CEOs.

I mentioned earlier about our shop keeping up with the latest technology. We don't do this just for the sake of having the latest toy. A great deal of thought goes into the need factor. Will the technology help us?

We waited an extra year, for example, to upgrade our computer system to make sure that we acquired the next generation of hardware and software. This will help us better serve our constituents. Our Web page, for example, is designed to help both

EXHIBIT 3.8   MAJOR CHALLENGES THAT NOT-FOR-PROFIT CEOS WILL FACE IN THE NEXT DECADE

- Technology and its use to save and serve
- Revenue, how and where
- Perceived value to current and future members or donors

members and nonmembers access information, link with several resources, and participate in the activities of the organization. Although this is not a unique service, the Web page provides services that were not available to constituents a decade ago.

"Revenue" received the second highest level of responses from the participating CEOs. This is also quite similar to the second highest response for Question 13 in the study. Revenue will continue to be a challenge, and revenue sources will change over the next decade. The challenge for CEOs is discovering what these funding sources may be. Not-for-profit organizations need to search for new sources of revenue while there is still time.

The third challenge that was cited by the participating CEOs was discovering ways to increase awareness of the value of the organization among current and future members or donors. This, of course, is the core question for all of us: Will our organization remain relevant? Every not-for-profit needs to find the answers to the following questions:

- Will the mission of the organization be needed in the future?
- Can the association continue to attract members?
- What kind of competition is out there?
- Can the organization produce enough revenue to fulfill its mission?
- Are the current services enough?

Determining if the mission of the organization will be needed in the future is very important. Thousands of not-for-profits cease operations every year and your association could be one of them. Never assume that the organization will go on forever without change; it is a huge mistake.

A fundamental question that key leaders need to ask is: Can the association continue to attract members? The retention of a CEO tends to be linked with membership growth and stability so it is important to obtain the right answer to that question for both personal and professional reasons. If the organization cannot attract sufficient members to make it viable, then three options need to be explored:

1. Should the organization widen its membership categories?

2. Should the organization merge with another organization?

3. Should the organization go out of business?

Hundreds of organizations will need to determine the answers to these questions.

Sizing up the competition is a very important aspect to the health of your not-for-profit. One of the CEOs who participated in the study felt very strongly that the not-for-profit sector is getting too crowded. He noted that associations are being organized each day—many with similar missions and all seeking funding for their programs. Can the not-for-profit sector sustain all of these organizations? Competition is also coming from for-profits and the public sector.

I have noticed a dramatic increase in competition in the last five years. My organization counteracts competition with a very businesslike approach. We make sure that we remain better than others by cultivating potential customers and maintaining our visibility and public perception.

There are a lot of considerations in determining if an organization can produce enough revenue to fulfill its mission. This is the most fundamental challenge. You may be able to look like an active association but, if your traditional revenue streams begin to dry up, your not-for-profit will be in deep trouble unless you make dramatic shifts in your revenue procurement programs. As we noted earlier, new funding sources need to be discovered in just about every not-for-profit organization.

Personal Enrichment Needs

Once you attain the CEO position, the immediate goal is to find every way you can to retain the position in the Corner Office. This is not an easy position to maintain. The CEO needs to be able to work with the board while providing a leadership role to the staff. These challenges and more all land on the CEO's desk. If you don't have an escape valve, you are going to be in trouble.

The CEO needs to get away from the office. I actually enjoy traveling on business to perform the work that needs to be done as well as meeting members and others in our field. It provides a wonderful way to test various programs or campaigns. I use my time away to think. There are many demands on the CEOs time and having to think about things is sometimes lost in our fast paced world. It seems that everything has to be done yesterday even if it is not done well. I detest operating like that so I often take the time to review current and future programs during "down" time on a plane or in a hotel room. Many of the most successful programs in my organization came from taking the time to get away and think.

Reading is also part of the job. I make sure to read not just the trade publications but also literature on a variety of subjects. I enjoy reading about the current trends in business, for example, and who is making the big splashes. It is often surprising what you can learn—many of the volunteers that we have are business leaders who are covered by these publications.

My organization's mission deals with outdoor activities so I have the pleasure of being involved in a number of fishing and hunting opportunities from both a work-related and personal standpoint.

I also have a few hobbies that keep me busy that are completely unrelated to my work. Over the years, I have always tried to keep a sports car around for a few moments of spontaneous fun. It is important to be realistic with your recreation—I thought about a buying a boat, but the time and effort to put it in the water just wouldn't work with my time schedule. The sports car is instant fun, however. Over the years, I have owned two MGBs, and my current car is a yellow Honda S2000. The Honda is the most fun because it is reliable and has a number of features that make it useful for most of the year, like a heater. If I have a stressful day, I simply put a CD in and head out. I even take a fishing pole with me just in case I see a good spot.

Family is an area that CEOs tend to place in a secondary role. Again, the pressure of getting the Corner Office and maintaining it calls for sacrifices. If you are the CEO of a national association like I am, you tend to travel a lot. Last year I was out of town 87 days. My wife, Sue, has been very supportive of it and, when I am home, Sue and I make sure that we eat dinner together every night. We do various activities that are non-pressure-driven for both of us. In other words, I become a follower, and I enjoy every minute of it.

The bottom line is that a full, well-rounded life will help CEOs retain their positions better than trying to spend all of their time working. If you don't maintain a balance in your life, you will get bogged down in the challenges that your not-for-profit faces. It will not do you or your association any good. Coming back from a break refreshed is much more productive.

SUMMARY

The CEO of a not-for-profit organization will face greater challenges in the years ahead, which could affect the length of tenure of these leaders. Tenure will be based on a number of factors, but performance will be the ultimate test. The lessons of the past have taught us that organizations do not last forever. Not-for-profits are organized to fulfill a mission. If the organization is unable to fulfill the mission or some other organization can fulfill the mission better, then the future of your not-for-profit is in question.

CEOs, however, have great opportunities to increase the strength and vitality of the not-for-profit that they lead. They cannot do it alone; however, CEOs need the support of both volunteer leaders and staff. It is the CEO who can create the excitement and vitality to rally everyone into a team to work together for the common good.

The CEO must be a strategic thinker and a true leader of the organization to get the results needed to keep the not-for-profit successful. The first six months is critical in the development of relationships within the organization as well as determining the needs of the organization. The six-month review of the organization's health acts as a message to the board that you are on top of things and it can be used as a rough draft for a more long-term planning document.

Establishing a healthy relationship with the board and other key volunteers is vital in the first days of becoming the CEO. Beyond reporting to them, they hold the key to how the organization will face the future. Therefore, you need to be up close and personal with every key volunteer.

The staff will act as the main vehicle to move the association into the future and the CEO needs to be the clear leader of the pack. Becoming the leader takes time because you will need to gain the confidence of the staff. The ultimate goal is that the staff will follow you anywhere.

The changes in the role of the not-for-profit CEO in the last decade have been dramatic. CEOs need more business-oriented skills as well as the unique skills that make them a not-for-profit leader. It is not an easy combination to attain.

The challenges of the future will be even greater. Not-for-profit CEOs will need to take advantage of technology to keep on the cutting edge and they will need to find new revenue sources to support programs to keep their organization as viable as possible. This will mean that successful CEOs who wish to retain their positions will need to become astute agents of change. The overall goal is to keep the association relevant while making sure that the soul or mission of the organization is untouched.

Case Studies of Successful Not-for-Profit CEOs

If we look at CEO effectiveness in a static sense—as a snapshot in time—it's evident that there are numerous different styles and approaches that work for different individuals.

David A. Nadler and
Michael L. Tushman

INTRODUCTION

The *National Study of Not-For-Profit Chief Executive Officers* summarizes the opinions of over 100 not-for-profit CEOs on attaining and retaining the Corner Office. The detailed results of this study can be found in Chapter 8.

This chapter will take that process a bit further by interviewing 12 of the CEOs who participated in the survey. Each of the individuals interviewed are CEOs who are recognized for their leadership and success in the not-for-profit community.

THE RESEARCH METHODOLOGY AND PRESENTATION

Each participating CEO was interviewed by the author. The questions were based partly on the survey as well as various other topics. In addition, the CEOs were asked to discuss the answers they gave on the survey. The synopsis of each of the personal interviews has been formatted in a consistent manner to assist the reader with (a) comparing the opinions of the 12 interviewees, and (b) comparing the overall opinions with the summary of all the CEOs who participated in the study discussed in Chapter 8.

SYNOPSIS OF THE PARTICIPATING NOT-FOR-PROFIT CEOs

Ed Benson

Executive Director (since 1992)
Country Music Association
Nashville, Tennessee

Highest education degree:	Bachelor of Arts
Major:	Business Administration
Certifications:	None
Career tenure:	Not-for-profits: 23 years
	For-profits: 8 years

Profile of current not-for-profit served:	International organization
	Budget: $15 million
	Number of members: 5,200
	Number of employees: 35
	Number of chapters: None
	Number of Incorporated organizations: 1
	IRS designation: 501(c)6
Past employers:	Vice president, the Benson Company, Nashville, Tennessee

The following is a summary of the interview that took place between Ed Benson and the author.

Walter Pidgeon: *Were there unique circumstances in your past that may have helped you to attain your current position?*

Ed Benson: I was the Associate Executive Director for 13 years and came out of the record business. I was the ideal candidate for the executive position because I understood the politics and knew "where all the bodies were buried." When I became the associate director in 1979 it was the result of a national search. At that time, the association was much smaller. I just grew with the organization and became the executive director in 1992.

WP: *Do you currently have a contract?*

EB: Yes.

WP: *What do you feel are the advantages and/or disadvantages of a contract?*

EB: The contract stipulates to the organization and to the executive both the legal aspects of the agreement and also the nature of the overall relationship. Volunteer leaders come and go and the contract helps to maintain a better working relationship between them and the executive director.

WP: *If you knew that you would become a CEO of a not-for-profit organization someday, would you have taken different steps to prepare?*

EB: No, I don't think so. My college work focused on business administration and psychology, which provided me with a sound base. I also spent three years in the U.S. Army, and I am a Vietnam veteran. That experience also taught me a few things. I started out working in my family's business, The Benson Company, which is a leader in the gospel and Christian music market. So, I knew the business that the Country Music Association represented. I also served on other industry boards and, through this, I gained a better understanding and perspective of the role that the volunteer plays.

WP: *What formal educational courses do you feel that every not-for-profit CEO should have taken?*

EB: I would suggest business courses including basic courses in finance, accounting, and other management areas.

WP: *What advice would you provide an individual who has set a career goal to become a CEO of a not-for-profit organization?*

EB: For *students* who aspire to become not-for-profit CEOs, I would make sure that I got the basics while I was in school, including taking the appropriate finance and management courses. I would also find courses and discover personal experiences that would focus on human dynamics to better understand what motivates people. As a CEO, you will need to motivate staff, members, and volunteer leaders to get the job done.

Also, I strongly suggest that you take an ethics course. CEOs need to be ethical to the core and sometimes it is the most challenging thing you do.

For *not-for-profit professionals* aspiring to become CEOs, I would strongly suggest that you diversify your background by switching gears every once in a while and taking other assignments. Successful CEOs are well-rounded individuals. Gain as much knowledge as you can and get an advanced degree if possible. An MBA is ideal. Never stop learning. Attend meaningful conferences like the American Society of Association Executives meetings.

For *for-profit executives* attempting to enter the not-for-profit world in the CEO capacity, I can tell you from my personal experience that it will take some adjustment. You need to treat such a position as more than just another job or you will fail.

WP: *Did you have and do you have mentors?*

EB: Yes, several. My late cousin Bob Benson was always an inspiration to me. Jo Walker-Meador, the past CEO of the Country Music Association (CMA), helped me to understand the association business and the unique role the CEO plays. CMA's Legal Counsel, Dick Frank, also guided me over the years.

Survey Responses and Additional Comments from the Interview

Note: Responses that are numbered (i.e., 1, 2, 3, etc.) are ranked responses, with 1 being the highest.

Please rank the chief reasons why you were able to attain your current CEO position.

1. Past experiences
2. Networking
3. Other: Respect among volunteer leaders

Additional comments: Strategic planning is also a major factor since 1988 at the CMA. We focus our resources to make the most difference for our members and our industry.

What are the major personal skills that have helped you to retain your current CEO position?

1. Fiscal control
2. Strategic planning
3. Volunteer management
4. Networking
5. Keeping on the cutting edge

What kind of career experiences would you recommend to aspiring CEOs to prepare them for the top position?

1. Finance
2. Volunteer management
3. Program related

Do you network with other not-for-profit CEOs?

Yes, to build knowledge on common needs and concerns.

What qualities, in your opinion, do not-for-profit boards seek in their CEOs?

1. Integrity, trust
2. Leadership traits
3. Successful administrative and fiscal management

4. Volunteer management skills

5. Staff management skills

Additional comments: Boards seek CEOs who have the ability to manage. That includes employees, volunteers, and other individuals and groups. Volunteers, for the most part, understand that they need a full-time leader to direct them—a CEO.

How did you become aware of your current CEO position?

I knew someone who was a member or in a leadership position of the organization.

Other: 10 years' experience working for the association

What were the major factors that helped you to successfully win your current CEO position?

1. Understanding what the organization sought in the new CEO

2. Ability to connect with the key volunteer leadership

Additional comments: I understood what the organization wanted from the CEO. I was hired as the associate director several years before due to a recommendation from a management study that was conducted to determine staffing needed to better serve the association and the industry.

What kind of preparation did you do prior to the interview?

N/A

What were the three major reasons you were selected for your current position?

1. Proven experience

2. Integrity

3. Loyalty

What did you do during your first six months as a new CEO to cement your relationships?

1. *Other:* Furthered strategic planning process with volunteer leaders

2. Met with key leaders

3. Did an overall evaluation of the organization

What measures have you taken to continue to strengthen your position at your current organization?

1. Maintain a high level of interaction with key leadership.

2. Keep my organization fiscally sound.

3. Make sure that a clearly defined strategic plan is in place.

4. Develop a relationship with the media or trade press.

5. Increase staff effectiveness.

How have you or would you prepare to attain another CEO position?

1. Maintain a network that would alert me to possible positions.
2. Keep on the cutting edge through training.
3. Increase my visibility with the volunteer leadership of the targeted organization.

In your opinion, what are the three major changes in the not-for-profit CEO role in the last decade?

- Entrepreneurial approach
- Strategic thinking
- Leadership

Additional comments: Today's not-for-profit CEO role is quite similar in function to that of a for-profit CEO. You need to satisfy your members, just as a for-profit must satisfy the customer.

What do you feel are the three major challenges that not-for-profit CEOs face in the next decade?

- Mergers and consolidations
- Instant communications required by constituents and stakeholders
- Nurturing volunteers to ensure future leadership in the organization

Additional comments: Mergers within our industry will be major factor. Right now less than 5 percent of our annual revenue comes from dues. The rest comes mainly from two events: (1) our summer festival, and (2) the CMA Awards Show on CBS each year. Yet, demand for services will only increase. Our Web site, *cmaworld.com*, is an example of our new services. It contains firewall access for the members and volunteer leaders sections, as well as a public part for consumers.

We would welcome any additional information or advice that you would like to provide that would help to prepare an individual to attain and retain a CEO position in a not-for-profit organization.

The challenge for not-for-profit CEOs is to maintain a grip on the rapidly changing business environment. I read several newspapers every day, the staff peruses articles and flags them for me, and we monitor news services for late-breaking news about our industry. We are in a state of information overload, and the volume is increasing.

Networking with fellow CEOs is so important. They act as sounding boards for ideas and management decisions.

Twenty-five percent of our 61 board members are new each year. I make sure that I meet with each new board member to provide an orientation program to make them feel comfortable with the position, outline what we expect from them and, most importantly, find out what they expect from us. Working with the board has resulted in wonderful relationships, both personally and on behalf of the association.

Anne L. Bryant

Executive Director (since 1996)
National School Boards Association
Alexandria, Virginia

Highest education degree:	Doctorate—EdD
Major:	Education and Labor Law
Certifications:	Certified Association Executive (CAE)
Career tenure:	Not-for-profits: 18 years
	For-profits: 13 years

Profile of current
not-for-profit served: National organization

Budget: $23 million

Number of members: 52 state and territorial organizations

Federation reaches 14,700 school board districts, including 95,000 school board members

Number of employees: 127

Number of chapters: None

Number of incorporated organizations: 2

IRS designations: 501(c)3 and a 501(c)3

Past employers: (Ranked: Number 1 is the first position held.)

1. Assistant to the Academic Dean, Springfield Technical Community College, Springfield, Massachusetts
2. Manager, Smith Bucklin, Chicago, Illinois
3. Vice president, Professional Education Division, P.M. Haeger and Associates, Chicago, Illinois
4. Executive director, American Association of University Women, Washington, D.C.

The following is a summary of the interview that took place between Anne Bryant and the author.

Walter Pidgeon: *Were there unique circumstances in your past that may have helped you to attain your current position?*

Anne Bryant: Both my personal and professional background fit well with the position that I have now. I have the academic base as well as the understanding of the association management field. Early on, I obtained valuable experience working in a management organization, where I was the director for more than one association at a time. That meant that I learned how to work with and use the talents of the volunteer leadership. They were critical to the success of the associations. It taught me a lot about strategic planning and consensus decision-making. Today's associations are more and more team driven, and the skills I gained through the years have served me well.

WP: *Do you currently have a contract?*

AB: Yes.

WP: *What do you feel are the advantages and/or disadvantages of a contract?*

AB: A contract gives the board and the executive director a clear understanding of employment, severance, and benefits.

WP: *If you knew that you would become a CEO of a not-for-profit organization someday, would you have taken different steps to prepare?*

AB: I would have taken more business courses like finance and accounting; I had to learn them along the way. My multi-management for-profit experience, however, really helped me to gain strong financial skills and to play a variety of roles in our field. During that time, I saw it all from both the for-profit and the association perspective.

WP: *What formal educational courses do you feel that every not-for-profit CEO should have taken?*

AB: Basic business courses in finance, accounting, strategic planning, governance, and management.

WP: *What advice would you provide to an individual who has a career goal of becoming a CEO of a not-for-profit organization?*

AB: *Students* who aspire to become CEOs should take course work that they really like, that really turns them on. This will help them to acquire a better educational experience. I majored in English, and it made me love literature, learn to write, critique others, and think conceptually.

Professionals in the field who aspire to be CEOs need only follow these three words to gain the top position; exposure, exposure, exposure. Keep asking for assignments outside your field of interest, solve problems, and work with other staff to help them and to also gain experience for yourself. Find ways to become a better decision maker and planner. Have passion for your work. Supervisors and boards are always looking for individuals who have these qualities, and they will help you become a future leader.

For-profit executives who aspire to be not-for-profit CEOs need to have a passion for the cause or industry that the association represents if they wish to be successful. They also need to be consensus leaders, someone who is comfortable behind the scenes. Our world is not top-down, it is grassroots up!

WP: *Did you have and do you have mentors?*

AB: Yes, I had several. John Gardner and Brian O'Connell come to mind. I also try to be a mentor for others as well. John Gardner encouraged me to take risks and try new paths. I put this into practice at the American Association of University Women where we made a shift in strategic direction in the organization by including research on younger women and girls. The program was quite successful. Brian O'Connell helped me see that I was ready to move to bigger professional opportunities. Mentors are truth tellers; they can say things to you that no one else could. It is a really wonderful service.

Survey Responses and Additional Comments from the Interview

Note: Responses that are numbered (i.e., 1, 2, 3, etc.) are ranked, with 1 being the highest.

Please rank the chief reasons why you were able to attain your current CEO position.

1. Past experiences
2. Other: Reputation as a builder and change agent
3. Ongoing training
4. Formal education
5. Networking
6. Certifications

Additional comments: I did a lot of homework and was well prepared; I thought strategically where the organization should be heading.

What are the major personal skills that have helped you to retain your current CEO position?

1. Producer—making goals
2. Keeping on the cutting edge
3. Volunteer management
4. Fiscal control
5. Planning
6. Member relations
7. Networking
8. Government relations

Additional comments: I would add listening to what people are saying or not saying. This often provides a wealth of clues. By the way, I ranked government relations low due to the quality of work that our government relations staff performs.

What kind of career experiences would you recommend to aspiring CEOs to prepare them for the top position?

1. Volunteer management
2. Finance
3. Fundraising
4. Program related
5. *Other:* Marketing
6. *Other:* Technology
7. Membership development
8. Government relations

Do you network with other not-for-profit CEOs?

Yes, to learn, to grow and to relax.

What qualities, in your opinion, do not-for-profit boards seek in their CEOs?

- Leadership traits
- Integrity, trust
- Staff management skills
- Ability to articulate and write a message
- Ability to raise funds
- Successful administrative and fiscal management
- Volunteer management skills
- Education credentials
- Government affairs experience

Additional comments: The qualities that boards seek in a CEO depend on what they are really looking for. Often, you can bring this out through the discussion by becoming an organizational consultant. You can help the search committee to realize your value, as well as assisting them in making sound decisions.

How did you become aware of your current CEO position?

A search firm contacted me.

What were the major factors that helped you to successfully win your current CEO position?

1. How I prepared and executed the interview meeting process
2. Understanding what the organization sought in the new CEO
3. Ability to connect with the key volunteer leadership

4. A well-prepared resume and cover letter

5. *Other:* A good search firm person

What kind of preparation did you do prior to the interview?

1. Obtained information about the organization via the Internet and other sources

2. Prepared questions to ask and anticipated questions to answer

3. Rehearsed

What were the three major reasons you were selected for your current position?

- Reputation in prior position

- Connection to search committee

- Articulation of future mission of NSBA

What did you do during the first six months as a new CEO to cement your relationships?

1. Met or interviewed key leadership and all staff across the organization

2. *Other:* Met key leaders outside the organization to gain their assessment of the organization. Met volunteers across the country, in regularly scheduled meetings, got input concerning our future strategic vision.

3. *Other:* Helped board and staff to create a new strategic vision for the organization

4. Ensured that proper fiscal controls were in place

5. Did an overall evaluation of the organization

6. Made sure program functions were in order

7. Evaluated staff

What measures have you taken to continue to strengthen your position at your current organization?

1. Make sure that the clearly defined strategic plan is annually revised, refined with the board.

2. Maintain a high level of interaction with key leadership and members.

3. Make sure that I am linked to the highest priority issues.

4. Keep my organization fiscally sound.

5. Insist upon an annual review based on mutually agreed upon goals.

6. Increase staff effectiveness.

7. Develop a relationship with the media or trade press.

8. Find opportunities to speak and write.

9. Keep on the cutting edge through training.

10. Raise more income.

11. Maintain a key role in the government affairs function.

12. Keep myself as visible as possible with members.

How have you or would you prepare to attain another CEO position?

1. Maintain a network that would alert me to possible positions.

2. *Other:* Let search firms know your interest.

In your opinion, what are the three major changes in the not-for-profit CEO role in the last decade?

- Time factor of volunteer leadership
- Economic pressure (doing more with less)
- Technology and the role it plays

What do you feel are the three major challenges that not-for-profit CEOs face in the next decade?

- Changing nature of associations; the role they play in people's lives
- Technology usage
- Fiscal restraints (doing even more with less!)

Additional comments: The role that associations play is changing. Technology is one of the areas that is forcing and enabling change. We will need to find the answers to many questions, including how we will be communicating to members, methods of attracting new members, and so on. How will we provide the added value to that member's life? What keeps their membership and convinces others to join?

We would welcome any additional information or advice that you would like to provide that would help to prepare an individual to attain and retain a CEO position in a not-for-profit organization.

Members and nonmembers alike expect shorter timelines. The problem with this new demand is that not all things can change quickly. Often, it takes time to orchestrate real change. Helping boards to use benchmarks as indicators of measurable advancement will help the association reach long-term goals.

Elizabeth J. Clark

Executive Director (since 2001)
National Association of Social Workers
Washington, D.C.

Highest education degree:	Doctorate—PhD
Major:	Medical Sociology
Certification:	Academy of Certified Social Workers (ACSW)
Career tenure:	Not-for-profits: 30 years
Profile of current not-for-profit:	National organization
	Budget: $18.6 million
	Number of members: 150,000
	Number of employees: 139
	Number of chapters: 56
	Number of incorporated organizations: 3
	IRS designations: 501(c)6, 501(c)3, a for-profit

Past employers: (Ranked: Number 1 is the first position held.)
1. Director, Department of Social Work St. Luke's Hospital, Bethlehem, Pennsylvania
2. Associate professor, Montclair State University Upper Montclair, New Jersey
3. Administrator, Albany Medical Center, Albany, New York
4. Executive director, NASW, New York State Chapter, Albany, New York

The following is a summary of the interview that took place between Betsy Clark and the author.

Walter Pidgeon: *Were there unique circumstances in your past that may have helped you to attain your current position?*

Elizabeth Clark: I believe that my varied background helped me to attain my current position. My academic credentials include three master's degrees, one in public health, one in social work, and the other in sociology, and a Doctorate Degree in medical sociology. I also had hospital administration experience, held the Academy of Certified Social Workers (ACSW) designation, and I was the executive director of NASW's New York State Chapter, which is the largest chapter in the country.

WP: *Do you currently have a contract?*

EC: Yes.

WP: *What do you feel are the advantages and/or disadvantages of a contract?*

EC: First of all, a contract provides security for both parties. It is a good tool to have to evaluate your performance at renewal time. CEO positions, particularly at the national level, are much more complex and require a detailed review process. The contract helps to outline what is expected of me and what obligations the association has in return.

WP: *If you knew that you would become a CEO of a not-for-profit organization someday, would you have taken different steps to prepare?*

EC: While I prepared for this role in so many ways, I might have taken additional courses in business, maybe even have obtained an MBA. I had to learn these skills the hard way. My skills have brought me here, and I have successfully adapted them to fit the position.

WP: *What formal educational courses do you feel that every not-for-profit CEO should have taken?*

EC: Financial management is the weakness of most not-for-profit CEOs. Course work in various management areas would be an asset. Another area that seems to be lacking is the art of writing. Future CEOs should take business-writing courses.

WP: *What advice would you provide an individual who has set a career goal to become a CEO of a not-for-profit organization?*

EC: *Students* should take the time to learn the fundamentals of finance. The not-for-profit community has a lot more restraints than for-profits. I would try to get as many experiences as I could through jobs and volunteering to understand and appreciate the not-for-profit sector, as well as how this sector relates to both the for-profit and government sectors.

    Professionals in the field seeking to attain a CEO position need to seek out as many training opportunities as possible and strive for a diverse career path.

    For-profit executives attempting to seek a not-for-profit CEO position need to understand the differences between the for-profit and not-for-profit sectors. They should explore the possibility before they actually take on a not-for-profit position. The not-for-profit sector is unique in many ways. Leaders in our sector have a lot more patience; they need to know that the rules are different. For example, knowing what percentage of funding can be used for lobbying, the need to keep administrative and fundraising costs low and program expense high.

WP: *Did you have and do you have mentors?*

EC: Yes, I had several mentors throughout my career:

Eleanor Cockerill, MSW—Eleanor Cockerill was one of my graduate school professors. She helped me understand that you could do a variety of things with a Masters in Social Work degree. She also gave me advice that I took to heart when she said, "Don't ever let yourself be locked into a job."

Joan Lingner, PhD—I worked with Dr. Lingner at the University of North Carolina at Chapel Hill. She taught me how to conduct meetings, and how to write grant proposals.

Jan Fritz, PhD—Dr. Fritz has a charismatic leadership style. She was president of a not-for-profit group when we met. She taught me how to "work a room" and how to keep a broad vision for an organization.

Survey Responses and Additional Comments from the Interview

Note: Responses that are numbered (i.e., 1, 2, 3, etc.) are ranked, with 1 being the highest.

Please rank the chief reasons why you were able to attain your current CEO position.

1. Past experience
2. Formal education
3. Networking

Additional comments: I prefer and had experience working in large systems: My past experience working as the executive director of the state chapter, my professional and academic background in social work and social work certification made the difference.

What are the major personal skills that have helped you to retain your current CEO position?

1. Fiscal control
2. Producer—making goals
3. Member relations
4. Volunteer management

Additional comments: When I came to my present position the organization was experiencing a deficit. I knew how to put the fiscal controls in place to turn it around.

What kind of career experiences would you recommend to aspiring CEOs to prepare them for the top position?

1. Finance
2. Fundraising
3. Program related

Do you network with other not-for-profit CEOs?

Yes. They provide good support; I see them at various meetings I attend.

What qualities, in your opinion, do not-for-profit boards seek in their CEOs?

1. Successful administrative and fiscal management
2. Leadership traits
3. Staff management skills
4. Integrity, trust
5. Ability to raise funds
6. Education credentials
7. Government affairs experience
8. Ability to articulate and write a message
9. Volunteer management skills

Additional comments: Most boards look for past success but they are really looking for leadership. Leadership in many ways is hard to define, however. During the interview I addressed the challenges that the association was experiencing. I took a leadership role within that meeting to advise them on what needed to be done to meet those challenges.

How did you become aware of your current CEO position?

I was a member of the organization.

What were the major factors that helped you to successfully win your current CEO position?

1. How I prepared and executed the interview meeting process
2. A well-prepared resume and cover letter
3. My negotiating skills
4. Understanding what the organization sought in the new CEO
5. Ability to connect with the key volunteer leadership

Additional comments: I did well in the interview. I was prepared to discuss the issues. I had a well-thought-out resume that was geared to the position in question.

What kind of preparation did you do prior to the interview?

1. Prepared questions to ask and anticipated questions to answer
2. Obtained information about the organization via the Internet and other sources

What were the three major reasons you were selected for your current position?

- Leadership skills
- Knowledge of organization
- Fiscal skills

Additional comments: Again, my interview was a major key. I took a leadership role in the process and provided ample backup material to make my case.

What did you do during the first six months as a new CEO to cement your relationships?

1. Did an overall evaluation of the organization
2. Prepared a status report for member leaders
3. Met key leadership
4. Evaluated staff

What measures have you taken to continue to strengthen your position at your current organization?

1. Keep my organization fiscally sound.
2. Maintain a high level of interaction with key leadership.
3. Keep myself as visible as possible with members.
4. Increase staff effectiveness.

How have you or would you prepare to attain another CEO position?

1. Increase my visibility with the volunteer leadership of the targeted organization(s).
2. Maintain a network that would alert me to possible positions.

In your opinion, what are the three major changes in the not-for-profit CEO role in the last decade?

- Need for increased fundraising
- Need for increased member relations
- Tighter fiscal controls

Additional comments: Other issues are increased fundraising pressures for all not-for-profits and increased emphases on media relations.

What do you feel are the three major challenges that not-for-profit CEOs face in the next decade?

- Attracting younger members
- Fundraising
- Moving to paperless state of operations

Additional comments: We need to change our model of service. Young people, for example, do not want to be attending a conference over the weekend. More online educational programs need to be instituted. A number of standing committees need to be dropped in favor of temporary task forces to ensure better use of members' time on the areas that really need to be done.

We would welcome any additional information or advice that you would like to provide that would help to prepare an individual to attain and retain a CEO position in a not-for-profit organization.

Have a clear understanding of why you want to become a CEO of a not-for-profit organization. Know the differences between for-profit and not-for-profit entities and understand that CEOs of not-for-profits are a special breed. While our sector may not move as fast, we have a good system of checks and balances.

Ann R. Cox

Executive Director (since 1992)
American Association of Occupational Health Nurses
   (AAOHN)
Atlanta, Georgia

Highest education degree:	Master's Degree
Major:	Nursing
Certification:	Certified Association Executive (CAE)
Career tenure:	Not-for-profits: 22 years
Profile of current not-for-profit served:	National organization
	Budget: $3 million
	Number of members: 10,000
	Number of employees: 22
	Number of chapters: 160
	Number of incorporated organizations: 2
	IRS designations: 501(c)6, 501(c)3

Past employers: (Ranked: Number 1 is the first position held)
1. Director of education, AAOHN
2. Director of professional affairs, AAOHN
3. Associate executive director, AAOHN

The following is a summary of the interview that took place between Ann Cox and the author.

Walter Pidgeon: *Were there unique circumstances in your past that may have helped you to attain your current position?*

Ann Cox: Yes, I had a number of transferable skills, including working with people, writing, and speaking before groups. I made the decision early in my career to stay in association management, and I am delighted with the results.

WP: *Do you currently have a contract?*

AC: Yes.

WP: *What do you feel are the advantages and/or disadvantages of a contract?*

AC: A contract clearly delineates authority. It also details the provisions of the CEO's compensation including salary, merit increases and other benefits. In addition, it outlines the termination and severance package.

WP: *If you knew that you would become a CEO of a not-for-profit organization someday, would you have taken different steps to prepare?*

AC: No. Since I made a career choice to stay in association management, I knew that I had to develop my skills and gain a variety of experiences. I became a Certified Association Executive (CAE) through the American Society of Association Executives, I took graduate courses and I sought on-the-job experiences. I planned for the day that I would become the CEO.

WP: *What formal educational courses do you feel that every not-for-profit CEO should have taken?*

AC: Certainly you need to have a good formal education base. In addition, aspiring CEOs should take advantage of continuing education to keep them up to date. The organizational development program that the Chamber of Commerce provides is a good example. Aspiring CEOs should not narrow their focus on either training or job experiences; CEOs need to have a broad knowledge base. CEOs need to have organizational knowledge including how systems and processes function; how to make things happen.

WP: *What advice would you provide an individual who has set a career goal to become a CEO of a not-for-profit organization?*

AC: *Students* aspiring to become a not-for-profit CEO someday need to understand that the CEO has to wear a number of hats so it is important they begin to understand the basics. Take the appropriate course work, gain people skills through involvement in sports, clubs or other activities while they are in school. They should volunteer at a not-for-profit to see for themselves what it is all about.

Professionals in the field aspiring to become CEOs need to stop, seek, and find opportunities to gain as many transferable skills as possible. They need to begin to understand the best timing to move to new opportunities and how to plan the process. Volunteer to gain insight on the way other organizations operate and how individuals participate in the process. When it is time to begin to select an organization to lead, make sure that you can be passionate about its mission. If you can't, it is not the right organization for you.

For-profit executives making the move from a for-profit position need to know that running a not-for-profit is much more of a dramatic change than they may think. In a for-profit you are selling a product like a rug, a not-for-profit generally is providing a service to its members. You need to motivate volunteers to help the process along and you have to know how to deal with a diverse board that represents a variety of member interests. There can be a lot of pitfalls and political fallouts in the process.

WP: *Did you have or do you have mentors?*

AC: I have had many, but I would like to take the opportunity to thank and recognize Bill Kelley, CAE (retired from the Elberton Granite Association) for seeing something in me early in my career and supporting me throughout my career. Mentors have helped me by opening doors, by providing guidance, and by helping me with gaining educational credentialing like the Certified Association Executive (CAE) designation through the American Society of Association Executives. A mentor is someone who is a grounding force. When times are challenging they are there to provide support. Many times they develop a sort of a spiritual relationship with you that is hard to describe, but they make such a difference.

Survey Responses and Additional Comments from the Interview

Note: Responses that are numbered (i.e., 1, 2, 3, etc.) are ranked, with 1 being the highest.

Please rank the chief reasons why you were able to attain your current CEO position.

1. Ability to work with diverse stakeholders (boards, members, staff, etc.)
2. Past experiences
3. Certifications
4. Ongoing training
5. Formal education
6. Networking

Additional comments: Never stop learning, and accept new challenges.

What are the major personal skills that have helped you to retain your current CEO position?

1. Ability to work with diverse stakeholders
2. Keeping on the cutting edge
3. Producer—making goals
4. Planning
5. Fiscal control
6. Volunteer management
7. Member relations
8. Government relations
9. Networking

What kind of career experiences would you recommend to aspiring CEOs to prepare them for the top position?

1. Different work experiences and a broad set of transferable skills
2. Attaining the Certified Association Executive (CAE) offered by the American Society of Association Executives
3. Volunteer management
4. Finance
5. Program related
6. Membership development
7. Government relations
8. Fundraising

Additional comments: Gain the skills that will help you to succeed, including the ability to articulate issues, being more strategic, and using technology to the fullest.

Do you network with other not-for-profit CEOs?

Yes, for support, benchmarking, advice and counsel, and motivation.

What qualities, in your opinion, do not-for-profit boards seek in their CEOs?

1. Integrity, trust
2. Leadership traits
3. People skills
4. Ability to articulate and write a message
5. Education credentials
6. Staff management skills
7. Volunteer management skills
8. Successful administration and fiscal management
9. Government affairs experience
10. Ability to raise funds

Additional comments: Boards want CEOs that can "walk on water." They want doers who can take care of the day-to-day operations and have the ability to "sell the goods."

How did you become aware of your current CEO position?

On staff, worked up to the position.

What were the major factors that helped you to successfully win your current CEO position?

1. Demonstrated performance
2. Understanding what the organization sought in the new CEO
3. Ability to connect with the key volunteer leadership

4. How I prepared and executed the interview meeting process

5. My negotiating skills

6. A well-prepared resume and cover letter

Additional comments: Having been an employee for several years, I had the advantage of knowing what needed to be done.

What kind of preparation did you do prior to the interview?

- Actually interviewed everyday through the year-long search process—demonstrated performance
- Prepared questions to ask and anticipated questions to answer
- Brought examples of my work
- Rehearsed
- Obtained information about the organization via the Internet and other sources

What were the three major reasons you were selected for your current position?

- Demonstrated performance
- Certified Association Executive (CAE)
- People skills

Additional comments: I was a known entity who had the business management skills, staff, and volunteer management record and the right credentials.

What did you do during the first six months as a new CEO to cement your relationships?

1. Did an overall evaluation of the organization

2. Did a legal audit

3. Began building trust with the board and staff

4. Created a personal plan of action

5. Ensured that proper fiscal controls were in place

6. Made sure program functions were in order

7. Evaluated staff

8. Evaluated volunteer leadership

9. Made significant changes and refinements

10. Prepared a status report for member leaders

What measures have you taken to continue to strengthen your position at your current organization?

1. Make sure that I am linked to the highest priority issues.

2. Keep on the cutting edge through training.

3. Maintain a high level of interaction with key leadership.

4. Increase staff effectiveness.

5. Make sure that a clearly defined strategic plan is in place.

6. Keep my organization fiscally sound.

7. Keep myself as visible as possible with members.

8. Find opportunities to speak and write.

9. Raise more income.

10. Develop a relationship with the media or trade press.

11. Maintain a key role in the government affairs function.

How have you or would you prepare to attain another CEO position?

1. Have people and headhunters contact me about opportunities.

2. Maintain a network that would alert me to possible positions.

3. Become a volunteer at the prospective organization.

4. Increase my visibility with the volunteer leadership of the targeted organization(s).

5. Keep on the cutting edge through training.

In your opinion, what are the three major changes in the not-for-profit CEO role in the last decade?

- Increased accountability
- Nothing stays the same
- Increased complexity

What do you feel are the three major challenges that not-for-profit CEOs face in the next decade?

- Increased accountability
- Nothing stays the same
- Increased complexity

Additional comments: The number one issue will be trust and the ability to prove it.

We would welcome any additional information or advice that you would like to provide that would help to prepare an individual to attain and retain a CEO position in a not-for-profit organization.

CEOs need to have a broad background in what makes an association function. CEOs need to "walk the walk." What I mean by this is that you need to be professional, have integrity, and you need to be in the game for the right reasons—to make a difference.

Katherine Mandusic Finley

Executive Director (since 2000)
Association for Research on Nonprofit Organizations
    and Voluntary Action
Indianapolis, Indiana

Highest education degree:	MBA and Master's Degree
Majors:	Marketing and History and Museums
Certifications:	Certified Association Executive (CAE)
	Certified Fund Raising Executive (CFRE)
	Certified Meeting Professional (CMP)
Career tenure:	Not-for-profits: 22 years
Profile of current not-for-profit served:	International organization
	Budget: $750,000
	Number of members: 1,300
	Number of employees: 4
	Number of chapters: None, but four special-interest sections
	IRS designation: 501(c)3

Past employers: (Ranked: Number 1 is the first position held.)

1. Research historian, Conner Prairie, Fishers, Indiana
2. Medical historian, Indiana Historical Society, and executive director, Indiana Medical History 3. Museum, Indianapolis, Indiana (shared position)
3. Assistant director—manager of communications, The Center for Philanthropy, Indianapolis, Indiana
4. Executive director, Roller Skating Association International, and executive director, Roller Skating Foundation, Indianapolis, Indiana

The following is a summary of the interview that took place between Kathy Finley and the author.

Walter Pidgeon: *Were there unique circumstances in your past that may have helped you to attain your current position?*

Katherine Finley: I believe that my varied professional background helped me to understand the role I needed to play for my current employer and made me a very attractive candidate for the position. First of all, I understood the field that the organization represented and I understood the research process. In addition,

I also had experience in managing an association and I had a credential that they respected, my MBA degree.

WP: *Do you currently have a contract?*

KF: No.

WP: *What do you feel are the advantages and/or disadvantages of a contract?*

KF: I had one with the Roller Skating Association and had to break it to take my present job. I have mixed feelings about them. It is nice to have one for security reasons. I don't have one in my present position, and I am doing fine. I sometimes wonder if contracts might make it easier to find ways to get rid of people, particularly at the end of the cycle.

WP: *If you knew you would become a CEO of a not-for-profit organization someday, would you have taken different steps to prepare?*

KF: I don't think so; from the start of my professional career, I wanted to find a way to become the CEO of a not-for-profit organization. To do this, I sought out as many experiences as I could to obtain the background that I thought I needed. I also obtained an MBA to have a recognized educational credential. I am currently in the process of attaining a doctorate degree in association management. I try to participate in as many educational opportunities as possible to keep myself on the cutting edge. To answer your question, I knew I was going to be a CEO someday so I prepared myself and I continue to do so.

WP: *What formal educational courses do you feel that every not-for-profit CEO should have taken?*

KF: Certainly not-for-profit CEOs should have taken courses in financial management and administration. In addition, public speaking and English are a must. Depending on the type of organization you wish to run, fundraising, government affairs, and communications should be in the mix. One of the areas often forgotten, however, is human resource management, particularly the legal aspects of the employee relationship.

WP: *What advice would you provide an individual who has set a career goal to become a CEO of a not-for-profit organization?*

KF: *Students* who aspire to become a CEO of a not-for-profit organization should try out the field while they are in school. Our association, for example, employs a number of interns who have aspirations of entering the not-for-profit field. Students need to know that even a master's degree is not enough to gain a CEO position without the experience needed to understand the role that needs to be played. Plan to start at the bottom and work your way up; it will make a world of difference. Then seek a CEO position at a small association to gain an overall perspective.

Professionals in the field who aspire to become a CEO should take a diverse path. Don't get typecast. Seek further education and find ways to serve as a volunteer to see for yourself what organizations and participants seek and want.

For-profit executives seeking a CEO position in a not-for-profit may be in for a shock. While we act like a business in so many ways we are not and our culture is different. If you don't understand that you will fail. Not-for-profits are driven by a mission, not by the bottom line. Therefore, the top professional leader needs to believe in the mission of the organization and not just be in it for the paycheck. The ones who successfully make the transition from the for-profit arena are those who make an effort to have an open mind, seeking education on the subject and becoming passionate about the role they are playing.

WP: *Did you have and do you have mentors?*

KF: Yes, I can think of a number of mentors in my past.

Bob Payton, executive director of The Center on Philanthropy at Indiana University, when I worked there from 1991 to 1993, opened my eyes to the philanthropic community. I have also had a number of board members who have been wonderful mentors at both the Roller Skating Association and my present position. At the Roller Skating Association, Harry Walker, Jim McMahon, Don Perkins and Dave Schafer, as board presidents, were very supportive of me and taught me a lot about the industry I represented. I also learned a lot about finance and fiscal responsibility from two treasurers—Jerry Shores and Bob Fortmann. There were also many other board members who helped me understand the industry and the association. They really made a difference. In my present position, I've also learned a lot from my board presidents at ARNOVA— Dennis Young, Elizabeth Boris, and Joe Galaskiewicz have given me perspective on running a professional association.

Survey Responses and Additional Comments from the Interview

Note: Responses that are numbered (i.e., 1, 2, 3, etc.) are ranked responses, with 1 being the highest.

Please rank the chief reasons why you were able to attain your current CEO position.

1. Past experiences
2. Formal education

Additional comments: We never know what past experiences will help us in the future; therefore, no experience is a bad experience. My research background, combined with my association management experience, made me both the ideal and the unique candidate for my current position. My competition had either research or association management experience; they did not have both.

What are the major personal skills that have helped you to retain your current CEO position?

1. Producer—making goals
2. Member relations
3. Planning
4. Fiscal control
5. Keeping on the cutting edge

Additional comments: I would add volunteer management. Not-for-profit CEOs need to know this skill very well. For example, my volunteer leaders change every year. CEOs need to know how to deal with all kinds of people even if the chemistry is not quite right.

What kind of career experiences would you recommend to aspiring CEOs to prepare them for the top position?

1. Finance
2. Fundraising
3. Membership development

Do you network with other not-for-profit CEOs?

Yes. One of the best ways for me accomplish this is to attend the American Society of Association Executives meetings and the Indiana Society of Association Executive meetings.

What qualities, in you opinion, do not-for-profit boards seek in their CEOs?

1. Leadership traits
2. Ability to raise funds
3. Successful administration and fiscal management
4. Educational credentials

Additional comments: Like it or not, it boils down to personality. Your track record might open the door to the interview, but it's the chemistry at the interview between the volunteer leaders and the candidate that closes the deal.

How did you become aware of your current CEO position?

I answered an ad.

What were the major factors that helped you to successfully win your current CEO position?

1. Understanding what the organization sought in the new CEO
2. How I prepared and executed the interview meeting process
3. A well-prepared resume and cover letter

Additional comments: I understood what the association was looking for through my research. I tailored my resume. The search committee felt comfortable with me.

What kind of preparation did you do prior to the interview?

- Prepared questions to ask and anticipated questions to answer
- Obtained information about the organization via the Internet, and so on
- Brought examples of my work

What were the three major reasons you were selected for your current position?

1. Had a good track record
2. Was familiar with the academic discipline represented by the organization
3. Brought examples of my work

Additional comments: My educational and professional background fit well.

What did you do during the first six months as a new CEO to cement your relationships?

1. Met key leadership
2. Did an overall evaluation of the organization
3. Prepared a status report for member leaders
4. Created a personal plan of action
5. Made significant changes and/or refinements

What measures have you taken to continue to strengthen your position at your current position?

1. Make sure that a clearly defined strategic plan is in place.
2. Maintain a high level of interaction with key leadership.
3. Keep myself as visible as possible with members.
4. Raise more income.
5. Keep my organization fiscally sound.
6. Keep on the cutting edge through training.
7. Find opportunities to speak and write.
8. Increase staff effectiveness.

How have you or would you prepare to attain another CEO position?

1. Check want ads.

2. Maintain a network that would alert me to possible positions.

3. Keep on the cutting edge through training.

In your opinion, what are the three major changes in the not-for-profit CEO role in the last decade?

1. Role in fundraising is more vital.

2. More focus is on ethics and justifying salaries, programs, etc.

3. More politics are involved in position.

Additional comments: Obtaining funds, either through earned income or philanthropic efforts, is more challenging.

What do you feel are the three major challenges that not-for-profit CEOs face in the next decade?

1. Competition for members and funds.

2. People are making membership choices based on more analysis.

3. Volunteer numbers will be limited and, therefore, the pool of leaders will be limited as well.

Additional comments: Your track record will count more. Desired CEOs will know how to network and increase the visibility of the organization. There will be a lot more looking over your shoulder.

We would welcome any additional information or advice that you would like to provide that would help to prepare an individual to attain and retain a CEO position in a not-for-profit organization.

Volunteer boards are looking for people of substance; they want CEOs who understand how to work with diverse groups both within and outside the organization. Don't ever give up, even though you might not get the first few positions. Maybe these organizations were not right for you. Get in the habit of asking search committees why you were not chosen; what you find out may be the key to securing a future CEO position.

Robert K. Goodwin

President, CEO (since 1995)
Points of Light Foundation
Washington, D.C.

Highest educational degree:	Master's Degree
Major:	Christian Ethics (I have completed the course work, but not the thesis for Master's work in Social Psychology)
Certifications:	None
Career tenure:	Not-for-profits: 12 years
	Higher education: 5 years
	For-profits: 15 years
Profile of current not-for-profit served:	National organization
	Budget: $22 million
	Number of members: 1,726
	Number of employees: 108
	Local chapters: 420
	Number of incorporated organizations: 1
	IRS designation: 501(c) 3

Past employers: (Ranked: Number 1 is the first position held)

1. Publisher, Oklahoma Eagle, Tulsa, Oklahoma
2. Sales manager, Webster International, Houston, Texas
3. Assistant deputy, Chancellors Office, Texas A&M University, College Park, Texas
4. Executive director, Whitehouse Initiative for Historically Black Colleges, United States Department of Education, Washington, D.C.
5. Chief operations officer, Points of Light Foundation, Washington, D.C.

The following is a summary of the interview that took place between Bob Goodwin and the author.

Walter Pidgeon: *Were there unique circumstances in your past that may have helped you to attain your current position?*

Robert Goodwin: In 1989, a White House initiative called for the formation of the Points of Light Foundation. I was chosen as the COO of the program. As the organization grew and began to seek a more independent role, I positioned myself and planned for the day that I would possibly become the CEO.

WP: *Do you have a contract?*

RG: Yes.

WP: *What do you feel are the advantages and/or disadvantages of a contract?*

RG: The clear advantage is the opportunity for explicit expectations, which can be evaluated by both the incumbent and the board. The board is protected when the incumbent is doing well and might be recruited for another opportunity. The organization is protected in the case of any flagrant conduct or performance failings. Each party is committed to performance within the bounds of the negotiated expectations. In the case of a rapidly growing enterprise, a disadvantage of a contract may be the absence of a clear means of renegotiating compensation of other benefits that might be desirable. This need not affect the ability of the board and incumbent from providing alternative forms of compensation, such as bonuses or raises not specified in the contract.

WP: *If you knew that you would become a CEO of a not-for-profit organization someday, would you have taken different steps to prepare?*

RG: No, my formal education has been a real source of help to me in my current CEO role. The art of dealing with people is so important in a CEO's role. Certainly ongoing training also has helped. There is no substitute for experience, however. A CEO needs to know what needs to be done and how to motivate others to support the vision.

WP: *What formal educational courses do you feel that every not-for-profit CEO should have taken?*

RG: Beyond the fundamental management courses that every CEO should take including finance and accounting, I strongly feel that CEOs need to understand the human condition and how to most effectively communicate with people. Educational opportunities including human relations, public speaking and communications would be a real benefit for any aspiring CEO.

WP: *What advice would you provide an individual who has set a career goal to become a CEO of a not-for-profit organization?*

RG: Take the time to understand the vital role that not-for-profits play in our society. Do it for the right reasons (i.e., to make a difference). Most importantly, take the time to experience for yourself the joy of volunteering.

WP: *Did you and do you have mentors?*

RG: I had many mentors; my father for example. My pastor, Rev. LeRoy K. Jordan, was a mentor when I was an assistant pastor at the First Baptist Church of North Tulsa. In addition, Oral Roberts; Charlie Kothe, a lawyer from Tulsa; Leroy Thomas, a banker; Jim Cheek, President of Howard University; Marian Heard; Norman

Brown; Steve Miller; George Romney; John Gardner; Dick Schubert, past CEO of the Points of Light Foundation (POLF); and all five past/current chairmen of the POLF to name a few. Mentors are so important in molding an individual.

Survey Responses and Additional Comments from the Interview

Note: Responses that are numbered (i.e., 1, 2, 3, etc.) are ranked, with 1 being the highest.

Please rank the chief reasons why you were able to attain your current CEO position.

1. Past experiences
2. Networking
3. Formal education
4. Ongoing training

Additional comments: A CEO has to be multitalented. I helped to build a number of partnerships for the POLF to succeed. We just could not have done it alone. I strive to project a vision, to attract various stakeholders and to amass both internal and external leaders to move our vision in the same direction.

What are the major personal skills that have helped you to retain your current CEO position?

1. Producer—making goals
2. Planning
3. Networking
4. Government affairs
5. Fiscal control
6. Volunteer management
7. Keeping on the cutting edge

What kind of career experiences would you recommend to aspiring CEOs to prepare them for the top position?

1. Program related
2. Fundraising
3. Government affairs
4. Volunteer management
5. Membership development
6. Finance

Do you network with other not-for-profit CEOs?

Yes, for collaborative opportunities and key learning.

What qualities, in your opinion, do not-for-profit boards seek in their CEOs?

1. Leadership traits
2. Ability to raise funds
3. Integrity, trust
4. Staff management skills
5. Ability to articulate and write a message
6. Education credentials
7. Successful administrative and fiscal management
8. Government affairs experience

Additional comments: The board of any not-for-profit organization wants its CEO to have the ability to successfully work with diverse groups of volunteers. They desire someone who is capable of sharing their vision. A CEO needs to know how to manage the various governance issues that arise in nonprofits.

Volunteer leaders want a CEO who is willing to immerse himself or herself completely in the organization and do what it takes to fulfill the mission. They seek a person who is able to articulate the organization's vision, find the resources to get the job done and attract the best staff possible. A CEO needs to be opportunistic by nature.

The CEO has to aspire to fulfill the organization's goals; not his or her personal goals. Sometimes personal goals run counter to doing your best and the CEO must always make sure that the organization's goals come first.

How did you become aware of your current CEO position?

I knew someone who was a member or in a leadership position of the organization through networking.

What were the major factors that helped you to successfully win your current CEO position?

1. Understanding what the organization sought in the new CEO
2. Ability to connect with the key volunteer leadership
3. How I prepared and executed the interview meeting process
4. A well-prepared resume and cover letter
5. My negotiation skills

Additional comments: Anyone who wishes to become a CEO of a not-for-profit must inspire confidence toward the organization's targeted groups, including staff, funding sources, members, or constituents and the general public. To become a CEO, you need to be able to set and reach goals. You are going to be judged on what you do, not on who you are. Interpersonal skills are needed to better relate to diverse audiences, to communicate well, and to understand the various points of view on the same subject. Having the ability to raise the needed funds to fulfill the mission of the organization will always be a major attribute. All of these qualities need to be brought out by the potential CEO during the interview process to ensure that he or she is identified as leader.

Aspiring CEOs must begin early in their career paths to gain attention in order to move up the ladder. One of best ways to do this is to be willing to do more than you are asked. Try to stand out in the crowd. Be known for what you can give, rather than what you want. Take any assignment that will demonstrate your abilities. Become known as the individual who does more than is expected of them. Boards are looking for CEOs who want to exceed expectations.

What kind of preparation did you do prior to the interview?

- Obtained information about the organization via the Internet and other sources
- Prepared questions to ask and anticipated questions to answer
- Rehearsed

What were the three major reasons you were selected for your current position?

- Background
- Communications skills
- Key contacts on board

Additional comments: I was hired from within. The organization knew who I was and had an idea of what I was capable of doing. Doing your current job well often leads to new opportunities.

What did you do during the first six months as a new CEO to cement your relationships?

- Met key leadership
- Created a personal plan of action
- Evaluated staff
- Prepared a status report for member leaders
- Made sure program functions were in order
- Did an overall evaluation of the organization

Additional comments: Because I was promoted from the COO position, my initial tasks were different than they would have been if I was starting as a new employee.

What measures have you taken to continue to strengthen your position at your current organization?

- Increase staff effectiveness.
- Maintain a high level of interaction with key leadership.
- Keep my organization fiscally sound.

- Raise more income.
- Make sure that a clearly defined strategic plan is in place.
- Make sure that I am linked to the highest priority issues.
- Maintain a key role in the government affairs function.
- Keep myself as visible as possible with members.

How have you or would you prepare to attain another CEO position?

1. Maintain a network that would alert me to possible positions.
2. Increase my visibility with the volunteer leadership of the targeted organization(s).
3. Keep on the cutting edge through training.

In your opinion, what are the three major changes in the not-for-profit CEO role in the last decade?

- Accountability
- Use of technology
- Fundraising success

Additional comments: A CEO has to be multitalented. I helped to build a number of partnerships for the POLF to succeed. We just could not have done it alone. I strive to project a vision, attract various stakeholders, and to amass both internal and external leaders to move our vision in the same direction.

What do you feel are the three major challenges that not-for-profit CEOs face in the next decade?

- Collaboration verses competition
- Fundraising/diversifying revenue
- Accountability issues

Additional comments: The increased use of partnerships, both with other not-for-profits as well as with for-profits, is going to be the key to fulfilling individual organizational goals. Also make sure that your programs are aligned with future consumer interests as times change and trends will begin to shift interest.

We would welcome any additional information or advice that you would like to provide that would help to prepare an individual to attain and retain a CEO position in a not-for-profit organization.

To continue to be a successful CEO, focus your organization on what it does best, drop programs that are not productive and help your organization become the leader in its field.

John H. Graham IV

President and CEO (since 2003)
American Society of Association Executives
Washington, D.C.

Highest Education Degree:	Bachelor of Arts
Major:	History
Certifications:	Certified Association Executive (CAE)
Career tenure:	Not-for-profits: 33 years
Profile of current not-for-profit served:	International
	Budget: $24 million
	Number of members: 24,000
	Number of employees: 110
	Number of chapters: 72 (allied societies)
	Number of incorporated organizations: 3
	IRS designations: 501(c)6, 501(c)3 and a for-profit

Past employers: (Ranked: Number 1 is the first position held)

1. District executive, Boy Scouts of America, Valley Forge, Pennsylvania
2. District executive M/M (supervising staff), Boy Scouts of America, Valley Forge, Pennsylvania
3. Field director, Boy Scouts of America, Valley Forge, Pennsylvania
4. Executive director, American Diabetes Association, Philadelphia, Pennsylvania
5. National development director, American Diabetes Association, New York, New York
6. Deputy, executive vice president, American Diabetes Association, Alexandria, Virginia
7. CEO, American Diabetes Association, Alexandria, Virginia

The following is a summary of the interview that took place between John Graham and the author.

Walter Pidgeon: *Were there unique circumstances in your past that may have helped you to attain your current position?*

John Graham: As you know, I have been an active member of the American Society of Association Executives (ASAE) for a number of years; I served on the board and the foundation. I was approached by the search committee to consider this position. I do believe that my liberal arts degree provided a good base, particularly taking courses in a wide variety of areas. My professional positions with the Boy Scouts of America provided me with an appreciation of the role that volunteers play in not-for-profits. The American Diabetes Association increased my association management skills.

WP: *Do you currently have a contract?*

JG: Yes.

WP: *What do you feel are the advantages and/or disadvantages of a contract?*

JG: A contract spells out the terms of employment and, equally important, separation. It makes it clear to the parties, the employee, and the board what is expected for what compensation.

WP: *If you knew that you would become a CEO of a not-for-profit organization, would you have taken different steps to prepare?*

JG: I don't think so, I gained a wealth of experience and background in the positions that I had. My professional positions with the Boy Scouts of America provided me with a very good base from which to work. They are very good at showing new employees, right from the start, the value of organization, volunteer management and fundraising. My time with the American Diabetes Association was exciting and productive as well. ASAE provided me with an opportunity for a change as well as an opportunity to provide a service to our profession.

WP: *What formal educational courses do you feel that every not-for-profit CEO should have taken?*

JG: Beyond the typical course work that you need to manage an association, not-for-profit CEOs need to have a good understanding of volunteer management. Most not-for-profit organizations today still rely on volunteers to fulfill their missions and it is critical that CEOs understand how to recruit, motivate and retain quality volunteers. Association leaders who do not understand the importance of volunteers will not be successful.

WP: *What advice would you provide an individual who has set a career goal to become a CEO of a not-for-profit organization?*

JG: CEOs have to portray confidence to everyone they associate with, both volunteers and staff. They have to know the process and how things get done. Having good ideas is not enough; you have to know how to move it from the vision stage to practical application. You have to make strategic decisions based on the organization's mission. Students should prepare by having some course work that enables them to understand human nature, what motivates and rewards people. This work is all about relationship building. Not-for-profit professionals should experience as many functions as possible in not-for-profit associations and get their CAE. For-profit executives need to first decide their motivation for moving on to not-for-profit work. Volunteers and volunteer boards are not just focused on the bottom line like for-profits. They really care about the impact the organization is having, which is a very different focus than just profits. For-profit executives should experience not-for-profit organizations before jumping in.

WP: *Did you have and do you have mentors?*

JG: Not really, I have had those who have helped me over the years but not what I would call mentors.

Survey Responses and Additional Comments from the Interview

Note: Responses that are numbered (i.e., 1, 2, 3, etc.) are ranked responses, with 1 being the highest.

Please rank the chief reasons why you were able to attain your current CEO position?

1. Past experiences
2. Ongoing training
3. Networking
4. Formal education
5. Certifications

What are the major personal skills that have helped you to retain your current CEO position?

1. Volunteer management
2. Producer—making goals
3. Fiscal control
4. Planning
5. Member relations
6. Government relations
7. Keeping on the cutting edge
8. Networking

What kind of career experiences would you recommend to aspiring CEOs to prepare them for the top position?

1. Volunteer management
2. Finance
3. Government relations
4. Fundraising

5. Membership development
6. Program related

Do you network with other not-for-profit CEOs?

Yes, for information sharing and learning.

What qualities, in your opinion, do not-for-profit boards seek in their CEOs?

1. Leadership traits
2. Integrity, trust
3. Successful administration and fiscal management
4. Staff management skills
5. Volunteer management skills
6. Ability to articulate and write a message
7. Ability to raise funds
8. Government affairs experience
9. Education credentials

How did you become aware of your current CEO position?

I was a member of the organization.

What were the major factors that helped you to successfully win your current CEO position?

1. Understanding what the organization sought in the new CEO
2. Ability to connect with the key volunteer leadership
3. How I prepared and executed the interview meeting process
4. My negotiation skills
5. A well-prepared resume and cover letter

What kind of preparation did you do prior to the interview?

1. Prepared questions to ask and anticipated questions to answer
2. Obtained information about the organization via the Internet and other sources
3. Rehearsed
4. Brought examples of my work

What were the three major reasons you were selected for your current position?

- Track record
- Leadership ability
- Known quantity

What did you do during the first six months as a new CEO to cement your relationships?

1. Did an overall evaluation of the organization
2. Met key leadership
3. Created a personal plan of action
4. Ensured that proper fiscal controls were in place
5. Made sure program functions were in order
6. Evaluated staff
7. Made significant changes and/or refinements
8. Prepared a status report for member leaders
9. Evaluated volunteer leadership

What measures have you taken to continue to strengthen your position at your current organization?

1. Make sure that clearly defined strategies and outcomes are in place.
2. Make sure that I am linked to the highest priority issues.
3. Maintain a high level of interaction with key leadership.
4. Keep my organization fiscally sound.
5. Keep myself as visible as possible with members.
6. Increase staff effectiveness.
7. Develop a relationship with the media or trade press.
8. Find opportunities to speak and write.
9. Maintain a key role in the government affairs function.
10. Insist on an annual review based on mutually agreed–upon goals. Keep on the cutting edge through training.
11. Raise more income.

How have you or would you prepare to attain another CEO position?

1. Maintain a network that would alert me to possible positions.
2. Increase my visibility with the volunteer leadership of the targeted organization.
3. Become a volunteer at the prospective organization.
4. Keep on the cutting edge through training.
5. Donate to the prospective organization.

In your opinion, what are the three major changes in the not-for-profit CEO role in the last decade?

- Metrics
- Governance
- Volunteer and staff relationships

Additional comments: Nothing is taken at face value. Tangible measurements are required; a CEO must understand that every decision that is made has implications. Therefore, CEOs must act and think differently than 10 years ago. They must be aware of constituent values.

What do you feel are the three major challenges that not-for-profit CEOs face in the next decade?

- Transparency
- Value proposition
- Maintaining effective communications

Additional comments: Technology will be one of our biggest challenges. Defining value or what members really want and then finding ways to provide it will be the key to attracting and retaining members.

We would welcome any additional information or advice that you would like to provide that would help to prepare an individual to attain and retain a CEO position in a not-for-profit organization.

Know what your organization's values are and execute your operations accordingly.

Robert (Rob) Keck

Chief Executive Officer (since 1981)
National Wild Turkey Federation
Edgefield, South Carolina

Highest education degree:	Bachelor of Arts
Major:	Liberal Arts
Certifications:	Certified to teach secondary and high school
Career tenure:	Not-for-profits: 26 years
	Education: 6.5 years
Profile of current not-for-profit served:	International organization
	Budget: $65 million
	Number of members: 510,000
	Number of employees: 240
	Number of chapters: 2,150
	Number of incorporated organizations: 1
	IRS designation: 501(c)3
Past employers:	Teacher, West Perry School District, Elliotsburg, Pennsylvania

The following is a summary of the interview that took place between Rob Keck and the author.

Walter Pidgeon: *Were there unique circumstances in your past that may have helped you attain your current position?*

Robert Keck: Absolutely. Being at the right place at the right time and knowing and having relationships with the decision-making board of directors. The people and communications skills I learned and refined as a high school teacher played a large role as well.

The communications skills that I refined as a teacher were a wonderful asset in setting the stage with chapters, volunteers, members, and partners.

Not-for-profit CEOs do not have to come from similar backgrounds; the key is how they use their talents to deal with people and to keep it simple. My teaching background helped me orchestrate short, simple messages that everyone could understand. It has made a real difference. My participation in competitive sports also played a huge role. Understanding the team concept fostered in both baseball and football helped me tremendously in team building before I was selected for the top job.

WP: *Do you currently have a contract?*

RK: No, and never have had one.

WP: *What do you feel are the advantages and/or disadvantages of a contract?*

RK: A contract detracts from the cohesiveness of the team concept I foster with my staff and volunteers. The fact that I don't have a contract makes me work harder to meet our mission, please the board I work for, and work harder to keep our team working together.

WP: *If you knew that you would become a CEO of a not-for-profit organization someday, would you have taken different steps to prepare?*

RK: No, I don't think so. It is important for any not-for-profit CEO to take a variety of course work to discover his strengths and weaknesses. My liberal arts degree has been a great help to me. The variety of subjects taught to me in college continues to assist me.

A simple formula for a CEO to be successful is to know one's weaknesses and surround oneself with those who can strengthen these areas. Everyone has weak areas; we cannot be all things to all people. But we can find others who can help us fill those gaps. The first step is to identify those weaknesses; you have to be honest with yourself. Then when you search for the right people to support your vision, you have a good starting point. This helps you have a higher-than-average success rate in selecting the right people to surround you. Sometimes you are not successful at selecting the right person, and the faster you recognize that you made a mistake in selecting the right person and replacing that person, the more effective you'll be.

Surrounding yourself with the right people helps you to grow both the organization you lead and yourself. A degree of common sense also is so important. Keep it simple and straightforward so everyone understands where you want to go.

WP: *What formal educational courses do you feel every not-for-profit CEO should take?*

RK: Much of what a not-for-profit CEO needs to do cannot be solved through an academic background. It involves how well that person deals with people, the trust people have in their CEO and how honest that person is with himself and others.

CEOs are constantly selling themselves and their organizations to others. CEOs are salesmen, yet many CEOs don't seem to focus on this part of the equation. I really feel strongly that not-for-profit professionals need to fully understand the art of selling. Basic and advanced courses in negotiations, marketing and the use of the media provide a wonderful base for leading an organization.

NWTF employees use these skills effectively to reach our audiences. We currently have three shows on cable TV, five magazines, four Web sites, and an electronic newsletter that have significantly increased our market penetration. These outlets help us reinforce what we are doing to fulfill our mission.

WP: *What advice would you provide an individual who has set a career goal to become a CEO of a not-for-profit organization?*

RK: Find out what not-for-profit really means. *Not-for-profit* does not mean you don't generate a profit. The bottom line is just as important in a not-for-profit as it is in a for-profit. The only difference between a not-for-profit and a for-profit is how the money is spent. CEOs need to understand the unique way not-for-profits find and spend revenue.

Also, it is important to secure the best finance person (CPA) possible to make sure you are maximizing financial and budgeting concerns. As a CEO you need to build a team atmosphere. Developing the budget, for example, is not a one-person exercise. At the NWTF, we involve the entire staff in the process and work with the management team to make sure everyone understands this process and has a stake in its development and execution.

Understanding the vital role of strategic planning is important as well. You cannot achieve your vision if you don't know how to begin and how to move the process along. At the NWTF we have a working three-year plan that we update constantly. The plan is tracked with the annual budgets and, again, everyone has a piece of it. The plan strengthens the team approach, and that is a vital part of our organization. My background in team sports taught me that you are only as strong as your weakest link. Each individual's work goes far beyond what is on our job descriptions; it is the commitment that everyone has for the mission of our organization. This position is not a job; it becomes a lifestyle. Learning how to deal with objection, turning negative attitudes into positives, and learning the art of negotiation will prove very important to your success

For *students* who aspire to become CEOs of not-for-profits someday, I would suggest they take courses in marketing, sales, public sales, public speaking and the media. I also suggest they seek opportunities for leadership roles through sports, student government, clubs, etc. Exposure to various leadership opportunities will pay large dividends. I recall a Rotary Leadership Camp that I was selected to attend between my junior and senior year in high school that dealt with leadership issues. That camp awoke in me my leadership potential. Potential leaders need to be nurtured more than ever. I also owe much to my days of scouting as a Cub Scout, Boy Scout, and Explorer. Leadership seeds are planted very early.

Professionals in the field who wish to work toward becoming a CEO need to understand and embrace the passion it takes to be a leader. A leader's key role is to inspire others to develop the same passion. To do this, you need to understand your organization's mission and to have a good idea how it should be fulfilled. You are not going to be able to do it all by yourself.

For-profit executives who wish to become a not-for-profit CEO need to make a few adjustments. The mission and the stakeholders are the bottom line in a not-for-profit. Polished people skills are required and tender loving care really makes the difference. In a not-for-profit you work for the volunteers and members who are your stockholders. While the bottom line is important, the selling of the vision to your members becomes an even bigger key to your success. Understand, profit is not only defined in dollars.

WP: *Did you have and do you have mentors?*

RK: Yes, many. Today our country is short of heroes and role models. This country's young people are hungry for role models who will shape tomorrow's future leaders. My dad, my mother and my grandparents were my firsts. They taught me honesty, respect, and basic life skills. They taught me that a simple thank-you can make a world of difference, and those two words are still one of the best tools we have to motivate people. "Thank you" is the "paycheck" to volunteers. My great uncle Bill Bibbus was another individual who taught me to always follow my dream and go after whatever it is I want to achieve. Never put off till tomorrow what I can do today. If you see an opportunity or experience that interests you, go for it.

My football coach in high school, Ted King, taught me the important role that a team plays. I still use these principles today. I was active in Boy Scouts as a youngster. Many mentors and leaders introduced me to a number of lifetime skills and added to my enthusiasm of the outdoors. Ned Smith, a wildlife artist, inspired me to be the best I could be. Curt Gowdy, host of ABC's "American Sportsman," and another personality, Harry Alleman of "Call of the Outdoors," inspired me to become a TV host.

Earl Groves, a past president of the NWTF, saw something in me I didn't see at the time and offered the challenge of my current role at the NWTF. He helped me understand what leadership was about and to believe in myself.

My pastor, Tony Hopkins, has helped instill in me the power of prayer. Being churched as a youngster laid a foundation of love and faith that has helped me through the most challenging of times.

Survey Responses and Additional Comments from the Interview

Note: Responses that are numbered (i.e., 1, 2, 3, etc.) are ranked, with 1 being the highest.

Please rank the chief reasons you were able to attain your current CEO position.

1. *Other:* Being at the right place at the right time

2. Networking

3. Past experiences

4. Ongoing training

5. Formal education

6. Certifications

What are the major personal skills that have helped you to retain your current CEO position?

1. *Other:* Having a very high percentage of picking the right people for my management team. Acknowledging my weaknesses and allowing the skills of my staff to shore them up.

2. Producer—making goals

3. Fiscal control

4. Planning

5. Volunteer management

6. Member relations

7. Keeping on the cutting edge

8. Networking

9. Government relations

Additional comments: People skills, having passion, and the ability to network with others

What kind of career experiences would you recommend to aspiring CEOs to prepare them for the top position?

1. *Other:* Learning to deal with people as a leader; people skills along with top-notch communications skills

2. Program related

3. Volunteer management

4. Fundraising

5. Finance

6. Membership development

7. Government relations

Do you network with other not-for-profit CEOs?

Yes, in a limited way. I partner on common needs for our organizations.

What qualifications, in your opinion, do not-for-profit boards seek in their CEOs?

1. Integrity, trust

2. Staff management skills

3. Ability to articulate and write a message

4. Ability to raise funds

5. Leadership traits

6. Successful administrative and fiscal management

7. Volunteer management skills

8. Education credentials

9. Government affairs experience

How did you become aware of your current CEO position?

I knew someone who was a member or in a leadership position of the organization through networking.

What were the major factors that helped you to successfully win your current CEO position?

- Ability to connect with the key volunteer leadership
- Understanding what the organization sought in the new CEO

What kind of preparation did you do prior to the interview?

Other: I was selected from the existing staff.

What were the three major reasons you were selected for your current position?

1. Leadership traits

2. Integrity, trust

3. Ability to articulate and rally volunteers

Additional comments: I was in the right place at the right time, and I sold myself to the volunteer leadership.

What did you do during the first six months as a new CEO to cement your relationships?

1. Evaluated staff

2. Created a personal plan of action

3. Ensured that proper fiscal controls were in place

4. Evaluated volunteer leadership

What measures have you taken to continue to strengthen your position at your current organization?

1. Keep my organization fiscally sound.

2. Make sure that a clearly defined strategic plan is in place.

3. Keep myself as visible as possible with members.

4. Raise more income.

5. Maintain a high level of interaction with key leadership.

6. Keep on the cutting edge through training.

7. Find opportunities to speak and write.

8. Develop a relationship with the media or trade press.

9. Insist on an annual review based on mutually agreed-upon goals.

10. Make sure I am linked to the highest priority issues.

11. Increase staff effectiveness.

How have you or would you prepare to attain another CEO position?

I have no interest in another CEO position.

In your opinion, what are the three major changes in the not-for-profit CEO role in the last decade?

1. Challenges of a lackluster economy

2. Thriving in a fast-food society

3. Increased need to use media

Additional comments: Accountability and technology have become major factors as well.

What do you feel are the three major challenges that not-for-profit CEOs face in the next decade?

1. Changing demographics

2. Using the media effectively

3. Competing for the best volunteers

Additional comments: Increased scrutiny of the not-for-profit CEO has occurred as a result of a few not-for-profit leaders who were caught with their hands in the cookie jar. CEOs need to be better prepared to sell their message. The limited time individuals have to volunteer and limited funding makes it more important than ever to position our organizations to be vital and attractive.

We would welcome any additional information or advice that you would like to provide that would help to prepare an individual to attain and retain a CEO position in a not-for-profit organization.

Acquire good people skills, be able to sell yourself and your organization, become media savvy, and learn how to acknowledge your weaknesses and how to shore them up. Understand the value of the words "thank you." Develop passion for your mission. Never fail to admit you were wrong. Embrace the job as a lifestyle. Hone your speaking and communications skills. Understand that the nonprofit is not in the business of making money, but rather in the business of spending money for the mission of the organization.

David Kushner

President and CEO (since 2002)
Professional Convention Management Association
Chicago, Illinois

Highest education degree:	Master's Degree
Major:	Human Resource Management
Certifications:	Certified Association Executive (CAE)
	Certified Meeting Professional (CMP)
Career tenure:	Not-for-profit: 29 years
	For-profit: 4 years
Profile on current not-for-profit served:	International
	Budget: $7.5 million
	Number of members: 5,000
	Number of employees: 31
	Number of chapters: 16
	Number of incorporated organizations: 3
	IRS designations: 501(c)6, 501(c)3, and a for-profit

Past employers: (Ranked: Number 1 is the first position held)

1. Teacher, St. James School, Johnson City, New York
2. Teacher, Whitney Point. Central, Whitney Point, New York
3. Field Representative, New York State United Teachers, Vestal, New York
4. Director, American Federation of Government Employees, Washington, D.C.
5. Owner, Kushner Group, Washington, D.C.
6. President and CEO, American Osteopathic Healthcare Association, Chevy Chase, Maryland

The following is a summary of the interview that took place between David Kushner and the author.

Walter Pidgeon: *Were there unique circumstances in your past that may have helped you to attain your current position?*

David Kushner: Each of my past positions was an integral step in my growth leading up to my current position. My work as a teacher provided me with a discipline that has helped me to focus on getting things done in a logical and progressive manner. It also fostered good communication skills.

When I was a field representative with the New York State United Teachers, I interacted with members from many districts including administrators, boards of education, and teachers. I was required to make independent decisions, which meant I had to be self-motivated. I needed a plan of action and I had to nego- tiate a variety of situations in each district, which forced me to become well organized.

At the American Federation of Government Employees I learned the art of politics, government operations, and how to lead a national staff, which was geographically dispersed. As a consultant through the Kushner Group, I was exposed to a number of industries, which broadened my perspective on leader- ship and quality management. This position also helped me gain experience in collaboration with other professional colleagues to gain the unique skills they could bring to large projects.

At the American Osteopathic Healthcare Association I had the opportunity to work with some wonderful people who were leading large medical institutions during very trying times. I saw how they had to manage their operations and balance the needs of very diverse constituencies, all the while keeping a close eye on the balance sheet.

All of these experiences provided me with a wonderful background to now lead the Professional Convention Management Association.

WP: *Do you have an employment contract?*

DK: Yes, I do.

WP: *What do you feel are the advantages and/or disadvantages of a contract?*

DK: A contract sets the terms of employment, establishes how your assessment will be done, and creates a more formal business relationship between the parties. It is an essential tool for a CEO to have.

WP: *If you knew that you would become a CEO of a not-for-profit organization someday, would you have taken different steps to prepare?*

DK: I do not think I would have done anything differently. The academic and profes- sional experiences that I have gained were logical steps in my career progression.

WP: *What formal educational courses do you feel that every not-for-profit CEO should have taken?*

DK: First of all, I would include all those courses that you listed on your survey. I would add that someone who is CEO-bound should take course work in orga- nizational behavior, human resources, planning, and practical courses in finance.

WP: *What advice would you provide an individual who has set a career goal to become a CEO of a not-for-profit organization?*

DK: *Students:* If you hope to become a CEO of a not-for-profit organization, I recommend getting as broad an exposure as possible to a number of management disciplines.

Professionals in the field: CEOs need to have broad experiences on which to depend for future decision making. Try to acquire some practical not-for-profit experience. Learn to stretch yourself. Talk with leaders in the field, with those in your organization and outside it to acquire insight on what you need to do to make it to the top.

For-profit executives: Those attempting to enter the not-for-profit arena may find that many of the skills attained over the years are transferable but the environment is a lot different. For-profit executives need to fully understand how things get done in the not-for-profit community.

WP: *Did you have and do have mentors?*

DK: Not in a formal sense; however, there are several people who I consider as "career guides."

Survey Responses and Additional Comments from the Interview

Note: Responses that are numbered (i.e., 1, 2, 3, etc.) are ranked, with 1 being the highest.

Please rank the chief reasons why you were able to attain your current CEO position.

1. Past CEO experience
2. Education background
3. Industry certifications
4. Foundation/philanthropic work
5. Networking

What are the major personal skills that have helped you to retain your current CEO position?

1. Good communications skills
2. Strategic planner/thinker
3. Good at member relations
4. Goal setter
5. Extensive volunteer experience
6. Experiences with government relations/advocacy

What kind of career experiences would you recommend to aspiring CEOs to prepare them for the top position?

1. Finance work
2. Management of volunteers
3. Membership development
4. Program management
5. Fundraising
6. Government affairs/advocacy work

Do you network with other not-for-profit CEOs?

Yes, to share ideas, learn from one another, for camaraderie, and for moral support.

What qualities, in your opinion, do not-for-profit boards seek in their CEOs?

1. Leadership
2. Integrity, trust, sound ethical foundation
3. Successful administrative and fiscal management
4. Staff management skills
5. Volunteer management skills
6. Strong communication skills
7. Ability to raise funds
8. Education credentials
9. Government affairs experience

How did you become aware of your current position?

Through networking and a job posting service

What were the major factors that helped you to successfully win your current CEO position?

1. A well-prepared resume and cover letter
2. How I prepared and executed the interview meeting process
3. Understanding what the organization sought in the new CEO
4. Having the ability to connect with volunteer leadership
5. Previous work in education and philanthropy

Additional comments: A well-done resume and cover letter helps you get in the door. Once you are at the interview you must find ways to stand out from the crowd. Ask well-thought-out questions, listen and respond with in-depth answers. Make sure that you find ways to connect to the interviewers on a personal level.

What kind of preparation did you do prior to the interview?

1. Obtained information about the organization via the Internet and other research
2. Prepared questions to ask and anticipated questions to answer

3. Rehearsed

4. Brought examples of my work

What were the three major reasons you were selected for your current position?

- Previous CEO experience in an association
- Background in education
- Direct experience in the industry

What did you do during the first six months as a new CEO to cement your relationships?

1. Did an overall evaluation of the organization's programs and strategic plan
2. Met key leaders across the country
3. Assessed staff
4. Created a personal plan of action
5. Ensured that proper fiscal controls were in place
6. Became familiar with volunteer leadership of the boards and chapters
7. Prepared a status report for member leaders
8. Made sure program functions were in order

What measures have you taken to continue to strengthen your position at your current organization?

1. Keep myself as visible as possible with members.
2. Maintain a high level of interaction with leadership.
3. Make sure that I focus on high-priority issues.
4. Keep the organization fiscally sound.
5. Make sure that the strategic plan is in place and being fulfilled.
6. Look for opportunities to speak and write.
7. Develop a relationship with the media or trade press.
8. Increase staff effectiveness.
9. Diversify sources of revenue.
10. Insist upon an annual performance review based on mutually agreed-upon goals.
11. Seek additional training.

How have you or would you prepare to attain another CEO position?

1. Maintain a network that would alert me to positions.
2. Increase my visibility with volunteer leadership of other organization(s).
3. Keep on the cutting edge through advanced training.
4. Be successful where I am now.

In your opinion, what are the three major changes in the not-for-profit CEO role in the last decade?

- Increased financial pressure
- Communications challenges resulting from the Internet
- Increased membership expectations with shorter time frames

What do you feel are the three major challenges that not-for-profit CEOs face in the next decade?

- Again, expanded access to information on the Internet for members
- Industry consolidations and incursion of for-profit companies into current association markets
- Media and public scrutiny

We would welcome any additional information or advice that you would like to provide that would help to prepare an individual to attain and retain a CEO position in a not-for-profit organization.

Maintain a personal focus on ethical behavior, increase your business skills, and become technologically savvy.

Paulette V. Maehara

President and CEO
Association of Fundraising Professionals
Alexandria, Virginia

Highest education degree:	Bachelor of Arts
Major:	Political Science and Music
Certifications:	Certified Association Executive (CAE)
	Certified Fund Raising Executive (CFRE)
Career tenure:	Not-for-profits: 26 years
	For-profits: 2 years
Profile of current not-for-profit served:	International Association
	Budget: $10 million
	Number of members: 26,000
	Number of employees: 61
	Number of chapters: 174
	Number of incorporated organizations: 2
	IRS designation: 501(c)6, 501(c)3

Past employers: (Ranked: Number 1 is the first position held)

1. March coordinator, March of Dimes, Honolulu, Hawaii
2. Assistant manager, American Red Cross, Honolulu, Hawaii
3. Assistant national director, American Red Cross, Washington, D.C.
4. Acting CEO/general manager, National Capital Chapter, American Red Cross, Washington, D.C.
5. Vice president of development, Project Hope, Millwood, Virginia
6. CEO, Epilepsy Foundation, Landover, Maryland

The following is a summary of the interview that took place between Paulette Maehara and the author.

Walter Pidgeon: *Were there unique circumstances in your past that may have helped you to attain your current position?*

Paulette Maehara: I believe two areas in my background helped me to attain my present position. The first is my background as a national manager starting with my role as acting CEO at the American Red Cross and my fundraising experience. The Association of Fundraising Professionals is very visible international organization that represents and supports fundraising professionals.

WP: *Do you currently have a contract?*

PM: Yes.

WP: *What do you feel are the advantages and/or disadvantages of a contract?*

PM: I believe a contract is an essential part of the CEO package. It defines the compensation package, including a retirement and protection for the CEO as well as the Association.

WP: *If you knew that you would become a CEO of a not-for-profit organization someday, would you have taken different steps to prepare?*

PM: For the most part, no; I might have sought an MBA, however. So much of what association CEOs do is related to the business side of the equation. Like a lot of association executives, I had to learn these skills on the job.

WP: *What formal educational courses do you feel that every not-for-profit CEO should have taken?*

PM: As you know, there are a number of undergraduate and graduate programs with majors in not-for-profit administration. If you have set a goal, early in life, to work for a not-for-profit you might want to check these programs out. Once you are on the job, the American Society of Association Executives has a vast array of educational programs to keep you up to speed. Anyone who becomes a CEO of a not-for-profit organization should have taken courses in finance, fundraising, human resources, and various aspects of legal work including contracts.

WP: *What advice would you provide an individual who has set a career goal to become a CEO of a not-for-profit organization?*

PM: *Students:* My advice to students who wish to enter the professional ranks of the not-for-profit community is to gain the skills of not-for-profit management and really understand the sector. The not-for-profit sector is different than the for-profit sector; you need to know the differences. Also, take the time to volunteer so you can better understanding how to manage individuals who are not on the payroll but can make a great deal of difference in the success or failure of an organization. Managing volunteers is your greatest challenge.

Not-for-profit professionals need to establish a network and keep in touch with peers to discover the opportunities that are available. Continue to increase your skills and look for training that will prepare you for the top position. The U.S. Chamber of Commerce association management training is a fine example.

For-profit executives: The greatest challenge for someone coming into the not-for-profit sector from the for-profit sector is to understand the difference in the dynamics of both of the sectors. What drives the not-for-profit sector is different, and no one will be successful working in the sector unless they know the differences. I would encourage anyone thinking of crossing over sectors to volunteer on a not-for-profit board first to see how the process works and, more importantly, to see if they would like to work in such an environment.

WP: *Did you and do you have mentors?*

PM: Yes, I do have mentors. The Honorable John Henry Felix has been and still is a mentor. I first met John when I was working in Hawaii. He taught me the importance of the volunteer governance process and how it relates to the success of an organization. My husband, Thomas H. Henderson, is also a mentor for me. He has been an association executive for 17 years. He is currently the CEO of the American Trial Lawyers Association.

Survey Responses and Additional Comments from the Interview

Note: Responses that are numbered (i.e., 1, 2, 3, etc.) are ranked, with 1 being the highest.

Please rank the chief reasons why you were able to attain your current CEO position.

1. Past experience
2. *Other:* My fundraising experience

What are the major personal skills that have helped you to retain your current CEO position?

1. Producer—making goals
2. Fiscal control
3. Other: Fundraising background
4. Volunteer management

What kind of career experiences would you recommend to aspiring CEOs to prepare them for the top position?

1. Volunteer management
2. Fundraising
3. Finance
4. Membership development
5. Government affairs
6. Program related

Do you network with other not-for-profit CEOs?

Yes; learn from peers.

What qualities, in your opinion, do not-for-profit boards seek in their CEOs?

1. Leadership traits
2. Ability to raise funds
3. Integrity, trust
4. Volunteer management skills
5. Successful administrative and fiscal management
6. Staff management skills
7. Government affairs experience
8. Education credentials
9. Ability to articulate and write a message

How did you become aware of your current position?

Executive recruiter

What were the major factors that helped you to successfully win your current CEO position?

1. Ability to connect with the key volunteer leadership
2. How I prepared and executed the interview meeting process
3. Understanding what the organization sought in the new CEO
4. A well-prepared resume and cover letter
5. My negotiating skills

What kind of preparation did you do prior to the interview?

1. Obtained information about the organization via the Internet and other sources
2. Prepared questions to ask and anticipated questions to answer
3. Rehearsed

What were the three major reasons you were selected for your current position?

- Past national management experience
- Leadership
- Fundraising background

What did you do during the first six months as a new CEO to cement your relationships?

1. Met key leadership
2. Created a personal plan of action
3. Did an overall evaluation of the organization
4. Ensured that proper fiscal controls were in place
5. Evaluated staff

6. Prepared a status report for member leaders

7. Made significant changes and/or refinements

8. Made sure program functions were in order

9. Evaluated volunteer leadership

What measures have you taken to continue to strengthen your position at your current organization?

1. Insist upon an annual review based on mutually agreed-upon goals.

2. Make sure that a clearly defined strategic plan is in place.

3. Maintain a high level of interaction with key leadership.

4. Keep my organization fiscally sound.

5. Increase staff effectiveness.

6. Keep myself as visible as possible with members.

7. Raise more income.

How have you or would you prepare to attain another CEO position?

Maintain a network that would alert me to possible positions.

In you opinion, what are the three major changes in the not-for-profit CEO role in the last decade?

- Shift from program to fundraising

- Emphases on outcomes

- The importance of open communications and transparency

What do you feel are the three major challenges that not-for-profit CEOs face in the next decade?

- Increased competition

- Fiscal restraints on not-for-profits

- Volunteers with less time

We would welcome any additional information or advice that you would like to provide that would help to prepare an individual to attain and retain a CEO position in a not-for-profit organization.

If you really want to become a CEO of a not-for-profit organization, be persistent. It may not happen the first or even second round. Keep yourself ready for when the opportunity comes your way.

H. Robert Wientzen

President and CEO (since 1996)
Direct Marketing Association
New York, New York

Highest education degree:	Bachelor of Arts
Major:	Sociology and Psychology
Certifications:	None
Career tenure:	Not-for-profits: 8 years
	For-Profits: 30 years
Profile of current not-for-profit served:	International Organization
	Budget: $34 million
	Number of members: 4,700
	Number of employees: 145
	Number of chapters: 7
	Number of incorporated organizations: 4
	IRS designations: 501(c)6, 501(c)3, 501(c)3, and a for-profit

Past employers:
U.S. Army, Captain
Procter & Gamble (various locations)
Advanced Promotion Technologies, Inc., CEO
The DMA (Direct Marketing Association), president and CEO

The following is a summary of the interview that took place between Bob Wientzen and the author.

Walter Pidgeon: *Were there unique circumstances in your past that may have helped you to attain your current position?*

Robert Wientzen: My 27-year marketing career with Procter & Gamble certainly provided me with knowledge about the field that the Direct Marketing Association (DMA) represents. The association leadership wanted someone who knew and understood the industry. I was also active in the DMA and served on the board for 7 years.

WP: *Do you have a contract?*

RW: Yes, when I first came to the DMA I had a multiyear contract. Now it is a year-to-year arrangement.

WP: *What do you feel are the advantages and/or disadvantages of a contract?*

RW: I believe contracts can be helpful, although not a requirement. They provide a clear arrangement between both parties. Sometimes it is best to have legal counsel handle it for you.

WP: *What formal educational courses do you feel that every not-for-profit CEO should have taken?*

RW: Not-for-profit CEOs need to gain more legal and political training, including how Congress really works. My background comes from a business perspective having been a CEO of a public corporation and a senior executive of a large complex company. I knew the industry but was new to the association field. I did have a good background as a volunteer, however. I was active in a number of not-for-profit organizations over the years and started a charity and served on their board for a number of years. These experiences really made a difference.

WP: *What advice would you provide an individual who has set a career goal to become a CEO of a not-for-profit organization?*

RW: *Students* who aspire to become CEOs of not-for-profit organizations should obtain a good understanding of the government relations process from both the federal and state perspective. Become familiar with accounting from a not-for-profit perspective, including how to read a balance sheet and how to develop and maintain a budget. Become aware of the various legal aspects of an association and how technology is going to play a greater role in the not-for-profit community, as well as the business world.

Not-for-profit professionals who aspire to become CEOs should find ways to become involved in other not-for-profit activities as a volunteer. Discover how not-for-profits do business and how they manage both volunteers and staff.

For-profit executives looking to enter the not-for-profit field in a CEO role can apply a lot of the skills that they have acquired in the for-profit arena. Leadership is one of the most sought-after attributes in the not-for-profit community. Due to time restraints, not-for-profits need more people to volunteer, particularly if you want to affect real change, and that takes real readership. Not-for-profit leaders can make a difference within an industry through discovering how their association can provide the value needed to orchestrate effective change.

WP: *Did you have and do you have mentors?*

RW: Yes, I do believe in mentors. Bob Goldstein, vice president of advertising at Procter & Gamble, was a great leader, teacher, and intellect. He was a great help to me, and a real mentor. Bob Wehling, also vice president of World Wide Advertising for Procter & Gamble, was also a mentor for me.

Survey Responses and Additional Comments from the Interview

Note: Responses that are numbered, i.e., 1, 2, 3, etc are ranked responses, 1 being the highest.

Please rank the chief reasons why you were able to attain your current CEO position.

1. Past experiences
2. Networking
3. Formal education
4. Ongoing training

What are the major personal skills that have helped you to retain your current CEO position?

1. *Other:* Vision
2. Keeping on the cutting edge
3. Member relations
4. Fiscal control
5. Producer—making goals
6. Volunteer management
7. Planning
8. Networking

Additional comments: I have helped to provide a vision for our industry.

What kind of career experiences would you recommend to aspiring CEOs to prepare them for the top position?

1. Government affairs
2. Membership development
3. Volunteer management
4. Finance
5. Program related
6. Fundraising

Do you network with other not-for-profit CEOs?

Yes, it is the best source of benchmarking.

What qualities, in your opinion, do not-for-profit boards seek in their CEOs?

1. Leadership traits
2. Government affairs experience
3. Volunteer management skills
4. Staff management skills

5. Integrity, trust
6. Ability to articulate and write a message
7. Ability to raise funds
8. Successful administrative and fiscal management
9. Education credentials
10. *Other:* Vision and leadership

Additional comments: Boards seek leadership qualities in their CEOs. They also seek core skills like government affairs and staff management.

How did you become aware of your current CEO position?

I was a member of the organization.

What were the major factors that helped you to successfully win your current CEO position?

1. Understanding what the organization sought in the new CEO
2. Ability to connect with the key volunteer leadership
3. How I prepared and executed the interview meeting process

What kind of preparation did you do prior to the interview?

Prepared questions to ask and anticipated questions to answer

What were the three major reasons you were selected for your current position?

- Vision
- Leadership
- Experience

Additional comments: My industry experience was the key factor. I also had a number of important contacts, as well as government affairs experience.

What did you do during the first six months as a new CEO to cement your relationships?

1. Created a personal plan of action
2. Evaluated staff
3. Met key leadership
4. Did an overall evaluation of the organization
5. Ensured that proper fiscal controls were in place

What measures have you taken to continue to strengthen your position at your current organization?

1. Maintained a high level of interaction with key leadership
2. Kept my organization fiscally sound
3. Kept myself as visible as possible with members

4. Developed a relationship with the media or trade press

5. Found opportunities to speak and write

How have you or would you prepare to attain another CEO position?

1. Maintain a network that would alert me to possible positions.

2. Increase my visibility with the volunteer leadership of the targeted organization.

3. Check want ads.

In your opinion, what are the three major changes in the not-for-profit CEO role in the last decade?

- Technology needs to be increased.

- Funding is more important and more difficult.

Additional comments: Being a spokesperson for the industry became a bigger challenge. Technology became more important than ever in successfully managing an association, including the meeting, planning, and marketing aspects. Demand on people's time has changed, and this has affected volunteering patterns.

What do you feel are the three major challenges that not-for-profit CEOs face in the next decade?

- Less volunteer time available

- More dependence on technology

- Global issues

Additional comments: We are going to have to be less dependent on volunteers. Dealing with the government will become even more complicated. If we experience another downturn in the economy, will associations have adequate funding to survive?

We would welcome any additional information or advice that you would like to provide that would help to prepare an individual to attain and retain a CEO position in a not-for-profit organization.

Although I spent most of my career in the for-profit arena prior to assuming my CEO role at the DMA, I also volunteered for a number of not-for-profit organizations. My favorite was a not-for-profit that I helped to start, called Lighthouse Youth Services, which is a children's organization that provides comprehensive youth and family services including emergency shelters, residential treatment, foster care, juvenile corrections, transitional living services for older homeless youths, and in-home service for families in crisis. I spent more than 25 years as the volunteer leader and chairman of the board. I am proud to say that when I left the organization, it was raising over $15 million a year. This experience and my business background provided me with a rich background to successfully run the Direct Marketing Association.

Roy L. Williams

Chief Scout Executive (since 2000)
Boy Scouts of America (BSA)
Irving, Texas

Highest education degree:	Bachelor of Arts
Major:	Business Certifications: Harvard School of Business, Strategic Perspectives in Non-Profit Management. Multiple BSA certifications.
Career tenure:	Not-for-profits: 32 years
	For-profits: 6 years
	4 years of military service
Profile of current not-for-profit served:	National
	Budget: $100 million National Council
	$600 million total organization
	Number of members: 4.7 million youth and 1.25 million adults
	Number of employees: 7,400
	Number of chapters (Councils): 310
	Number of incorporated organizations: 311
	IRS designations: 501(c)3

Past Employers: (Ranked: Number 1 is the first position held)

1. District executive, BSA, Ft. Worth, Texas
2. District executive, BSA, Abilene, Texas
3. Finance director, BSA, Little Rock, Arkansas
4. Council Scout executive, BSA, Topeka, Kansas
5. Division director, National Council, BSA, Irving, Texas
6. Council Scout executive, BSA, Providence, Rhode Island
7. Regional director, BSA, Phoenix, Arizona

The following is a summary of the interview that took place between Roy Williams and the author.

Walter Pidgeon: *Were there unique circumstances in your past that may have helped you to attain your current position?*

Roy Williams: I believe by working hard at each position, I opened the door to the next advancement. As you know, The Boy Scouts of America (BSA) advances its executives through the ranks rather than hiring individuals from outside the organization. In this type of environment, individuals are judged on how they are doing in their current position. If they are doing well, an opportunity for advancement will come. Top management is always looking for talent, energy, and enthusiasm.

WP: *Do you have a contract?*

RW: No, I have a letter of employment.

WP: *What do you feel are the advantages and/or disadvantages of a contract?*

RW: I have never had a contract, only letters of employment. My employment is subject to a 30-day notice. Every professional at the BSA works under the same arrangement. Long-term contracts are not a good idea. If you think you need one, you might not want the job. Good performers are always in demand.

WP: *If you knew that you would become a CEO of a not-for-profit organization someday, would you have taken different steps to prepare?*

RW: I don't think so; I have a business degree, which has been a real asset for me over the years. A lot of what not-for-profit executives do to run organizations like the BSA is quite similar to running any for-profit business. Our local Scout executives, who are CEOs of our 300+ councils across America, deal with the same issues that for-profits do. They have personnel issues, they need to generate revenue streams and they need to attract customers by providing the best products possible. In not-for-profits, however, it is not just about raising funds, although it is a necessity to do so, it is about the services that we provide. Life is not as simple as it once was; not-for-profits need to be much more sophisticated in how they operate. Not-for-profit CEOs need to have the educational and practical background to meet these challenges. When I started, many nonprofit CEOs were program people. That has changed.

WP: *What formal educational courses do you feel that every not-for-profit CEO should have taken?*

RW: A business major with a psychology minor would be a perfect combination. "Getting things done through others" is the key to success for anyone who wishes to be a professional in a not-for-profit organization. To be successful, you have to know how to deal with people and understand volunteers' needs. That is a great advantage to anyone who wishes to be a not-for-profit professional. One of the college-level programs that offers quality course work is American Humanics, Inc. This Kansas City-based organization helps to support more than 100 colleges and universities that provide programs in not-for-profit administration.

WP: *What advice would you provide an individual who has set a career goal to become a CEO of a not-for-profit organization?*

RW: *Students* should become involved with a not-for-profit organization while they are in college. This will provide an opportunity to see firsthand both the positive aspects of not-for-profit work and also the challenges and other factors that make it a demanding job. Individuals often have misconceptions about the role that a professional plays in a not-for-profit. I would suggest that students who are really interested in pursuing a career in the not-for-profit community volunteer in not one but several organizations. In this manner they will get an overall picture of the sector and they may find an area that they would like to focus on for their first professional position after college.

    Professionals in the field: I would suggest that they focus on their current job but be visible. Lots of people are watching and the world will beat a path to the door of anyone who is doing their job well. I never had to look for greater responsibility, it came to me. Keeping your eyes on your current position, in many respects, will help to guarantee your future. Teaching at conferences is a great way to be visible.

    For-profit executive: Individuals coming into the not-for-profit arena from a for-profit experience need to understand the culture of the sector and the organization that they will lead. Each not-for-profit has a unique culture that needs to be understood or the leader will not be successful. The skills of a for-profit executive will be assets including various business applications and the art of dealing with people.

WP: *Did you and do you have mentors?*

RW: Yes, I had several. I was blessed to have mentors who saw in me the energy to succeed. They were not always my supervisors; several were peers. They helped me to identify my spiritual side, to strengthen my commitment to my family and to help me to achieve career goals. Mentors are absolutely critical. They protect you from yourself. If one has the right mentors they often guide you away from shortsighted goals. I have a favorite song. Its title is "Thank God for Unanswered Prayers." Mentors often have to use what I call a velvet hammer, but many times it is only body language. Frankly, most good people do not know all their mentors. Some of my best mentors were hardest on me. They were always trying to get the best out of me. Men like Ben Love, Jere Ratcliffe, Ron Moranville, Mike Hoover, Tom Ford, Don Knecht, and Vick Vickery were mentors and role models. These were people I worked for. I have had friends in the business: coworkers like Cliff Eng and Ron Hegwood. These people are all retired now. Most of my mentors are now senior-level volunteers in scouting. My best two mentors, as corny as it may sound, were my mom and my wife. My wife, Barbara, had to quit several teaching jobs over the years so that we could take a promotion. I always asked her how she felt first. We would talk about it. I could read her. Her attitude was, where you go, I go. That kind of support is rare these days, but it is critical.

Survey Responses and Additional Comments from the Interview

Note: Responses that are numbered (i.e., 1, 2, 3, etc.) are ranked, with 1 being the highest.

Please provide the chief reasons why you were able to attain your current CEO position.

Past experience, track record, and reputation.

Additional comments: Past experiences were the key to being chosen as the chief scout executive. I was well known by the national board and they knew my strengths and weaknesses.

What are the major personal skills that have helped you to retain your current CEO position?

1. Volunteer management
2. Member relations
3. Planning
4. Fiscal control
5. Producer—making goals

Additional comments: Integrity and belief in people; don't hesitate to give volunteer leaders the good and the bad news; board leadership understands that the business cycle has both ups and downs over the years.

What kind of career experiences would you recommend to aspiring CEOs to prepare them for the top position?

1. Volunteer management
2. Fund raising
3. Membership development
4. Finance
5. Program related
6. Government affairs

Do you network with other not-for-profit CEOs?

Yes, mostly through a group called Leadership 18. I probably spend more time talking to for-profit people because there are more of them.

What qualities, in your opinion, do not-for-profit boards seek in their CEOs?

1. Integrity, trust
2. Leadership traits
3. Volunteer management skills
4. Staff management skills

5. Ability to raise funds

6. Successful administrative and fiscal management

7. Ability to articulate and write a message

Additional comments: As a regional director for the BSA, I sat in on over 40 selection committees to choose council scout executives; the candidates represented a quality pool of professionals. The selection committee usually sought out the intangibles that they could not visualize until they met the candidates. Those who were selected had something the others did not. Personality and the ability to bond with the selection committees was the critical factor each time.

How did you become aware of your current CEO position?

- I was a member of the organization.
- I knew someone who was a member or in a leadership position of the organization.

What were the major factors that helped you to successfully win your current CEO position?

1. Ability to connect with the key volunteer leadership

2. Understanding what the organization sought in the new CEO

3. How I prepared and executed the interview meeting process

Additional comments: A lot had to do with my performance record. While such a record cannot predict how one will perform in the future, it is a pretty good indicator. I also provided a solid list of references to verify my background.

What kind of preparation did you do prior to the interview?

There were 10 finalists. We all had to do an unscripted video. They brought us all together in a studio. The selection committee was sent the videos. I worked at it but did not do very well. In our case, I think the committee was really interested in seeing how we handled tough questions in person. Many interviews are lost, not won. I did not prepare that much. I wanted to be relaxed. People who over-prepare often cannot listen and react. I have seen that happen many times. I think it is wise to give the committee materials ahead of time. Your record will often generate questions, which is what you want. You can then answer with short responses. Most people who don't get the job talk too much. My experience over the years has been that the more they talk, the better they like you.

What were the three major reasons you were selected for your current position?

- Proven track record
- Energy and enthusiasm
- Well-known by selection committee

Additional comments: Once you are involved in the top professional positions at the BSA you get to be pretty well known. They knew that I was not in scouting for the money, that I had a deep passion for the program. People want passion and energy in leaders.

What did you do during the first six months as a new CEO to cement your relationships?

1. Met key leadership
2. Created a personal plan of action
3. Evaluated staff
4. Did an overall evaluation of the organization
5. Ensured that proper fiscal controls were in place
6. Evaluated volunteer leadership
7. Made sure program functions were in order

What measures have you taken to continue to strengthen your position at your current organization?

1. Maintain a high level of interaction with key leadership.
2. Keep my organization fiscally sound.
3. Make sure that a clearly defined strategic plan is in place.
4. Make sure that I am linked to the highest priority issues.
5. Increase staff effectiveness.
6. Insist upon an annual review based on mutually agreed-upon goals.
7. Raise more income.

How have you or would you prepare to attain another CEO position?

1. Increase my visibility with the volunteer leadership of the targeted organization.
2. Become a volunteer at the prospective organization.

In your opinion, what are the three major changes in the not-for-profit CEO role in the last decade?

- Leadership
- Strategic planning
- Staffing

Additional comments: Hiring smart is absolutely critical. The job is too big to do it alone. Also, the style of leadership has changed. The old style of "follow me" has given way to more of a group decision-making process. Leadership requires you to get most of your people aimed in the same general direction, which is easier said than done.

What do you feel are the three major challenges that not-for-profit CEOs face in the next decade?

- Funding
- Attracting quality people
- Competition

Additional comments: Funding is becoming more and more critical. Thousands of not-for-profits are being organized each year. The local United Way, for example, used to have 25 organizations to fund; now it may have hundreds. Attracting quality people will continue to be the key to success.

We would welcome any additional information or advice that you would like to provide that would help to prepare an individual to attain and retain a CEO position in a not-for-profit organization.

- Stay long enough with a job to build a track record.
- Have a sincere enthusiasm for the work or mission of the organization.

Additional comments: I see a lot of professionals in the not-for-profit field who are so busy looking down the road that they never build a track record. Boards want to hire those who will live with their work. If you hop around too much, they assume you will bail on them, too.

Summary

As you have seen, the individuals who took the time to participate in the personal interview process are exceptional people. Although they all come from very diverse personal and educational backgrounds and became CEOs of not-for-profit organizations in a variety of ways, they all have one thing in common: they wanted to be leaders. Among the group, some have spent their entire career in the not-for-profit community while others have only entered this sector in the later part of their career. Every one of the interviewees, however, brings with them an inner desire to serve and they also bring the proven skills to be successful. These skills include both professional and personal attributes that made them stand apart from the crowd.

Although each of these professionals has attained a significant career position, they know that retaining that position requires hard work, additional training and constant personal renewal.

Although most of the details comparing how these individuals attained and retained their positions in comparison to the CEOs who participated in the overall survey are discussed in Chapter 2 and Chapter 3, it is important to note here that the key to their success is hard work. None of these executives had their positions handed to them. In the survey, everyone felt that being a producer and making goals is a critical part of what CEOs need to do to retain their positions.

When the interviewees were asked what they think boards seek in CEOs, they ranked integrity, trust and leadership traits very high. This provides yet another clue about the caliber of the interviewees.

I was impressed with the openness of each of the participating CEOs. Every one of them offered a number of solid suggestions for everyone from students beginning the process, to executives climbing the ladder within the not-for-profit community, to for-profit executives thinking of entering the not-for-profit field and, finally, to current CEOs looking to make the move to the next career level.

Overall, these executives have provided a good road map for anyone who seeks the not-for-profit CEO position. Chapters 5, 6, and 7 will provide some of the details of how to create a personal road map to the Corner Office.

Suggested Methods of Attaining a CEO Position

The key to success is holding in your conscious mind what you want to achieve and then striving in everything you do to make the image reality.

Dr. Norman Vincent Peale

INTRODUCTION

This chapter is designed to present a number of ideas and methods of obtaining the CEO position in a not-for-profit. Chapter 2 demonstrated that the CEO position is not for everyone and it certainly is not easy to obtain. However, this shouldn't deter you from seeking the position if you feel strongly that you have what it takes to run a not-for-profit organization.

This chapter addresses two main questions:

1. How can you tell if you are ready to pursue the CEO position?
2. If you are ready, what you have to do to attain the CEO position?

Peter Drucker was one of the first people to recognize management as a discipline worthy of deep and formal study, and he has been a longtime admirer of the not-for-profit sector. On many occasions, he has observed that the not-for-profit sector out-performs the for-profit sector in how they manage people and in getting things done.

It is only fitting, therefore, to embellish on a concept that Mr. Drucker recently observed in the for-profit sector. In a recent interview, he compared U.S. CEOs to those in the rest of the world. Drucker noted, "Our most important educational system in the U.S., unlike Europe, is in the employee's own organization. . . . When [the Europeans] move into this country, they are overwhelmed by the expectations they face. Look at the career path for many people here. Jeffrey Immelt, the CEO at

GE, worked in about half a dozen different categories—in sales, in design, in different product groups. In contrast, the head of Siemens never held a job outside Germany until he became CEO."

In many respects, Drucker's analogy of the American for-profit CEO model mirrors what it takes to be a successful not-for-profit CEO. Most of the participating CEOs in our study confirmed this principle. The respondents generally had a very diverse range of experiences and they did not specialize in one particular discipline. In fact, their educational backgrounds and, even, a lot of their professional experience, had very little to do with the current position that they hold today.

What the respondents' career paths have in common, however, is the leadership-based aspects of the positions they held and the core knowledge they obtained. As a result, most of the participating CEOs have backgrounds that, while untraditional, make them well suited for the Corner Office.

KNOW YOURSELF

No matter what career choice you make, one of the most important things in life is to really know yourself. This sounds a little weird, but it is essential. Come to terms with your strengths and your weaknesses; what makes you comfortable and what makes you uncomfortable. It is crucial to know what you do well and, maybe even more importantly, what you do not do well.

This sounds so simple to do, yet egos and outside pressures always seem to get in the way. Somehow, most of us never take the time to do it. We fall into the trap of trying to be all things to all people, and it starts at an early age. Do you remember having to show your report card to your parents? You may have earned a B+ average, but there was usually one subject that was lower than the rest. For me, it was mathematics. I can still hear my mother say, "I am proud of the B+ average, but you need to spend more time and energy on math." Well, it just never happened. I hated math and I was never very good at it; it simply was not a strong point for me.

Later in life, the same thing would happen in a number of job-related situations. I would outperform everyone in the office in most of the areas but my boss always lectured me on the one area that I merely did okay on. I finally realized that, in certain areas, I could never achieve the standards that some others could attain.

Well, guess what? I am only human and so are you. Each of us has the ability to excel in certain areas, while in other areas our performance is quite average. The secret is to know which is which. Supervisors have become a lot more aware of this and, as a result, they have become better at placing people in positions in which they can excel.

Every organization looks for quality people to fill a specified job, but the truly successful organizations look for employees who can perform across departmental lines due to a particular skill or skills that they possess. If an employee works well in a sales-related position but is also a gifted public speaker, why not use that gift to enhance the organization's public relations activities? The employee will enjoy the experience and, most likely, will do even better at his or her main job.

The lesson here is that not-for-profits need to encourage skill enhancement in the areas that employees excel in and the areas that are of interest to them. They need to create positions that take advantage of these skills and they need to provide training in areas of employees' interests.

Once aware of the particular strengths and weaknesses among the staff, the successful CEO will make sure that employees focus on their strengths, and that the talents among the staff are diverse enough to handle all the tasks that need to be performed. A CEO who can achieve this can produce a high level of personal satisfaction for each individual on the staff. This, in turn, produces a team that can achieve anything. While this sounds perfectly logical, in the real world it is nearly impossible. Nevertheless, it is what every not-for-profit CEO should be striving for. Chapter 3 covers this topic in more detail.

Aspiring CEOs need to think in terms of leading others to greatness. However, they also need to prepare themselves for greatness. What are your strengths and what are your weaknesses? Eric Vautour of Russell Reynolds Associates, a prominent search firm in Washington, D.C., notes that search committees often ask candidates to tell them their strengths and weaknesses. Strengths are easy to state; weaknesses are not. Candidates tend to hide weaknesses rather than stating what they are and, more importantly, how they compensate for them. Often, the right answer is simply that you surround yourself with individuals that excel in your weak areas.

The Use of a Self-Assessment Tool

Students

Self assessment for students focuses on the first steps that need to be taken to prepare for a professional career in the not-for-profit community. Students are still in the process of maturing both emotionally and educationally. The major objective for a student is to establish a sound base. As a student, there is time to take the appropriate course work and to dream of the day that you will head a not-for-profit organization.

Question 1: Why do I want to become a not-for-profit CEO?   This question encourages responses from both a personal and a career viewpoint. This is the core question, and it should be taken seriously. Even though your response may vary over time, it is important to document in writing why you wish to pursue such a career. Your response should be discussed at length with your college counselor, with a mentor in the field, and anyone else who can give you sound advice.

Question 2: How do I prepare for the CEO position?   Start by listing the various courses and activities that will be needed to establish a sound base. Establish goals and make a record of when they are accomplished. When you set a goal, create a timeline for its completion. This will provide you with a record of your accomplishments, as well as giving you a lesson in time management.

Each individual will need to determine his or her own specific path, but consider the following list of courses and activities that were suggested by the CEOs who participated in the study. This covers basic core classes and experiences, allowing you to branch out from there:

- Core college-level courses (e.g., finance, accounting, public speaking, business writing, marketing)
- Higher-level course work (e.g., business management, human relations, political science, sales, negotiations, human resources, planning)
- Extracurricular activities (e.g., sports, student government, clubs, fraternities/ sororities)
- Off-campus activities (e.g., job, volunteering, internship)

As we discussed in Chapter 2, CEOs are generally well-rounded individuals with solid educational credentials and professional backgrounds. As a whole, they also are involved in many other activities that help them lead.

In college, most of the participating CEOs were active in sports, student government, and various club activities. Students who aspire to become CEOs should emulate these leaders. Become involved in the college community. These experiences will improve your confidence, social skills, and leadership abilities.

Off-campus activities are also valuable. Many students have a part-time job to pay for school. While most of these jobs seem like a waste of time, they can provide a wonderful learning experience. They teach self-reliance and they instill a good work ethic, both of which will be a help later in life.

Volunteering should also be part of your off-campus plan. Remember, as a future CEO, your success will rely heavily on how you interact with volunteers and how they perceive you in your role. You can't understand a volunteer until you are in their shoes. By volunteering as a student, you can observe how the CEO and other professionals work with the volunteers and how, in turn, the volunteers react to them. You will encounter good and bad examples of this relationship. This experience will be really valuable when you enter the professional ranks.

Consider applying for an internship. Most not-for-profits have interns. Every semester, my association invites several students to intern at our national headquarters where we provide them with a rich experience. It is a really valuable experience, and many of the interns from my shop have gone on to successful careers in the business, government and not-for-profit work.

Question 3: From whom am I seeking help and support? Friends, professors, parents or someone in the not-for-profit field? This is an important process to begin to establish a networking base and to begin to move into the professional ranks. These individuals can be strong supporters. Don't take any of them for granted and, by all means, continue to add more people to the list. Some of them will become valuable mentors.

Question 4: After I graduate, how do I plan to reach my goal? This is sort of the "dream category," but it is important to write down your thoughts on this subject. These are the goals you are working on accomplishing right after graduation. Your thoughts and goals will probably change, but this is all right.

During their college days, most current CEOs never thought they would enter the not-for-profit profession and, one day, strive to attain the Corner Office. I did, however. From the time I was sixteen, I wanted to work in the not-for-profit community. I was lucky enough to be accepted into a college with a major in human relations focusing on not-for-profit administration. At the time, only three colleges had an accredited program in this area. If the plan had stopped there, however, I never would have attained my goal.

Your post-graduation plan is as important as what you do at college. If you can't translate your work at school into a full-time professional position, then what good is it? With my plan in place, I secured my first professional position a couple of months before I graduated. My plan consisted of working during the summer with the organization that hired me, securing mentors within that organization, securing references from my supervisors, and aggressively seeking professional employment during the fall of my senior year.

I recommend that you sign and date your self-assessment tool each time you revise it. It is a personal commitment to yourself. You should also place a date at the top of the document every time you revise it, and you should schedule a time for future revisions and place the date at the bottom of the document. You should revise this document at least once per semester. This document should be a living "plan of action" that you refer to on an ongoing basis.

Attaining the CEO position takes time but, if you prepare well in college, you will enter the professional ranks of the not-for-profit community with the necessary tools you need to make it to the Corner Office. Proper preparation will make it an enjoyable journey, producing the results that you want. Continue to use the self-assessment tool after you enter the professional ranks; just adapt it to the recommendations covered in the next section, Professionals in the Field.

Professionals in the Field

The self-assessment tool for the professional in the field is designed to act as a personal playbook for individuals who are serious about becoming the CEO of a not-for-profit organization. This assessment tool is really about simplicity and gaining momentum. As a full-time professional, there is very little time to think about your future; you have deadlines and goals to make.

If you are still thinking about making a bid for the Corner Office despite this hectic schedule, you probably have ambition and you are certainly enjoying the work. (Both qualities are essential to make it to the Corner Office.)

Question 1: Why do I want to become a not-for-profit CEO?   This question focuses on your career objectives as well as your personal objectives. It is a question that is even more important for professionals in the field than students. As a player in the not-for-profit game, you probably have a general idea of what it takes to become a CEO. If you still want the Corner Office in light of the hard work it will take, you must be dedicated to this goal. It is appropriate to put your thoughts in writing. It will act as a reminder of why you are putting the extra time and effort into achieving your goal.

Question 2: Do I have enough preparation for the CEO position in terms of my educational background and project-building experiences?   This question is the most important question for professionals in the field. Once you have made the decision to become a CEO, you need to determine if you have enough formal education. Several of the CEOs who were interviewed for the book needed to take additional course work to fully prepare themselves for the greater responsibilities of their leadership roles. I have gone back to college several times. While my undergraduate degree was specifically tailored for not-for-profit administration, I found that I had to take courses in finance and marketing to properly prepare me for the CEO position.

It is important to make sure that you have certain basic courses on which to build your career plan. If you need more formal course work, complete it as early in your career as possible. Strongly consider earning an advanced degree. Of the CEOs who participated in the study, 66.99 percent had master's or doctorate degrees. That is a telling fact.

Trade-driven courses are a must these days. These courses help you to keep up with the latest advances in your industry and the latest technologies that are available. Remember, successful CEOs embrace change and stay ahead of the curve. Aspiring CEOs need to do the same.

Work toward becoming certified in a particular area of your business. For example, if you need to raise funds, become a Certified Fund Raising Executive (CFRE) through CFRE International. If meeting planning is an important part of your future, become a Certified Meeting Professional through Professional Convention Management Association. There are many secondary certifications that are valuable credentials for a CEO. The credentials will also help you keep up to date through the various course work that is required for recertification every few years.

There is one certification that you must acquire and maintain if you are serious about attaining the Corner Office. This is the Certified Association Executive (CAE) certification that is available through the American Society of Association Executives. It is the standard in the not-for-profit industry.

Become involved with various project-building experiences as a way of learning your craft. Projects help you gain practical experience and allow you to become proficient in a number of areas. CEOs have to know how to run the entire shop; they do not necessarily need to know how to do all of the individual tasks. The aspiring CEO should focus on two areas:

1. Becoming familiar with all the tasks that are required to run an association

2. Becoming proficient at core areas that CEOs need to know, such as finance

The study lists a number of areas that aspiring CEOs need to know. There are others, but if you can be proficient in these, you are in very good shape. Many of these building experiences can be obtained on the job by incorporating them into your current tasks.

You may even want to ask your supervisor or the current CEO if you can be assigned to tasks that will provide you with one or more of these experiences. Usually, your supervisor will understand why you want these experiences and, if they are secure in their positions, they will welcome someone who aspires to greater responsibility. If not, maybe it is time to move on.

Question 3: How can I obtain career positions that include the experiences I need to become a CEO?   This question focuses on obtaining the kinds of on-the-job experiences that are needed by aspiring CEOs. Many of these opportunities can be easily arranged. Most associations have projects that include staff supervision, volunteer management, communications, government relations, fundraising and finance. While they may be presented under different titles, all of these functions are conducted in most not-for-profit organizations.

These are the opportunities that aspiring CEOs should seek. They are the opportunities that will give you most useful experiences as well as the most visibility in your organization. These are the experiences that not-for-profit boards look for when they hire a new CEO.

One of the challenges, however, is to avoid stagnating in one area of the business or you will be typecast. Many talented professionals fall into this trap of making everyone but themselves the hero. Even though you might be the best person in a particular area, if you aspire to become a CEO, you must move on to the next challenge. The secret is to get as many valuable experiences as possible.

Question 4: From whom am I seeking help and support? My supervisor, the CEO, fellow not-for-profit professionals and others?   Many aspiring CEOs do not pay adequate attention to this area. The CEO position is often gained through the network that the aspiring CEO creates. Even within your current association, you can gain a wealth of information and experiences that will increase your chances of being in the running for your organization's CEO position someday. To be successful within your current association, you need to create a network that includes a number of the key volunteer leaders in your organization. These volunteers need to know how good you are and how dedicated you are to advancing the mission of the organization.

If your best chance of obtaining a CEO position is outside of your current organization, you need to determine who are the best individuals who can assist in this process are. These individuals may include the following:

- Volunteers in the organization
- Top professionals in the organization
- Individuals outside of the organization who are respected by key individuals within the organization
- Search firms
- Individuals who can help you become more visible to key people in the organization

Remember, it is a person-to-person game. You may have what it takes to be a CEO, but you will be judged on how well you work with people. If a number of the key leaders think that you have what it takes, you will be in the running.

Question 5: What is my plan of attack for obtaining a CEO position, and what is the appropriate timeline?   Every aspiring CEO should have a plan of action. The plan may change as various circumstances change but it can be updated very easily. Every participating CEO, as well as most CEOs I have known, found that the actual path to the Corner Office was quite different from how they had originally planned it. The plan needs to be flexible, but it will provide structure and it will help you be persistent. Many of the CEOs indicated that it was their persistence that made the difference.

In the beginning, I thought that I would stay with one not-for-profit organization for the duration of my career. I stayed with the first organization for 14 years, but I finally realized that I had to leave if wanted to be a CEO. It was one of the most difficult career decisions that I have ever made, but I have never regretted it. The decision was based on a number of job specific factors and an assessment of what I really wanted to do with my professional life. It was a completely different direction than what I had originally planned, and it refocused me on my goal of becoming a not-for-profit CEO.

Your plan needs to remain flexible, and so do you. If one avenue doesn't work, find another way to do it. Remember, it doesn't matter how you get there as long as you get there. Use your network and your past experiences to come up with innovative solutions in the planning process.

Always sign your assessment document every time you update it. This habit reinforces your commitment to the plan. Make sure you place a date at the top of the plan every time you refine it. This will help you remember the last time you updated the plan. Also, make sure that you place the planned revision date, usually one year, at the bottom of the form to remind you when it is time to update or revise your document. It is important to keep this document fresh.

For-Profit Executives

The number of for-profit executives entering the not-for-profit sector is growing. This seems to be the result of two factors:

1. Less opportunities in the for-profit sector
2. Better compensation for not-for-profit positions than in the past

Many of the CEOs in the survey had for-profit work experience prior to becoming a not-for-profit professional. Some had experience working in and out of the for-profit and not-for-profit sectors over time.

For-profit executives seeking employment in the not-for-profit sector will probably have had a successful and productive career in the for-profit arena. For the most part, they come to the not-for-profit world with a wealth of experience that can be a real asset to the organizations that they lead. However, this experience needs to be channeled properly.

The self-assessment tool may seem a little basic to many for-profit executives wishing to enter the not-for-profit field, but the astute ones will use it as a guide to make the transition smooth.

Question 1: Why do I want to become a not-for-profit CEO?   This question needs to be answered both in terms of personal and career goals. The answer to this question is just as important for the for-profit executive entering the not-for-profit community as it is for students and professionals in the field.

In many respects, running a for-profit concern may not seem very different than running a not-for-profit organization, particularly a trade association. In the case of the trade association, the candidate will more than likely have vast experience in the industry that the organization represents. The candidate may even have been on the board or have had a volunteer leadership position with the association. Still, other for-profit executives may decide to completely change their career paths and target a social service organization.

While the transition may seem easy for these candidates, it is important for them to recognize that there are subtle differences between the for-profit and the not-for-profit sectors. These differences can be crucial in determining the success or failure of the new CEO. The two sectors are simply not the same; each sector requires a different kind of leadership style to be successful.

Your personal assessment should enumerate and analyze the reasons why you chose such a career change. It should also explore what you hope this move will do for you both personally and professionally.

Question 2: Will my background and experiences be a good fit for a CEO position?   Take this opportunity to compare your background and educational credentials to what is needed and sought after in the not-for-profit sector. In most cases, a formal education and background in business is a real plus. Figure out how you can adapt this knowledge to the not-for-profit environment and, most importantly, how you can communicate this specific knowledge to future employers.

Question 3: What are the areas that I need to work on, and how do I improve in these areas?   List the areas that you need to devote your time to and set goals and deadlines for improving these areas. Some areas that you may want to address are filling in gaps in formal course work or taking not-for-profit courses that are available through various associations. Tailor your formal and informal training to the non-for-profit world; experiences in volunteer management, membership promotion and not-for-profit governance should be high on the list.

As a business executive, you are certainly used to networking to make a sale or to promote your company. Networking is also very important in the not-for-profit community and it is a valuable tool in seeking the not-for-profit CEO position. Many of your fellow for-profit executives may have contacts in the not-for-profit world. Some of them may even be in the volunteer leadership of the organizations that you have targeted. Many times, the process of obtaining the CEO position can be shortened or enhanced through this networking process.

Question 4: From whom am I seeking help and support? Experts in the field, including not-for-profit CEOs, associations that represent not-for-profit CEOs, and former for-profit executives who have made the switch to the not-for-profit sector?   For-profit executives entering the not-for-profit field really need to focus on this question, especially those seeking the CEO position. Form an extensive network of experts and consult with as many sources as possible.

An expert in the not-for-profit field can help make the transition a lot smoother. Call on and get to know as many not-for-profit CEOs as possible. They will provide you with a strong support network, often making themselves available by phone or e-mail to render advice on pressing matters. A number of associations are available to provide materials and expertise in this area as well. Perhaps the best source of information and advice is an ally that recently made the transition from the for-profit world to the Corner Office of a not-for-profit.

Question 5: What is my current plan for finding and attaining a CEO position?   It is important to put a specific timeline on this plan. Start by listing the immediate avenues and action steps that you need to take to attain the CEO position. If you have time to search for the position, make sure that your plan involves networking and researching one or more associations. Along the way, you will probably discover other opportunities and paths to pursue.

You should sign the document even though it is designed to be a personal plan. Also, set a timeline for revising the plan and place that date at the bottom of the form. This will help keep the document fresh and it will keep you on target.

TAKE A REALISTIC LOOK AT THE PRIZE

With the self-assessment tool to guide you it is now time to set a realistic timeline for attaining the Corner Office. It is important to remember that it will take time to attain the CEO position.

Students

Students have plenty of time to plan their path to the top. Be careful to use all of this time wisely, however, as time has a way of getting away from all of us. We have all had the experience of getting behind in our course work. The big exam is tomorrow and, suddenly, you still have 300 pages to read and you need to memorize your notes. So, you do what you have to do—you pull an all-nighter and make it through okay. You might pass, but you could have done a whole lot better with the right preparation.

Likewise, the road to the Corner Office is much smoother and easier to build with the right preparation. While in school, your main goal is to craft a self-assessment tool and to begin the process of completing the core course requirements necessary to become a not-for-profit CEO. Take maximum advantage of opportunities both on and off campus. This is the last time that you will ever be able to devote your entire life to education. By using this time to the fullest, you can put yourself years ahead of the competition.

Professionals in the Field

Not-for-profit professionals are already in the running for the prize and, for them, time is becoming more and more precious by the day. As a professional in a not-for-profit, your obligations, both personal and professional, seem to increase by the hour. There never seems to be enough time to think of about your career or the future. This is why the personal assessment tool is so important.

As a busy professional, you need to find the time to reflect on your future. If you don't, no one else will. Even a well-meaning boss who is providing training and advancement opportunities is not doing it entirely on your behalf.

Every professional needs to manage his or her own future. In doing so, you are seeking the kinds of educational programs and job experiences that will build your personal future. Remember, this future may not necessarily be with your current employer.

I had a mentor who told me that you have to think of yourself as a business. Entertainers have done this for years. They are the value and product in their company even though they may have a hundred people working for them. You may work for a particular not-for-profit but, if your name is John Smith, you are really working for "John Smith, Inc."

Over the years, this one piece of advice has helped me through both good and bad times. Only you are in charge of your destiny.

For-Profit Executives

For profit executives need to have a realistic view of what it takes to become a not-for-profit CEO. For-profit executives bring a number of transferable skills to the table but they often have misconceptions about what a not-for-profit is all about. I have seen for-profit executives who tried to run a not-for-profit the same way that they would run a for-profit. It doesn't work—some of the operational functions may improve but the core elements of the organization often wither.

Leading a successful not-for-profit requires a delicate balance between employing traditional business principles and serving the mission of the organization through volunteers and members. For-profit executives make fine not-for-profit professionals if they make an effort to adapt.

For-profit executives should test the waters if possible. Volunteer for several organizations. Determine what kind of support structure is needed to make a valuable contribution to a not-for-profit organization. See what it really takes to run a not-for-profit. Make sure that becoming the CEO of a not-for-profit organization is the right move for you as well as for the organization that you may lead.

EDUCATION: WHAT'S IN AND WHAT'S NOT

The road to the Corner Office starts with a solid educational base. Many attain this base before they enter the job market, while others attain it as they move up the ranks. In any case, education should be a lifetime experience.

Can you imagine trying to run an organization using 20-year-old technology or even older management techniques? In an age where we discard three-year-old computers and programs, it is not logical to think that the people within the organization wouldn't stay current in education. The CEO needs to know what's in and what's not on the educational front.

There are two kinds of education that every CEO needs. The first is the formal education often taught at the university level. Exhibit 5.1 provides a basic list of course work that every aspiring CEO should have. If you did not take some of these classes while earning your degree, you should go to night school or explore online courses. Every CEO needs these courses to be successful.

The second kind of education is the informal professional or continuing training received on the job or in job-related seminars. You should jump at every opportunity to take continuing training as it enhances your education base. Exhibit 5.2 provides a list of some of the fields of study that you need to explore. You ultimately want to have an overall understanding of what it takes to run a successful organization.

There are several ways of obtaining this training at the university level and through specific organizations. At the university level, there are two programs that are the best out there, and they will put you a huge step ahead of the competition. I am a graduate

---

EXHIBIT 5.1   CORE COURSE WORK RECOMMENDED FOR CEOS OF NOT-FOR-PROFIT ORGANIZATIONS

- Finance
- Accounting
- Business management
- English
- History
- Public speaking
- Business writing
- Political science
- Marketing

EXHIBIT 5.2   RECOMMENDED FIELDS OF STUDY FOR CEOS OF NOT-FOR-PROFIT ORGANIZATIONS

- Communications
- Meeting planning
- Volunteer management
- Board relations
- Program planning
- Fundraising
- Membership development
- Government relations
- Human resources
- Staff management
- Budgeting
- Investing
- Use of media
- Technology
- Strategic planning
- Negotiations

of both programs. They really helped me jump start the beginning and middle stages of my career.

The first program, American Humanics, is a national organization that supports over 70 colleges. These colleges provide majors in not-for-profit administration at the undergraduate and graduate level. For further information contact:

American Humanics, Inc.
4601 Madison Avenue
Kansas City, MO 64112
800-531-6466
www.humanics.org

The second program is at The Union Institute and University (UIU). UIU offers a number of higher education opportunities as well as degree programs at any level ranging from bachelor to doctorate degrees. The programs are engineered so that full-time professionals can earn their degree while continuing to work.

I assisted with the development of UIU's doctorate program in Association Management and I arranged a partnership between the school and the American Society of Association Executives. Exhibit 5.3 illustrates the six areas of concentration for the doctorate program including leadership, constituency development, communications and marketing, strategic thinking: defining the field, organizational structures and functions, and administration and finance. For further information contact:

Union Institute & University
440 East McMillan Street
Cincinnati, Ohio 45206-1925
800-486-3116
www.tui.edu

Chances are good that a college or university near you offers courses in not-for-profit administration. If you need to take a particular college course, contact your nearest college or university even if it is not on the list. Remember, you may be able to find online courses as well.

When it comes to ongoing or refresher seminar programs to increase your knowledge of not-for-profit issues, the American Society of Association Executives is the organization:

American Society of Association Executives
1575 I Street, NW
Washington, DC 20005-1103
202-626-2742
www.asaenet.org

In addition, many other organizations exist both nationally and locally that can provide support for any particular area that you may need.

EXHIBIT 5.3   UI&U ASSOCIATION MANAGEMENT INITIATIVE

Source: Jinelle F. Runberg, Union Institute and University

KNOW THE TURF

You have to know the game to be a player. This sounds simple, but there are some full-time professionals in the not-for-profit community that don't understand the industry's core principles. Those who do understand the core principles have a grasp of the following:

- The mission of their organization
- The current programs and activities of the organization
- How their organization fits into the overall not-for-profit sector
- How the not-for-profit sector fits into our nation and the world in general

The people who understand these principles far outnumber those who don't, but it is sad to think that some of our fellow not-for-profit professionals do not know the game. As CEOs, we have an obligation to teach our staffs about the important role that they play on behalf of the organization's constituents as well as for the common good in general. Not-for-profit professional leaders must set an example by keeping informed and finding relevant ways to demonstrate to our staffs why the not-for-profit sector exists. As Chapter 1 illustrated, the not-for-profit sector's evolution is a story about the advancement of humankind and the foundation of democracy.

GET PAST THE BRICK WALL

I came across an article recently that described how older workers are hitting a brick wall due to age discrimination. The article noted that age discrimination is now starting as low as 45 years old.

Sometimes, it is funny to look back at the obstacles that we all have in our lives. When I graduated from college, I looked like I was 15 years old. This began to be a real problem for me in my relationship with a 50-year-old factory worker, who was my key volunteer. He thought that I was wet behind the ears. I won him over, however, by asking him to show me the ropes and by showing him that I was not afraid to work hard.

Around this time, I was drafted into the U.S. Army and I served in Vietnam as a psychological operations officer. When I returned, I discovered three things. First, I didn't look 15 anymore, so the volunteers related to me better. Second, due to the antiwar environment at the time, I couldn't openly discuss my experiences in the service even though I had many professionally significant experiences unrelated to the war. Finally, I discovered that I had lost three years in the work force, putting me far behind my peers. So, I was able to avoid one brick wall, only to face two others.

This is just a part of the process. Everyone has different obstacles to overcome, and you will never get rid of all the brick walls in your life. When dealing with these walls over the years, I began to identify four options:

1. Bounce off of the wall.
2. Avoid hitting the wall directly.
3. Anticipate the wall.
4. Avoid the wall altogether.

The bottom line is that you can't do anything about brick walls most of the time—you can try to climb it, cut a hole in it, or knock it down. Instead of wasting valuable time thinking about the what-ifs, the best approach is moving on to bigger and better things. While many of these walls are painful at the time, each makes you stronger and more aggressive in the quest to reach both your personal and career goals. It would have been nice to avoid the brick walls in my life, but I don't think that I would be where I am today without them.

Find a Mentor

Most of the CEOs who participated in the study indicated that having mentors was one of the key elements in their success. These CEOs seem to have a very special relationship with their mentors; one that is both satisfying and inspirational. Aspiring CEOs seriously need to examine how they can secure one or more valuable mentors. See Exhibits 5.4 to 5.6.

The benefits of having mentors in your network as a close advisor are essential:

- Mentors can help you better understand your good and bad experiences.
- Mentors can provide frank, straightforward answers to your questions.
- Mentors can give you a needed push.
- Mentors can help to open new frontiers that you never thought could exist.
- Mentors can help keep you on track.

Everyone needs mentors. So, how can you find a mentor? Mentors may come your way by accident or you may have to go out and find them for yourself.

Exhibit 5.4 provides students with a guide in selecting, approaching, and evaluating the process. A number of the CEOs who participated in the study mentioned

---

EXHIBIT 5.4   THE MENTOR SEARCH FOR STUDENTS

1. Who to select:
    a. Look for individuals who can make a difference in your life.
        - Select someone who can help you right now.
        - Select someone who can help you mold your future.
2. The approach:
    a. Ask to meet with each prospective mentor personally.
    b. Prepare a one-page request:
        - Why you need a mentor
        - Why you wish him or her to be your mentor
        - What you are asking the mentor to do for you
    c. Be prepared to adapt your request; your prospective mentor may want to add or simplify the request.
    d. If the mentor agrees, develop a plan and schedule together.
    e. Send a thank-you letter confirming the arrangement.
3. Evaluation:
    a. Do a self-evaluation often to determine if it is still working.
    b. Ask the mentor to evaluate the arrangement.
    c. Determine if the arrangement is worth continuing.

EXHIBIT 5.5   THE MENTOR SEARCH FOR THE
PROFESSIONAL IN THE FIELD

1. Who to select:
   a. Select someone who you know and trust perhaps from your past—a teacher, minister or past supervisor.
   b. Select a key leader where you work, maybe even your CEO.
   c. Select a person outside your organization who is well known in the field.
2. The approach:
   a. Ask to meet with each prospective mentor personally.
   b. Prepare a one page request:
      • Why you need a mentor
      • Why you wish him or her to be your mentor
      • What you are asking the mentor to do for you
   c. Be prepared to adapt your request; your prospective mentor may want to add or simplify the request.
   d. If the mentor agrees, develop a plan and schedule together.
   e. Send a thank-you letter confirming the arrangement.
3. Evaluation:
   a. Do a self-evaluation often to determine if it is still working.
   b. Ask the mentor to evaluate the arrangement.
   c. Determine if the arrangement is worth continuing.

the mentors that they had in the early days. Several were mentored by one or both of their parents. Parents have a profound effect on their children, but these CEOs were talking about a much deeper commitment than that. These were parents who made it a major mission in their lives to provide the extra caring needed to launch their child into a successful life.

Several participating CEOs singled out teachers, college professors, and coaches who made a difference. Most of these executives felt that their mentors made a measurable difference not only in their careers but in their personal lives as well.

You should continue to have mentors even after you become a professional in the field. Exhibit 5.5 is a guide for this process. I still regularly visited one of my mentors until two years ago, when he passed away. I have had the privilege of having a handful of great mentors. They helped me acquire a college education and advance in my career and they reminded that life is more than "9 to 5" proposition.

Exhibit 5.6 is a guide for those who have entered the not-for-profit field from the for-profit arena. Executives who have successfully accomplished this switch often mention the mentors they have in their professional lives. They talk about their mentors in the same positive way that not-for-profit CEOs do. For-profit executives

EXHIBIT 5.6   THE MENTOR SEARCH FOR THE FOR-PROFIT EXECUTIVE ENTERING THE NOT-FOR-PROFIT FIELD

1. Who to select:
   a. Look for a CEO from the for-profit sector.
   b. Select a CEO who has successfully made the transition from the for-profit to not-for-profit sector.
   c. Seek a CEO who has been primarily spent his or her career in the not-for-profit sector.
2. The approach:
   a. Ask to meet with each prospective mentor personally.
   b. Prepare a one-page request:
      • Why you need a mentor
      • Why you wish him or her to be your mentor
      • What you are asking the mentor to do for you
   c Be prepared to adapt your request; your prospective mentor may want to add or simplify the request.
   d. If the mentor agrees, develop a plan and schedule together.
   e. Send a thank-you letter confirming the arrangement.
3. Evaluation:
   a. Do a self-evaluation often to determine if it is still working.
   b. Ask the mentor to evaluate the arrangement.
   c. Determine if the arrangement is worth continuing.

entering the not-for-profit work force will have a much smoother transition if they take the time to find a mentor who can help them with this process. You are never too old to have a mentor.

LISTEN TO THE EXPERTS

The participating CEOs have spoken about what it takes to become a CEO of a not-for-profit organization. They told us that a solid educational base is essential and that good old–fashioned hard work is the key. They indicated that CEOs need to understand and appreciate the underlining principals of the sector, and they need to know how to be leaders.

A search firm is usually not involved with the entry level or first CEO positions that most new CEOs attain. This is because the entry-level positions are usually at organizations smaller both in terms of membership and budget size. In this case, the smaller not-for-profit appoints a search committee made up of volunteer leaders from the organization. They conduct the search and report their recommendations to the board.

Outside search firms, however, have become a major partner in the hiring process for medium and large sized organizations. Chapter 7 discusses search firms and how they factor into the equation.

Eric Vautour is a principal at Russell Reynolds Associates, a Washington, D.C.–based search firm. He specializes in conducting searches for not-for-profit CEOs, particularly for large associations. He emphasizes that candidates should never try to beat the system by enhancing their resume or exaggerating about their current compensation. This information is easily obtained about any candidate. Anyone who raises funds can tell you that getting information on an individual's background is easier than ever before.

Vautour also advises not to hide any past employment situations; they are always discovered. It is always better to tell your story first. In addition, let the search committee know your strong and your weak points. Tell them how you handle both. No one is good at everything; how you deal with your weak points is of primary interest to the search committee or a search firm. When confronting the issue of weaknesses, tell them that you surround yourself with people who compliment your abilities and who fill in these voids.

PUT TOGETHER THE PACKAGE YOU NEED

Once you have obtained a sound educational base, acquired a rich background of experiences, and created an active network of colleagues, you are ready to let the world know that you want a CEO position. This process can be achieved in several ways:

- *Use your network to get your message to the right people.* Your network can open a door or two, greatly increasing your chances of landing a CEO position.
- *Rise through the ranks at your current employer.* This process may take longer and it is certainly more challenging, but it has its merits.
- *Respond to a want ad.* While this seems like the obvious approach, it is really the hardest method.

Networking is the best way to attain any new position, particularly a CEO position. If you decide to take this route, you will need a comprehensive plan of attack. The plan should consider

- Who to network with
- How to reach the people you should be networking with
- How to convince them to be part of your network
- What you want them to do

Rising through the ranks of one organization is not simple. Your worst enemy is being taken for granted. You need to constantly be aware of how your work is being perceived and how you are being rewarded for it.

I have been there. I worked for one particular organization for several years, and I made many of my supervisors very successful due to my productivity. Yet, I was never properly thanked for my achievements. The last year that I was with this group, I discovered that I was one of the top producers in the organization and, again, I received nothing in return. I began to notice that others who produced less were receiving promotions and surpassing me in rank. One even became the CEO of another division. Basically, I was more valuable to my supervisor than I was to the organization, and I was not given the advancement opportunities that I had earned.

Other CEOs have the opposite experience. They rise quickly through the ranks of one organization and take over as the CEO. In many respects, it is matter of circumstance. It is also a matter of how managers deal with employees. Supervisors should not merely extract as much out of an employee as possible. True leaders recognize that they have a responsibility to the people that they direct. Part of this responsibility is to encourage personal growth in the employees and, when the time comes, to encourage them to move on to the next level.

Successful supervisors continually produce new leaders. As a result of this process, they always seem to attract quality people to replace them. Employees are more eager to work for someone who will recognize their talents and encourage them to move up. Personally, I have never seen the advantage of holding anyone back; it is a lot more satisfying to see employees move ahead in life.

The bottom line for aspiring CEOs who want to make it to the Corner Office by working through the ranks of one organization is to cover these bases:

1. Make sure your organization's supervisors are leadership builders and not credit takers.

2. Make sure that you can see the steps to the top. Is it really possible to attain the Corner Office?

3. Make sure that you have the time to wait it out.

Responding to a want ad may be the least desirable option for finding a CEO position, but it can still work and it should be a part of your search. It should not be the only part of your search, though. I have been preaching the network game all along, but I have a secret to tell: I found out about my current position by answering an ad in the *Wall Street Journal*. The ad was rather large and it caught my attention for two reasons:

1. It is rare to see an ad in the *Journal* for a not-for-profit CEO position.

2. The mission of the organization fascinated me.

I applied and, within 90 days, I was the new CEO. So, part of your plan should include looking through various mainstream and trade publications for ads. Just recognize that this is not the most efficient way of finding a CEO position.

Once you identify a potential position to research or apply for, how do you get started? The details of each position and the circumstances of its timing will dictate your approach. Position searches generally fall into three categories:

1. The position is not open but will be shortly.
2. The position just opened and you are one of the first to know about it.
3. The position is being advertised in the want ads.

A position that is not open but will be shortly calls for a cultivation approach. The position may be opening because the current CEO is retiring or it may be available for many other reasons. This is a job for networking. The networking plan will depend on whether you are an insider or an outsider.

If you are an insider, you can learn a lot of information that is unavailable to outsiders. You will also have a good idea of who you need to cultivate for more information or who you need to talk with to get your name thrown into the ring. This will mean getting closer to board members and, even, search committee members. It may also mean getting closer to the current CEO who, in some circumstances, may have some influence on who will become the next CEO.

If you are an outsider, your access will obviously be more limited. You can start by accessing information from the organization's Web site, and maybe even speaking to some insiders, as well. Perhaps you know a member of the organization or, better yet, a volunteer leader. If not, maybe you can become a member of the organization. The main objective is to obtain as much information as possible and to gain visibility with a few key players.

If the position has just become available and you are one of the first to know about it, you have short time advantage. The first thing you need to do is to gather all the information you can get from the organization's Web page and from anyone you know who may have knowledge of the organization.

Check your network to see if anyone in it may know someone associated with the organization. If so, ask if they would be willing to approach this person on your behalf. This is an excellent opportunity to possibly bypass a search system. Even if this only gets you an interview, it will help you avoid the weeding-out process.

The next best thing to do is to find out who will be conducting the search. Try to contact them to ask what type of an executive they are seeking and if they have any advice for you in the search process. You may gain an inside ally or some valuable information.

The objective is to determine the needs of the organization and to discover the qualities they seek in the new CEO. This information is extremely valuable because you can use it to tailor any written materials you submit and you can target your interview discussion to the areas that they are looking for.

Armed with all of the relevant information, you will need to develop a tailored search package that includes the traditional cover letter and resume and, perhaps, some support materials. If you need help in this process, there is a great book on the subject, *Planning Your Career in Association Management,* written by Paul A. Belford and published by the American Society of Association Executives. Paul is the principal at JDG Associates, a search firm that specializes in filling not-for-profit CEO positions.

The materials package you need is fairly standard. You will need a cover letter that is tailored to the position at hand. The letter should be the product of the research that you conducted. In short, it should address the association's needs and how you are the ideal candidate to fill those needs. The resume should be no more than two pages and it should contain all the traditional items. Consider a resume that lists your skills. These resumes always get my attention.

What about extra materials? Use them if they are particularly relevant, but use them sparingly. As an interviewer, I find that introducing too many extras, particularly at the first meeting or interview, tends to complicate the process and, frankly, it looks like you are trying too hard. However, as a candidate, I like to have a surprise or two for the search committee.

If you are aware of a major need of the association or a particular attribute that the search committee is looking for in their new CEO, you may want to submit something extra if you can relate the need or attribute directly to a story of personal achievement. Limit the extra material to one page and be sure to attribute the success to everyone but yourself. Be sure to mention how much of a difference it made to your members and constituents.

Looking for CEO positions in the classified ads is usually considered the least productive way of obtaining a CEO position. Often, it is. However, all comprehensive search plans should include this method as a component.

If you find a position in the want ads that fits your background, follow the steps outlined in Exhibit 5.7 to determine if you want to apply and then how to gain access to the organization. This process has become a lot easier with the Internet.

HOW TO FIND *THE* POSITION

Finding openings is easy, finding *the* position is much more difficult. It is often tempting to apply for any CEO position that comes your way. This makes sense if you need a job, but the exercise is not just about getting a job, it is about a way of life that makes it worthwhile to go to work.

I have had a number of positions in my career and, of course, there were some that I would not have wanted for an entire career. Some of these positions came at times

EXHIBIT 5.7   GAINING ACCESS TO THE NOT-FOR-PROFIT LEADERSHIP

1. Check the organization's Web site and other sources for:
   a. General information on the organization
   b. The mission
   c. Current issues and programs
   d. Overall size:
      • Budget
      • Membership or number of donors
      • Number of volunteers
      • Number of staff
   e. Discover the key leadership, including contact information:
      • Check for board members.
      • Identify the key staff.
      • Check publication, articles and news releases to determine the volunteers and staff that are quoted the most.
   f. Check the fiscal integrity of the organization:
      • Is it increasing its budget each year?
      • Does it have a number of funding sources, or does it depend on a few?
      • How does it raise revenue?
2. Prepare a two-page summary of the organization, including a list of key leaders, both volunteer and professional.
3. Check with your network and mentors to see if they know something about the organization and someone in the organization. If so, ask them to intercede on your behalf.
4. If you cannot find anyone to intercede on your behalf, determine the best person within the organization to contact. Most of the time, it will be a key volunteer.
   a. Explain why you contacted the person.
   b. Ask what kind of CEO the organization is seeking.
   c. Very briefly review your background.
   d. Ask the person's advice on becoming a candidate.
   e. Thank the individual for his or her help.
   f. Send a follow-up thank-you letter.

---

when I needed a job to provide for my family. They fulfilled that purpose, but not much more. I was miserable in them.

Luckily, most of the positions I have held offered new challenges and new surroundings that allowed me to grow. These are the sorts of positions that you can't wait to dig into everyday and they are the sorts of positions where you don't count the minutes until you leave, instead you count the successes. These are the kinds of jobs that aren't really a job at all, they are more of an avocation; one that you might take up even if you were not paid.

My career as a not-for-profit leader fulfills all of this and more. If you're a student, a professional in the field, or a for-profit executive thinking of entering the not-for-profit field, then you must look at the role of the CEO as a calling and not just another job. Frankly, the not-for-profit community doesn't need job seekers. We need dreamers; people who bring unbridled enthusiasm and unlimited talent to the table. In short, the not-for-profit sector needs real leaders who can make a difference. Job seekers need not apply.

The Cultivation Process for the CEO Position

By this point, you have completed your homework and have selected one or more not-for-profits to cultivate. You have accomplished this through networking, using your mentors, and sending a targeted search package to the appropriate people.

Now you begin the wait. Suddenly, the search committee calls and wants to meet with you, so you make an appointment and travel to see them. The meeting may be held during their annual out-of-town conference. Perhaps, you are invited to stay overnight. How do you prepare for this part of the process? What can you do before, during, and after the search committee meeting to land the CEO position?

Exhibit 5.8 provides you with a starting point. Most search committees start by sending you a packet of information on the organization. This may include general items such as the CEO position description, an overview of the association or some general statistics about the membership base. Often, there is much more information that you need to know.

At the bare minimum, you should have a copy of the last annual report, the latest financial statement, a summary of the current staff positions, an outline of the governance structure, a description of the program activities and a summary of how they raise revenue. If you don't receive this information, ask them to provide it. You may be the only one who does.

Good organizations will welcome such a request and the search committee will have a very favorable impression of you for asking. Any organization that seems annoyed or refuses to send any or all of this information may not be very well organized, may not have these documents readily available or, worse, may be hiding something. In any case, by receiving or not receiving these items you are already gathering positive or negative information about the organization.

If you don't receive the financial statements, you can access the organization's annual IRS Form 990 through the Internet. Completing Form 990: Return of Organizations Exempt From Income Taxes for the Internal Revenue Service, is a yearly requirement of all not-for-profits having a gross income of more than $25,000 per

EXHIBIT 5.8   SUGGESTED STEPS FOR CULTIVATING THE PROSPECTIVE NOT-FOR-PROFIT ORGANIZATION

1. When the call comes to go for an interview, make sure you have all the background information you need to prepare properly. If not, request it.
2. Prepare for the interview by
   a. Anticipating questions
   b. Developing a list of questions
   c. Developing one-page summaries
   d. Rehearsing
   e. Determining what to wear—always look the part of a CEO
3. Take charge of your interview:
   a. Make an entrance.
   b. Bring a briefcase with notepad and the one-page summaries.
   c. Act as natural as possible. Smile and look people in the eye, and add just a hint of a smile in your voice.
   d. Answer all their questions as if you heard the questions for the first time.
   e. Ask questions that go to the soul of the organization and ask a particular person in the room to respond.
   f. Leave them with a hint that the position sounds interesting, and we should talk about it again.
4. Follow up with a thank-you letter that includes a well-thought-out question concerning the organization's future. Focus the question on a leadership issue.
5. Evaluate the meeting, including making notes on everyone on the search committee and the kinds of question they sought. Determine what kinds of questions you might ask if you are called back.

year. Form 990 contains the financial status of the organization for that year. It also contains other information, including the names of board members. If the CEO is on the board, it will list the salary of the CEO as Form 990 requires a listing of any board member who is compensated. To access this information, go to *www.irs.gov.*

If you still need more information on the organization, make inquiries with other organizations that they may relate to, including allied groups of the American Society of Association Executives (ASAE). These allied groups are in most major metropolitan areas. Most of the allied groups are managed by management firms, but some have full-time executives. If you would like to contact an allied organization in your area, ASAE can be reached at 202-626-2723. Other organizations exist that fulfill similar functions.

The information that you have gathered may not provide all of the details that you desire but it is good place to start. Don't forget to check out the organization's Web

eat source of information. If not, the organization. The information-

the interview about what you know been able to find out

eed, you are ready to design your plan

of the interview process. With proper now that you took over. However, they rp individual who is worthy of serious v plan should include the following:

pared to answer

iat you want to make sure that the search es

two categories:

answers to

nmittee how smart you are

The questions that you need to ask will examine the areas and issues that will determine if you really want the position. These include:

- The fiscal health of the organization
- The governance structure of the organization
- The effectiveness and skills of the staff
- The board structure
- How the CEO position relates to the volunteer leadership of the organization
- Any other issues or concerns

Asking questions is a great way of showing the search committee how interested you are. It is a great technique when you notice a search committee not really paying attention to you, for example. In fairness, you may be the third or fourth candidate they have seen that day or they may have already found the person that they think is the best possible candidate. Sometimes it is wise to ask an offbeat question; it helps to get the search committee to refocus on you. The question may pertain to the position or, if appropriate, it may even be an off-the-cuff question. For example:

> In the lobby this morning, I took a moment to glance at your recognition wall.
> I notice that John Smith was recognized for providing a major gift to your

capital campaign. Is that the same John Smith that is the current the CEO of the Smith Corporation?

If the answer is yes, it shows the search committee that you already know someone associated with their organization. If turns out to be a different John Smith, it shows the search committee that you might already have someone to cultivate as a possible donor for their organization. Tell the committee something about the John Smith you know. In both cases, you have told the search committee that you know a few key people and that you are very observant. Both are good qualities for a future CEO.

- The other side of the equation is anticipating the questions that the search committee will ask you. Be prepared for a variety of questions pertaining to your background, education, and personality: *Background questions provide you with an opportunity to shine.* Tell them about the positions that you have had and highlight your major accomplishments. Be sure to provide examples that demonstrate your management and leadership style. You should have at least two or three examples in mind.

- *Your educational background is simple.* Tell them what degrees you have earned and tell them the subjects that you liked and excelled at. Be sure to mention any unusual areas of study, especially if they relate well to the organization.

- *The personality questions are the real purpose of the interview.* Your background and educational credentials have been checked long before the time you are sitting in front of the search committee. What the search committee is trying to determine is how you will fit into the culture of the organization.

The search committee wants someone who will embrace the mission of the organization. They also want someone who can work well with the board and the staff. Approach the interview almost as you would approach a social event. It is important to look like you are enjoying the opportunity to be with the search committee. Smile, laugh, and have a sense of humor, but be sure you show your serious side as well.

Search committees can come up with some wild questions. Don't let it get to you; try to answer the questions as best you can. The wild questions are often used to test how you will react under pressure or stress. Develop and polish a few key selling points about yourself and bring them up during your conversation with the search committee. The strongest selling points will be the particular skills or experiences that you have that fit the needs of the organization that were determined from your research. Don't attempt to present too many points; the search committee can only comprehend and remember so much. One or two strong points will make you memorable.

The Interview

Arrive on time and come dressed like a CEO. If your best suit is five years old, buy a new one that is in style, but not flashy. Make sure you know the exact location of the interview—scout it out the night before or arrive early and grab a cup of coffee somewhere.

Bring reading material with you that deals with leadership or some other cutting edge dynamic. Often you will need to wait for a few minutes before you go into the interview. The book keeps you from looking nervous or looking like you are wasting time. The individual who greets you is often one of the members of the search committee. It is the first impression you will make, and the book might even start a conversation.

As you enter the room, look everyone in the eye and go around the room to introduce yourself. Shake each person's hand firmly. When you are asked to sit down, take out a note pad and pen and lay it on the table. You may never use it, but it acts as a symbol that you mean business. Don't move your body too much during the interview, instead, move your head. At the end of the interview, thank the committee for inviting you. Get up and shake each person's hand again and thank each person personally with a smile on your face. Your exit should look like a winner's exit.

A follow-up letter should be sent immediately to the chair of the search committee. The letter should thank the committee for the opportunity to interview for the organization and it should encourage them to contact you if they have any additional questions.

If you get called back for a second interview, it means you have made the cut. Congratulations! The second interview will be even more personality driven and it will involve a deeper examination of your core skills. Be prepared to provide more in-depth examples of how you lead and how you can get things done. Also, you will need to be prepared to respond to an offer of employment. It may not happen at the second interview, but it is a possibility.

Offers for the position can be strange at times. One time, I interviewed for a position out of town and, after the interview, I went out to dinner, came back to my hotel room, did some work, watched TV and went to bed at 11:00 P.M. About an hour and a half later, I received a call from the chairman of the board.

The call woke me up, of course. Half awake, I listened as he said that he wanted to see me in his room right away. I got dressed and went to his room, where I was offered the position at 1:30 in the morning. I did what everyone should do under such circumstances; I said that I would think about it and get back to them.

When the offer comes, always take the time to think about it. It is a big decision that will change your life, and it is worth taking a day or two to consider. If you decide to take the position, this is the time to begin to negotiate your compensation package. Some people feel more comfortable involving an attorney in the negotiation process and others don't. In either case, a lawyer should have a look at the contract or the letter of agreement.

If you accept the position, make sure that you negotiate enough time to wrap up things with your current employer. This includes providing your current employer with a detailed checkout report even if they don't require one. The checkout report will be a real asset to the person who assumes your position, and it will serve to document your accomplishments. It also provides one last pledge of loyalty to the organization.

Make sure that your current employer can call you at any time to ask a question or seek advice. Keep a copy of the checkout report. A smooth exit is important to your current employer, and it demonstrates your level of conduct to your new employer. It also protects you.

SUMMARY

The steps to the Corner Office are not always easy to negotiate. Individuals seeking the CEO position need a sound education, a rich career background, and certain personality qualities. The CEOs who participated in the study had plenty to say about the qualities that a CEO needs to possess, including passion for the cause, integrity, and leadership. The CEO also needs core business skills and a sound planning background as well as the ability to work with people and the drive to get things done.

This chapter provided a number of techniques on how to attain the CEO position but the ultimate test of those who aspire to become a CEO of a not-for-profit organization is the willingness to pay the price to attain and retain the position. It is not an easy position. Only a few are chosen, and some do not succeed.

The CEO's Survival Kit

*The greatest thing in the world is not so much where we are, but in which
direction we are moving.*

Oliver Wendell Holmes

INTRODUCTION

Recently, a full-page advertisement appeared in the *Wall Street Journal* featuring
Judy Warrick, senior advisor of Investment Banking at Morgan Stanley. The headline
of the ad read: *The New CEO: Rethinking the Corner Office.* The ad, which focused on
the for-profit sector, said, "Once a coveted job, being a CEO is not what it used to
be; in 2002, nearly 40 percent of CEOs were fired for poor performance, up 25 percent from 2001." A CEO appointed in the early 1990s was three times more likely to
be fired than a CEO tapped before 1980. Here are a few additional facts from the ad:

- With shorter grace periods and higher performance bars, results rarely meet
  expectations.

- Often those who solve problems or exploit opportunities earn the board's confidence and the top job. But when the future is different from the past, yesterday's stars are unlikely to be tomorrow's heroes.

- The next CEOs need much more. Some skills are universal, some unique to each
  industry. But unless skill sets match future demands, trauma is more likely than
  triumph.

- The future demands more than executing someone else's vision.

- Corporate governance now means taking personal responsibility along with
  personal consequences.

- Beware of the CEO who looks in the mirror and sees the future.

- The CEO sets the tone. The personality at the top becomes the personality of the corporation.
- The person who runs the show matters.

Wow. This one-page ad basically sums up the landscape that chief executive officers are facing in today's for-profit environment. It is fascinating to compare the challenges that for-profit CEOs face with the challenges that not-for-profit CEOs face. In a number of ways they are very similar. A great deal of ideas and business solutions can be borrowed from the for-profit sector and used quite effectively in the not-for-profit arena.

Likewise, the for-profit sector could learn a few things from the not-for-profit community. This is particularly true in the area of governance and leadership. However, this chapter will focus on what the successful not-for-profit CEO can gain from any source including the for-profit community.

The legendary for-profit corporations like General Electric became what they are today through the leadership and drive of their CEOs and boards. In the late 1980s, GE began to reduce bureaucracy, empower people, and reinvent ways to more effectively do business. As a result, GE became one of the most admired and innovative companies in the world. The entire process was built on a simple concept that the individuals closest to the work knew it the best. The implementation of this philosophy unleashed an unstoppable wave of energy, creativity, and productivity throughout the organization.

Results have always been the important equation in the business environment. Bruce Tulger notes in his book *Winning the Talent Wars,* "The market value of results has always been an important equation in business. In the new economy, however, it's the critical equation and there is going to be a perpetual tug of war between individuals and organizations, between talent and management over who is going to control and leverage the market value." Tulger feels that this will call for a more transactional approach to employing people.

In the midst of all this for-profit turmoil, there is a growing suspicion that leadership itself does not matter. Those who are suspicious of leadership would argue that the structure of the organization, market conditions, and other factors have a much greater impact on business outcomes. In his book *Creating Leadership Organizations,* Joseph A. Raelin rejects this argument, stating that this viewpoint focuses on the theory that only one person in an organization possesses leadership, when in reality that is far from the truth.

The world around us can have a profound effect on the health and vitality of both the for-profit and not-for-profit communities. Yet, in the worst of times, for-profits and not-for-profits have not only survived, they have thrived.

What is the difference between the for-profit companies or not-for-profits organizations that succeed and those that fail? The answer is leadership. The successful entities have leaders who are capable of anticipating and embracing change. They have leaders who understand that they have to sacrifice, be flexible, be innovative, be imaginary and take calculated risks to survive. In short, they have leaders who care.

Therefore, a CEO must take three initial steps to retain her or his position:

1. Care deeply about the mission of the organization.
2. Share the vision and become a major part in developing the vision.
3. Spend more time than anyone else thinking of ways to advance and improve the organization.

If you are not really committed to the principles and mission of your not-for-profit organization, the logical question must be asked: "How effective can you be?" If your motives are pure and you really want to make a difference, then you will find the suggestions in this chapter helpful to retaining your position.

The CEO's Survival Kit outlines the steps that each CEO needs to take to succeed. These steps should be taken the minute that the CEO walks into the association, and they should continue until the CEO leaves the organization. The Survival Kit outlines the following:

- Maintaining your personal edge
- Optimizing the first six months
- The review document
- Achieving a full partnership with the board
- Creating a staff team
- Keeping watch
- Making a difference

MAINTAINING YOUR PERSONAL EDGE

The first and most obvious way to retain your CEO position is to maintain your personal edge. You have made it to the top and you did it through a lot of hard work and by obtaining the required training. Now is not the time to slack.

The hard work will be easy. It is what you are used to doing. The important thing will be to focus on the areas that will do you the most good. The CEO position is different than other positions in that you cannot be bogged down in one or two areas even though they may need your expertise. A CEO has to be constantly looking over the whole playing field. The key to success for a CEO is to find talented individuals who will work hard and intelligently in the required areas and report back to you for advice and more work.

The personal areas that you can continue to work on, however, are the training and personal relationships that can assist you in retaining your position. The training aspect should cover a broader area than you have learned to date, including:

- Leadership skills

- Personal skills enhancement

- Training related to the mission of the organization

- Technology

- Networking/opening doors

Be sure to be involved with at least one leadership training opportunity per year. Search carefully for courses that teach a new angle or approach to old problems. Many of the courses may be a refresher but you will always get something new out of them and they will help you focus on your leadership role or enhance the way your staff and volunteers can become better leaders.

Personal skills enhancement varies from person to person, but it is important to keep up with as many skills as possible. I only wish that I learned how to type in high school, for example; my productivity would be greatly increased over the two-finger approach.

Taking courses or learning through experience is a great way to learn more about the issues or nuances that relate to the mission of your organization. Learning these skills will help you understand your constituents and it will help you talk the talk a little better. It is a noble thing to do for the CEO that cares about his or her mission.

Technology training is required learning for any successful CEO. Never get behind in this area; know as much as you can. Perception is reality; if you're on the cutting edge, so is your organization.

Opening doors is another way to use training to your advantage. Training is a great way to increase your exposure in the community. You never know who you will meet; it may be the opportunity to meet an influential individual or it may afford you the opportunity to be invited to a place that you might not otherwise have access to. This aspect should never be overlooked.

Personal relationships become much more important when you are a CEO. In your role as the CEO, you will have the opportunity to meet thousands of people from all walks of life by chance or by design. Either way, each meeting affords you the chance to tell both your organization's story as well as your personal story. Here is a practical outline of who should be on the list:

- Individuals with key leadership roles in your organization

- Individuals who wield the real power in your organization

- Powerbrokers in the industry or field that your organization represents

- Individuals who fund your organization

- Individuals who can give you sound advice from time to time

- Fellow CEOs

Individuals with key leadership roles in your organization are very important to have on your side. Simply put, you need to be up front and personal with each and every one of them. They hold the keys to your future in many ways.

Individuals who wield the real power in your organization may not be as obvious to detect at first. These individuals may be past leaders, current donors, or a key program people. In any case, the CEO needs to know, understand, and appreciate the role that these individuals play and must do everything possible to support them.

The CEO represents his or her particular industry or field to the entire world. The successful CEO is active in that world and becomes an appropriate player based on the need and traditions of the organization that she leads.

Those who provide funding to the organization should hear from the CEO on a regular basis. In-person meetings are ideal but a telephone call or a thank-you letter is the least that can be done for individuals who support your organization's mission.

Don't forget your network of advisors and, also, be sure to add to your list of advisors throughout your tenure as the CEO. Individuals who helped you to attain the CEO position can continue to help you retain your position.

Create, expand, and maintain a group of fellow CEOs who will take your calls and provide you with sound advice. Be sure to keep up to date with them by meeting them for a drink or calling them regularly to stay in touch. Make sure it is not a one-way street; help them work out their issues as well. This may be your best support network; chances are that they have encountered the same issue you're dealing with or they know someone who has.

The key to maintaining your personal edge is to work on it everyday. Having a little bit of an ego is fine; after all, you've earned it. Just don't let it get out of hand. At the end of the day, you are only as good as your last success story and all of your achievements are the result of lots of hard work from many people. The not-for-profit CEO who thinks they can do anything often finds something new and different to do—collecting unemployment compensation.

Once the initial celebration of getting your first CEO position is over, you should ask yourself, "What steps should I take in the first days and weeks of taking this position in order to be successful?"

If this is your first CEO position you will notice a difference right away. Before, your supervisor greeted you on your first day as you entered the building. The supervisor assigned tasks and, maybe, sent you through an orientation program. You are on your own when you enter the building for the first time as the new CEO.

Even if this is not your first CEO position, it is always a shock. Of course, you will be more prepared for your role, but you will notice cultural and organizational differences at your new organization.

In either case, several people may greet you, but they will be in the subordinate role rather than the supervisory role. Often, they will be looking for direction themselves.

They can provide a lot of information, helping you locate everything from the stapler to important documents but, when you enter your office and close the door, you are alone. The staff will be waiting for you to come out and say something profound and to point them in the right direction.

Successful CEOs walk into their organization on the first day with a plan of action that has two primary purposes:

1. Getting up to speed as quickly as possible on the current issues and responsibilities of the CEO

2. Gathering enough information to understand how and where to lead the organization into the future

The first challenge is always enlightening. Typically, the CEO position has been vacant and the responsibilities of the CEO were either not done or they were partially picked up by staff members who are anxious to get rid of them. During the first days of your administration, you need to find out what duties you need to perform and you need to take back the duties that staff members have been doing in the absence of a CEO. Make sure you take all of the duties back; you are in charge and you want to make sure that you hold the power and the key roles that the CEO traditionally holds in the organization. It is important that you become proficient at all of these duties as quickly as possible since they are, in reality, a part of your job.

Optimizing the First Six Months

The most important part of your job as the new CEO is to begin to gather information on the organization. From this data, you will need to get a pretty good reading on the current status of the operation so that you can begin to determine what the organization needs to do to move ahead.

In order to determine this, the CEO should be prepared to carry out a six-month personal plan that will determine how to best manage the day-to-day activities while providing leadership and planning for the future. The plan should be started on your first day.

Exhibit 6.1 provides a guide for the new CEO of a not-for-profit organization. The plan is designed to get you started; you will need to fill in all the details. If your organization is smaller or larger than what is outlined in the sample plan, just adapt the plan to your needs. All of the same principles apply regardless of size.

You begin the process of informing everyone about the quality of your leadership the minute you walk through the front door of your new office and announce that you are the new CEO. First impressions count and they are quite important. The way you dress and the way you greet everyone makes an impression. Just as you prepared for your interview, you should prepare for the staff's evaluation of you. This is why the six-month plan starts out with an outline for the first day and the first week.

EXHIBIT 6.1   A SUGGESTED PLAN FOR THE CEO'S FIRST
SIX MONTHS

The First Day
- Meet the entire staff to immediately open dialogue.
- Meet with key staff to establish relationships.
- Meet with executive office staff to establish guidelines.
- Arrange the office to your liking. Try to make it a bit different than the last CEO's arrangement.
- Find out how to use core technology.
- Contact the top volunteer leader and tell her or him you are onboard.
- Call your old office to let them know that you are at the new position, and if they need anything, don't hesitate to call.

The First Week
- Meet with your key staff individually to determine functions versus reality.
- Receive an orientation on key aspects of the operation.
- Meet individually with staff members briefly, just to get a feel for each person and to place a name with a face.
- Send a letter to all board members.
- Meet with the communications director to begin to discuss the vital role of visibility.

The First Month
- Call all board members to let them know what is happening. Begin the cultivation process by seeing a few in person, if it is possible.
- Hold a full staff meeting at least monthly and keep holding such meetings for as long as you are there.
- Meet with key staff to discuss their relationship with the staff.
- Make sure that your key staff hold weekly meetings with their staff, and drop in on the meetings once in awhile.

The Second Month
- Make a trip that would feature you as the new CEO.
- Make a trip for something that is outside the mission of the organization but provides good exposure to inform your staff that you are more than just the new CEO.
- Meet with key board members in person, or at least by conference call. Tell them that you have begun a review of the entire operation to determine its status and that you will produce a report in about four months.
- Meet with the entire staff to inform them about the review and let them know that you will need their help to complete it.
- Begin the review by asking key staff to lead in the information-gathering process.
- Meet with the entire board, and when you do, provide them with some exciting news.
- Start walking around.

(continues)

EXHIBIT 6.1   A SUGGESTED PLAN FOR THE CEO'S FIRST
SIX MONTHS *(continued)*

The Third Month

- Complete the first draft of the review using the information gathered by the staff.
- Conduct a full staff meeting to go over the draft of the review and ask their advice.
- Contact key board members on a conference call to go over the draft review and ask for their advice.
- Make changes in the review based on everyone's comments.
- Continue to walk around.
- Take another outside trip.
- Make a major speech on behalf of the association to obtain visibility coverage.
- Begin to selectively take out staff to lunch to ask their opinion.
- Do one major visual change in the office.

The Fourth Month

- Conduct a full staff meeting to go over refinements of the review and get final opinions before it is presented to the executive board.
- Present the review to the executive committee. This should be done in person, to gain their advice and approval.
- Refine the review based on executive board comments and advice.
- Produce the final review draft and send it around to key staff for one more look.
- Recognize staff individually for doing something right.

The Fifth Month

- Get out of your executive office more often to walk around and meet with staff.
- Get out of the overall office more, with and without staff.
- Put the final touches on the review and publish it.
- Begin to draft the board brief of the review.
- Develop an audiovisual presentation on the brief.

The Sixth Month

- Present the review and board brief to the board.
- Find a way to make the findings of the review or brief known to the full membership, and maybe even the field your organization represents.
- Begin to refine the staff structure by promoting and moving people around.
- Begin to give hints of the need to create a strategic plan to find ways to meet the needs discovered by the review.

The First Day

You need to make an impact and immediately begin to gather information on your first day. One of the most important goals for the first day is to meet with the entire staff. If possible, arrange the meeting in advance but, otherwise, make this the first priority the minute you show up. The meeting should take place as early as possible, preferably within the first half hour of the day.

The purpose of the meeting is to look everyone in the eye and tell a little about yourself. Ask the staff to introduce themselves and tell you about their position, even in large offices. As participants are introduced, walk up to them, greet them, shake their hand, comment on the nature of their work and ask questions that tell the staff that you have done your homework. Let them know that you have a good idea of what the organization is all about. Joke a little, show your human side and be positive even if the organization is in trouble.

Once you have met the entire staff you will want to have a separate meeting on the same day with the key staff. These are generally the individuals who manage other staff members. The purpose of the second meeting is to begin to evaluate what needs to be done immediately and what will need to be done in the future. Your approach should be a little more personal than it was with the entire staff. It is important for them to know that you will treat them fairly and that you are interested in their work.

The third group that you will want to meet with is your executive office staff. These are your support people; the primary individuals who will help you to be successful. You want them to be on your team from the beginning. Their knowledge of the organization, staff, and volunteers will be incredibly valuable. Let them know your expectations during this meeting and give them an idea of how they can meet your needs based on the available resources.

At some point during the day, make sure that you are introduced to the existing technology in the office. This includes everything from how to use the phone to using the copier. This will give you a good idea of what needs to be done on the technology front. Also, make sure that you are issued all the hardware you will need including cell phones, PDAs, laptops, and so on.

Before the day is over, make sure you contact your volunteer leader and tell him or her you are onboard and what you have done so far. Schedule a meeting with this volunteer leader for a week or two from now so you can begin the process of working together to advance the organization's mission. This will be one of the most important relationships that you develop during your first year. If you can successfully work with this volunteer leader, you will have a much better chance of working well with the volunteer leaders that come later.

Call the key person in your old office to say that you are onboard with the new organization. Let them know that you are available to help them anytime with questions or advice. This call accomplishes five things:

1. It finalizes the exit from the old organization.
2. It extends the hand of friendship.

3. It tells them that you felt good about working in your former position.

4. It lets them know that you appreciated the opportunity to grow in your last position.

5. It protects you by demonstrating that you still want your past organization to succeed and that you are willing to help out when you can.

Most of the time you will only receive a few calls from your old organization but it helps you to keep this group of people in your network. It also sends a message to your current staff that you have deep respect for the organization that you worked for in the past and that you will have the same respect for the organization that you now lead.

Make sure you arrange your office to your liking. Everyone's office should have a personal touch. Don't do this during office hours, however. Place items of interest on your desk and on the wall, but don't overdo the awards or make it appear cluttered. A few nice pieces is a good touch; too much is distracting. You don't need to impress anyone on your staff with your awards; a few interesting awards or certificates are good for your board to see, however.

When the staff arrives on the second day, they will see that you stayed late and personalized your office. It is a clear demonstration that you are ready to go to work. The first day is the most powerful day of your administration. First impressions are always important. If you started out well, you are on your way.

The First Week

Now that the first day is behind you, the next step is to begin to get a handle on the operation side of the organization. Remember, the two goals are to get know and understand the current needs of the association and determine what the needs will be in the future. The best way to do this is to meet individually with your key staff to determine the basic functions of the association and how well they are being carried out.

The information they provide you with will determine the ways that you measure success within each function and how each person on the staff relates to these functions. The total evaluation of these leaders will take some time, yet this process can give you some good impressions of each person. Later that week, you will want to begin to develop a profile on each staff leader based on their past records and your first impressions.

Instruct the key staff members to provide you with an orientation on all the aspects of the operation. Have them prepare a presentation broken down by department and let the departments' staffs provide you with the details of what they are doing. This will provide you with a quick understanding of what the organization is currently doing and it will give you a good look at the quality of the staff as well.

Begin to meet with each staff member on a one-on-one basis so you can get to know each one as an individual. This is more difficult to do with larger staffs but it is possible even if the staff is scattered nationwide. The personal touch makes all of the difference to your staff and you can begin to find the gems in your organization. The gems will come from all levels of your staff. Some have a greater role potential, some are misplaced and others provide a vital service in the positions that they hold. If motivated properly, each of them can play a vital role in helping you move the association in the right direction.

Send a letter to the entire board announcing your arrival and your activities to date. Let them know that you will contact them in the near future to discuss an important matter. Let them know that you need their advice on this matter.

Meet with the communications director to begin to discuss the vital role of visibility. This is an area that most CEOs do not take the time to do. The association may be going great things, the staff and volunteers may be doing outstanding things, and the CEO may have the best ideas in the world but, if no one knows about it, no one wins. The visibility effort has to be a priority from the beginning. This is one of the most important goals for the CEO in terms of retaining the position. The meeting with the communications director should review:

- The materials needed to support the CEO:
  - A current biography for the CEO
  - A planned introduction for the CEO
  - Standard remarks in materials concerning the CEO
  - CEO photos
- The role you will play in visibility:
  - Writing a regular column for the organization's newsletter or journal
  - Making speeches
  - Outside writing

The communication department is often instrumental in advancing other areas of the organization from fundraising and membership acquisitions to volunteer recruitment, attracting staff, and government affairs. The key is timeliness; make sure that everything that can advance the organization is revealed quickly to the various target audiences.

The First Month

Continue to call your key volunteers to keep them up to date. This includes telling them both the good news and the bad news. Communication is your best offense in fulfilling your goal of retaining the CEO position.

Also, schedule appointments to visit with the volunteer leaders on a one-to-one basis. These are important visits and they take a lot of time to accomplish but are well worth the effort. I make it a priority to get to know my board members. I want to know who they are, what they think, and why they are involved with the organization. This is vital information in order to have a meaningful relationship with each board member. Board members are the CEO's best allies; you want to avoid having them as your enemy.

Begin to hold staff meetings of all kinds; short ones, long ones, retreats, you name it. These meetings are good for finding out what is happening and guiding the staff in the same direction you are going.

The meetings also build a team. The team effort, as one of the participating CEOs noted, is everything. Much more can be done through a team effort than can be done through a bunch of individuals trying to do everything by themselves.

The staff meeting is as much a social affair as it is a reporting device. At my shop, we hold a weekly staff meeting: week one, executive staff; week two, departments; week three, full staff; and week four, individual staff. The staff crosses over department lines all the time to support particular issues or functions, so these meetings help us pin down where each person will be working for the next week and beyond.

These meetings should be used to build a team effort. I run the executive staff meeting and the full-staff meeting, and I drop in on the department meetings and individual meetings every so often to just observe. Remember that these are not your meetings, however. All you want to do is make sure that the meetings are taking place and they are being conducted well.

Once you have survived the first month, you are on your way. The next big hurdle is making it to the six-month mark. Most of what you wish to introduce is yet to come. You are still in a discovery stage, but you can start to stage the changes that you want to make.

The Second Month

Exhibit 6.1 provides a list of action steps for the CEO to follow in the second month. As the exhibit notes, it is extremely important to get out of the office to represent the not-for-profit. This should happen no later than two months into your tenure. The first trip should be an activity that features you as the CEO, providing visibility for both you and the association.

You should schedule another trip that highlights a skill or area of expertise from your background. Say, for example, you are good public speaker. Perhaps you could arrange to speak at a key national meeting that is unrelated to your association. This will show that you are a lot more than just the CEO of the organization and it demonstrates that you have several avenues of increasing the visibility of the association. Don't forget to let the communications director know about these trips so you can gain maximum exposure for both events.

This is also the time to meet with the executive committee. The meeting can be done in person or by a conference call. The purpose of this meeting will be to update them on what you have done so far and to get a clearer idea about what they think your priorities should be in the coming months.

Since this is your first official meeting with the executive board, you want to make sure that it is conducted well. The examples, the materials, and the way the meeting is conducted should all be first-rate. At the same time, it should look like it took minimal effort to pull it off. As the new CEO, you should take the lead role in this meeting to show your leadership.

One of the main purposes of this meeting is to inform the executive committee that you are conducting a review of the entire operation to determine its status. Inform them that this is necessary so you can gauge the immediate and long-term needs of the organization. Indicate that the review will take about four months and that you will prepare a report of your findings for the board. The executive committee will surely ask questions and have comments about the study. Be sure to list any suggestions or comments they have and incorporate these ideas into the study.

Meet with the entire staff and inform them that you will be conducting a review of the entire operation and that you will need their help in completing it. Tell them that the purpose of the review is to determine the current status of the organization so that you can properly plan for the future.

Meet with your key staff so you can begin to develop the review process and to determine how the information will be obtained. Make sure that the key staff is fully informed about the purpose and scope of the review so that they buy into the effort. Ask for their advice and suggestions on how to conduct the review.

Make an effort to meet with the entire board during the second month. If it is not possible to do in person, a conference call is all right. However, in-person attendance may be easier to accomplish than you think because most of the board members will be curious about how you are doing. Obviously, you will be reviewing the status of the operation, but be sure to convey a little good news even if the overall picture is negative. Also, tell them a story that shows a little progress in the organization so they can visualize forward movement, even if it is just a small step forward.

Begin to walk around the office. This is something I do on a regular basis; I want to see what is happening in the shop. Stop in and talk to staff members about the job at hand or anything of interest just get a reading on how employees are doing and if they need help. This process is healthy for both the CEO and the staff. It allows both parties to get to know each other a little better and each party begins to understand the role and challenges that the other faces.

The Third Month

By the time you make it to the third month you should feel pretty comfortable in your position. You should have a good idea about the quality of the entire staff and, in particular, the quality of the key staff. You should understand the flow of the office and the level of work that can be done. It is now time to make your first moves.

This is the time to complete the first draft of the review using the information gathered by the staff. The gathering process should have been informative to you, but it also should have informed the staff to the good, fair, and poor aspects of the organization.

During the final stages of the gathering process, be sure to ask the staff for their opinions on the review exercise as well as their opinions on the information that was found. Some of the discoveries will be a surprise to the staff and some will not. If you have engaged the staff enough in this process, they will understand what you are trying to do.

Once you have all of the information you need, provide the key staff with a draft outline and ask them to help you create the final review document. Allow each department to take charge of providing the necessary information and input for their area. Remain in the facilitator role until you receive the rough data back from each department.

Begin to process the data using as much key staff support as possible. Keep asking for comments and suggestions as the review document begins to take shape. Once you have completed a rough draft of the review document, it is time for others to see it and to comment on it.

Hold a full staff meeting to go over the draft of the review document. Solicit everyone's advice and comments and let them know how you are going to use the document. The advice from the staff will further refine the document and it will assist in the staff's buy in process.

It is very important that the staff understands the purpose of the review document and how they will benefit from it. Make sure the staff understands that this is not a vehicle designed to lay blame or come up with excuses to lay people off. Let them know that the process is designed to discover what the organization is doing right and to find ways to increase the organization's service. This could mean having to hire additional staff! The review is simply a method of determining the direction that the not-for-profit needs to take to best serve its constituents.

Hold a conference call with key board members and go over the rough draft of the review document to ask their advice. It is also important at this time to make sure that key volunteers understand the vital role that the review is providing in the planning process and for the future of the association.

The key board members will react well to your leadership move of conducting the review. It shows initiative and it will make a lot of sense to business-oriented people. Be sure to point out the good areas and comment on them at length. This is not an exercise of tearing down the organization's past but, rather, of celebrating it by building on its strong points.

Yes, you will also need to subtly mention the areas that need refinement and the areas that may need to be completely overhauled or abandoned. Be sure to introduce these changes gently, however. Start by planting a few general ideas on how the organization can be improved. Don't be too specific; however, that will come later. Remember, you are only on a fact-finding mission in the review process.

Once the key board members have had time to look over the review document, ask them for their advice. Focus on the top five concerns that the study has identified and provide a few suggestions on how to improve these areas. Again, ask the board's advice. Hopefully, at least one key volunteer will suggest a few refinements. Run these ideas past the other board members. This exercise will produce other ideas and additional key volunteers will be engaged in the process.

When you incorporate these suggestions into the document, make sure you give full credit to everyone who participated. Send the new draft out to the key staff and the key volunteer leadership for comments.

Meanwhile, back at the office, continue to walk around. By now, your staff should be getting used to your practice of just dropping in on them for a friendly chat. Hopefully, they are feeling more comfortable with this practice and they are beginning to open up to you. These conversations should be getting better each time that you sit down with each person.

You should be increasing your outside travel even more now and at least one additional significant trip should take place. Each of these outside experiences should be shared with the staff. This can be done directly by taking a staff member along if appropriate, or it can be done indirectly by simply commenting on the travel itself. The motive here is to show that you are out representing the association and that things are happening.

In addition, schedule to make a major speech on behalf of the association to obtain visibility. You are strengthening your position every time you appear as the CEO of the organization and make a speech that supports its mission.

Begin to selectively invite staff members to lunch to ask their opinions on various aspects of the association. By now, the staff knows you and, hopefully, they see you as an energetic leader who wants to make a difference. Most people will be flattered to be asked out to lunch. Don't delegate the asking part to someone else. The entire experience should be conducted on a friendly level and not seen as a command performance even though it is.

The lunch should be conducted in a public place for a number of reasons. The purpose of the meeting is to get a feeling from the individual about how things are going. Look to see if some of your ideas are beginning to find their way down the pipeline. In addition, see if the individual feels free enough to provide an idea or two. If so, your open operations approach is working. The last thing you want to determine is the potential of the person and where you think he or she will fit in the operation in the future.

Sometime in the third month, make one major visual change in the office. Make sure the change is something that everyone will understand and benefit from. One of the changes I made in an association soon after I came on board was to invest in a new copier. From the first day I came into the office, all I heard about was that the copier was broken or jammed again. The existing copier was way beyond its normal shelf life, but the association was struggling financially so it had not been replaced.

I had the operations director do a simple analysis of the replacement value versus the time drain on the staff. It was obvious that we needed a new copier with more features and capacity, so we decided to look around and obtained a very good lease deal. The copier just appeared one day and news spread around the office within minutes.

The entire staff was surrounding the machine when I went over to make a copy and asked, "What do you think?" I got a round of applause. Never underestimate the power of listening for real needs and fulfilling them.

The Fourth Month

In the fourth month, you will begin to refine all that you have done so far. At the full staff meeting, you want to go over the refined copy of the review document and get any final opinions before it is presented to the executive committee. By now, the staff clearly understands that the review document is a major priority for you and they should be comfortable with it because they have been involved in the process. Hopefully, they also understand that the document will be a major benefit to them as well. This is the time to complete the document and to celebrate the staff's contributions.

It is time to present the review document to the executive committee. This should be an in-person meeting if at all possible. It is important to see the reactions of each executive committee member. You want to encourage comments on your ideas, seek further advice and, ultimately, get tentative approval of the document. The committee will almost certainly add refinements and suggestions, but that is fine. This improves the quality of the document and makes the committee buy into the process even more.

Refine the review document yet another time based on the comments of everyone who contributed. Hold on to the document for a couple of days after you have finished it in case you come up with some more ideas or refinements. Then produce a working draft and send a copy to each key staff member for one final look. No matter how many times you look over a document like this, you always miss something. Develop a final working draft copy once the key staff sends back their comments.

Before the month is over, recognize one or more staff members for doing an outstanding job. Make sure you recognize them in front of the entire staff and give them a useful gift such as dinner or theater tickets. This will generate interest from the other staff members and it will increase morale. It also sets a precedent for doing this in the future.

The Fifth Month

Continue to get out of your office and walk around and meet with staff. By now, you should no longer be the boss; you should have become a partner and colleague. The staff should consider you a fellow worker who is interested in helping them to be successful. At this point, they have begun to trust you and they may even like you. They consider you the team leader and they like being on your team.

Begin to use this working relationship to sell your vision even though it still may be vague. At this point, you should have a good idea of what the organization is all about from the review that you conducted. Use this knowledge to begin to orchestrate change, even if the change seems to be small or incremental.

Increase your time out of the office both by yourself as well as with the staff. Traveling with the staff is good for helping to accomplish the goals of the organization, as well as having a one-on-one opportunity to discuss a number of issues with the individual staff members. Business travel, as we all know, is not a glamorous experience. Often you are waiting for a plane or driving in a car for several hours. This time is valuable for getting to know, appreciate, and encourage fellow staff members. Find out what they think about the current assignment, learn what their career goals are, and find out their interests.

Put your final touches on the review document and print it up. The document has served you well so far—it has helped you to get valuable information about the association, it has helped you transform your staff into a team and it has helped you begin to develop a working relationship with your board. Not a bad start.

Now it is time to draft a *board brief* based on the review document. Exhibit 6.2 can provide a guide for you. Remember, the review document is a large document that details everything about the organization. Not everyone on the board will want a copy, but they should be aware of the basic findings of the review.

This is the purpose of the board brief. This document should be just what the name implies; brief and to the point. It should outline the condition of the association by areas and it should provide your recommendations for how these areas can be improved or maintained. If possible, an audio/visual presentation is a great help in presenting the board brief.

The Sixth Month

Present the review document and the board brief to the board. This should be an in-person meeting so you have the opportunity to go over your findings and recommendations. Your report should focus on the board brief but you should also refer to

EXHIBIT 6.2   THE BOARD BRIEF

Page one: Title page should include the following:
                       Name of organization
                       Prepared especially for the Board of Directors
                       Prepared by: CEO

Page two: Contents page

Page three to end:

Opening statement: Reason for the study
                       How the study was conducted
                       Limitations of the study
                       People who participated in the study:
                       • Volunteers
                       • Staff
                       • Other

   I. Brief History of the Organization
   (short paragraph)

  II. Review of the Fiscal Integrity of the Organization
   (short on wording, high on graphics)

 III. Financial Resources
   (Keep the wording as brief as possible, and use graphics wherever possible.)

 IV. Operations
   • Legal counsel and legal issues, if any
   • List of insurance policies and coverage
   • List of outside consultants and agreements in force
   • List of leased items, including office
   • If you own your own building, what it is worth
   • Summary of equipment, and so on
   • List of technology and its use
   • List of a complete inventory
   • Other

  V. Board of Directors
   • List of current board members
   • List of past board members
   • List of prospective board members

- Summary of current issues before the board
- CEO evaluation process
- Other

VI. Personnel Report
- List of staff and functions, including open positions
- Current support
- Other

VII. Member and/or Donor Relations
- Recruiting fundraising process
- A summary of all types or sources
- Other

VIII. Government Affairs Function
- What functions exist
- Current issues
- Status of a political action committee (PAC)
- Other

IX. Meetings, Educational Functions and Other Programs
- Complete evaluation of meetings over the last three years
- Other

X. The Visibility Function
- Complete list of internal publications produced
- Evaluation of the media placement program
- Web site review
- Use of e-mail
- Other

XI. Volunteer Management
- Evaluation of volunteer management program, including use of volunteers
- Other

XII. Recognition
- Review the of the recognition plan
- Other

Summary and Recommendations:

(Summarize what you have found, and highlight the positives. Note the areas that could use refinement, areas that may need to be replaced, and a few ideas for new activities, actions, or programs that likely will need further study. If a strategic plan is in place, suggest that the plan may need to be updated. If no plan is in place, suggest that a strategic planning process needs to be created.)

the review document often to verify that it was the source for everything you are talking about.

This event should be staged as a celebration of the accomplishments of the past and prospects of a bright future if certain areas can be addressed. Clearly define the areas that need improvement, and provide reasonable solutions for each situation. Field questions and have your key volunteer leaders help you sell the documents and the recommendations to the board.

Find a way to make the findings of the review document known to the full membership of your organization and, perhaps, to the field that your organization represents. Develop a story to sell these findings and explain how the information is going to be used to advance the cause. This is another way to strengthen your position. Make sure you are quoted in reference to these findings.

Now that the review document is done and the board has approved it, chances are that the findings reveal a need to change course to fulfill the organization's mission. This may be a good time to refocus the staff structure to assist the organization in making these refinements. The changes should not be drastic but, rather, should consist of small changes such as promoting from within or slightly refining staff duties.

You have been studying the staff for six months. You know what you have and, chances are, there are one or two individuals with great potential who could do much bigger things if they had a chance. It is time to give them that chance. There is nothing more satisfying than opening up new career opportunities to people who are eager make a name for themselves. Your actions will be noticed by other staff members and some of them will be inspired to work harder.

Now is also the time to move people around to better fit current needs. This will be well received if you treat the staff with dignity and approach the process with the attitude that everyone is getting a fresh start and a new opportunity to grow. This may be the time to bring in some new talent as well. If you have laid the groundwork properly, the staff will not be surprised to see a new employee or two coming through the door.

This is the time to hint about the need for creating a strategic plan to address the needs or shortcomings revealed in the review document. Start by laying the groundwork with your key staff and then roll out your plans to the full staff. The objective is to use the findings in the review document to make the case to develop a strategic plan.

The CEO needs to explain to the staff that the strategic plan will help steer the association in the right direction in the future as well as addressing the needs and shortcomings that were revealed in the review document. The strategic plan is your next logical step in keeping everyone engaged and moving ahead.

THE REVIEW DOCUMENT

As the six-month plan emphasized, the review document can perform a number of important functions at the beginning stage of a CEO's tenure. The review document is designed to perform five functions:

1. Provide quick and accurate information to the new CEO concerning the entire not-for-profit operation.

2. Illustrate to the board that you know your business and that you are taking immediate steps to improve the organization.

3. Alert the staff that you are taking charge and that you have the skills to succeed.

4. Provide a quick evaluation of the staff.

5. Determine who the key volunteer players are.

The review document has the ability to jump-start the new CEO's agenda, greatly enhancing the probability that the professional leader will be there long enough to make a real difference.

In order to make a proper evaluation of the association, the CEO needs to have accurate information on its current condition. The evaluation should include the current status of the organization as well as the possibilities for the future. Not-for-profits vary in the role they can play based on their mission and resources. Always look at the mission first to determine:

- Is the mission really fulfilling a need?
- Is the mission exciting enough to attract volunteers and donors?

If the answer is yes to both questions, then you must determine if the organization has the ability to move in the right direction and if you are the proper person to lead that charge. I have walked away from a number of "opportunities" after determining that I was not the right person for the position.

The review is designed to alert your board that you have arrived and that you are immediately beginning to roll up your sleeves and get to work. They will be impressed that you are taking the initiative to begin this process. The review also alerts the staff that you have come to the not-for-profit with a plan of action and they will respect you for it. The staff always wants a leader; they want someone to show them the way and to make them feel that someone is in charge. The review process will cement this relationship.

The review process is also a great way to evaluate your staff. It will help you to discover untapped talent, to see if the staff functions correspond to what really needs to be done and to find the dead wood.

The review will begin to expose the key volunteer players. These players may or may not be your current leaders. They may be a combination of past leaders and potential future leaders. This is very valuable information for the new CEO. The review will also reveal voids in the volunteer leadership.

When conducting the review, you should research each area using the channels that are currently in place. For example, you should start with the accounting department when you are addressing the fiscal health of the association. This methodology will engage the entire staff.

It is your study, but you should encourage everyone else to gather the information. This will save you time as well as getting the staff and volunteers to buy into the process. It is a great way to build the team approach as well.

The review document should cover the following areas:

- A brief history of the organization
- Review of fiscal integrity
- Financial resource strength
- Operations
- Board of directors
- Member and/or donor relations
- Government affairs function
- Meetings, educational functions, and other programs
- Visibility function
- Volunteer management
- Recognition

A Brief History of the Organization

When you began the process of researching this position, you were probably told about the history of the organization and its founders and other folklore. Your review will cover these areas but you will probably discover new information as well.

One of the best opportunities that this exercise provides is the chance to talk with past professional and volunteer leaders. Don't let this opportunity slip by. During the review, take the time to contact as many of the past leaders as possible and be sure to add their comments to the history section to bring it alive. It will help you sell your points to your current leadership.

See if you can keep in touch with the past leaders to ask their advice. Most of them will be flattered and will be happy to advise you throughout your career at the association. Make sure that they are still receiving the association's newsletter and other mailers. These past leaders can continue to support the organization by providing a sense of history and they may even be able to open a few doors for you.

The history of the organization is an important tool to use to remind current members of the reason why the organization was founded in the first place. Create an updated history of the organization using stories and quotes from past leaders. Make sure this information highlights the richness of the organization. If nothing else, the historical background of the organization will be useful sometime in the future when your association reaches a milestone.

My current organization celebrated its twenty-fifth anniversary about five years into my tenure. We created a history wall in our lobby that consisted of five panels depicting the various events of the last 25 years and a smaller panel listing all of the volunteer leaders over that time. The display consisted of photos, literature, and art work. We unveiled the display at a special board meeting where we invited all of our past volunteer and professional leaders to attend. It was a great success in recognizing the founders who built the organization and it was a great chance to get "approval" from them on the current and future direction of the organization.

The history wall stands as both a living memorial to those pioneers and an excellent tool for educating new staff members and leaders about our past. In addition, we developed a handout that talks about the wall and our history for anyone who is curious about our origins. We intend to add another panel to the history wall every five years to record the accomplishments that were made during that time.

One of our association's mottos is, "We are in the process of making history for others to follow." This means that anyone of the staff members or volunteers could be featured on the history wall in the future if they make a real difference today. The lesson is that the historical origins of every not-for-profit are not only in its past but in its future as well. History is a living thing that can be much more dynamic if everyone puts their heart and soul into it.

Make sure that your historical review includes a number of major accomplishments. The review needs to include the traditional facts such as the date the organization was founded, but, more importantly, it should contain the accomplishments that generate excitement. What was the driving force for creating the organization? What good did it do? Who did it help? In most cases, you will find a rich history that can be used to remind everyone that the not-for-profit made a difference.

Once you have assembled the complete history from record sources and the verbal accounts of past leaders, it is time to develop the copy. Don't write it yourself. Meet with your communications director or someone who you feel is appropriate, and ask them to write a draft. Give the individual a sense of direction and let them have at it.

Review of Fiscal Integrity

Fiscal integrity is the first and most important area for a new CEO to review in detail. This part of the overall review, however, is not a substitute for your immediate need to know the current status of the organization's financial health and its general accounting practices. The objective of this review is to discover the association's culture and general fiscal practices over a period of time. Hopefully, much of the information you seek was revealed to you during the interview process, but it might not have been.

I assumed a CEO position some years back and, upon arrival, discovered that the association had balanced its budget only twice over a 12-year period. As a result, the reserve had been depleted considerably. The problem was rather simple; spending was not in check and revenue production was not emphasized. I immediately instituted a purchase order procedure, placed a greater emphasis on achieveing a balanced budget and making money on all activities, increased income from members and donors, and performed regular checks on all of these requirements. While I was CEO, the organization never had a problem in this area again.

Remember, the volunteer leadership may not reveal everything to you in your interview, either, because they are unaware of the problems themselves or they do not want to scare good candidates away. I was never scared away from any reasonable problem. In fact, organizations that are experiencing certain basic management problems need to attract strong candidates to serve as their CEOs. If the new CEO is prepared for the challenge, these opportunities are a great way to attain the Corner Office and to make a real difference in the future of an organization.

The review should provide everything you need to fully evaluate the fiscal integrity of the organization. This may include the organization's current accounting practices, copies of a minimum of the last three audits, a complete listing of the association's investment portfolio, insurance policies, a listing of the major sources of income, assets, and anything else that might affect the fiscal strength of the organization.

As the new CEO you want to know everything. Don't assume anything. Years ago, I took over the CEO position at an association and discovered several surprises. The previous CEO of this organization had died suddenly and, after a six-month search, I was chosen. I had reviewed a number of documents before I assumed the position and I was well aware that the organization was a financial mess, but I was young and eager and so I took the position.

I began my review as soon as I came on board. Among the many things I discovered, one really illustrates the point. One of the organization's missions was to provide materials to other not-for-profits to distribute throughout the country. Since this was a small organization with small offices, these materials were stored in four printing houses located in various parts of the country. The value of these materials was well over $250,000 and, at the time, the association's yearly income was in the neighborhood of $500,000. The organization leased its office space and it had no reserve. When income came in, it was immediately used to pay expenditures, so the program inventory was the biggest asset that the association had.

Since these materials were stored in remote locations, I contacted the four printing houses so I could do an inventory. I quickly discovered that three of the four printers did not exist. The fourth printer did exist and admitted that he had our program materials in storage. I asked the printer to make an inventory of the materials he had in stock, which he refused to do. Then, I had our legal counsel draft a letter to the printer demanding the return of all of our materials. After nearly a year, we received two small boxes of materials from the printer containing all of the materials he had stored for us.

In continuing my investigation, I discovered that the organization had paid these printers to print and store these materials over the years, but I could not find a single authorization to distribute them. Obviously, most of the materials never existed. After reviewing the situation, it turned out that the printer and the past CEO had a very close relationship. Clearly, money had passed hands with no services rendered, costing this particular organization a huge financial loss and, more importantly, a lost opportunity in fulfilling the mission of the organization.

In my case, I had to remove the $250,000 asset from the books and explain the situation to the board. This situation took almost a year to resolve but became clear that it was going to be a problem very early in the review process. I got in front of the problem right away and I let the board know about the situation as soon as I discovered it. Of course, the board wasn't happy about the bad news, particularly since they were at least partially responsible for it.

All you can do in a situation like this is to turn a negative into a positive. I used this situation to make significant changes in the fiscal operations of the association. Most importantly for me, I discovered this problem very early in the review process so the criminal responsibility and consequences for this situation did not land on my shoulders. I assumed the responsibility of cleaning the problem up, of course, and it ultimately strengthened my position.

Once you and your financial staff have gathered the information you will want to meet with them to review each document. Then, you will want to work together to compile this information into a logical report.

You and your chief financial person should meet with the outside support people, usually an accounting firm, that the association relies on to help maintain the fiscal integrity of the organization. Meet them at their offices as it gives you a good opportunity to see how they run their operations. Ask for a tour of the office and ask about the other services that they provide to their clients. You may discover that the accounting firm can provide additional services or that you need a new outside consultant.

My current association's manager of finance and support is the primary contact person with our outside accountant firm, but I sit down with the accountant in charge as often as possible. This is a habit I formed when I was the CEO of smaller associations. Good accountants provide a number of services beyond the annual audit. This can include anything from handling money coming into the office to improving the overall accounting practices of the organization.

The primary question you want to ask your accountant when you first meet him or her is, in their opinion, "What is the fiscal health of your organization?" Since you have already completed your internal review, you may think you have a pretty good idea about your organization's fiscal health. Your accountant may have a completely different point of view, however.

A good CEO does not like surprises. I am direct with my approach to the accounting firms that serve my organization. I want to know what they are thinking and I want to know what they would like to see from our financial management process. I want to come to an understanding about the best way to conduct our fiscal affairs. This includes everything from how to set up and maintain the books, to what should be saved, to what to maintain from hard copies, to electronic files. The objective is to discover your accountant's ideal financial process and to work with the firm to meet these requirements.

The only thing you should try to negotiate is simplicity. Not-for-profits do not need and should not have complicated accounting or reporting systems. The business side of a not-for-profit is not that complicated. Negotiate any way you can to make the accounting system more easy to administer, more simple to review, and more easy to understand by the staff and volunteer leaders.

If your organization is fortunate enough to have a reserve or an endowment, you will need to conduct a review of your investments. You need to meet with your broker, which, again, should be done at his office. Discuss the investment plan that is currently in place and review any recommendations for the future.

The not-for-profit portfolio, to ensure that the principal is protected, is usually invested in the most conservative vehicles possible. Endowment funds should be placed in low-risk vehicles to ensure that the interest is adequate enough to provide income for the intended purpose. The CEO needs to have a running knowledge of the current investments and the projected goals of these investments. If your organization does not have an investment policy, make sure that you initiate one.

Volunteer involvement should be encouraged in helping the CEO and other staff perform some of these duties. The opportunities for volunteer involvement will vary in different not-for-profits, however. At my shop, we have a number of ways to safeguard our fiscal integrity to ensure that the organization's staff and board are fulfilling their fiduciary duties including:

- Internal controls recommended by our accounting firm are performed by the staff and overseen by the CEO.
- The board reviews quarterly financial reports.
- An outside accounting firm conducts an annual audit. The volunteer audit committee meets annually with the auditor to review the audit and inquire about the financial status of the organization. Then, they present the audit to the board for approval.
- The volunteer audit committee approves the annual budget and presents the budget to the board for approval.
- The treasurer and the chair of the audit committee work closely with the CEO to ensure that all financial procedures are in place and working.

- The investment committee provides advice to the CEO and helps oversee the portfolio of the association.

The CEO can use all the help that she or he can get in the area of the fiscal integrity in the not-for-profit. While a CEO needs to make sure that this area of the operation is on solid ground, there are other areas that demand much more of her time. That is why you need to develop a solid yet simplified procedure that you can administer with the staff and volunteers.

Financial Resource Strength

Once you have determined the fiscal integrity of the organization, you need to review your sources of income. It does not matter where the money is coming from—membership dues, benefit programs, annual meetings, program income, or donations—revenue is revenue, and you cannot exist without it.

Many not-for-profits have more than one organization within their operation and this must be factored in as well. At my shop, we have a 501(c)4 organization to run our government affairs function and a 501(c)3 organization to run our legal and educational affairs services. Many organizations may even have a for-profit subsidiary that helps them serve their constituents and produce revenue.

This is the second most important area to get control of as the new CEO. Meet with the staff leaders who are in charge of any area that produces revenue and ask them to provide you with a list of all revenue sources as well as a breakdown of what these sources produced in the last three years. Meet with the appropriate staff members individually on each of the major sources of income, for example, the annual meeting and convention. You should come away from this process with a clear picture of the current status of the income that is being generated, how it relates to the organization historically and how it relates to the projected trends and needs of the organization.

It is important to review the projected trends of the organization. Once you have gathered the background information, you need to determine two things:

1. Are the revenue sources from current activities on the rise?
2. How does the association compare to the industry standard?

The first area is pretty easy to determine. You will be able to ascertain this from the review of what your various revenue sources produced in the last three years. You simply have to see which activities are producing well and which are not. Be sure to look at the extent of new revenue opportunities that have been introduced over the past couple years.

The second area is a little more difficult to determine. That is why you need to keep abreast of current and future trends by maintaining your network of outside contacts with other CEOs of not-for-profits. You can cross-reference these trends with a number of other information sources. As you examine the trends and changes that will have an effect on your revenue sources, you will see that some of them are reversible and others will be beyond your control to change.

Several fundamental changes are afoot that will affect the existence of not-for-profits and how they do business. These kinds of changes have always been around in one form or another and they will always be a part of the not-for-profit landscape. Current trends suggest, for example, that diversity and new generational attitudes will change who will become members of associations and how they will expect to be served. Constituencies have changed since associations began, however.

Not-for-profits leaders who embrace these changes will need to refine both the culture of their organizations as well as the methods in which they issue the services that they provide. For example, many associations rely on annual meetings to fund their operations. The question is, will this format of service appeal to their target audience in the future? If not, what will take its place? If the organization gradually switches to a new format to serve future members, will that service produce enough revenue to offset the annual meeting format?

Needless to say, the new CEO needs to get on top of these kinds of issues. They need to determine the health and vitality of current revenue sources and be on a constant search for new sources of revenue that can replace dwindling programs. The health of the CEO's organization depends on this ability.

Operations

The next area you should focus on is the overall operations of the organization. The goal is to become aware of all the details of the operation so you can make educated decisions regarding what to maintain, what to improve, and what to be drop.

The legal aspects of not-for-profits are generally handled by the operations department. This would include any legal issue other than issue-driven work. Most not-for-profits have legal counsel on retainers or have made other arrangements. Whatever the arrangement, this is a person you want to meet. Go see your attorney in person and ask her for her impression of your organization. Ask the attorney to provide any advice that she thinks is relevant. Make sure that this is a person you know well enough that you can have full confidence in her abilities when and if you need it.

Every organization has insurance. The appropriate question, however, is: "What is the right insurance?" Your operation's staff will provide you with copies of the organization's policies but you will need to find out what the policies really cover. The last thing you need is a situation that isn't covered simply as a result of not reviewing your insurance plan.

Ask your insurance agents to visit so you can go over the policies and have them tell you what they cover. During the visit, ask if the current policies offer adequate coverage and if there are ways of getting better coverage. Ask if you would save money by combining several policies.

Ask your staff to provide you with copies of any agreement that the organization has entered into with any outside consultants or other entities. This includes professional services, real estate leases, equipment leases, vehicle leases, or any other obligation. Ask your staff to produce a list of assets including furnishings, buildings, or vehicles. Ask your staff where this information is stored so you can refer to it when you need to.

Ask your staff to provide you with a list of all the technology that is in place. The list should have the age of each piece of equipment and it should indicate if there is a replacement plan in place. In addition, the list should indicate any equipment that has a service contract and whether the contact is adequate or not.

Compile a list of which banks you use and why you use them. Although this is a fiscal integrity issue as well, it is also an operations question that needs to be addressed from the perspective of administrative and fiscal efficiency. Complete an inventory of any items that are considered assets or products to give away or sell. This inventory should indicate the value of the item as well as its age and salability. Overall, this process will help the new CEO to better understand the support mechanisms of the organization and what will be needed to strengthen the operation.

Once, before I was a CEO, I worked in an organization that determined that it would make good sense to own its own building. At the time, a building came up for sale that would have housed the organization as well as generating additional income from both retail and office leases. The organization discovered, however, that their current lease had more than 10 years left on it. The organization tried to buy out the lease, but the cost was prohibitive.

Instead of moving ahead with the new office, the group was forced to lease yet more space to accommodate a growing staff. The CEO then spent considerable time and money updating the entire office. The result, of course, was a missed opportunity due to a few miscalculated moves.

The lesson here is, never sign your life away. A 10-year lease is not good, no matter how much money you save. If you inherit a situation like this, never complicate a bad deal. Live with it or find another way around it. If I had been the CEO in the previous example, I would have found a legitimate way to break the lease. If I were forced to stay, I never would have leased additional space, nor would I have spent a cent on renovating the office.

If I was stuck in those offices, I might have used this situation to illustrate why we needed to move, and I could have developed a capital fund drive to buy the new building outright. The campaign might have taken three years to complete, but in the meantime, I would have been actively searching for a tenant to sublease the current office space. I might have also considered buying the building that housed the association. The point is that there is always a way to move ahead even though the obstacles seem insurmountable.

The operations of a not-for-profit can make or break a CEO. It is imperative that the professional leader ensures that the operations of the organization are a truly supportive arm of the organization. Volunteer involvement is normally nonexistent with this facet of the organization. This is the area that volunteers expect the professional leader to oversee.

Board of Directors

The next area to examine is the key group of volunteers that you report to—the board of directors. They are the body of people that are most important to satisfy. Several facets of this relationship should have been negotiated during the hiring process:

- The roles that the board and the CEO play in the organization
- How the CEO will report to the board
- The CEO's evaluation process

The roles that the board and the CEO play can vary from association to association, but boundaries for the two roles should be maintained. These boundaries prevent the board from micromanaging the organization and they prevent the CEO from having too much power and influence.

In my experience, no matter how much you negotiate the terms of this relationship, a testing of the boundaries always occurs at the beginning of the CEO's tenure. The testing of boundaries will occasionally resurface throughout the CEO's tenure as well. The CEO needs to be continually vigilant in this area. The continued success of the not-for-profit depends on this balance of power being maintained.

Typically, the reporting process consists of the CEO reporting to the entire board but, in reality, the CEO works closely with the top volunteer and the executive committee. The executive committee usually consists of elected officers and other key players. The number of executive committee members should be kept below ten. Make sure that you negotiate a clear reporting process so you are not reporting to everyone on the board. The top leaders need to support you in this fight if it ever arises.

The volunteer leadership and the CEO must feel comfortable with the CEO evaluation process. Over the years, I have developed a system that is pretty effective and seems to be well received by most volunteer leaders. My evaluation is based on the bottom line. Did we do better than last year? Did we make our goals?

Since we keep open books at my organization, all of the key volunteers know what we have done. The goals that are set are based on the plans that the board and staff agree on and on the budget that is approved by the board. I provide a set of goals based on the key categories within the strategic plan.

At the end of the year, I provide a detailed report of how the goals were met. The key leaders meet to review the materials and they evaluate my performance. It is a simple process and it works. Each year this gives me an opportunity to tell the organization's story as well as my personal work story. This helps everyone focus on the direction we are taking. In addition, the process strengthens the CEO's position by showing how far we have come as well as the exciting places we are going.

The review should include a listing of all of the current board members with information listed beside each name, such as the number of years each member has been involved, their tenure on the board, the areas that they like to work on, and any other relevant information. The listing should also include past board members and their current relationship with the organization. Finally, the list should have the names and statistics of future candidates for the board.

Volunteer involvement is the prime issue here. Finding as many ways to properly engage the organization's leaders is a constant goal that every CEO must take on. The more you help to create a volunteer environment based on a true partnership with the CEO and the staff, the more successful the not-for-profit will be and the more secure your position will be.

Personnel Report

The CEO will want to review the entire staff in detail. This evaluation should be conducted through the personnel director or whoever is in charge of that duty. Some of the information may need to be acquired from other key staff members as well. The important thing is that the information that you are gathering should be kept confidential, with only one or two trusted individuals helping you gather the required data.

The first thing to assemble is a complete list of the current staff. Make sure you get a brief description of each staff member's background and education and find out when they started. The list should include a job description for each individual. This will become valuable information as you begin to match function to actual need. You should have an organizational flow chart so you know who reports to whom.

Find out what kind of support is provided for the staff including coaching, internal/external training, or other educational opportunities to help them succeed in their work. If there are any positions open, ask why. Find out how many employees quit or were fired in the last three years and what the causes were.

The review is a good starting point for the CEO to determine the quality of the overall staff. Individual evaluations and team building will take time but the information you have obtained is a start.

Member and/or Donor Relations

Generally, there are two ways that not-for-profits procure operating funds:

1. Through a membership base
2. Through a donor base

Not-for-profits that rely on a membership base to fund their organizations generally receive their funds through annual dues and other activities that members pay for. Organizations that are membership based tend to be trade associations or professional societies for the most part. However, some of the largest member-based organizations are issue based.

Not-for-profits that rely on donors come in two general forms:

1. Independent organizations that raise funds for a cause
2. Subsidiary foundations that raise funds to support a cause related to the core organization

Although a membership-based organization differs from a donor-based organization in many ways, they also have a lot in common. The difference lies in the kind of return that each participant desires. A member wants information or services in return for the dues that that they pay while a donor generally provides funds for a cause they wish to support.

From the standpoint of the organization, there are many similarities between donors and members. Each needs to be discovered, nurtured, asked to participate, recognized, and cultivated to keep them interested in the organization.

Your review should look at the process as much as at the results. You should ask for a three-year composite of the number of participants by category to determine if your membership or donor level is up or down. The review should include the reason why these numbers are increasing or decreasing. It should also explain how the organization recruits and cultivates their members and donors so the CEO can understand the process and determine if it is adequate.

Volunteer involvement in membership-based funding tends to be less than donor-based funding. A membership-based funding volunteer may help recruit some members and may participate in some of the activities that are provided to the members. In a donor-based organization, volunteers are used more heavily to solicit funds.

Government Affairs Function

Not-for-profit organizations vary a great deal in whether they have a government affairs function. Trade associations generally are the strongest users of the government affairs function as it is often the primary reason they exist. Some professional societies have well-designed programs, while others have what really amounts to public affairs programs. Of course, both trade associations and professional societies are classified under Section 501(c)6 of the IRS code.

Some advocacy organizations are classified under Section 501(c)4 of the IRS code. These organizations tend to use the government affairs function as the main service program for their constituents.

The largest group of not-for-profits falls under Section 501(c)3 of the IRS code. These organizations are mostly donor based since contributions are tax deductible. The IRS has placed certain restrictions on 501(c)3 organizations in the area of government affairs activities. Unfortunately, the not-for-profit leaders of these organizations have traditionally tended to interpret these restrictions as meaning that they are not allowed to have government affairs program at all. This is far from the truth. In my book, *The Legislative Labyrinth: A Map for Not-For-Profits,* I demonstrated how every not-for-profit can take advantage of the government affairs process to fully represent their constituents.

The CEO needs to conduct an in-depth review of the government affairs program at their organization. If your organization has a government affairs program, meet with the person in charge of it and find out what the department has done in the last three years. Have the government affairs director make a list of the issues, accomplishments, and costs. Find out what kind of volunteer and staff involvement it has taken to produce these results. If your organization has a political action committee (PAC), follow the same review process with it.

If your organization does not have a government affairs program, you should take this opportunity to explore the advantages and disadvantages of establishing one. Find out why the organization does not have a government affairs program and determine if this is an area that would benefit your organization's constituents.

Volunteers can play an active role in the government affairs process. This is particularly true at the grassroots level. Volunteers can be a big help in contacting legislators or other officials on the issues that affect your organization.

Meetings, Educational Functions, and Other Programs

If there is one thing not-for-profits do, it is conduct meetings and programs. We have meetings for just about everything; in fact, we have meetings to plan more meetings. Not-for-profit organizations are people-oriented entities that have traditionally used gatherings to meet the needs of running the organization as well as serving constituents.

The CEO's review of this area should be used to determine the purpose, quality, and need of the organization's meetings and programs. This is one of the toughest areas to quantify, particularly if the association relies on more than one meeting or program to generate revenue.

At this point, you want to determine the following:

- Does the meeting program fulfill a need or an important function?
- What is the attendance record?
- Is the meeting or program making money?
- Are there similar activities in another association or in the overall field?

- What would happen if the activity didn't exist?
- Can other meetings or programs be combined to fulfill the same purpose?

You are trying to determine the current impact of the meeting or program as compared to how it performed historically. You also need to determine if this is the best way to continue to deliver the needed message or educational component to your constituents in the future.

The most important question to ask is, "Does the program or meeting fulfill a need?" This is often a very difficult question to answer. You can begin to get an idea from the attendance records over a period of time, say three to five years. However, attendance records only tell you about the level of participation; they do not necessarily tell you about the quality of the program. The meeting may have been held in the wrong place or at the wrong time of the year.

The same is true about profitability. If a meeting begins to lose the interest of your members, it may have simply run its course and is longer needed.

Another aspect you need to consider is that other not-for-profits or for-profits may be better positioned to provide this meeting or program. If someone else is already holding a similar meeting, you need to determine if your organization is losing attendees to the competition. Maybe you think the meetings should be dropped, but what do your members think? Perhaps this meeting and other questionable programs can be repackaged or combined to attract enough attendees to make it worthwhile.

CEOs need to focus on finding alternatives to current programs and meetings. These alternatives must satisfy members and produce enough revenue to take the place of the old revenue sources. If current trends continue, for example, associations will need to move away from staging large-scale meetings. As more and more information is available online and time becomes more of a premium, members are less and less interested in attending long meetings out of town.

Will meetings remain a major vehicle for not-for-profits to convey their educational and motivational messages? This question is hard to answer. People will probably always want to get together to discuss issues and to be educated but, perhaps, they will want to obtain these services at a more local level and rely on information gathered online. Perhaps the meetings of the future will become more social or issue driven than educational. Week-long national conventions may slowly fade away to be replaced by short one-to-three-day specialty meetings with an online component leading up to it. The point is, the review process should take these possibilities into consideration and figure out how they can become advantages.

The areas that still seem to need to be conducted in person include issues work, fundraising, and projects that require selling the organization or oneself. This should figure into your review and how you will strategize going forward from the review.

As a CEO, you have to find ways to serve the needs of your current members. Today's needs may still be mostly meeting based and the challenge may be to figure out how to generate revenue within this format. You will need to keep an eye to the future to exploit the possible changing trends away from using conventional meetings and program formats as the only way to educate, inform, and generate revenue, however. This one issue may become a major factor in the retention rate of CEOs going into the future. As a CEO, you need to keep on top of this shifting trend and to make sure that the organization that you lead remains ahead of the curve.

Visibility Function

The visibility function is the best tool that a CEO has to increase his or her success. While most organizations have recognized the need for some kind of a communications program, many organizations do not take full advantage of this tool. One of the participating CEOs noted that the use of media and other forms of exposure is fundamental to the success of today's not-for-profit.

As a result, the new CEO will want to undertake a thorough review of this function. Be sure to engage the communications staff and key leaders in this exercise.

Create a list of all of the internal publications and materials. Get a sample of all of these publications, a copy of all of the external releases sent out for the last year, a list and copy of all media placements for the last year, and a copy of any support materials for the staff to use to train members or make speeches. In addition, ask for copies of any support items for volunteers. Ask to see any audio/visual materials including radio and television spots and examine the organization's web page. Observe how the organization uses e-mail or other vehicles to increase the exposure of the organization.

You are trying to see how adept the organization is at increasing its visibility. In many cases, you will find that this area has not been exploited nearly enough. Your association's brand can have a lot of power and impact on your bottom line if its visibility is kept high.

Your review should concentrate on what the organization has done to date and how it can increase its visibility level in the future given the current financial and organizational resources. Every organization is unique and requires different approaches but every not-for-profit needs visibility.

By examining the internal publications, member-driven publications, and other written materials, you will be able to determine the general consistency of quality and effectiveness of the communications department. Is the flow of the materials consistent or do the designs of the materials conflict with each other? Ask questions such as: What do these publications cost? How do you evaluate their effectiveness? How long have they been produced for and what are the plans for upgrading or replacing these items?

External literature such as press releases tells a story about what the organization felt was important at the time. Review the press releases both in terms of rating the visibility factor of the organization and in gaining knowledge of past activities. Ask how many media placements these releases produced. Effective media programs go far beyond simply sending out press releases; they orchestrate media placement.

At my shop, we cultivate hundreds of media players through direct contacts. These contacts include telephone calls, belonging to press associations, in-person visits, and holding specific events for media players so they can get to know our organization. As a result of this ongoing effort, we have significantly increased our media coverage and this visibility has helped us become the leading resource for the media on our issue. It has also increased our visibility with our constituents and potential members.

Support materials designed to help staff and volunteers represent the organization at meetings or through speeches and training exercises help to increase the visibility of the organization. You will also want to be familiar with the complete inventory of audio/visual materials currently available as well as what may be needed in the future.

Determine the status of the organization's website. How is it used to serve the current members? How is it used to attract future members? Is your website the resource in your field? The web page is the tool of the future and it should be an important part of your visual strategy.

You will also need to review the e-mail strategy of the organization. Hopefully, the association is using e-mail whenever they can to save time and money in contacting members and conducting business. The use of e-mail for fundraising and other program-related uses is on the rise. At my shop, one of our most effective tools is our weekly one-page e-mail newsletter. The e-mail highlights three major issues and provides links to our Web page for the complete story. The newsletters are very easy to do, and they are very effective in telling our story to target audiences from members to media sources. Everyone seems to love the format and the content.

In short, the visibility factor is the key to the CEO's success.

Volunteer Management

The new CEO needs to determine the extent to which the volunteers are involved with the organization. This will depend a lot on the mission of the organization. Trade associations tend to make use of volunteers a little differently. Most of the individuals they recruit represent businesses that are members of the organization. In one sense they are volunteers but, in many ways, they act as representatives of their companies. They still play an important role in the success of the association, however. Often, for example, these member leaders can tell your story to legislators or media sources much more effectively than the staff ever could.

Professional societies tend to attract a large number of members who wish to be involved in a variety of committees and, eventually, to strive for a seat on the board. These seats can become quite competitive at times. The CEOs of these organizations are usually faced with the continual challenge of attracting volunteers who will keep the organization moving steadily ahead.

Social service organizations usually attract volunteers who wish to work for a particular issue or cause. For the most part, organizations falling under the classification of Section 501(c)3 need to attract large numbers of volunteers to fulfill their missions. They have a distinct advantage over other not-for-profits in that donors can declare their contributions as tax deductions.

Although the distinctions just listed are generally valid, a number of organizations have multiple related associations within their structure with different IRS classifications. This allows the organizations to be more flexible and to offer a greater mix of benefits to their members. Of the CEOs who participated in the study, 53.47 percent represented organizations with two or more IRS designated entities within their structure.

The new CEO needs to know the current role of volunteers within the organization. To obtain this information, ask the staff for a listing of the volunteers and the positions or roles that they play. Since this information may need to be obtained from several departments, make sure that you request and obtain consistent information so you can make a proper evaluation. At this point, you want to get a sense of how volunteers are utilized to fulfill the mission of the organization. Later, you can obtain a detailed overview of every volunteer.

Every not-for-profit can benefit from the use of volunteers. Once you have discouraged the current use of volunteers, you can determine if the current volunteer management program is adequate or if it needs to be enhanced.

Recognition

One of the most powerful tools that a not-for-profit has is the power of recognition. Organizations need to recognize individuals who are involved with the organization both internally and externally.

Recognition can take many forms. One of the participating CEOs noted that a simple thank thank-you can really make a difference. As the new CEO, you want to obtain a list of the current recognition programs at your organization. Find out what kind of recognitions were used by past CEOs. You should also review how the recognitions process has been managed and what kinds of records were kept.

Every not-for-profit should have a formal recognition program. The program should be administered by one person to ensure that the recognition program maintains a high standard, that everyone who earns recognition gets it and that all of the recognitions are recorded.

Occasionally an individual may state that they do not want to be recognized. Most of the time, what they are saying is that they want to be recognized in a way that is not currently offered. The not-for-profit recognition program needs to find out what the recipient desires and to be flexible enough to accommodate them.

Exhibit 6.3 provides a framework for starting a quality recognition program. The easiest and, perhaps, most effective recognition tool is saying thank you. This can be done in so many ways that are not time consuming or expensive. It can be said to the person when the act is performed, it can be said in a letter or a card or it can be said during a phone call. These personal gestures go a long way.

I make it a habit to personally sign all fundraising requests, as well as thank-you letters to every single donor. This amounts to thousands of letters per year and they always seem to arrive at my desk when I am busy doing something I think is important at the time. I make an effort to stop and sign all the letters and, often, write a personal note as well. I am convinced that this helps to increase the bond between our donors and the organization. Everyone who has a financial stake in our organization knows me well, and they know that they can contact me any time. This is the kind of relationship that every CEO should strive for.

At our shop, we have made it a habit to recognize individuals and entities by listing them in a number of places so that others may see what they have done for the organization. We have a *giving wall* and a *history wall* at our headquarters that recognizes individuals who have given their time and money. We also list individuals who have donated their time or money in our monthly publications, in our annual report, in news releases, and anywhere else we can. We recognize individuals in person at our meetings or on stage at other functions.

We often have gatherings at the homes of key players. Though they don't expect it, we send flowers to the host after the event and, of course, we follow up with thank-you letters. It is the unexpected small recognitions that do the most good.

EXHIBIT 6.3   **SAMPLE LIST OF RECOGNITIONS**

- Thank-you letters to anyone who helps in any way
- Direct telephone calls to say thank you
- Listing in newsletters, annual, etc.
- Stories about them in both internal and external publications
- Recognition at meetings
- Flowers
- Certificates of appreciation
- Personal plaques
- Group plaques
- Art or sculpture
- Dedication opportunities
- Other

The staff needs to be recognized as well. There are many ways to thank the staff for a job well done. Although increased compensation or bonuses are certainly a good way to thank your staff, they may not always be the most effective way. Generally, not-for-profit staff members are involved with the association for more personal reasons, not the least of which is a real belief in the mission of the organization. CEOs need to figure out what drives the staff and come up with a recognition program that reinforces this drive. At my shop, we tend to work hard together as a team in an almost family-like environment. We schedule times to recharge ourselves through planned staff events that are both check-up sessions and opportunities to socialize. It is the socialization part that makes all the difference in the world.

Not-for-profits need to have an array of formal recognitions. These may vary but will generally fall in the area of recognition for service and volunteering or recognition for providing funding. Organizations should take advantage of the visibility factor in determining how to distribute these recognitions. The best plans maximize the impact of the recognition to the individual as well as providing good exposure for the not-for-profit.

Achieving a Full Partnership with Your Board

If you followed the six-month plan and used the review document process, you are already working on developing your partnership with the board. The culture of each not-for-profit, at least in the beginning, dictates how you initially need to work with the board. This does not mean that you need to continue to work in this manner.

If you have been in a professional role in the not-for-profit community for any length of time, you will have seen a wide variety of ways in which volunteer boards work with CEOs. In Chapter 1 you read that the first employees of these organizations were not considered professional at all; rather, they were viewed as specialists or support staff. The full-time manager of a not-for-profit generally held the title of secretary for the first half of the last century. Even today, not-for-profit boards work in a variety of ways with their CEOs. Titles for these positions vary and may include executive director, executive vice president, president, or CEO.

So, the relationship between a not-for-profit CEO and the volunteer board is still really in a transitional phase. The new CEO needs to begin to negotiate the relationship at the time of employment and she needs to continue to refine the relationship throughout her tenure to maximize the benefits for the organization.

Ideally, the CEO should be fully in charge of the day-to-day operations including supervising staff, office operations, and program support. The board should oversee the CEO, make policy decisions, attract other volunteers, and get the needed funding to operate. The CEO needs to make sure this delicate balance is maintained. This relationship should be discussed right from the beginning and it should be fully understood by both parties and committed in writing.

The review document can help to cement your relationship as a significant player with the board. Throughout your first six months, you have kept them apprised of the progress of the review, you have presented your ideas on the review, you have incorporated the ideas of others, and you have refined the review. Now you are ready to present it to your board. The review document will be too large to present to the board, so you will need to develop a summary of that document (see Exhibit 6.2).

Make sure that you do it in person even if you have to wait for a few extra weeks. You should be the primary presenter, but bring in other key staff to support your efforts. This will show the board that you have already begun to build your team and the staff involved will see the leadership role that you are playing with the board. If the review is well received by the board, you will be on your way to a good and successful relationship with your volunteer leadership.

The review should be used to identify the areas that need to be worked on and to build a consensus on how to do it. If you are able to convince your board to refine a few of the recommended areas, this will provide you with an opportunity to show them how well you can perform. If a strategic plan or any other major undertaking is needed in the near future, your ability to achieve these first few tasks will determine if the board will trust your judgment on the bigger opportunities that lay ahead.

What you have done is to lay the groundwork for the future that everyone will want to be a part of. While this will take time, you have saved valuable time by getting your playing field identified early in your administration.

CREATING A STAFF TEAM

One of the major goals of a CEO is to create an environment that will make the staff want to follow you wherever you go. This can only happen if you work hard to fully support the staff as well as successfully selling them on your vision. In short, you must develop a team approach.

Once you have completed the review document, you will know more than anyone else about the staff and the current status of the operation. The manner in which you use this information will determine if you can win the hearts and minds of your staff.

A true leader is not afraid of having staff that knows more than they do about any particular subject. If you know more than everyone in the office, then why do you need any of them? The key to leadership, particularly with a knowledge-based entity like a not-for-profit, is to have the most talented staff possible.

At my shop, I have a staff that knows much more than I do about a number of the issues or operations that make our organization successful. What I need to know is how to motivate my staff to use their skills to the fullest. These efforts include the following:

- Coaching
- Finding training to fit everyone's needs
- Providing the latest technology to support the team
- Providing support in materials and supervision
- Anything else you can do to keep the individuals and the team happy

Sometimes a CEO is more of a facilitator than anything else. The challenge for the new CEO is to make sure that there is enough talent on the staff to perform the day-to-day operations and to come up with creative solutions to advance the mission of the organization.

As you and your staff begin to work toward your vision, you will see growth in some staff members, you will see other staff members who do the work but don't grow, and you will see other staff members who slowly get left behind. In all three cases, you need to continue to support these staff members in every way possible, and you need to let them make the best decisions for themselves and for the association.

The individuals who are growing in their positions need to be given new opportunities to recognize them for a doing a good job as well as giving them even more room to grow. Staff members who do the work but don't grow in their positions are really saying that they want to continue to do the same kind of work and to be paid fairly. There is nothing wrong with this philosophy and most of the staff members that fit this profile are great team players.

Individuals who don't want to contribute or who don't want to continue to keep up may need to find another opportunity. This is often one of the hardest parts of a CEO's role. However, keeping staff members that are not performing is detrimental to the work that should be getting done as well as to the morale of the other staff members. The CEO's role in this case is to find a dignified way to encourage these staff members to move on.

The staff can be a great help in fulfilling the vision of the CEO or they can be a major obstacle that stops you dead in your tracks. The not-for-profit CEO's role as a staff leader is to get the staff to buy into the CEO's vision and to support the staff in working toward that vision.

KEEPING WATCH

Even the best CEOs need to keep watch. Like it or not, no matter how much you attempt to help everyone, someone could be out there trying to get rid of you. These individuals can be on your staff or on your board, or they may be a member or someone outside the organization. The best way to combat this problem is to keep on top of your work, develop close ties with as many key individuals as possible, and keep your eyes and ears wide open.

It sounds simple, but keeping on top of your work is always a good way to keep the wolves away from the door. Keeping on top means not just fulfilling a bunch of goals each year but doing your work with gusto, being at ease with the position, and acting like you are having the time of your life. This kind of persona has strength to it and it is contagious. It therefore brings people to you who want to share the experience and moves others away who might want to harm you.

Developing close ties with key people is the most effective way to stop those who may stop you dead in their tracks. The most important body to win over, of course, is your board—they hired you, and they can also fire you. You should be working with your board anyway, but do it with as much gusto as possible. Go beyond the formal arrangement between you and each board member and get to know and be friends with the person. Talk with board members often, meet with them, and find ways to do recreational activities with them like playing golf or going hunting or fishing with them. Keep close to your staff. While you need to maintain a certain distance, it does not have to be that far. I enjoy being around my staff both at work or at some kind of recreational activity. They get to know me, and visa versa.

I also keep myself available for any member who wants to contact me about anything, and I keep my channels open to a number of associates that relate closely to the field my organization serves. Because of this, there is a loyalty factor that is earned over the years. They know who and what I am and they respect that. As a result, this network helps to fortify me from those who may try to harm me.

Yet, with all of this support, a CEO still needs to keep his eyes and ears wide open to hear the prevailing winds. Sometimes you need to act on situations that come up to protect yourself. It just comes with the territory. If you have done your best and you have established a network both within and outside of your organization you will do fine.

MAKING A DIFFERENCE

New CEOs retain their position by working hard and making sure that all of the bases are covered. The retention of the Corner Office is largely based on success as measured by goals and perceived performance. However, the successful and conscientious CEO always looks at one other factor: making a difference.

Leaders look at the role that a not-for-profit plays quite differently than mere managers. A true leader will guide an organization down the road toward fulfilling a significant vision and making a difference rather than just settling for doing business as usual.

Every CEO has the opportunity to move the not-for-profit they lead toward a vision that really makes a difference. At first, the CEO may be the only person who has this vision but, over time, others will begin to share the vision and soon everyone will be working to achieve the vision. When the vision is finally realized, the CEO looks at the experience with pride and begins to create a new vision that, again, will make a difference.

A century from now your vision may be the basis of an unbelievable discovery or an important movement in history. The CEO of a not-for-profit really has the power to make a difference; don't miss out on your destiny.

SUMMARY

CEOs of not-for-profit organizations have the opportunity to be successful if they really work at it. The CEOs who participated in the study agreed that hard work is the key to keeping the Corner Office. Boards of directors seek qualified candidates to lead their organizations. They are not interested in excuses or failure.

Being successful means starting out on the very first day with a winning attitude and a plan of action. Start by using the six-month plan and the review document outlined in this chapter. This will put you well on your way to gaining valuable information about the organization, gaining the trust of the staff and beginning to cultivate the board.

The CEO role is fast moving and leadership driven, and it requires talent far beyond knowing what functions need to be performed on a day-to-day basis. The CEO needs to be a strategic thinker with an eye toward the future to catch the opportunities that may come his or her way. The CEO also needs to have the talent to turn these opportunities into practical applications that benefit the organization's constituents.

CEOs have the power to retain their positions simply by working harder than anyone else, having a vision for the future, and having a genuine concern about the mission of the organization that they lead.

CHAPTER 7

Positioning Yourself to Attain a Higher-Level CEO Position

If you want to succeed, you should strike out on new paths rather than travel the worn paths of accepted success.

John D. Rockefeller Jr.

INTRODUCTION

Time has a way of slipping by quite quickly. Before you know it, you have been at the helm of your not-for-profit for a long time, and you have questions:

- You wonder if you have accomplished everything that can be done at your current organization.
- You may begin to think that there might be an opportunity to serve another organization.

With these thoughts in mind, you may also wonder if you really want to go through the process of looking for a new position. After all, your current position probably has been rewarding and the search for a new position will entail the interviewing ordeal and possible rejection.

So, is it really worth your time to begin to look around? You may find yourself in the following circumstances:

- Your current position is one you really like and you seem to be well respected by both the volunteer leadership and the staff. You may be hesitant to leave as a result of this.
- You have been successful at your current CEO position but you are the kind of person that gets antsy after a few years at the same job. Is it really wise to move on to another position in this case?

Either way, moving on is a difficult decision for anyone. This is particularly true of a CEO who has been successful and is finally beginning to reap the rewards.

It's funny—opportunities seem to find successful people. You might even find yourself in the position of being approached about a new CEO opportunity. In this case, you will have been taken by surprise, but you will need to act quickly to secure the opportunity. Of course, this leaves you with even less time to consider leaving your current position.

Successful CEOs should always be prepared to take a look at new opportunities. You never know what is going to be offered. It is worth the time even if it only verifies that you have a much better position than what is being offered.

The ultimate decision is yours, of course. The important thing is to make sure that the move is the right decision for you, your family, and for a both organizations that will be affected. Seasoned CEOs involved in a search for a new position tend to fall into the following categories:

- CEOs who feel like they have done what they wanted to do in their current positions and who want to take the next step in their careers
- CEOs who have been approached for a better position
- CEOs that have stayed too long at the dance

TIME FOR THE NEXT STEP

CEOs come in all kinds of packages. Some CEOs like the excitement of coming into an organization that desperately needs professional leadership. They enjoy helping the organization transform to better serve their constituents and, when that is achieved, they are not interested in maintenance work. Others like to be with an association for an extended period of time. They feel that they can help an organization grow through a long-term leadership role. Neither of these examples is wrong. Everyone has a different performance approach and a different idea about the length of time they feel comfortable in a position.

Many other factors play a role. Here are a few examples:

- A professional who took over the CEO role 10 years ago and built an organization into a powerhouse may not wish to run an organization that is now five times larger.
- A professional who is running an organization that has grown about as far as the CEO feels that she can take it and understands that she needs a change as well.
- A CEO who understands that the association now requires another kind of CEO to move the group to the next level.

Whatever the reason, if you as a CEO feel that it is time to take the next step in your career, you should begin to carefully examine the options.

The Ultimate Recognition

If you are a CEO who has been noticed for your work and approached about a better position, then you have received the ultimate recognition for your work. This means that the search committee or search firm is confident that you are more than qualified to assume the new CEO position. If they are offering you an even better opportunity than your current position, it is a wonderful compliment. CEOs need to be prepared to react to these opportunities. To do this, you need to be well aware of your options:

- Some CEOs have concluded that they are very satisfied at their position and that they do not want to move on. These individuals can respond quickly.
- Others may want a better CEO position but they are afraid of making the wrong move. This is the majority of CEOs.

Leaving Before the Stroke of Midnight

CEOs that have stayed at the dance too long have another kind of problem. Some organizations tend to eat up CEOs more quickly than others. One association I know of goes through a new CEO every 18 months to two years, no matter who the CEO is or how qualified the person is.

Unfortunately, in some not-for-profits, the CEO is given a very short honeymoon before there is a move afoot to oust them or find fault. CEO prospects need to recognize this problem before they take a position. These trends are often easily discovered by finding out how many CEOs the organization has had in the last 10 years and, if possible, talking to a few of them.

History repeats itself in many organizations. If you are the CEO of such an organization or if you find yourself noticing certain signs beginning to appear that your days may be numbered, the search for a new CEO position should take on a much more aggressive approach.

WHAT THE PARTICIPATING CEOs TOLD US

The CEOs who participated in the survey had career tenures ranging from 5 to 40 years. The highest percentage fell in the 20- to 30-year range. You can see from Exhibit 7.1 that 68.32 percent of these leaders have held more than one CEO position. These CEOs, therefore, have a wealth of experience in leaving an organization as a CEO and assuming another CEO position. Exhibit 7.2 summarizes their thoughts on this process.

An overwhelming majority of the participating CEOs told us that maintaining a network is the best way to find another CEO position. The need to create such a network is discussed in Chapter 2 and in Chapter 5.

234 POSITIONING TO ATTAIN A HIGHER-LEVEL CEO POSITION

EXHIBIT 7.1	PARTICIPATING CEOS AND THE TOTAL NUMBER OF CEO POSITIONS HELD	
Positions		**Percentage**
1		24.75
2		16.83
3		24.76
4		14.85
5 and over		11.88
Unknown		6.93

EXHIBIT 7.2	THE BEST WAY TO ATTAIN ANOTHER CEO POSITION	
Rank	**Response**	**%**
1	Maintain a network	60.39
2	Stay visible with volunteer leadership	11.88
3	Keep on the cutting edge	5.94
4	Check want ads	3.96
5	Others	11.88

This network, however, may need to be a bit different than the one you had earlier in your career. The network you need now should contain the following:

- Individuals who understand your strengths and your weaknesses
- Leaders in an industry related to organizations that interest you
- Not-for-profit leaders whose expertise covers your fields of interest
- Respected leaders who are easily recognized in your field
- Close allies within your current organization

To keep your stability, you need individuals who can advise you on your strengths and your weaknesses. They should not hold back in telling you what they feel you can or cannot successfully do in a particular position. For example, you may be the perfect candidate to lead a trade association but might not be suited to lead a medical society.

Leaders in the industry that are related to organizations that interest you can help you in many ways. They can, for example, take these actions:

- Alert you to upcoming CEO positions in associations within their field
- Recommend you as a candidate
- Use their influence to open doors by researching the organization and meeting the right people

There are a number of not-for-profit leaders in your field of interest that can alert you to position openings if they know and respect you. These individuals see and hear about a number of openings over the course of any given year. If they are in your network, they will keep you in mind and alert you to these opportunities.

Respected and recognized leaders in a given area are not always available to everyone, of course. If you can get to know these people, however, they can be used to influence the right people and open doors to the best opportunities. They can also recommend you for the prime positions. The key to the search plan of the seasoned professional leader is using your carefully assembled network to locate CEO opportunities.

Allies within your current organization can provide vital support in helping to sell you as a proven CEO to others. They have seen you in action and they are impressed. Many times, CEOs do not involve current volunteer leaders in their organization in order to protect themselves. This can be a wise decision but there are other options available. If you been with the organization for a while, you might call upon a past volunteer leader who respects you and who can be trusted to perform this duty. You might also want to look at past organizations where you had trusted volunteer leaders who can provide support in this process.

The participating CEOs also responded that "increasing your visibility with the volunteer leadership of your targeted organizations" may be a good move. This response ranked a distant second, however, at 11.88 percent. This makes sense, of course, if you already know which association or what kinds of associations that you want to target.

Increasing your visibility with the volunteer leadership of an organization is difficult for short-term searches. However, if you are targeting a particular position and you have the time, it is an effective way to gain favor. You may even consider becoming a volunteer in your targeted organization if it is appropriate. I have seen this work several times in my career.

"Keeping on the cutting edge through training and other means" came in a distant third at 5.94 percent. It is really just a given that a qualified CEO candidate will be up to date on every aspect of running an organization. That means that you must constantly increase your knowledge base to be ahead of other candidates.

"Checking want ads" came in last at 3.96 percent. While good opportunities certainly exist in the want ads of the trade publications, the vast majority of CEO positions are never advertised. Often, when an ad does appear, it is late in the search. One of the biggest problems with answering want ads is that they usually attract hundreds of inquiries. It is much more difficult to have your resume stand out from all the other candidates.

The participating CEOs also mentioned the following:

- Do extensive research on the targeted organization.
- Identify organizations that need your skills.
- Make sure that you have a good track record.
- Let search firms know your interest.

The participating CEOs indicated loudly and clearly that successful CEOs choose their own career paths. They have the ability to choose to stay and build one organization or move on to other challenging opportunities.

SEARCH FIRM RELATIONSHIPS

CEOs seeking another CEO position will inevitably encounter search firms that have been hired by the not-for-profits to find the best candidate for their organization. For larger organizations, this is a wise and astute decision. A lot is riding on making a good decision, and the volunteer leaders may not have the time or expertise to do a quality search.

Eric Vautour, Russell Reynolds Associates, Washington, D.C., has completed a number of searches, particularly for large associations. He notes that conducting a proper search to find a qualified person to fill a CEO position is a much more extensive undertaking than most people realize. A number of associations want to hire the same type of person they had in place for several years. This is often not a wise move. The organization may have grown and it may have different issues that need to be addressed than when the last CEO was hired. Vautour explains that search firms conduct extensive research to help not-for-profits develop a profile on the type of leader that the organization needs.

Many times search firms find candidates holding a CEO position in which they have proven to be very successful, and they will often approach these candidates about taking on the new position. Vautour indicates that this can often be a real challenge and that it is accomplished by showing the candidate that this is a rare opportunity to use their strengths to make a difference and to do work that they enjoy.

Vautour has some advice to anyone who may be contacted by a search firm or who may wish to seek a CEO position in general:

- *Be honest.* Do not exaggerate on your resume or exaggerate about your compensation level. Most of these facts can be found very easily.
- During the process, *probe the search committee* to find out as much as you can about the organization.

- *Be prepared to discuss your strengths and your weaknesses.* Everyone has weaknesses; the key is to tell them how you found ways to overcome them.

When asked if it is wise for an individual beginning a search to alert search firms, Vautour stated that it is certainly okay. However, he added that each search is unique, and the objective is to find the right candidate for a particular position at that moment in time.

Finally, he noted that if you are offered a position you should know how to negotiate well enough to get what you feel is appropriate. However, he cautions about making enemies in the process. His opinion is that most boards feel it is appropriate for a candidate to have an attorney review the agreement or contract before signing it.

Paul A. Belford, principal of JDG Associates, Rockville, Maryland, is noted for his ability to distinguish the difference between leaders and managers. In his recent book, *Planning Your Career in Association Management,* he notes that search committees seek the following:

- Service-oriented attitudes
- Management skills
- Leadership skills

Paul emphasized that volunteer leaders tend to seek a service-oriented attitude. They want a CEO who considers service as one of the major parts of the position. Although they seek other attributes as well, they look favorably on someone who will promote the association's goals and well-being.

Volunteer leaders want a CEO who can quickly win credibility with the staff and with the board through the management skills that he or she possesses. In order to function, an organization must seek and find resources; the CEO must be aware of these needs and deliver them. Volunteer leaders also want a leader who brings a sense of purpose to the organization and sets direction. A leader motivates others to achieve a shared goal by setting a good example and cajoling them with a good personality.

Any CEO looking to attain a higher level CEO position must be prepared to present themselves to search committees made up of volunteer leaders as well as hired search firms. Any individual who takes the time to research, prepare and execute a personal search plan will eventually be successful.

PREPARING FOR THE NEXT CEO POSITION

If you want to have the option of moving on to new leadership opportunities in other organizations, you need to work toward that goal, starting on the first day you attain a CEO position. Many of the steps you will take for the next position are the same ones that will help you to retain your current position, as well as making a lasting contribution to the organization and constituency that it represents.

Some of the areas that you need to concentrate on are:

- Determining what you really want to achieve in your career
- Keeping your search package up to date
- Expanding your existing network
- Determining the best approach to make
- Developing a distinctive record of achievement
- Cultivating people
- Making an external name for yourself
- Creating a winning interview strategy
- Knowing what compensation package you desire
- Making sure that your career goals fit well with your personal way of life

Determining What You Really Want to Achieve in Your Career

Determining what you really want to achieve in your career is not as easy it sounds. If you are a successful CEO, you are a busy person. There seems to be no time to think about your career path. Yet even if you thought a lot about your career, most seasoned CEOs would be the first to admit that their career paths did not go the way they had originally planned. Many CEOs, myself included, took a much different career path than they ever could have dreamed of.

While I trained to become a not-for-profit professional and had aspirations of becoming a CEO from the beginning, I originally thought that I would ascend to the top through one organization. I may have continued on this path had it not been for a mentor who correctly advised me to pursue other paths. While this was a major departure from my original plan, it was the best career decision I ever made. I have deviated from the planned path many other times since then, but I always focused on the goal of becoming a CEO.

Along the way toward achieving my goal of becoming a CEO, I began to understand that the journey was not about attaining a position but, rather, being positioned to make a real contribution to the not-for-profit field. This realization helped me to focus on the kinds of organizations that I could serve, and it refined the approach I took toward my work. I really don't work for a living; I enjoy every minute of my career.

Everyone should strive for a position that he or she feels this strongly about. Several of the CEOs who participated in the study were so satisfied with their positions that they plan to stay until retirement. Bravo to them; they have found what so many others seek. If you are still looking for your calling, that is okay, too; the important thing is to determine what you want to do in your career life and don't let anyone talk you out of it.

Keeping Your Search Package Up to Date

Have you ever had a search firm call you up to offer you the opportunity of becoming a candidate for a CEO position and then ask, "Could you send your resume by the end of the day?" I have on a few occasions.

Early in my career, prior to becoming a CEO, I received a call from a search firm that was searching for a CEO for a small association. We had a positive conversation and he asked me to send my resume to him the same day. Without thinking, I told him no problem. When I hung up the telephone, however, I began to realize that I had not updated my resume in some time. Moreover, the only copy I had was more than 50 miles away at my home. I hurriedly called the search firm back and told them that it would take me a couple of days to complete my resume. I am not sure if it made any difference, but I never heard from the firm again.

The point is, every CEO should create a search package that is up to date and ready for *the* call that you may receive out of the blue. Even if you never receive the call, it will be ready when you begin the search.

At this stage in your career the search package should be more sophisticated than just a resume. The package should include the following:

- A resume that can be easily adapted to a particular organizational search
- A curriculum vitae (CV), which may be more appropriate for certain types of organizations
- Cover letter samples plus a handful of short paragraphs that can be inserted into the various cover letters, depending on how you want to sell yourself to a particular organization
- Backup materials that demonstrate your achievements
- A master list of 15 to 20 individuals who can provide references from which you will select the best three to five references for a particular position
- A list of significant achievements that you can draw on, at a moments notice, to highlight your current situation
- Any other item that will help sell you as a candidate

The best approach for developing your search package is to always have more than you need. Many times, the item you put in your files as an afterthought is the very thing you need to refer to or send. Keep a hard copy of all of these items of your office, at home and accessible by computer so you are prepared when you receive a call from a search firm. When the call does come, you will want to retrieve the information instantly—particularly your list of achievements.

Expanding Your Existing Network

Having an active network is not a luxury for a CEO, it is a basic need. This is particularly true for CEOs searching for a greater leadership role. By this time in your career, you should have a well established network and mentoring base. These individuals will serve you well in the process of searching for a new position. Always leave room for more people in your network, however; you never know who can open doors for you.

Determining the Best Approaches to Make

Part of your strategic approach for your next CEO position should be figuring out how you can become known to your targeted not-for-profits. Once you have determined the organizations that you wish to approach, you need to compile detailed information on these groups. This includes a profile of the current CEO. With this information, you can create a cultivation plan that includes making yourself visible to them. Here are a few ideas:

- Your current role as a CEO of another organization may be the perfect excuse to interact with the CEO and key volunteer members of your targeted association.
- Become a volunteer with the organization.
- Offer to write an article for one of the targeted organization's publications.
- Offer to make a speech or do training at their conferences.
- Invite leaders of the targeted organization to join you in a government affairs issue that your current organization is involved in.
- Organize a joint activity between your current association and the targeted group.

The ideas are endless. The important thing is that making such a contact with your targeted organization makes you a known entity if the time ever comes that you have the opportunity to be a candidate for their CEO position.

Developing a Distinctive Record of Achievement

Working hard and being successful are the keys to opening new doors. Search committees and search firms are looking for success, but they are also looking for someone that stands out from the crowd. They are looking for something that sets one individual apart from the others. They want individuals who have quantifiable achievements in the traditionally measurable areas of success, but they also want other qualities, including:

- Leadership
- Dedication
- Understanding and appreciation of the mission of the organization

- Passion
- Ability to make great strides in the good times and to survive during the tough times
- Trustworthiness and loyalty
- Ability to work with their staff to build a team

A lot has been discussed about leadership. Boards of excellent not-for-profits want their CEOs to be leaders and they deserve to have a leadership-driven professional in the Corner Office. Leaders are not managers—they are individuals who welcome challenges and orchestrate change. Through their enthusiasm and strategic thinking, they are able to persuade others to follow them. CEOs looking to step up to bigger positions need to clearly demonstrate these leadership qualities. They need to show that they can do the following:

- Effectively tackle any challenge
- Think and act strategically
- Get results
- Bring diverse groups together
- Inspire others
- Be strategic teachers
- Find the needed resources

The most important area that seasoned CEOs need to demonstrate is how well they perform during challenging times. Often, this is not found in the list of achievements that are on resumes or support materials. Everyone is eager to report a 25-percent increase in revenue for the three years of an economic boom, but they are not so forthcoming about breaking even or achieving a 3-percent gain during a recession. However, anyone with experience knows that achieving a 3-percent gain during a downturn in the economy is much more difficult than making 25-percent gain during a boom.

I make sure that my organization's board understands this every time I present them with our year-end figures. Not many candidates bring this up during the search process and it is a mistake. If you have helped to balance your organization's budget during the hard times, make sure you provide the search committee documented proof. This quality alone will separate you from the crowd.

In an article in Association Management Magazine titled "When Talking's Tough: Ten Essential Communication Tips for Leading in Hard Times," author Deborah Bright provides a good list of talking points for demonstrating that you know how to meet the challenges of low periods:

- Think before speaking.
- Stay focused by combining the short and long-term picture.

- Handle emotions effectively.
- Be hopeful, instill hope, and do something.
- Recognize that quality gossip is good.
- Be transparent when answering questions.
- Point out successes in a timely manner.
- Follow through on commitments.
- Listen well.
- Avoid surprises with the board.

Cultivating People

Successful CEOs constantly cultivate people. However, when you decide to enter the search game, this process needs to be intensified. The more people you can leave with a good, lasting impression of you, the greater:

- Your chances of discovering new CEO opportunities
- Your chances that the individuals in your network will keep you in mind for future opportunities

Recently, our organization held a fundraising gathering at the home of an influential person who invited about 25 of his friends to hear our story. It was a great affair, and the host did a great job with representing our cause. After the event, the host mentioned another CEO from an organization that we work very closely with. He praised this CEO both personally and professionally and, by the way, this CEO deserved every bit of the praise that he received; he is one of the best in our field. By the end of the conversation, however, I was left wondering if we had made anywhere near the same impression! The point is that not-for-profit CEOs have the power to make a lasting impact. This power can be used to find out important information about a number of topics including your search.

Making a lasting impression with any of the people you meet will go a long way in helping you to achieve your long-term career goals. I made it a habit to use my network of influential people to further my career. Even now, in my current position, I have formed partnerships with other organizations and accomplished meaningful goals by networking with people that I have not worked with for over two decades. I kept up with many of these people over the years. Yet, with others, I was able to rekindle the relationship due to the impression I made several years ago. One of these relationships resulted in the successful launch of a new program at my organization.

Quality people count in our business. They are an essential tool for a successful career but, more importantly, they make a difference in how well you can serve your constituents. Finding quality people to work with makes the journey more successful and more enjoyable.

Making an External Name for Yourself

One of the best ways to get noticed is to make an external name for yourself. This is a real challenge at times, due to the workload of the average not-for-profit CEO. While it seems impossible, every CEO can do something to be recognized. Here are a few suggestions:

- Teach a seminar course.
- Become an expert is one or more areas.
- Do research.
- Write an article or a book.
- Become a consultant.
- Become a speaker.
- Become a celebrity in your field.
- Find unique ways to become known.

I used to teach seminars a lot in my younger days and I still try to teach at least one course every year to stay in the game. I find the experience exhilarating. If you enjoy educating others, it is a great way to get your name out there, particularly if the course you are conducting is at a national meeting. Usually, you will be listed on the program and the people in attendance who see you in this role will consider you an expert.

Speaking of being an expert, you are already an expert in a number of areas. Why not flaunt it a little? The world is full of experts and will welcome one more. Pick an area and find ways to share your knowledge.

Do research that grabs the attention of your field or the not-for-profit community in general. More research is needed in so many areas of our work. Don't be intimidated by the process or by those who tell you can't do it. Everyone can contribute. Pick an area that you are an expert in and find an area within that field that needs to be developed or refined. It will make a great contribution to your profession and you will get noticed.

A number of CEOs do consulting on the side to keep themselves sharp. The volunteer leadership of good organizations understands that CEOs stay longer and are more creative if they use their talents to help other organizations once in awhile. These experiences often result in wonderful ideas that can be implemented at the CEO's primary organization.

Becoming a speaker is a natural thing to do for most CEOs as they tend to find themselves speaking before groups several times a month anyway. You can turn your speaking skills into an opportunity by working on a few speeches that are more general in nature. Test them out at a few local meetings and then take it up a step or two.

Becoming a celebrity is not as far-fetched as it sounds. Several CEOs, due to the nature of their work, have become celebrities. They end up on talk shows discussing issues that may be related to their associations, and many associations even have their own talk shows. This visibility opportunity is a great way to gain favor for future positions.

Find unique ways to increase your name recognition. Your imagination can help you find ways to get out where the action is and where you can be noticed.

Earn a reputation that relates to the not-for-profit community in some fashion. This will separate can you from other CEOs when you are in the running for a new position.

These outside experiences also help you in your current position:

- They act as refresher course for the CEO.
- They generate new ideas that come back to the CEO's organization.
- They increase the visibility of the organization through the CEO's actions.
- They increase the volume and types of business that can be generated by the CEO's organization.

Creating a Winning Interview Strategy

When all of your preparation finally results in gaining the attention of your targeted organization, you want to make sure that you are well prepared to interview for your dream job. We have already discussed the importance of preparation and the strategy of taking charge of the meeting. You should enter the meeting with a sense of worth and accomplishment but, most importantly, be prepared to have an enjoyable experience no matter what happens.

Obviously, the astute CEO will spend a lot of time preparing for the meeting. Don't forget to have two or three prepared stories or examples that demonstrate to the search committee that you are well prepared to assume the position.

Knowing What Compensation Package You Desire

At this stage in your career, you have a good idea of what you need and want in terms of compensation. If you did your homework, you know roughly what the organization is offering. It is also a good idea to have a list of the benefits that you would like to include in the package. This list is not for the search committee but, rather, for you to refer to ensure that you don't forget an important benefit in the heat of the negotiation process.

If a search firm is involved, the firm may help you negotiate your contract. You may also want to involve legal counsel in the negotiation process or, at least, have them review the draft contract. If you are going to involve counsel, it is wise to have secured a person you can trust prior to beginning your search.

Making Sure that Your Career Goals Fit Well with Your Personal Way of Life

This last area is really the most important area to consider both before and during the search process. For example, you may have found the CEO position of your dreams, but if it requires moving across the country:

- Will the move cause problems with your loved ones?
- Will you like the new location?
- Will you leave behind friends or way of life that is important to you?

First and foremost, before you begin your search, you need to have a clear understanding of your family's expectations and desires. If your significant other is employed, will it be a problem if an opportunity opens up out of town? If your children are old enough to have formed lasting friendships or if they will graduate from high school in two years, is this a problem? How far away is the family comfortable moving? All of these types of questions need to be worked out prior to conducting your search so you can focus on the right position for everyone.

You need to look at what you want to do and where you want to do it. Would you like to be a CEO of a not-for-profit organization in California or on the east coast? You need to weigh the pluses and minuses. I worked in Washington, D.C., for 14 years and the commute to my town was two hours each way. I grew to hate the commute, and I would look forward to business travel or, sometimes, working at home.

When I began the search for my current position, one of my goals was to live near the office. I still have to travel to Washington several times a year, but now I do it by air. My commute to my current association is less than 10 minutes, and I am 20 minutes from the airport. I saved 3 hours and 40 minutes per day just by cutting out the commute, and I feel like a whole new person because I changed my way of life for the better. Make sure your new position does not change an important aspect of your life for the worse; it simply isn't worth it.

If you have ever relocated, you know that it involves leaving behind close friends, favorite activities, and a way of life that you are accustomed to. If your new position requires you to move, you must decide if you can give these things up or if you can work out a practical way to maintain them. These are difficult decisions, but they must be discussed prior to beginning your search.

Summary

Successful CEOs have a choice of what they want to do with their careers. Some CEOs want to stay in one association and build the group into a powerhouse; some choose to move on to conquer new challenges. The important thing is that successful CEOs have a choice.

Choice is an earned gift that consists of a lifetime of preparation and hard work. The CEOs who participated in the study understood what it took to attain their first CEO position and they understand the challenges of retaining this unique and wonderful role. Some CEOs may choose to go on to greater glory in another organization and, if they do and they are prepared, they have a greater chance of obtaining that new position.

Although some CEOs will be sought out by others for a new CEO role, others will make the decision to actively seek a new position. In either case, the candidate must be prepared. By their very nature, the truly successful CEOs are always prepared for any challenge that may come their way. Likewise, the successful CEO candidate will always be ready to provide the necessary documents and support for a search firm or a search committee.

CEOs need to be aware of their surroundings so that they can identify opportunities as well as warning signs. Not-for-profits differ greatly in how they regard their hired help. Even CEOs who have performed well may not survive due to other factors within an association. Certain changes such as board shifts can trigger situations that a CEO can have little control over. This is why it is a sound policy to have a prepared contingency plan in place.

The person who holds the Corner Office has one of the best opportunities for an exciting career while being afforded the opportunity to make a difference at the same time. The position has come a long way from the days of playing a secretary's role. The CEO in a well designed not-for-profit has been given the leadership role to conduct the day-to-day operations, to be a full partner within the board, and to be a strategic leader. If this describes your goals, the Corner Office is just where you should be.

CHAPTER 8

Summary of the National Study of Not-for-Profit CEOs

> *Applied evaluation research is judged by its usefulness in making human action and interventions more effective and by its practical human utility to decision makers, policymakers, and others who have a stake in efforts to improve the world.*
>
> Michael Quinn Patton

INTRODUCTION

The National Study of Not-For-Profit CEOs was conducted in the fall of 2003 to discover how current not-for-profit CEOs attained and retained their positions. Information was gathered through a survey that was sent to 425 not-for-profit CEOs. A copy of the survey is featured in Chapter 2 (see Exhibit 2.2). Of the 425 surveys, 200 were received by CEOs through the mail and 225 were received via e-mail or in person. Exactly 105 CEOs participated, or 24.7 percent of the targeted group.

The data provide a great array of empirical information. Much of the data substantiate what we perceived to be valid before the survey was conducted. The survey also reveals a number of standards and practices that have helped the participating CEOs to be successful over a long period of time.

CAREER PROFILES OF THE PARTICIPATING NOT-FOR-PROFIT CEOS

Exhibit 8.1 provides a visual representation of the nationwide contribution to this effort. The 105 participating CEOs represented 26 states and the District of Columbia.

EXHIBIT 8.1   GEOGRAPHICAL OVERVIEW OF WHERE
PARTICIPATING CEOS RESIDE

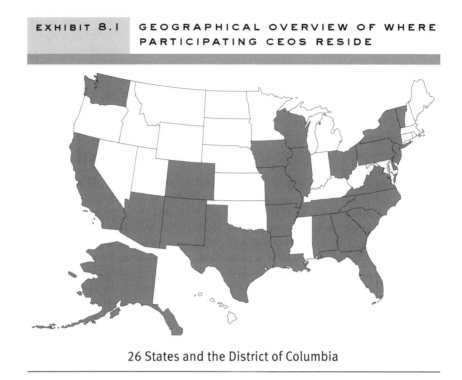

26 States and the District of Columbia

The participating CEOs represented a variety of missions and types of organizations including:

Trade associations	44.55 percent
Professional societies	42.57 percent
Social service organizations	11.88 percent
Other organizations	1.00 percent

The official titles of the participating CEOs were

President and/or CEO	38.61 percent
Executive director	56.44 percent
Executive vice president	4.95 percent

While this cannot be used to measure the overall field, it is interesting that the president and CEO title is growing in use while the executive vice president title is not being used as much. The proper title of a CEO seems like a small thing, but it really is not. The right title provides power and dignity.

Exhibit 8.2 reveals the desire by not-for-profit boards of directors to seek and find individuals who have attained higher degrees. Our sampling reveals that 65.99 percent of the participating CEOs have a master's or doctorate degree, or twice the number with undergraduate degrees. The implications of these findings are obvious; academic credentials do matter.

EXHIBIT 8.2 HIGHEST ACADEMIC DEGREE ATTAINED BY PARTICIPATING CEOS

Type	Percentage
Doctorate (Ph.D., JD, etc.)	15.85%
Master's (MA, MBA, MS)	50.14%
Bachelor's (BA, BS)	30.69%
Associate	0.99%
High school	0.99%
Unknown	1.34%
TOTAL	100.00%

The participating CEOs majored in a number of different disciplines. The study seems to indicate that the area of discipline for an academic major really does not make much of a difference in how or why these CEOs have been successful. As one CEO noted, his liberal arts degree served him as well as any business-related degree would have since it provided him with a rich, diverse background and taught him how to deal with people.

The five top degree choices of the participating CEOs were:

1. Various course majors in business administration
2. English and/or journalism
3. Health and science fields
4. Education
5. Law

When asked what certifications that they had achieved and maintained, 28.71 percent of the CEOs listed the Certified Association Executive (CAE) certification. This certification is obtained through the American Society of Association Executives and is bestowed on individuals who have maintained good standards in their leadership role with the not-for-profit community. In addition to this certification, 32.67 percent of the participating CEOs have obtained other certifications, usually focused on areas of personal or organizationally related specializations.

When asked about their career path, 34.65 percent of the participating CEOs indicated that they have spent their entire careers in the not-for-profit community. The majority of respondents spend at least some time working in the for-profit sector before entering the not-for-profit arena. Many spent considerable time there.

Exhibit 8.3 indicates the number of years that our participants spent in the not-for-profit and for-profit sectors. Note that 42.57 percent of our CEOs spent 5 to 10 years in the for-profit community and 62.37 percent spent from 5 to 40 years overall.

Although the survey did not measure the differences in success between CEOs with for-profit experience and those without for-profit experience, it would be interesting to determine if that would be a factor. The survey results were unable to determine the tenure of 5.91 percent of the CEOs.

A number of responses were measured to determine the diversity of the CEOs and their organizations in order to ensure that the survey was representative of a good cross section of the not-for-profit community. Exhibit 8.4 reveals that some respondents run organizations with huge budgets; however, the majority of respondents were spread across a good blend of budget sizes.

Exhibit 8.5 also provided evidence of a fair cross section of organizations. Of the respondents, 37.63 percent run organizations with a staff of five or less.

Exhibit 8.6 provides another clue about the size of the organizations that the participating CEOs run. It is almost a dead heat between organizations with local chapters and those without. Of the respondents who run organizations with local chapters, the number of individual chapters range from less than 10 to more than 7,000, with 12.87 percent of the associations having less than 10.

The number of IRS-designated entities and how they play a role in the participating CEOs' organizations is fascinating. Exhibit 8.7 provides three different ways to look at the data.

The first way is to examine the number of IRS designations. The responses indicated that 53.47 percent of the organizations had two or more IRS entities, with an average of 2.3 overall. Note that 501(c)3 and 501(c)6 organizations, 43.2 percent and 41.75 percent respectively, far outnumber the 501(c)4 and for-profit categories. The core or main organization's IRS classification was 34.65 percent for 501(c)3 organizations and 54.46 percent for 501(c)6 organizations. The number of for-profit subsidiaries in this study, 11.17 percent, provides evidence of the growing need for better ways to serve constituents and to find new revenue sources.

EXHIBIT 8.3	CAREER TENURE OF PARTICIPATING CEOS		
Number of Years	**Not-for-Profit**	**For-Profit**	**Government**
40 or more	0.99%		
35	1.98%	1.98%	
30	21.78%	8.91%	
25	17.82%	3.96%	
20	18.81%	1.98%	0.99%
15	12.87%	2.97%	
10	10.89%	12.87%	0.99%
5	13.86%	29.70%	
Unknown	1.00%		
TOTAL	100.00%	62.37%	1.98%

EXHIBIT 8.4   BUDGET SIZE COMPARISON

Size by Millions	Percentage
200+	0.99%
100	0.00%
50	1.98%
25	4.95%
15	2.97%
10	10.89%
5	13.86%
2.5	12.87%
1	21.78%
Below 1	29.71%
TOTAL	100.00%

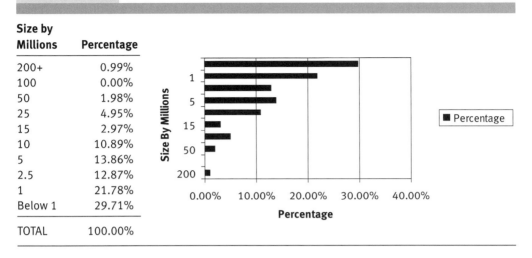

EXHIBIT 8.5   NUMBER OF STAFF

Number	Percentage
1,000 or more	1.98%
250	0.99%
125	1.98%
100	6.93%
50	5.94%
40	6.93%
35	5.94%
30	1.98%
25	6.93%
20	7.92%
15	3.96%
10	10.89%
5	20.79%
Below 5	16.84%
TOTAL	100.00%

EXHIBIT 8.6   LOCAL CHAPTERS

Do You Have Local Chapters?	Percentage
Yes	52.00%
No	49.00%
TOTAL	100.00%

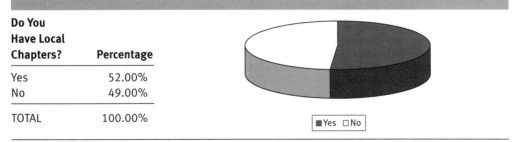

(continues)

EXHIBIT 8.6   LOCAL CHAPTERS *(continued)*

Those with Chapters by Numbers	Percentage
7,000	0.99%
2,500	1.98%
1,000	0.99%
200	2.97%
150	1.98%
100	3.96%
75	1.98%
50	5.98%
45	1.98%
40	1.98%
30	0.99%
25	1.98%
20	3.96%
15	1.98%
Below 10	12.87%
Unknown	2.43%
TOTAL	49.00%

EXHIBIT 8.7   IRS CLASSIFICATION CODES OF PARTICIPATING CEO ORGANIZATIONS

Number of IRS Designations	Percentage
1	46.53%
2	25.74%
3	20.79%
4 or more	6.94%
TOTAL	100.00%

IRS Designations by Category	Percentage
501(c)3	43.20%
501(c)4	1.94%
501(c)6	41.75%
For-Profit	11.17%
Other	1.94%
TOTAL	100.00%

EXHIBIT 8.7   IRS CLASSIFICATION CODES *(continued)*

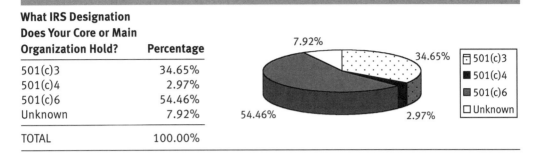

What IRS Designation Does Your Core or Main Organization Hold?	Percentage
501(c)3	34.65%
501(c)4	2.97%
501(c)6	54.46%
Unknown	7.92%
TOTAL	100.00%

EXHIBIT 8.8   NUMBER OF POSITIONS PRIOR TO FIRST POSITION

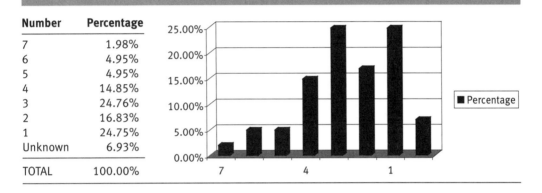

Number	Percentage
7	1.98%
6	4.95%
5	4.95%
4	14.85%
3	24.76%
2	16.83%
1	24.75%
Unknown	6.93%
TOTAL	100.00%

EXHIBIT 8.9   NUMBER OF CEO POSITIONS

Number	Percentage
6	1.98%
5	0.99%
4	1.98%
3	13.87%
2	28.71%
1	46.53%
Unknown	5.94%
TOTAL	100.00%

Our next way of qualifying the participating CEOs was to determine how seasoned the CEOs are. Exhibit 8.8 provides interesting data. Of those surveyed, 24.75 percent held only one position prior to becoming a CEO. Although most of the CEO positions within this category represented smaller organizations, this is still quite a revealing statistic. Even if you look at the group as a whole, most of the CEOs held four or less positions prior to becoming a CEO.

Exhibit 8.9 reveals the level of movement within the test group. Of the respondents, 46.53 percent are in their first CEO position while 47.53 percent are in their second to sixth CEO position. Once again the data substantiates that the survey hit a good cross section of the not-for-profit world, providing us with valuable information from both the new CEO's perspective and the seasoned CEO's perspective.

The survey also asked the participating CEOs if they have a contract. This question is a little off topic, but was included as it is part of an ongoing debate among most not-for-profit CEOs. For the results, see Exhibit 8.10. Of the respondents, 64.36 percent reported that they do have contracts. Since there is not a right or a wrong answer to this question, we asked each CEO to indicate what they thought were the advantages or disadvantages having of a contract.

The top three responses for having a contract were:

1. It protects both the employee and the association.

2. It creates a clear sense of responsibility.

3. It provides a clear sense of authority.

EXHIBIT 8.10   DO YOU HAVE A CONTRACT?

Answer	Percentage
Yes	64.36%
No	35.64%
TOTAL	100.00%

35.64%

64.36%

☐ Yes ■ No

What Do You Feel Are the Advantages and/or Disadvantages of a Contract?

The Most Frequent Yes Responses (1 being the most frequent)

1. Protects both the employee and the association

2. A clear sense of responsibility

3. A clear sense of authority

4. Clarifies the benefits package both during employment and if the termination occurs

5. Provides both a sense of security and fairness

6. Forces to hold ongoing evaluations

7. Provides a clearer set of goals an expectations

The Most Frequent No Responses (1 being the most frequent)

1. Brings up more negative than positive feelings

2. Generally not enforceable

3. Association volunteer leadership refuses to do it

4. Seems like those with contracts are let go more often

5. Freedom to leave anytime I want to

6. Several disadvantages (e.g., use as a weapon)

The top three responses for not having a contract were:

1. It brings up more negative feelings than positive feelings.
2. It is generally not enforceable.
3. The association's volunteer leadership refuses to do it.

Some organizations, particularly trade and professional societies, have been using contracts for some time as a way to attract and retain quality leaders as well as clarifying the role that the CEO plays. Social service organizations have generally lagged behind when it comes to the use of contacts. The use of contracts, in my experience, depends on the makeup of the organization including the overall cultural, volunteer leadership, and professional mix. This is an area that will continue to be debated for some time.

PARTICIPATING CEOs' ADVICE AND INSIGHT ON THE SURVEY QUESTIONS

The survey part of the questionnaire contained 15 questions. The method of response varied to provide a little more interest and to maximize individual responses. It proved to be quite successful in obtaining a number of individual responses which help to make the overall study much more interesting and powerful.

Individual responses are listed under "Comments." These responses are a composite of all of the responses; for example, if several CEOs made similar responses, the answer is simply listed as a general response that covered that particular category.

Several questions asked the CEOs to rank their answers. It was enlightening to see what the CEOs considered their first, second, or third priority. Exhibits 8.11 through 8.25 tally these responses by placing them under columns by rank. For example, for Question 1 (see Exhibit 8.11), the "1" column represents the highest-ranked response: 10.89 percent of the participating CEOs ranked "Formal education" as the number-one reason why they were able to attain their current CEO position.

All of the tabulations are based on the total number of respondents and the number who responded to a particular question. For example, if the response is 10.89 percent, it simply means that 10.89 percent of the participating CEOs favored that answer to the question.

Question 1: Please Rank the Chief Reasons Why You Were Able to Attain Your Current CEO Position.

This initial question provided some interesting findings. Exhibit 8.11 details the responses to Question 1. "Past experiences" was by far the number one choice at 69.3 percent, as compared to 11.88 percent for "Networking" and 10.89 percent for

EXHIBIT 8.11	QUESTION 1: PLEASE RANK THE CHIEF REASONS WHY YOU WERE ABLE TO ATTAIN YOUR CURRENT CEO POSITION.

Responses	1	2	3	4	5	6
Formal education	10.89%	23.76%	21.78%	10.89%	5.94%	0%
Certifications	1.98%	5.94%	8.91%	7.92%	10.89%	2.97%
Past experiences	69.3 %	13.86%	0.99%	0%	0%	0%
Networking	11.88%	17.82%	20.79%	3.96%	3.96%	0.99%
Ongoing training	1.98%	2.97%	9.9 %	19.8 %	0%	0%
Other	3.97%	7.92%	3.96%	1.98%	1.98%	1.98%
TOTAL	100%					

Comments

1. Respect among volunteer leaders
2. Ability to work with diverse stakeholders
3. Marketing background
4. Engagement in the field of specialization
5. Competency and integrity
6. Business ethics
7. Past experience in similar association
8. My government affairs experience
9. Inside knowledge of the association as a former member
10. My member relations experience
11. Knowledge of the association issues
12. My track record of getting results
13. My direct industry involvement
14. Clear knowledge of the goals of the association
15. Ability to work with volunteer boards
16. My experience as a past member volunteer
17. My referrals
18. Right place at the right time
19. Spent many years in the industry
20. Success in a similar position
21. My test scores
22. Being recognized as the right person as an inside candidate
23. Knowledge of the nonprofit process
24. Ability to build trust and unity
25. Through the roles that mentors played in my life

"Formal education." This is a significant finding in that it clearly demonstrates that those who wish to attain the CEO position need more than a good education or a good network; they need a wealth of experience to be considered for the position. The comments section revealed some good advice as well:

- The ability to work with volunteer boards
- The ability to build trust and unity
- The need for competency and integrity
- The importance of in-depth knowledge of the non-profit process
- A good marketing background

Question 2: What Are the Major Personal Skills That Have Helped You to Retain Your Current CEO Position?

The responses to this question followed a similar path as Question 1. By far, the number one response was "Producer—making goals" at 36.64 percent for the first choice and 60.4 percent for the top three choices. See Exhibit 8.12 for the details. This reflects what all CEOs face in today's environment: First and foremost, they must produce.

"Fiscal control" came in a distant second at 14.85 percent as the first choice. When you look at the top three responses combined, however, it totals 52.47 percent bringing it much closer to number one. "Member relations" was ranked third as the number one choice at 11.88 percent and at 36.63 percent one of the top three choices. Keeping

EXHIBIT 8.12	QUESTION 2: WHAT ARE THE MAJOR PERSONAL SKILLS THAT HAVE HELPED YOU TO RETAIN YOUR CURRENT CEO POSITION?								
Responses	1	2	3	4	5	6	7	8	9
Producer—making goals	36.64%	10.89%	12.87%	8.91%	0.99%	2.97%	0.99%	0.99%	0%
Fiscal control	14.85%	20.79%	16.83%	12.87%	9.9 %	2.97%	3.96%	0%	0%
Government relations	8.91%	9.9 %	9.9 %	4.95%	0.99%	7.92%	6.93%	13.86%	0%
Volunteer management	8.91%	7.92%	7.82%	10.89%	12.86%	7.92%	6.93%	3.96%	0.99%
Planning	4.95%	11.88%	11.88%	13.86%	18.81%	9.9 %	9.9 %	1.98%	0%
Networking	2.97%	1.98%	5.94%	5.94%	9.9 %	7.92%	2.97%	4.95%	1.98%
Member relations	11.88%	14.85%	9.9 %	6.93%	11.88%	8.91%	12.87%	3.96%	0.99%
Keeping on the cutting edge	4.95%	7.92%	7.92%	4.95%	9.9 %	10.89%	3.96%	4.95%	0.99%
Other	3.96%	1.98%	0.99%	1.98%	0.99%	0%	10.89%	0%	0%

Comments

1. People skills
2. Ability to speak to the public
3. Able to work with diverse individuals and groups
4. My staff motivation skills
5. Strategic insight
6. Issues and management skills
7. Knowledge of the industry
8. My team-building skills
9. Communications background
10. Time management
11. Low-key management style that keeps board stress to a minimum
12. Overall management skills
13. Versatility
14. Multitask oriented

members or contributors happy continues to be a major task of the not-for-profit CEO.

Although the top three choices are certainly key areas, it is interesting to see how low some other categories are. The two categories that are most surprising are "Networking" and "Planning." Both of these skills are vital to long-term success. Networking is important in continuing to expand the CEO's horizons as well as the organization that he or she represents. Planning is a crucial skill in making sure that the organization is on track both in day-to-day activities as well as the long-term vision.

The comments section provided a few additional skills that are important:

- The ability to speak to the public
- Issues and management skills
- Team-building skills
- Versatility
- Time management

Question 3: What Kind of Career Experiences Would You Recommend to Aspiring CEOs?

As the first two questions revealed, career experiences seem to be the key to the success of the participating CEOs. Exhibit 8.13 highlights the career experiences that the participating CEOs recommend. The number one recommended experience was "Finance." Of the respondents, 22.77 percent ranked this their number one choice and 67.23 percent listed it in their top three choices. The respondents obviously feel a CEO's success depends largely on how they handle financial matters.

"Volunteer management" came in second with 16.83 percent of the respondents, ranking it as their number one choice and 45.54 percent listing it in their top three choices. Volunteer management will become even more crucial due to the shrinking volunteer pool and greater budget restraints.

"Program-related" ranked third at 16.83 percent as the first choice and 38.61 percent in the top three choices. "Membership development" ranked fifth as the first choice at 10.89 percent, but it came in third place at 41.58 percent for being listed in the top three choices. "Government relations" scored 37.62 percent for being listed in the top three choices. Clearly, the responses to this question indicate that CEOs need to be well versed in several areas of their organization's operations.

One choice that ranked low was "Fundraising," earning 1.89 percent of the responses for first choice and 10.89 percent for the top three choices. Some CEOs may have lumped this function into the finance response and, for some CEOs, *fundraising* is not the term they use when referring to the procurement of funds. However, the key to not-for-profits has been and will remain funding. This question may reveal the need for more emphasis on training aspiring CEOs on the vital role that fundraising plays in not-for-profit.

| EXHIBIT 8.13 | QUESTION 3: WHAT KIND OF CAREER EXPERIENCE WOULD YOU RECOMMEND TO ASPIRING CEOS? |

Responses	1	2	3	4	5	6
Program related	16.83%	6.93%	14.85%	10.89%	16.83%	3.96%
Fundraising	1.98%	5.96%	2.97%	11.88%	12.87%	9.9 %
Finance	22.77%	30.6 %	13.86%	8.91%	1.98%	3.96%
Membership development	10.89%	8.91%	21.78%	14.85%	9.9 %	4.95%
Volunteer management	16.83%	18.81%	9.9 %	9.9 %	9.9 %	4.95%
Government relations	14.85%	7.92%	14.85%	5.94%	9.9 %	11.88%
Other	9.9 %	1.98%	1.98%	0.99%	0%	0.99%

Comments

1. Obtain a diverse and difference work experience.
2. You need a broad set of transferable skills.
3. People management and organizational development
4. Try to attain any position that requires some management skills.
5. Active participation in the profession represented by the organization is sometimes a plus.
6. Obtain a high level of association management skills.
7. Investigate the various ways to gain training (i.e., The Institute of Organizational Management).
8. Find ways to work with volunteer boards as both a professional and a volunteer; it will be of great value.
9. Gain skills and knowledge in working with people including labor relations.
10. Look within to strengthen your personal management skills.
11. Develop your communication skills.
12. Make it a point to become skilled in government affairs.
13. Know how to increase revenue streams.
14. Find opportunities early in a career to manage an entire area in all respects.
15. Become a strategic planner and visionary.
16. Become aware of the importance of an organizations mission and how not-for-profits run.
17. Increase your skills in managing your time and show others.
18. Always keep promises.
19. Never stop being educated.
20. Know the skills of goal setting.
21. Acquire business management skills.
22. Understand and refine skills to work successfully with groups including boards of directors.
23. Volunteer to be on volunteer boards to better understand the role.
24. Become as well rounded as possible. Do not specialize; know as much as you can about all aspects of an organization.
25. Keep in touch with industry and member needs.

The comments section provided additional responses worth considering:

- Try to attain any position that requires some management skills.
- Become a strategic planner and a visionary.
- Volunteer to be on not-for-profit boards so that you may better understand their role.
- Become as well rounded as possible. Do not specialize—know as much as you can about all aspects of an association.
- Look within to strengthen your personal management skills.

Question 4: Do You Network with Other Not-For-Profit CEOs?

The overwhelming majority of respondents felt that networking with other not-for-profit CEOs was important in retaining their positions. Exhibit 8.14 shows that 96.7 percent of the respondents answered yes to this question and also lists the top five reasons why the CEOs network.

The number one reason that CEOs network is moral support. This comes as no surprise to me. Over the years, I have found that talking with other CEOs often provides the counsel I needed to make important decisions, to move ahead on projects, to work with troublesome volunteers, or to deal with staff issues.

The second reason why CEOs network is to find solutions. This is the main reason why successful CEOs find ways to meet with each other. I have found that the best way to make the networking process work is to find ways to meet one-on-one with other CEOs. I have done this throughout my career and it has been very helpful. I have a number of CEOs that contact me for the same reason.

"Information sharing and learning," "Motivate innovation," and "Stay on the cutting edge" were listed third, fourth, and fifth, respectively. Successful CEOs understand that in order to stay on top in the not-for-profit arena you have to be agile and understand that the playing field is constantly changing. Not-for-profits have a lot more competition these days, not only from other not-for-profits but also from for-profits. Innovation can either be an opportunity or a disaster if you are not prepared for it.

In the past, for example, members joined a number of not-for-profits to gain information about a cause or a trade. Today, they do not have to join an organization to get information. They don't need to go to meetings or buy publications. All they have to do is to go on the Internet to find what they seek. Ironically, this information is often available for free on the Web site of the very organization that they used to have to join. Can associations still remain relevant? Yes, but not in the same way they did a generation ago. The bottom line is that CEOs who are networking are finding the answers.

EXHIBIT 8.14   QUESTION 4: DO YOU NETWORK WITH OTHER NOT-FOR-PROFIT CEOS?

Answer	Percentage
Yes	96.70%
No	3.30%
TOTAL	100.00%

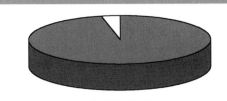

Yes ☐ No

Top Five Reasons

1. Moral support
2. Find solutions
3. Information sharing and learning
4. Motivate innovation
5. Stay on the cutting edge

Other Comments

1. Build knowledge on common grounds based on needs and concerns.
2. Build on a collaborative approach.
3. Validate ideas.
4. Borrow ideas.
5. Lobby.
6. Stay plugged in.
7. Tap others' expertise.
8. Build on best practices.
9. Remain as diverse as possible.
10. Find partners.
11. Keep up to date on news and events.
12. Gain a certain kind of support that you cannot get from your staff.
13. Networking often speeds up problem solving.
14. Reliable source for a second opinion.
15. Feel that it is part of my continuing education.
16. Mentoring
17. Talk with those who speak the same language.
18. Learn from both successes and failures.
19. Networking aids in career growth.
20. It is often a realty check.
21. Gain from hearing real-life experiences.

The comments section provided additional insights:

- *Build on best practices.* It really saves time and you don't have to repeat the same thing over and over again.

- *Networking is often a reality check.* Sometimes we get so wrapped up in what we are doing we forget that our ideas and plans need to fly in the real world. It is a good idea to bounce new thoughts or new directions off a fellow CEO.

- *Talk to those who speak the same language.* Even though you may have a quality staff and dedicated volunteers a CEO's role is different. It is always refreshing to sit down and discuss current challenges and opportunities with a fellow member of the club, another CEO.

Question 5: What Qualities, in Your Opinion, Do Not-For-Profit Boards Seek in Their CEOs?

Not-for-profit CEOs are sought, hired, and kept at the sole discretion of the board of directors. Before making it to the CEO level, you were hired and supervised by a fellow professional that judged you on a number of different levels from performance to attitude. When you seek the Corner Office, you are suddenly playing with a completely new set of standards and rules.

For starters, you will be reporting to a part-time group that may or may not have any idea what they need in their new CEO. This is part of the responsibility of a CEO candidate—to guide the board or search committee through the hiring process. This begins at the interview. For more on this subject, see Chapter 2.

Exhibit 8.15 provides a summary of the responses to the question, "What qualities do not-for-profit boards seek in their CEOs?" The participating CEOs provided two very astute answers to this question. The number one answer was "Integrity, trust," ranking 41.5 percent as the first response and 68.23 percent for the top three responses. The second response was "Leadership traits" scoring 37.6 percent as the first response and 56.41 percent for the top three responses.

All the other available responses dealt with functionary skills or acquired training. Although these skills are certainly necessary in performing the role of a CEO, the top two choices of the respondents go to the very core of what makes a great leader.

In recent years, volunteer boards have come to realize that a number of candidates have the background and many of the tangible skills that they desire. This is not enough, however; they are looking for more. The personal qualities of the candidate separate the chosen from the also-rans.

Of course, it is often very difficult to showcase these qualities. These are the kinds of qualities that are recognized over the long term, when they are being used constantly day after day among the board members of the organization. A well prepared

EXHIBIT 8.15 QUESTION 5: WHAT QUALITIES, IN YOUR OPINION, DO NOT-FOR-PROFIT BOARDS SEEK IN THEIR CEOS?

Responses	1	2	3	4	5	6	7	8	9
Integrity, trust	41.5 %	16.83%	9.9 %	5.94%	0%	0.99%	0%	0%	0%
Staff management skills	1.98%	8.91%	11.88%	20 %	15.84%	7.92%	5.94%	0.99%	0%
Volunteer management skills	1.98%	1.98%	2.97%	10.89%	16.83%	7.92%	10.89%	3.96%	5.94%
Ability to articulate and write a message	1.98%	5.94%	12.87%	17.82%	15.84%	16.83%	10.89%	3.96%	2.97%
Leadership traits	37.6 %	9.9 %	8.91%	6.93%	2.97%	1.98%	2.97%	0%	0%
Ability to raise funds	0.99%	0.99%	3.96%	0.99%	4.95%	2.97%	8.91%	6.93%	2.97%
Successful administrative and fiscal management	7.92%	11.88%	24.75%	10.89%	9.9 %	3.96%	2.97%	2.97%	0.99%
Education credentials	1.98%	0%	3.96%	4.95%	3.96%	11.88%	8.91%	16.83%	4.95%
Government affairs experience	3.96%	3.96%	4.95%	3.96%	4.95%	4.95%	2.97%	17.82%	14.85%
Other	0%	0%	2.97%	0%	0.99%	0%	0%	0.99%	0%

Comments:

1. People skills
2. Ability to network
3. Planning skills
4. Balancing budgets

candidate can provide hints of these skills in the interview process, and good references can help to show a history of such qualities.

The bottom line, however, is that successful long-term CEOs have these qualities. They are values that help attract and retain a quality staff, they are the values that drive volunteers to the highest levels of performance, and they are values that capture the interests of funding sources.

Integrity, trust, and leadership traits are the core qualities of a successful CEO. If you have them, you are well on your way to the Corner Office.

Question 6: How Did You Become Aware of Your Current CEO Position?

This question provides insight on how top positions are found. The responses to this question are outlined in Exhibit 8.16. Only 18.81 percent of the respondents indicated that they answered an ad. Of the remaining respondents, 61.38 percent marked another available response and 25.74 percent provided their own response, for a total of 87.12 percent. Clearly, searching for a CEO position by monitoring ads is not the preferred plan.

Of the respondents, 19.8 percent indicated that they were a member of the organization that they now lead, and 18.8 percent responded that they knew someone who was a member or in a leadership position of the organization that they now run. The highest response indicated that the respondent got their position through networking, with 22.77 percent of the respondents checking this answer.

Overall, this is a strong indication that successful CEOs do not rely on the opportunity coming to them; rather, they seek out the position through a number of means. They believe that in order to secure the top position, you need to be in the game where the action is. The respondents found the right opportunities and they had allies that could help them open the right doors and land the position.

The comments section provides additional insight. Note the number of times that the CEO was in the right place at the right time:

- Employed by the organization
- Advanced through the ranks
- Previous employer
- Asked by last CEO to succeed him
- Hired on a six-month contract to bring group back to stability, then asked to assume the CEO position

Although each one of these circumstances is different, they all have a common thread. Each of these CEOs positioned themselves to be part of the action and then found ways to show what they could do.

EXHIBIT 8.16	QUESTION 6: HOW DID YOU BECOME AWARE OF YOUR CURRENT CEO POSITION?

Responses	Percentage
Were you a member of the organization?	19.8 %
Did you know someone who was a member or in a leadership position of the organization?	18.81%
Did you gain awareness through networking?	22.77%
Did you answer an ad?	18.81%
Other	25.74%

Comments:

1. I was employed by the organization.
2. I was recruited by a search firm.
3. I advanced through the ranks.
4. A previous employer contacted me.
5. I received a referral by the retiring CEO.
6. I was contacted by board chair.
7. I was asked by the last CEO who succeeded him.
8. I was hired on a six-month contract to bring group back to stability, then asked to assume the CEO position.
9. I networked extensively with the previous CEO.
10. I was referred by associates.
11. I founded the association.
12. I replaced my father.
13. A job referral service contacted me (ASAE).
14. A search committee contacted me.

Question 7: What Were the Major Factors that Helped You to Successfully Win Your Current CEO Position?

Exhibit 8.17 clearly demonstrates that three responses were chosen relatively evenly by the participating CEOs:

	Responses	
	Top 3	#1
How I prepared and executed the interview meeting process	68.31%	30.69%
Ability to connect with the key volunteer leadership	65.34%	23.76%
Understanding what the organization sought in the new CEO	62.37%	26.73%

| EXHIBIT 8.17 | QUESTION 7: WHAT WERE THE MAJOR FACTORS THAT HELPED YOU TO SUCCESSFULLY WIN YOUR CEO POSITION? |

Responses	1	2	3	4	5	6
My negotiating skills	0.99%	0.99%	6.94%	10.89%	21.78%	2.97%
A well-prepared resume and cover letter	6.93%	6.93%	8.91%	21 %	11.88%	0%
How I prepared and executed the interview meeting process	30.69%	15.84%	21.78%	5.94%	1.98%	0%
Understanding what the organization sought in the new CEO	26.73%	23.76%	11.88%	5.94%	0.99%	0.99%
Ability to connect with the key volunteer leadership	23.76%	27.72%	13.86%	6.93%	1.98%	0%
Other	7.93%	0.99%	6.92%	1.98%	0.99%	0%

Comments:

1. Demonstrated performance
2. Understanding the organization and members needs
3. Background and professional experience
4. My key use of references
5. Past relations with the industry
6. Experience and knowledge of the association and goals
7. Track record of producing as a volunteer for the organization
8. Reputation after three years as the assistant
9. Perceived value for the association
10. My willingness to relocate
11. Knowledge of the association issues
12. My area of expertise as demonstrated by my dissertation
13. Right place at the right time
14. My history with the association
15. My tenure of service
16. Recognized through my consulting work with the association
17. The stability I brought to the organization
18. My industry experience
19. Lifetime experience in the association
20. My leadership skills

This question provides insight on where the respondents chose to put their emphasis to win the prize. Note that a well-prepared resume did not score well. One can assume that all the respondents had a well-thought-out resume but, if you are playing the game right, you are way beyond that.

Negotiating skills scored low, at least in relation to the top three responses. There is a jump in the response rate to 35.64 percent if the fourth through sixth responses are grouped together. These responses reflect that negotiating skills, while certainly important, are not as important as the first three.

While preparing well and executing the interview meeting process is vital, the ability to connect with the key volunteer leadership and understanding what the organization seeks in a new CEO actually wins the prize. This is what makes it possible for you to be considered "their type of person" and provides you with the insight to sell yourself by emphasizing and highlighting the right things.

The participating CEOs added several good points under the comments section:

- Know the perceived value that you bring to the association and make sure you communicate it.

- *Make good use of references.* This point is often overlooked as reinforcement to what you have presented to your prospective employer. If possible use references that are familiar to the leadership of the organization. They have high credentials themselves and are close enough to you that you can brief them before and after your interview. Make sure that they emphasize the qualities that you possess that can directly relate to what the particular association is seeking.

- *I sold the stability that I brought to the organization.* Volunteer boards are always looking for a CEO to stabilize the organization. When a CEO position needs to be filled, there may be a major problem that needs to be addressed or just the necessity to hire a sound person to run the show. In either case, the volunteer board of directors wants to make sure that the process they are going through produces a qualified candidate who will stabilize the organization. They do not want to go through the recruiting process every few years. If you are perceived as a candidate that can stabilize the association in question, it will help you separate yourself from the other candidates.

Question 8: What Kind of Preparation Did You Do Prior to the Interview?

The number one response to this question, "Obtained information about the organization via the Internet, and other sources," ranked 28.71 percent. "Prepared questions to ask and anticipated questions to answer" was close at 27.72 percent. Combined, these two responses ranked 56.43 percent. Exhibit 8.18 details the range of responses to this question.

By ranking the answer that was listed most often in the top two choices, however, the response "Prepared questions to ask and anticipated questions to answer" came in higher at 59.4 percent as compared to "Obtained information about the organization via the Internet, and other sources" at 40.59 percent. The overall numbers are slightly

EXHIBIT 8.18	QUESTION 8: WHAT KIND OF PREPARATION DID YOU DO PRIOR TO THE INTERVIEW?				

Responses	1	2	3	4	5
Obtained information about the organization via the Internet, and other sources	28.71%	11.88%	5.94%	3.96%	0.99%
Prepared questions to ask and anticipated questions to answer	27.72%	31.68%	7.92%	0.99%	1.98%
Brought examples of my work	5.94%	4.95%	12.87%	8.91%	0.99%
Rehearsed	6.93%	5.94%	12.87%	11.88%	0.99%
Other	17.82%	3.96%	0.99%	0%	0%

Comments:

1. Researched industry
2. Talked with members
3. Maximized ideas that would help the organization
4. Explained why I could help the organization
5. Had a strong working relationship with members
6. I had an active search process going on
7. My interview approach was tailored to each association that I interviewed with
8. Since I already worked at the organization, I explained how I could make a difference
9. Talked with the current CEO
10. Spent six years on the board
11. Researched and found the strategic plan for the association and provided a presentation on how I could attain the goals
12. Although I was young, the board gave me the opportunity to show what I could do
13. Focused my remarks on the strategic and vision that the organization want to achieve
14. Met with industry leaders to determine current and emerging issues
15. Performed well in previous position
16. Demonstrated a strong understanding of the challenges that the organization faced
17. Learned about all the key players from a former insider
18. Visited with first line consultants
19. Learned the lesson that preparation for the interview is very important
20. Never had an interview; I was recommended and asked to take the position
21. Prepared very little for the interview

higher due to a few respondents selecting number one and two rankings for more than one response. The other two answers, "Brought examples of my work" and "Rehearsed" received much lower responses.

The respondents' choices show that they focused on researching the organization and preparing to ask and answer the proper questions based on this research. This allows the CEOs to obtain information and to make a good impression.

The participating CEOs provided additional information on how they made it through the interview process in the comments section:

- *Maximized ideas that helped the organization.* It is always a good idea to have an innovative idea to share if the occasion presents itself. It shows that you have vision and that you can think on your feet.

- *Never develop just one approach.* Always tailor your approach to each organization based on the research that you have obtained.

- *I demonstrated a strong understanding of the challenges that the organization faced.* Having the right information so you can sell how you would help the organization to face current challenges begins the buy-in process and it helps you stand out from the crowd.

- *Learn about all of the key players from a former insider.* Although this might not be possible for some of your opportunities, it does point out the need to know as much as you can about the type of people you will be meeting with in the interview. It also gives you the chance to learn what the priorities may be in a particular organization. Your research will help you to at least have a general idea of who you will be meeting with and it will help you prepare a few approaches to use.

One participating CEO did not have an interview at all; what a lucky person! A few of the respondents prepared very little for the interview. These individuals might have been well known by the organization's leadership or well aware of the challenges that the organization faces. These are very rare circumstances, however. Most CEO candidates will need to prepare for the interview if they want to make the cut.

Question 9: What Were the Three Major Reasons You Were Selected for Your Current Position?

This was a fill-in-the-blank question and, therefore, the responses are not officially ranked. Exhibit 8.19 highlights the answers. Similar responses are grouped together under one category.

The most common response to the question was "Background and proven experience." This is consistent with the answers from previous questions. Again, volunteer boards want someone who knows what to do and isn't afraid of doing it.

The second response was "Leadership skills." The value of true leadership cannot be overstated and boards know that they need a CEO with certain qualities that encourage the staff and members to want to follow them.

"Knowledge of the organization" came in third place. It was enlightening how many CEOs were involved with their organizations professionally or as a member before taking the CEO position. Clearly, many associations are picking their CEOs

EXHIBIT 8.19   QUESTION 9: WHAT WERE THE THREE MAJOR REASONS YOU WERE SELECTED FOR YOUR CURRENT POSITION?

Top Five Reasons

1. Background and proven experience
2. Leadership skills
3. Knowledge of the organization
4. Management ability
5. Fiscal know-how

Comments:

1. Conveyed a compelling vision
2. Integrity and trust
3. Familiarity with the academic discipline represented by the organization
4. My certifications
5. Marketing experience
6. My loyalty to the organization
7. Knowledge of the industry
8. Reputation
9. Known quantity
10. People skills
11. Government relations background
12. Personality
13. An innovator
14. Support from the industry
15. Comfort level
16. Credentials
17. Ability to articulate clearly and persuasively
18. Advance degree
19. Perception that I would stay a long time
20. Sold ability to perform
21. Understood needs and explained how to meet them
22. Had industry respect
23. Crisis management skills
24. Held a key industry position
25. Held a key leadership position
26. My ability to think quick on my feet
27. The perceived cost value was high
28. Ability to raise funds
29. Insight as a former member
30. Understanding needs and having solutions
31. My confidence
32. I was a great fit
33. My dissertation and how it related to the mission
34. Ability to motivate staff
35. My visionary skills
36. My passion and enthusiasm
37. Ability to work with boards
38. Reputation with constituents
39. My contacts
40. Saw in me the ability to take the organization to a new level
41. The prep I gave to the search firm
42. My institutional memory of the organization
43. Advocacy experience
44. They saw me as a hungry candidate
45. My research in the field
46. Maturity
47. Willingness to relocate
48. My degree
49. My shared value system

from within. If you are not currently involved with the targeted association, however, you can still gain knowledge of the group through research and talking with the right people.

"Management ability" came in fourth place. It is important to note that it came in below leadership. This is a good thing. Of course, CEOs have to know how to manage an organization, but this skill can be easily measured by past experiences and positions. Leadership is a different quality. It is not as easily measured, but it is more desirable because a leader can move mountains and make meaningful change.

"Fiscal know-how" was fifth. This is a basic skill that every CEO must have to keep the organization sound.

Take the time to read the "Comments" section, as it contains the written responses of the participating CEOs. The following responses are the most compelling:

- *Integrity and trust.* This is a must for any successful CEO.
- *Reputation.* This is important both on and off the job.
- *People skills.* The job is too big to do it alone; you need to attract others.
- *The ability to articulate clearly and persuasively.* These are the basic tools of the trade.
- *Understanding needs and having solutions.* The power of listening to what is needed and finding ways to fulfill that need is vital.
- *The ability to work with boards.* Work with them like you are almost their equal.
- *Maturity.* Everything you do needs to look and feel like it is well thought out.

Question 10: What Did You Do During the First Six Months as the New CEO to Cement Your Relationship?

Exhibit 8.20 clearly shows that two responses outranked any of the others. "Met key leadership" ranked the highest at 30.69 percent. This answer received the highest rating at 51.48 percent when comparing the top three responses. "Did an overall evaluation of the organization" was a close second at 26.73 percent and was mentioned in 47.52 percent of the top three responses.

The participating CEOs clearly favored meeting with the key leadership first. This is a wise thing as it will allow you to determine who the players are and how they feel about the issues.

Doing an evaluation of the organization at the beginning of your tenure makes a great deal of sense. Every new CEO should do an evaluation, regardless of how he or she attained the position or how successful the organization is. It is the only way to document and measure status of the organization at the time you took over. The evaluation should cover at least three areas:

1. The overall operational status of the organization
2. The immediate needs of the organization
3. The long-term needs of the organization

EXHIBIT 8.20 QUESTION 10: WHAT DID YOU DO DURING THE FIRST SIX MONTHS AS A NEW CEO TO CEMENT YOUR RELATIONSHIP?

Responses	1	2	3	4	5	6	7	8	9
Met key leadership	30.69%	12.87%	7.92%	5.99%	10.89%	0.99%	0%	0%	0%
Created a personal plan of action	6.93%	9.9 %	4.95%	11.88%	7.92%	4.95%	1.98%	2.97%	1.98%
Evaluated staff	6.93%	9.9 %	12.87%	11.88%	4.95%	8.91%	1.98%	2.97%	0.99%
Made significant changes and/or refinements	5.94%	1.98%	4.95%	0.99%	1.98%	1.98%	8.91%	1.98%	4.95%
Prepared status report for member leaders	0%	5.94%	8.91%	8.91%	4.95%	6.93%	7.92%	7.92%	0.99%
Made sure program functions were in order	6.93%	10.89%	14.85%	13.86%	9.9 %	9.9 %	3.96%	7.92%	4.95%
Did overall evaluation of the organization	26.73%	10.89%	9.9 %	5.94%	5.94%	1.98%	2.97%	0%	0%
Insured that proper fiscal controls were in place	5.94%	16.83%	13.86%	11.88%	12.87%	3.96%	0%	1.98%	0%
Evaluated volunteer leadership	0%	1.98%	5.94%	2.97%	2.97%	4.95%	5.94%	2.97%	9.9 %
Other	7.92%	0.99%	3.96%	0.99%	0.99%	1.98%	0.99%	0%	0%

Comments:

1. Talked with hundreds of constituents
2. Began building trust with the board and the staff
3. Conducted a legal audit
4. Helped staff divine the strategic plan
5. Successfully handled an IRS audit
6. Did a number of meetings to directly meet members
7. Included volunteers in our strategic planning process
8. Listened, listened, listened
9. Memorized names and faces
10. Produced immediate results on several issues
11. Worked on lobbying issues that are key to the association
12. Instituted strategic planning
13. Ensured the staff that they would be an important part of the team
14. Met key leadership at their locations
15. Upgraded our communications effort
16. Communicated with former staff, officers and current board members to get a handle on the job
17. Created visibility for myself and the organization
18. Found ways to show that I was in charge

A number of other functions are important to evaluate including the staff and the volunteer leadership. You should also create personal plan of action during this evaluation process.

The comments section provided additional advice from the respondents including:

- *Begin by building trust with the board and the staff.* This is a very good move.

- *Conduct a legal audit.* Always make sure that everything is in order. You are in charge now and you are also to blame. Make sure you let your volunteer leadership know what you find and have a plan for refining whatever needs attention.

- *Create visibility for yourself and the organization.* Make sure that the members and the field know who is in charge and are aware that the association is on the move.

- *Listen, listen, listen.* This is great advice. Listen much more than you talk during the first six months. You are looking for problems and opportunities.

Question 11: What Measures Have You Taken to Continue to Strengthen Your Position at Your Current Organization?

The participating CEOs sent a clear message that maintaining a high level of interaction with key leadership was the most important measure that a CEO can take to strengthen their position. This response was first at 35.64 percent, and it was mentioned in the top three responses 63.36 percent of the time.

Coming in at a distant second place was keeping the organization fiscally sound, at 11.88 percent for the number one choice. This answer was listed in 45.54 percent of the top three responses. Third place was increasing staff effectiveness, ranked at 8.91 percent for the first choice and 21.78 percent for the top three choices. Exhibit 8.21 provides a detailed breakdown of the responses to this question.

The important lesson is that CEOs need to be highly involved with the key leadership of the organization that they are leading. This strengthens the CEO's position more than any other factor. Remember, a job done well doesn't mean a thing unless the key volunteer leaders are aware of it and perceive it that way.

Keeping the organization fiscally sound is also important. This is one of the main responsibilities of a CEO. It is essential to be keenly aware of the day-to-day aspects of making sound fiscal decisions from developing budgets based on need and reality to making sure that the organization stays within proper guidelines. Increasing staff effectiveness can also strengthen a CEO's position. Without the right staff performing the needed functions, the mission of the association will not be achieved.

Although all of the other survey responses have value, the participating CEOs understood the need to focus on strengthening their positions.

EXHIBIT 8.21 QUESTION 11: WHAT MEASURES HAVE YOU TAKEN TO CONTINUE TO STRENGTHEN YOUR POSITION AT YOUR CURRENT ORGANIZATION?

Responses	1	2	3	4	5	6	7	8	9	10	11	12
Maintain a high level of interaction with key leadership	35.64%	14.85%	12.87%	8.91%	1.98%	4.95%	2.97%	0%	0%	0%	0%	0%
Keep myself as visible as possible with members	3.96%	12.87%	5.94%	4.95%	13.86%	2.97%	4.95%	3.96%	2.97%	2.97%	0%	0%
Keep my organization fiscally sound	11.88	15.84%	17.82%	15.84%	7.92%	7.92%	0%	0%	0%	0.99%	0%	0%
Raise more income	3.96%	3.96%	0%	4.95%	6.93%	4.95%	3.96%	7.92%	10.89%	3.96%	1.98%	0.99%
Keep on the cutting edge through training	2.97%	6.93%	4.95%	5.94%	0.99%	2.97%	6.93%	2.97%	4.95%	4.95%	6.93%	0.99%
Make sure that a clearly defined strategic plan is in place	9.9%	7.92%	11.88%	9.9%	6.93%	1.98%	1.98%	6.93%	0.99%	1.98%	1.98%	0.99%
Insist upon an annual review based on mutually agreed upon goals	0.99%	1.98%	2.97%	2.97%	7.92%	1.98%	1.98%	2.97%	0.99%	3.96%	7.92%	7.92%
Find opportunities to speak and write	0.99%	0.99%	0.99%	0%	4.95%	8.91%	5.94%	2.97%	8.91%	3.96%	4.95%	1.98%
Develop a relationship with the media or trade press	1.98%	0.99%	0%	2.97%	3.96%	4.95%	6.93%	6.93%	2.97%	3.96%	3.96%	7.92%
Make sure that I am linked to the highest-priority issues	4.95%	11.88%	7.92%	9.9%	4.95%	10.89%	7.92%	0.99%	0.99%	0%	0.99%	0%
Maintain a key role in the government affairs function	3.96%	5.94%	6.95%	4.95%	6.93%	3.96%	5.94%	2.97%	0.99%	4.95%	0.99%	3.96%
Increase staff effectiveness	8.91%	2.97%	9.9%	7.92%	8.91%	5.94%	9.9%	5.94%	6.93%	2.97%	0.99%	0%
Other	3.97%	2.97%	3.96%	0%	0%	0%	0%	0%	0%	0%	0%	0%

Comments:

1. Surround myself with superior staff and expose them to the board
2. Found ways to increase the member base
3. Improved services to members
4. Developed an exciting business plan and made it work
5. Executed key objective
6. Keep our technology on the cutting edge
7. Maintain the highest visibility for myself and my organization
8. Keep my association as the prime source of knowledge and information concerning our issue
9. Push new and exciting programs
10. Make sure that the association is organizationally sound
11. Maintain a realistic and sound business plan
12. Reconstructed the organization's governance to better fulfill the core mission
13. Find ways to regularly communicate with our members
14. Recognize both volunteers and staff for their work

The comments section provided additional words of wisdom:

- *Surround yourself with superior staff and expose them to the board.* You cannot do it all, and you need to find quality people to fill these voids. Letting your board know that you have secured such people only strengthens your position.

- *Make sure your association is the prime source of knowledge and information concerning your issue.* Becoming the lead group for your particular issue or area helps your association take on a leadership position, as perceived by current or potential members. It puts the CEO in a great position as well.

- *Push new and exciting programs.* No one likes the same old thing. Creating new programs or repackaging mature programs or issues helps to stimulate new interest and enthusiasm.

- *Recognize volunteers and staff for their work.* Everyone wants to be thanked and recognized for what they do. It is not only the right thing to do; it is also a great way to strengthen your position.

Question 12: How Have You or How Would You Prepare to Attain Another CEO Position?

The number one answer to this question was "Maintain a network that would alert me to possible positions." Exhibit 8.22 reveals that 60.39 percent of the respondents chose this as their number one choice. "Increase my visibility with the volunteer leadership of the targeted organizations" was a distant second at 11.88 percent.

Clearly, the participating CEOs believe that networking is the best to attain another CEO position. Note that "check want ads'"was near the bottom of the list. The respondents recognized that the higher CEO positions can realistically be found only by being in the game and having the right people to alert them to new opportunities.

The comments section provided several more suggestions:

- *I let several search firms know my interest.* This is not a bad idea.

- *I did extensive research on the targeted organizations.* This is a great way to focus on the right course.

- *I identified organizations that needed my skills.* This is a good move; this way you are selling your strengths.

Question 13: In Your Opinion, What Were the Three Major Changes in the Not-for-Profit CEO's Role in the Last Decade?

This question produced a number of good responses. The listing below is a composite of the replies. Exhibit 8.23 lists the top three responses. The responses focused

EXHIBIT 8.22   QUESTION 12: HOW HAVE YOU OR WOULD YOU PREPARE TO ATTAIN ANOTHER CEO POSITION?

Response	1	2	3	4	5	6	7
Check want ads	3.96%	12.87%	15.84%	3.96%	0.99%	3.96%	0%
Increase my visibility with the volunteer leadership of the targeted organization(s)	11.88%	26.73%	9.9 %	12.87%	0%	0%	0%
Maintain a network that would alert me to possible positions	60.39%	15.84%	3.96%	0.99%	0%	0%	0%
Keep on the cutting edge through training	5.94%	19.88%	19.8 %	7.92%	1.98%	0%	0%
Become a volunteer at the prospective organization	0%	4.95%	5.94%	4.95%	10.89%	0.99%	0%
Donate to the prospective organization	0%	0%	0%	1.98%	5.94%	9.9 %	0%
Other	11.88%	0%	0%	0%	0%	0%	0%

Comments:

1. I let several search firms know my interest.
2. I responded if head hunters contacted me.
3. I improved performance at my current position.
4. I did extensive research on the targeted organizations.
5. Seek to identify organizations that need my skills.
6. Make sure that you have a good track record.
7. Put your future in the hands of a good search firm.
8. Attract opportunity by performance.

on technology, stability, and finding new ways to raise revenue. The recent call for greater accountability was also in the minds of the respondents, many of whom listed trust and integrity issues.

The organization's leadership seeks a CEO who understands the need to keep the association on the cutting edge but they also realize they need new sources of funding to take the place of mature income sources. They demand leaders who are fully accountable.

Successful CEOs never wait for others to tell them what to do; they are always 10 steps ahead. Technology, for example, is just another word for change; something that successful CEOs embrace. Finding new ways to raise revenue should be an ongoing search. No matter how you raise your funds, it will become dated. The ways we procure funds will have changed just a decade from now. Organizations that do not realize this won't be around in a decade to observe this trend.

The comments section provided a number of additional suggestions:

- *Increase emphasis on the entrepreneurial approach.* Innovation, imagination, and the ability to think outside the box are the hallmark of a successful CEO.

- *Increase the value of the core knowledge base.* The knowledge base for an association, in many cases, is the most valuable asset it has. Use it wisely and you will be quite successful.

- *Increase the complexity of issues.* Yes, this can be a good thing! It makes your organization that much more valuable.

- *Create a vision.* Vision is the ultimate selling tool. Every organization needs to know where it is going. The destination must sound enticing and the end result has to be exciting. No one wants to work for a boring organization that seems to be going nowhere.

- *Create an atmosphere of mutual respect between the volunteers and staff.* Successful organizations work as a team. In organizations where volunteers treat staff as equals, the staff strives to make each volunteer experience a memorable one.

- *Maintain value-added services.* Not-for-profits compete with other not-for-profits, for-profits, and even government programs. To attract and maintain members, associations need to provide timely programs and activities that are simply better and more exciting than anyone else's.

- *Be relevant.* This is something that that every CEO needs to keep in mind. Not-for profit organizations remain relevant by keeping the customer in mind. The question must always be asked—what do our members want and need?

- *Be a leader, not a steward.* CEOs are leaders; they are not in the maintenance business.

EXHIBIT 8.23   QUESTION 13: IN YOUR OPINION, WHAT ARE THE THREE MAJOR CHANGES IN THE NOT-FOR-PROFIT CEO'S ROLE IN THE LAST DECADE?

Top Three Reasons

1. The ability to acquire and use technology to the fullest
2. The increased need to find new ways to raise revenue
3. The call for greater accountability

Comments

1. Increased emphasis on the entrepreneurial approach
2. Need to increase member relations
3. Doing good is no longer enough
4. Increased demand for strategic planning
5. How to do more with less
6. Less volunteers
7. More justifying both salaries and programs
8. New communications challenges
9. Finding new ways to raise funds
10. Increased values of our core knowledge base
11. Nothing remains the same
12. Increased need for people skills
13. Shorter tenure of both volunteers and staff
14. More politics involved in the CEO position
15. Increased membership expectations
16. Increased complexities to everything
17. CEO has more power and responsibilities
18. The need to examine all the possibilities
19. Decrease in available funds
20. The changing demographic
21. The need to create alliances
22. Justifying the organizations mission
23. Increased demand for integrity and trust
24. Increased complexity of issues
25. Increased role of government affairs
26. Broader job description—more to do
27. Increased regulatory and compliance issues
28. The increased role that the economy is playing
29. Grant competition
30. New generations are tending to be less involved
31. New governance models
32. Growing international involvement
33. Change directs more quickly
34. The need for more vision
35. Difficult to attain and retain quality staff due to competition from for-profit arenas
36. The management of volunteers who have less time to give
37. The management of staff is more difficult
38. Satisfying the need of more diverse members
39. Maintaining a revenue stream
40. Mutual respect of volunteer staff
41. Constantly proving value
42. Maintaining members commitment
43. General organizational apathy
44. Increased need for strong business skills
45. Change in the way we do lobbying
46. Convincing boards to embrace change
47. Lack of experienced volunteer leaders
48. Less dedicated younger staff
49. More direction needed to staff
50. Relevancy
51. Maintaining value-added service
52. Dealing with a vastly changing member industry
53. Increased need for media interaction
54. More emphases on evaluation
55. Being a leader rather than a manager
56. Running not-for-profits like a business
57. Increased diversity in the professional ranks, including female CEOs
58. Need for both staff and members to be informed more about both organization issues and outside issues that may effect them or the association
59. Leadership versus stewardship
60. Fundraising and grant work

Question 14: What Do You Feel Are the Three Major Challenges that Not-For-Profit CEOs Face in the Next Decade?

It is interesting to observe the similarities and differences between this question and the previous one dealing with the changes that CEOs faced in the last decade. Exhibit 8.24 provides the top three responses of the participating CEOs.

The number one response to this question was "Technology and its use to save and serve" and the second-place answer was "Revenue: how and where." These answers were very similar to the first- and second-place responses for the last question.

The third most popular response, "Perceived value to current and future members or donors," marked a departure from the similarities in the responses to these two questions. This response puts a high value on relevance, a challenge that has been mentioned several times already. Every CEO must continually measure the relevance of their organization based on customer needs and demographics. At least two questions must be asked:

1. Is the organization's mission still timely?
2. Can the organization attract enough interest through memberships or donations to fulfill the mission?

If you cannot answer yes to either one of these questions, then the organization's leadership must determine if it should pursue any of these options:

- Can the organization adapt itself to meet these challenges on its own?
- Is it appropriate to merge with another organization?
- Should the organization go out of business?

Chapter 1 highlights a number of organizations that were timely in their day but are no longer around because they simply aren't needed anymore. Many of these organizations at one time provided needed services, yet over time they were perceived as unnecessary and they simply faded away. This is not a negative process; in fact, it is a rather healthy process. Current not-for-profit leaders simply need to ask themselves where their association fits into the equation.

The comments section provides a number of insightful predictions:

- *The competition for money and members.* Those who understand this and find ways to compete will be winners.
- *Attracting younger members.* This is a must. Those who find ways to cater to younger audiences will still be in business a generation from now.
- *Dealing better with economic fluctuations.* The real need is to diversify the way organizations obtain funds by encouraging creative thinking.
- *Embracing change and using it to your advantage.* Change can be your best friend. A CEO has to orchestrate real change

EXHIBIT 8.24   QUESTION 14: WHAT DO YOU FEEL ARE THE THREE MAJOR CHALLENGES THAT NOT-FOR-PROFIT CEOS FACE IN THE NEXT DECADE?

Top Three Reasons

1. Technology and its use to save and serve
2. Revenue: how and where
3. Perceived value to current and future members or donors

Comments

1. Competition for money and members
2. Mergers and consolidations of members
3. Attracting younger members
4. Collaboration versus competition
5. More information explosions
6. Fewer volunteers
7. Increased tendency for individuals to make membership choices based on research
8. Instant communication and how it relates to every day operations
9. Increased perceived need for self development
10. More focus on developing organization leaders
11. Increased accountability
12. Greater use of government affairs within all not-for-profits
13. Greater demand for member value
14. Increase competition from other not-for-profit entities
15. Need to define the balance between work and life for staff and volunteers
16. Finding unique avenues to offer current and to attract new members
17. Challenging volunteers to step up
18. Keeping quality staff
19. Should the organization remain independent or merge to better serve
20. Financial accountability
21. Better ways to communicate with members
22. Find ways to put into place competitive compensation to attract and maintain quality staff
23. Keeping organizations transparent
24. Globalization of member businesses
25. Doing more with less
26. Building meaningful networks to increase the effectiveness of the organization
27. Increasing trust and integrity
28. Dealing better with economic fluctuations
29. Embrace change and use it to your advantage
30. Finding more non-dues income
31. Refining the governance model to encourage the proper division of duties between volunteers and employees
32. Look more to specialization rather than generalization
33. Find ways to deal with increase competition
34. Become program driven rather than administratively driven
35. Join with others to stop the greater control of government in all we do
36. Be willing to take more risks
37. Find out how to successfully require more work from staff while increasing the quality and loyalty of them
38. Increase the focus on more revenue generation from all we do
39. Need to develop more mentors for both members and staff
40. Becoming more versed on employment law and HR requirements
41. Increase the emphasis on value
42. Need to deal with a new generation of volunteers who may not wish to give back to the same degree as past generations

43. Encourage both members and staff to continue to be educated
44. Find ways to deal with the increase of legislative issues
45. Educate members that due to decreases in volunteer support staff may need to be added
46. Replacing corporate and government funds
47. Learn that it is not being a not-for-profit, but being an entity that serves the community
48. Counteract the "let others do it" mindset by directly educating members
49. Streamline your governance to be lean and noble
50. Greater emphasis on selling the sizzle and member benefits, not the cost
51. Avoid being seen as old history
52. Maintain your core mission but change to perform it
53. Diversity your revenue sources
54. Position your association to do great things
55. Repackage yourself to be more appealing
56. Focus on impact and results
57. Attract the most effective board members who want to make a difference
58. Build a sense of community that includes everyone (i.e., members, leaders, staff and others outside)

- *Becoming program driven rather than administratively driven.* Sell the sizzle and watch the crowd form.
- *Being willing to take more risks.* Always remember that doing nothing is the biggest risk of all.
- *The need to develop more mentors for both staff and volunteers.* Not-for-profit organizations need to get back to using the mentor approach. Find them for yourself and become one for someone else.
- *Increasing the emphasis on value.* This is the best way to attract and retain members or donors.
- *Building a sense of community.* The mindset that we are all in this together can really strengthen a group.

Question 15: We Would Welcome Any Additional Information or Advice That You Would Like to Provide That Would Help to Prepare an Individual to Attain and Retain a CEO Position in a Not-For-Profit Organization.

The participating CEOs provided a wealth of information and advice for those who wish to attain and retain the CEO position. Exhibit 8.25 provides a composite of the responses. The following comments were particularly relevant:

- *Maintain a personal focus.* Not much is said about what a CEO personally needs to do to be successful. The successful CEOs I have met all have a personal focus.

EXHIBIT 8.25   QUESTION 15: WE WOULD WELCOME ANY ADDITIONAL INFORMATION OR ADVICE THAT YOU WOULD LIKE TO PROVIDE THAT WOULD HELP TO PREPARE AN INDIVIDUAL TO ATTAIN AND RETAIN A CEO POSITION IN A NOT-FOR-PROFIT ORGANIZATION.

Responses

1. Know what your organization values.
2. Maintain a personal focus.
3. Become technology savvy.
4. Achieve the highest ethical standards.
5. Increase your business skills.
6. Keep a pulse on member needs—what keeps them up at night.
7. Benchmark best practices in association management.
8. Find ways to keep on learning throughout your career.
9. Prepare to start in a lower position and learn all the key areas.
10. Learn how to seize opportunities.
11. Make sure that all staff is compensated well.
12. Be honest, have integrity, be straightforward, and be yourself, and you will gain the trust of others.
13. The more education the better; you must stay one generation above your members and at least two weeks ahead of them.
14. Anticipate needs, meet expectations, and lead.
15. Be familiar with Roberts's rules.
16. Maintain and strengthen relationships with each board member and volunteers.
17. Never believe that you know enough; always stay open to learning.
18. Talk with current and former leadership to discuss issues that are important to them.
19. You have to have a certain level of God-given initiative, interpersonal skills, and drive. Some things can not be taught, learned, or copied.
20. Get involved in outside leadership opportunities like allied groups of ASAE.
21. CEOs today must have exceptional communications skills.
22. Be flexible and learn to take calculated risks.
23. Always have mentors and be one for others.
24. Learn how to manage the association rather than learning the business of the association members.
25. Greet, meet, and speak as much as possible.
26. Learn to build coalitions; today's issues are too big to go it alone.
27. Choose quality over quantity and sincerity over all matters.
28. Thank and reward volunteer leaders; they are a scarce breed.
29. Earn and recertify as a Certified Association Executive (CAE).
30. Maintain a strong network.
31. Interact with your peers.
32. Don't get too comfortable.
33. Don't get too far out ahead of your board members.
34. Don't become a brown-noser to your board. They have hired you to do a job, don't be afraid to do it.
35. Learn to be a leader and don't focus on if you are running a not-for-profit or for-profit.
36. Believe in working your way up inside the organization.
37. Be prepared to put the time in as a staffer to learn and to prove yourself.
38. You must understand the needs of your members.
39. Keep those who support you closer; keep your adversaries closer.
40. Be loyal to your organization.

41. Always act with integrity.
42. Recognize that not-for-profit CEO jobs are becoming fewer.
43. The larger the association, the more result oriented it will be.
44. Understand the search firm process, since most of the larger opportunities will involve them.
45. Do not get drawn into the politics of your association.
46. Be fair to all staff—no favorites.
47. Reward staff for achievement.
48. Don't forget to be good to yourself.
49. Make sure that all of your records, from financial to mission-related, comply to the highest standards.
50. Although your focus should be running the organization, it never hurts to be familiar with the industry or cause in which you represent.

They have a vision that they wish to achieve and, no matter what, they find ways to turn their vision into a reality.

- *Keep a pulse on your members' needs.*

- *Find ways to keep learning throughout your career.*

- *Learn how to seize opportunities.* Opportunities present themselves to us everyday. We need to know how to recognize them and how to take advantage of them.

- *Get involved in outside leadership opportunities.* Volunteer. Be aware of the outside world and how your members think.

- *Greet, meet, and speak as much as possible.* The major function of the CEO is to represent the organization and to bring new ideas back to it.

- *Don't forget to be good to yourself.* We often forget to reward ourselves, which is a mistake. The CEO needs it as much or more than anyone in the organization.

SUMMARY

More than 100 CEOs of not-for-profit organizations representing a cross section of the sector participated in the study. They provided a wealth of information and advice to those who aspire to the Corner Office and to those who seek to retain the number one professional position in the not-for-profit organization. Some of the data reaffirms what seem to be logical avenues to success. In other cases, some surprising responses offered new insight into how the not-for-profit CEO's role is changing.

More accountability is needed. According to the respondents, individuals who aspire to the CEO role need to be better prepared than a decade ago, and the respondents feel that this trend will continue for the foreseeable future. The participating CEOs felt that a good CEO needs to be a generalist who must know what needs to be done. The respondents felt that CEOs needed to be much more astute on how to delegate responsibilities to full-time staff and volunteers.

Although the participating CEOs were highly trained and held impressive academic credentials and certifications, a high percentage of them felt that this was not the prime reason that they secured their position. The majority of CEOs saw past experience as the key to their success in terms of knowing what to do as well as being favored by volunteer boards or search committees. The respondents felt that success was built on a number of factors such as fiscal management, integrity, and trust. They also felt that CEOs need to possess leadership traits.

The participating CEOs indicated that successful CEOs need to know how to work with people through boards, leading staffs and interacting with outside friends and adversaries. Overwhelmingly, the respondents sought council with other CEOs as both peers and mentors for several reasons including moral support. CEOs, with all of their power, are still human. They need the contact and support that everyone needs and they get it from the individuals who best understand their role; namely other CEOs.

The road to becoming a CEO must include a personal marketing plan. Networking to gain attention is the favored way to discover new opportunities as opposed to answering an ad or waiting to be discovered. Even the interview process is handled differently by successful CEOs. Several indicated how they took charge of the interview through preparation, connecting with key leaders and understanding the organization's culture and needs.

The secret to success within the search committee selection process is to understand and appreciate how the process works. CEO candidates need to know that the approach to a volunteer-based search committee relies on the human factor. Boards often think that they know what they need in the new leader, but their notions are frequently based on dated information and personal experiences that often cloud their true needs. CEO candidates can increase their chances of securing the position by offering sound advice and expertise during the interview process.

In the early days of their tenure, more than half of the participating CEOs found that working with key leadership to understand the needs of the group and the expectations of the board was fundamental to their success. They also indicated that it is a good idea to provide the board with an evaluation report early in the tenure that summarizes the current status of the organization. This helps the CEO pin down perceived needs and creates a reference point for the future.

The respondents overwhelmingly advocated networking as the prime way of securing another CEO position. Being a player was the key.

When asked to identify the major changes that CEOs have had to face over the past 10 years and the challenges that they will face over the next 10, nearly all of the respondents focused on how to deal with change. The chief role of the CEO is to react well to change and to create change of her or his own when it is strategically advantageous to do so. Change is the number-one challenge that CEOs face; however, it is also the number one opportunity they have at their disposal. CEOs who are good at taking advantage of change are highly successful and in demand.

When asked to provide any additional advice or comments not included in the survey, one of the CEOs gave some friendly advice: "Maintain a personal focus." This is very good advice. CEOs can easily get caught up in the heat of the moment and forget the role that they play. In doing so, they become ineffective and may soon be looking for another line of work.

Another respondent said, "Learning to seize opportunities is a key element in the life of a successful CEO." Many times we do not take advantage of opportunities that come our way. This may be due to not knowing how to recognize opportunities or not knowing how to take advantage of them. Successful CEOs never let an opportunity slip by, and many will tell you opportunity is the very area that can make or break a CEO's term.

A Message to Volunteer Leaders

The definition of a board . . . is an organized group of people with the authority collectively to control and foster an institution that is usually administered by a qualified executive and staff.

Cyril O. Houle

Although *The Not-For-Profit CEO: How to Attain and Retain the Corner Office* is primarily for individuals who aspire to attain and retain a CEO position, it can also help volunteer leaders by giving them a better understanding of how to attract quality professional leaders. The book may also give them a better grasp of what CEOs require from volunteers and members to succeed.

A qualified professional leader has traveled a long way to get to your not-for-profit. This leader has extensive training. Of the CEOs who participated in the study, 66.99 percent had at least a master's or doctorate degree. The entire study detailing this fact and all the other qualities of the participating CEOs can be found in Chapter 8, "Summary of The National Study of Not-For-Profit Chief Executive Officers."

Your CEO has also continued training and considers keeping on the cutting edge a vital part of his or her ongoing educational goal. The CEO has a vast array of experience. In fact, 69.3 percent of the participating CEOs considered past work experience to be the number-one prerequisite to attaining a CEO position.

The participating CEOs understood that the role of a CEO of a not-for-profit is both an honor and a privilege. These CEOs were selected from a random sampling from the membership list of the American Society of Association Executives, a national professional society made up of not-for-profit professionals who maintain their edge through training and networking. Therefore, the participating CEOs are an average cross section of CEOs who care and who have the same feelings about the role that they play in their organizations.

Not-for-profit volunteer leaders, in general, need to better understand the vital role that dedicated professional leaders play in the success of a not-for-profit organization. More importantly, they need to understand the vital role that they play in the success of the professional leader. The most important role that the board of a not-for-profit organization performs is selecting and supporting the professional leader. If volunteer leaders select the right person and they support that person properly, the not-for-profit will serve its purpose at the highest level.

In order for not-for-profit volunteer leaders to properly support the professional leader of their not-for-profit, three areas must be examined and held to predetermined stringent standards:

1. How to seek qualified candidates

2. How to obtain the best candidate

3. How to retain a quality CEO on board

Best Methods to Seek Qualified Candidates for a Not-For-Profit CEO Position

- Key members of the not-for-profit's volunteer leadership determine what educational credentials, experience, background, and leadership qualities are required for the CEO position. The key leadership develops a two-page job description based on this need.

- The key leadership appoints a small search committee to seek the new CEO. The search committee determines how to conduct the search, including whether to use a search firm.

- If a search firm is employed, the leadership must make sure that the organization clearly defines the qualifications that it seeks in the new CEO. It also needs to indicate that it wishes to maintain a leadership role in the process.

- If the search committee will be receiving the resumes, the review process should not include the not-for-profit's staff. During the sorting of the resumes, make sure that the qualities that you seek are the keys to selection; your best candidates may come from unique backgrounds.

- Develop a detailed packet of information that will be provided to each prospective candidate that you select. The packet should include the following:

  o A full history of the organization

  o A current list of volunteer leaders and positions

  o A list of staff and their functions

  o The association's publications

  o A brief overview of the plan, if a strategic plan is in place

- ◦ A summary or copies of last three years' audits
- ◦ An overview of programs and activities
- ◦ A summary of any problems the organization is currently facing
- ◦ The job description and a short description of what the volunteer leadership is looking for in terms of the candidate's qualifications and experience. (The description should have an overview of what the organization expects the incumbent CEO to accomplish.)
- Select finalists and contact them by telephone. Get the following information:
  - ◦ Discover if the person is interested.
  - ◦ Schedule a conference call with them and two members of the search committee.
  - ◦ Obtain the best address to send the packet of information to.
  - ◦ Conduct the conference call with each finalist. Explain the position in detail. Ask questions to evaluate the finalist. Finally, determine if the finalist is still interested.
- Select the final candidates and schedule to have them meet with the search committee.
- Allow the final candidates to ask for more information.
- Let the final candidates know what the interview process will include. That should include the following information:
  - ◦ The number of candidates being interviewed
  - ◦ The interview process
  - ◦ When each candidate will be notified about their status
  - ◦ When the decision will be made
  - ◦ Finalists who are not chosen will be encouraged to ask why.

THE RECOMMENDED STEPS TO OBTAIN A QUALITY CHIEF EXECUTIVE OFFICER

1. Be open and friendly with every candidate.
2. Conduct the interview in such a way as to gain the needed information as well as to provide enough information to the candidate so he or she can make a good decision.
3. When you provide the history of the not-for-profit, tell the entire story including both the good and bad (e.g., the reason the last CEO was let go).
4. Tell the candidates, after they have provided you with ample information, what you are really looking for in the next CEO.

5. Allow ample time to let each candidate show her or his personal skills and encourage them to provide samples of their work.

6. Give each candidate equal billing even though you feel that an in-house candidate or a candidate that has already been interviewed seems to be your choice. You may be surprised at what you discover.

7. Be reasonable where and when you interview.

8. Don't prolong the agony: get the job of selecting the candidate done in a reasonable time and let everyone know the outcome as quickly as possible.

9. Bring the leading candidate or finalist in one more time so the candidate can ask questions about the organization including its governance, fiscal policies, staff, programs, and any other questions.

10. Allow the final candidate to visit the not-for-profit's offices to see the layout, meet with the staff, and talk to key volunteers.

THE MOST EFFECTIVE STANDARD TO RETAIN A CHIEF EXECUTIVE OFFICER

- Develop a clear statement of agreement or a contract with the new CEO that covers the following:
  - The relationship that he or she will have with the volunteer leadership
  - The role that the volunteer leadership wants the CEO to play
  - The complete reporting process in the organization
  - The CEO's full compensation package including salary, incentives, and traditional benefits
- Work with your new CEO to create an annual review process for both the not-for-profit and the CEO. Both parties should be reviewed at the same time. Make sure that the CEO and the volunteer leadership understands the role each should play in the annual review process including identifying challenging but realistic, quantifiable goals that advance the organization's mission.
- Meet the new CEO in person during the first 30 days of employment to discuss, in detail, what the volunteer leadership expects him or her to do in the first year. Provide some indication about where you feel the association should be in three to five years.
- Make sure that you provide enough room to let the CEO lead.
- Don't isolate the CEO. Make her or him an equal partner with the volunteer leadership.
- Bestow recognition and praise on the CEO in front of the staff and membership. This will help the CEO strengthen his or her position.

- Let the CEO do work outside the association, both in the organization's field of interest and beyond. This practice will elevate the CEO to an even stronger level of leadership.

- Encourage your CEO to find ways to stay on the cutting edge through self-enrichment programs and training.

- Provide a meaningful retirement package that is specially designed for upper-management personnel. Give the CEO something that is personal to work for.

- Encourage the CEO to do the following:
  - Think strategically.
  - Use his or her imagination.
  - Be innovative.
  - Work with the volunteer leadership to create a challenging but realistic vision for the future.
  - Lead.

- Reward the CEO when she or he does something above the call of duty.

SUMMARY

The selection and support of the chief executive officer of a not-for-profit organization is the most important role that the volunteer leaders of the board play. The CEO will be the key representative of the organization to which the volunteer leaders have devoted their time and energy over an extended period of time. The CEO will run the day-to-day operations and he or she will be a player on the board. The position is so vital that placing the wrong person in the role or not supporting the right person can have significant short-term and long-term effects on the association.

If the key volunteers are serious about fulfilling the mission of the not-for-profit that they lead, they must create the highest standard in which to seek, obtain, and retain a chief executive officer. If they do, they will attract and encourage a CEO to stay in that position for a longer period of time. This will result in a more stabilized operational structure and it will result in greater success in fulfilling the mission of the not-for-profit.

It really does matter who sits in the Corner Office of a not-for-profit. The volunteer leaders have the power and the duty to put the right person there.

Bibliography

Chapter 1

"An Acte to Redresse the Misemployment of Landes, Goodes, and Stockes of Money Herefore Given to Charitable Uses," 1601.

Brenner, Robert H. *American Philanthropy*. Chicago: University of Chicago Press, 1988.

Ellis, Susan J., and Katherine H. Noyes. *By the People*. San Francisco: Jossey-Bass Publishers, 1990.

Ernstthal, Henry L. *Principles of Association Management*. 4th ed. Washington, DC: American Society of Association Executives, 2001.

Fisher, James L. and Gary H. Quehl. *The President and Fund Raising*. New York: MacMillan Publishing Company, 1989.

Harrison, Frederick C. *Spirit of Leadership*. Germantown, TN: Leadership Education and Development, 1989.

Independent Sector. *Giving and Volunteering in the United States*. Washington, DC, 2001.

Independent Sector. *The New Nonprofit Almanac In Brief*. Washington, DC, 2001.

Miltner, John R. *A Study of the Characteristics of Successful Chief Development Officers in Selective Public Colleges and Universities,* a dissertation. Cincinnati, OH: Union Institute, 1990.

Principles of Association Management. Washington, DC: American Society of Association Executives, 1975.

U.S. Census Bureau. "County Business Patterns, 1977–2001." The U.S. Nonprofit and Voluntary Membership Association Segment. Washington, DC, 2001.

Webster, George D. and Alan P. Dye. "Association Legal Checklist." Washington DC: U.S. Chamber of Commerce, Association Department, 1983.

Chapter 2

Harrison, Frederick. *Spirit of Leadership*. Germantown, TN: Leadership Education and Development, 1989.

Pidgeon Jr., Walter P. *Universal Benefits of Volunteering.* New York: John Wiley & Sons, Inc., 1998.

Pidgeon Jr., Walter P. *The Legislative Labyrinth.* New York: John Wiley & Sons, Inc., 2001.

Wellington, Sheila. *Be Your Own Mentor.* New York: Random House, 2001.

Chapter 3

Butterfield, Bruce. "What Comes After What We Know." Aristotle Web site. Washington, DC: Forbes Group (June 6, 2003).

George, Bill. "Today's CEOs are Being Swayed by Every Voice — Except Their Own." *Fortune Magazine* (September 29, 2003).

Herman, Robert D. and David O. Renz. *Nonprofit Organizational Effectiveness: Practical Implications of Research on an Elusive Concept.* Kansas City, MO: Henry W. Bloch School of Business and Public Administration, 2002.

Hymowitz, Carol. "The Best Leaders Have Employees Who Would Follow Them Anywhere." *The Wall Street Journal* (February 10, 2004).

Jones, Del. "CEOs of the Future Get Formal Training to Take Giant Leap." *USA Today,* Money Section (December 1, 2003).

Langley, Monica. "In Tough Times for CEOs, They Head to Warren Buffett's Table." *The Wall Street Journal* (November 14, 2003).

McCambridge, Ruth. "A Gateway to 21st Century Governance: Are You Ready?" *The Nonprofit Quarterly* (Fall, 2003).

McDonald, Tom. "Best Behavior: The Key to Motivating Employees is to Let Them Use Their Brains." *Successful Meetings Magazine* (September 1996).

Pidgeon Jr., Walter P. *The Legislative Labyrinth: A Map for Not-For-Profits.* New York: John Wiley & Sons, Inc., 2001.

Pidgeon Jr., Walter P. *The Universal Benefits of Volunteering: A Practical Workbook for Nonprofit Organization, Volunteers, and Corporations.* New York: John Wiley & Sons, Inc., 1998.

Raelin, Joseph A. *Creating Leadership Organization: How to Bring Out Leadership in Everyone.* San Francisco: Berrett-Koehler Publishers, Inc., 2003.

Reungold, Jennifer. "Still Angry After All of These Years." *Fast Company Magazine* (October, 2003).

Rhoads, Christopher. "Success Stories: Companies Around the Globe are Finding Ways to Buck the Economic Downturn." *The Wall Street Journal* (September 22, 2003).

Tharpe, Don I. "Turbulence-Free Transition." Washington, DC: American Society of Association Executives, *Association Management Magazine* (January, 2002).

Wakin, Edward. "Making Creativity Contagious." *Beyond Computing Magazine* (October, 1996).

"Walking the Talk: Measuring the Performance of Your Corporate Culture." SMM's Performance eNewsletter (February 23, 2004).

Chapter 4

Hambrick, Donald C., David A. Nadler, Michael L. Tushman. *Navigating Change*. Boston: Harvard Business School Press, 1998.

Chapter 5

Belford, Paul A. *Planning Your Career in Association Management*. Washington, DC: American Society of Association Executives, 2002.

Broening, Thomas. "Peter Drucker Sets Us Straight." *Fortune Magazine* (January 12, 2004).

Fisher, Ann. "Older, Wiser, Job Hunting." *Fortune Magazine* (February 9, 2004).

Harrison, Frederick C. *Spirit of Leadership*. Germantown, TN: Leadership Education and Development, 1989.

Chapter 6

Hanan, Mack. *Manage Like You Own It*. New York: AMACON, American Management Association, 1994.

Harrison, Frederick C. *Spirit of Leadership*. Germantown, TN: Leadership Education and Development, 1989.

Pidgeon Jr., Walter P. *The Legislative Labyrinth: A Map for Not-For-Profits*. New York: John Wiley & Sons, Inc., 2001.

Pidgeon Jr., Walter P. *The Universal Benefits of Volunteering: A Practical Workbook for Nonprofit Organizations, Volunteers, and Corporations*. New York: John Wiley & Sons, Inc., 1998.

Raelin, Joseph A. *Creating Leadership Organizations*. San Francisco: Berrett-Koehler Publishing, Inc., 2002.

Senge, Peter M. *A Conversation with Peter F. Drucker*. San Francisco: Jossey-Bass, 2001.

Tulger, Bruce. *Winning the Talent Wars*. New York: W. W. Norton & Company, 2001.

Ulrica, Dave, Steve Kerr, Ron Ashkenas. *The GE Workout*. New York: McGraw Hill, 2002.

Warrick, Judy. "The New CEO: Rethinking the Corner Office." *Wall Street Journal* (March 1, 2004).

Chapter 7

Belford, Paul A. *Planning Your Career in Association Management*. Washington, DC: American Society of Association Executives, 2002.

Bright, Deborah. "When Talking's Tough: Ten Essential Communications Tips for Leading in Hard Times." American Society of Association Executives, *Association Management Magazine,* (November, 2003).

Harrison, Frederick C. *Spirit of Leadership.* Germantown, TN: Leadership Education and Development, 1989.

Chapter 8

Patton, Michael Quinn. *Qualitative Evaluations and Research Methods.* 2nd ed. Newbury Park, CA: Sage Publications, 1990.

Additional Sources of Information

Source	Find Out About
American Humanics, Inc. 4601 Madison Ave. Kansas City, MO 64112 800-531-6466 *www.humanics.org*	Supports more than 70 colleges and universities who offer majors in not-for-profit administration.
Union Institute & University 440 East McMillan Street Cincinnati, Ohio 45206-1925 800-486-3116 *www.tui.edu*	Undergraduate and graduate degree programs, including a doctorate degree in Association Management through a partnership with the American Society of Executives.
American Society of Association Executives 1575 I Street, NW Washington, DC 20005-1103 202-626-2723 *www.asaenet.org*	A host of education programs in association management and the Certified Association Executive (CAE) designation.
Association of Fund Raising Professionals 1101 King Street, Suite 700 Alexandria, Virginia 22314 703-684-0410 *www.afpnet.org*	The resource for fundraising information and training.
Points of Light Foundation 1400 I Street, Suite 800 Washington, DC 20005 202-729-8000 *www.pointsoflight.org*	The best source for information concerning community service and volunteer issues.

Index

HEIRLOOM BULBS

For Today

2365 Rice Boulevard, Suite 202,
Houston, Texas 77005

10 9 8 7 6 5 4 3 2 1

ISBN 978-1-933979-95-3
Library of Congress Cataloging-in-Publication Data on file with Publisher.

Creative Direction by Ellen Cregan
Design by Marla Garcia
Printed in China by South China Printing Co. Ltd, An RR Donnelley company

HEIRLOOM BULBS

For Today

Chris Wiesinger

"THE BULB HUNTER"
and Cherie Foster Colburn

Introduction by Dr. Bill Welch

Art by Loela Barry and
Johan Kritzinger

bright sky press
HOUSTON, TEXAS

To all of you, who over the last six years have fed me, lodged me, believed in me, trusted me, forgiven me, loved me, and celebrated with me.

CHRIS WIESINGER

For the men in my life:

Greg, the father of my two beautiful daughters (and, conveniently my sweetheart for the last 30 years);

My father, Bob Foster, for introducing me to gardening (although it was called "pulling weeds" at our house);

Chris, for trusting me to tell his story;

And for my Father God, to Him be all glory and honor.

CHERIE FOSTER COLBURN

To our parents in our native South Africa – Erich and Gerda Barry and Sarel and Marié Kritzinger – for instilling a passion for art and nature; our British mum Joanie and art mentor Rensche for their encouragement and support; Chris and Cherie for recognizing our talents; and our Lord for joining us in a new life together....

The 'JoLoè Art' Team

LOELA BARRY & JOHAN KRITZINGER

PRIVATE
PROPERTY

"I WANTED TO KNOW THE NAME OF EVERY STONE AND FLOWER
AND INSECT AND BIRD AND BEAST.
I WANTED TO KNOW WHERE IT GOT ITS COLOR,
WHERE IT GOT ITS LIFE—
BUT THERE WAS NO ONE TO TELL ME."

George Washington Carver
1864–1943

WHY A NEW BULB BOOK?

Before I was a year old, my family moved to Houston, Texas from my birthplace, Lafayette, Louisiana. Eight years later we left the South, bound for Bakersfield, California, and Dad's new job there. We were a gardening family, at least in our definition of the word. Fruit trees, vegetables, and flowers all grew around our home. Saturdays often meant a trip to the local garden center to pick up something new. I watched with envy while my dad mowed the lawn each week and kept the bedding plants and small orchard in check. My older brother took over the task of mowing when he was deemed old enough, eventually handing the responsibility over to me, a right of passage I eagerly awaited.

On one fall outing to the garden center, I noticed stacks of boxes with pictures of vibrantly colored flowers on them in the corner. Inside the boxes were what looked like little brown rocks. I convinced my mom to let me buy a "rock" and took it home with a tiny piece of paper, instructions that promised to transform my rock into a beautiful red tulip. Five months later, spring arrived. Doors and windows open to the catch the breeze, California's cool, dry air drafted through the house that first day of my gardening spring. Having located various spots around the house to snooze in the sunshine and open air, I was catnapping at the front entryway. Just as I was about to close my eyes, I looked out the front door into the entry garden bed. There was my red tulip! I had noticed the foliage coming up from the spot where I'd planted the rock—the first indication that it wasn't a rock after all—but the dazzling bloom appeared almost magically. Unfortunately, that afternoon some petals were lost due to a spring shower. But it was okay. Now I knew I was a successful gardener, and I would look forward to the next year's bloom.

But when it came time for my plant to come back, only the bulb's foliage appeared. I thought all was fine, and I practiced a patience I often boasted about and looked forward to the next year's bloom. But that year, the foliage didn't even come up. I dug down to investigate and found the rotted remains of my little red tulip bulb. I could say I was devastated, or horticulturally scarred, but in reality, I was just curious about what had happened to my bulb.

That experience and the questions that came with it eventually became a quest for me. I pursued a horticulture education at Texas A&M University. In a senior level course, I was required to write a business plan for a plant nursery start-up. I decided to respond to some of my personal issues in the assignment, researching the viability of a nursery that offered bulbs that would survive, multiply and bloom—year after year—in warm climates.

My initial research required calling world sources for bulbs. Each one told me the same thing: there is no such thing as a warm climate, naturalizing bulb. Pondering this dilemma, I spent several weekends exploring country roads around the state of Texas, thinking these would be my final months there. On one of my trips, I looked out my truck's window and noticed daffodils marking the old foundations of a dilapidated house. Just down the road, more daffodils encircled huge trees and lined a crumbling sidewalk. Upon closer inspection, they weren't just daffodils, but hyacinths, gladiolus, lilies, rain lilies, and crinums. Maybe, just maybe, I thought—if I looked hard enough—I would find a lonely red tulip standing in the mix.

This was the start of the Southern Bulb Company, which has become a story of its own and would take another whole book to tell. The most important thing my academic and professional experiences with bulbs have taught me is that the old, tried and true heirloom bulbs should be the stars of our Southern gardens instead of some of the plants now popular that have no hope of survival in the heat and humidity. I've come to know these bulbs intimately, seeing them face hardships alongside me, going through drought and flood, heat and cold. My hope is that when you get to know the individual personalities of these beautiful friends of mine, their ease of cultivation—combined with their charm—will win your heart as they have mine.

Since my first bulb trauma, I have come to understand not all bulbs are meant for all places. *Heirloom Bulbs for Today* is different from typical gardening books because its purpose follows my experience and my desire for everyone with access to soil to find success gardening with bulbs. I believe understanding these heirlooms means more than seeing their beauty or learning the best technique to grow them or incorporate them into your landscape. I want you to understand that each bulb blooming today has a tale to tell: it has traveled from somewhere, from someone. It was carried in the pocket of an immigrant coming to a New World, or symbolized the love of a child on a parent's grave, or was divided from an old clump in grandmother's garden to provide a "start" for a daughter's new home. Each bulb comes to us with a full and seasoned past.

So, besides the facts and figures and information on what works and doesn't work with the bulbs profiled for you here, I include stories that touched me in my work with heirloom bulbs: how I found them, how they came to America, landmarks where the plants have merged with history, and ways to use them, both inside and outside your home.

We'll start with bulbs most gardeners have success with, and then move to bulbs that are great for more

limited regions. Then I'll introduce some exciting, romantic bulbs that require very specific conditions, and finally, show you what to do when you just love a bulb, but it's not right for your particular environment. This book may be used to map out a bulb hunt of your own, and you can visit historic sites where heirloom bulbs grow with reckless abandon as they have for decades, or even centuries. You can use the resources included to force your favorite bulbs to bloom on demand for indoor gardens, for gifts, or for a breath of spring during the middle of winter.

My adventures finding these bulbs are just the beginning. More important are the adventures you will have with them. May you find pleasure not only in images and information collected here, but also in taking part in resurrecting our horticultural heritage. By welcoming heirloom bulbs into your garden and home, you continue a lasting legacy, ensuring these plants are cherished by yet another generation.

Chris Wiesinger
The Bulb Hunter

Introduction by
DR. BILL WELCH

Chris Wiesinger has become a nationally recognized figure in the heirloom bulb movement in a relatively short time. Tom Christopher, then-Garden Editor for House & Garden *magazine, was among the first to bring Chris to the attention of the gardening public through a series of articles on "tastemakers." A color spread in the* New York Times *followed, as well as articles in* Southern Living *magazine and other publications. So began the process that made Chris a popular lecturer and supplier of these rare old bulbs to the public.*

In the 1980s I had begun to popularize the idea of using hardy, tough plant "survivors" for trouble-free landscapes, although there were few commercial sources at the time. Available bulbs had been rescued from old landscapes or came from gardeners who had shared with each other. As the use of these bulbs became more popular, my books *Perennial Garden Color* (Taylor Publishing, Dallas, 1989) and *Antique Roses for the South* (1990) furthered the general awareness of these concepts, and a third book, *The Southern Heirloom Garden* (1995) with Greg Grant, increased the gardening community's understanding of "time tested" plants and our Southern gardening heritage.

In the mid 1980s I became interested in networking with other garden historians through The Southern Garden History Society that included some of the staff at Mt. Vernon; Monticello; Old Salem, NC, and other public and private gardens and universities. As those relationships developed, I found myself with a group of friends who were equally passionate about these living symbols of success that document our gardening heritage.

One of the joys of my work at Texas A & M University is that some really outstanding students come my way.

As an Extension Landscape Horticulturist I spend most of my time providing educational material and programs for Master Gardeners, nursery professionals and garden club members throughout Texas and the South, but occasionally I lecture in classes in the department and interested students seek me out for my special interests in landscape design, heirloom plants and garden history. Chris Wiesinger was one of those students. Texas Garden Clubs, Inc. has provided a scholarship in my name and each year a committee including myself selects an undergraduate and a graduate student. I particularly remembered seeing Chris' application, because being a Ross Volunteer and leader in the Aggie Corps requires a major time commitment, and Chris was also an honor student.

Chris arrived for our initial meeting in uniform and was very polite. We were both intrigued with his class project for Dr. Fred Davies' horticulture class: a business plan for a nursery specializing in heirloom bulbs. I shared experiences of starting The Antique Rose Emporium with Mike Shoup in 1982, and we both could see the similarities. Chris became increasingly excited as we spoke of various heirloom bulbs that have naturalized across the South and have been shared by generations of gardeners but generally ignored by the commercial bulb growing syndicates. We deepened our mutual interests as I introduced him to a network of people throughout the South who knew about these bulbs and knew where they could be found--from people connected to historical sites to wonderful seasoned gardeners, all with many personal experiences and stories to share.

In a user friendly manner, *Heirloom Bulbs for Today* groups bulbs on the basis of their ease of culture and adaptability to various areas. Each bulb has an engaging and beautifully drawn portrait by Loela Barry and detailed photographic studies by Johan Kritzinger. Chris provides stories about finding each of the bulbs as well as accessible horticultural information that will enhance the reader's knowledge of how they may use these heirlooms in their own gardens. Through our conversations, Chris often mentioned the dedication and talent of co-author Cherie Colburn, without whom the transcript would never have reached print. Cherie not only displayed a commitment to excellence and perseverance in seeing this project fulfilled, but her passion for sustainability and younger gardeners shines through as well. Join me to explore the pages of this beautiful book as Chris weaves his talents into the rich tapestry of our Southern gardening heritage.

Dr. William C. "Bill" Welch
Author, Professor and Texas AgriLife Extension Service Landscape Horticulturist, Department of Horticultural Sciences
Texas A&M University

BEFORE YOU DIG IN TO THIS BOOK...

What is an heirloom bulb?

For our purposes, an heirloom bulb is one found in American gardens before World War II. These specific bulbs we have chosen to profile are just an introduction to the many beautiful heirloom bulbs that exist. And, we profile some bulbs here that do not fit that criteria exactly. These bulbs are here because they are cultivated varieties of plants that *do* meet the requirements and are destined to become heirlooms.

What's in a name?

As a student of horticulture, Latin pronunciation was not my forté. And I was not always careful about using the correct, botanical name of a plant. I just didn't see the necessity of it. My mentors in the American Rose Society and other garden groups were ecstatic to see somebody under the age of sixty involved in gardening. But the necessity of knowing Latin names of plants hit me hard when I was speaking to the National Rock Garden Society, Potomac Chapter, at the National Arboretum. I was walking with a member of the group when she made a remark about the person leading our garden tour. "He really knows a lot of plants," she said "but his Latin is shoddy." As I thought about this comment later, I got self-conscious about my own "shoddiness" when it came to botanical name-calling.

Why does it even matter? Why demand this strict adherence to a formal language instead of the beautiful names folks have bestowed on beloved plants throughout time? It matters because this is the only name that a specific plant will always have everywhere. Although the Latin name of the plant might change over time because of new discovery or classification, the Latin name remains the name of *that* particular plant, no matter where you are. Whether I speak to a flower enthusiast from Bristol, England, Bristol, Connecticut, or Bristol, Tennessee, all will know which plant I refer to when I mention a *Hyacinthoides hispanica,* but each will picture a very different flower when I talk about a bluebell. At least two of them will be totally confused when my "bluebell" remarks do not line up with their personal experience.

Soiled again!

My experience with bulbs is primarily in Texas. Specifically, my bulb farm is in northeast Texas. But since plants do not recognize state lines, the vegetation regions, soil types, cold hardiness, and rain fall are applicable not by state, but by regions with similar conditions. You will find that many of the heirloom bulbs are not native, but they do well in the United States. That's because they may be found in other areas of the world that are extremely similar. For instance, South African plants tend to grow well in Southern California, Mediterranean plants in Central Texas, and Central American plants in Florida.

To give you an idea of how important the *soil* information is in deciding which heirloom bulbs will thrive in your landscape, let me tell you how I learned this lesson. It was the hard way, and the *expensive* way! Texas has ten different vegetation regions, including the Blackland Prairies, actually a series of prairies with a variety of terrain from slightly rolling hills to flat lands, that stretches from the northern part of the state and slices south through its heart. These prairie soils engulf Dallas and reach into Austin and San Antonio. Soil in the Blackland Prairies is dark clay. It becomes brick-like and may crack during a dry summer. Rainwater can bypass large patches of soil because the earth is too hard to absorb it. While this soil is not good for many plants, it happens to be ideal for what was nicknamed the Texas Tulip, known botanically as *Tulipa praecox.*

Growers and gardeners alike were thrilled to have found this bulb growing with reckless abandon on old homesites. A new discovery! A naturalizing tulip for Texas! With such excitement we built up our supply and released the bulb for sale at midnight during a big promotion. By 7 a.m., we had nearly sold out. Fast forward a year and a half, and I hurt from reading responses received when I e-mailed customers to check on their bulbs. It was utter failure. Many avid gardeners had diligently prepared their beds and done everything the "right way." Their bulbs rotted. Humid Houston was a disaster. But many of my customers in the Blackland Prairies had simply dug a hole into unprepared ground and stuck the bulb in with no special treatment whatsoever. Their reports were glowing; they had great success using these "no-brainer" bulbs.

It had become painfully clear: although the cold hardiness was the same in many of these areas, the soil, humidity and other factors all played a part in the importance of a bulb not only surviving, but thriving. Some bulbs are "cross-vegetational" and are superstars. But for others, it is important to weigh all factors. Granted, the nickname "Texas Tulip" is not fair one. Garden writer Felder Rushing reports this tulip growing around Jackson, MS, and I have personally seen it in northern Georgia. The cold and rainfall vary in these three areas. But all these areas have black, clay soils that crack during dry times.

On the back pages of *Heirloom Bulbs* we have included a soil map and the cold hardiness map based on USDA studies. While there is no perfect map that will tell you everything, using these two maps together and relating them to the descriptions written about each bulb you can get a better idea of each plant's needs and achieve success growing heirloom bulbs.

The biggest complaint!

"All of the foliage came up, but my bulb did not bloom this year."

This is the number one complaint of all bulb gardeners who report a bad experience. Here are some of the main reasons why a red spider lily, for instance, might have skipped its bloom.

1. *The bulb:* It just didn't feel like blooming. Not much you can do about this, because when you want a garden with personality, you have to deal with personalities.
2. *Moving:* If the bulb was shared with you, it was probably allowed to dry out for too long. Under the ground the bulbs will often keep some roots growing all year long. When those roots dry out, the bulb goes into a longer dormancy period.
3. *A very dry summer:* During a particularly dry summer, those roots can also dry out under the ground.
4. *Winter sun:* Foliage continues to grow after the bulb blooms, even in winter. It can be deceiving, seeing it bloom in shady areas. But when trees lose their foliage in the winter, the bulb's foliage is able to collect the amount of sun it requires for its photosynthetic needs.

How should I plant them? Which end is up?

When you view the illustration of each plant given, note its requirements. Most bulbs simply could care less how they are planted, as long as soil covers them a bit. Plant the bulb sideways if you are unsure; just make sure you get it in the ground. Others do best under a specific planting regimen, and refuse to comply with expectations if these needs are unmet.

Where should I plant them so that they will survive and bloom?

Look at not only the light conditions, but the water and soil conditions needed for each bulb. If you find a plant that you simply have to have, provide a home where it will be happy, and your results are assured. For most of us though, it is easiest—and better environmentally—to look at the existing conditions of a location and then find a bulb that will thrive in that habitat. There is often huge variability within our landscapes, so don't generalize. Take a closer look at your site.

- Where does the sun stay during the heat of the day?
- Is there enough sun/shade to meet the bulb's needs?
- Which trees lose their leaves in the winter?
- Where does water stand after a rain? (whether because of clay soil or a low spot)

These are just a few of the questions to ask in considering the lay of the land.

Where should I plant bulbs so they look good?

Bulbs can meet a number of needs in the aesthetics of a properly designed landscape.

- mass plantings
- perennial combinations
- potted combinations
- seasonal interest

See how you can incorporate them in a fun, new way. Bulbs are not usually evergreen, but when paired with other plants that mask departing foliage, they can look great year-round, providing constant color and change to their surroundings without constant re-planting and cost.

How to use this book

Many gardening books are available. Some have excellent information about bulbs. Some are easy to use. The purpose of our book is to combine these two elements into a guide for growing and knowing bulbs in a unique way. With the art, photos, growth information, and stories, we hope to reveal each profiled bulb's personality, including its aesthetic beauty, a little history, how I found it for re-introduction into the trade, and its current use and horticultural implications.

In his work, *Philosophia Botanica*, Carl Linnaeus, the Swedish botanist known as the father of modern taxonomy, said, "If you do not know the names of things, the knowledge of them is lost, too." By recognizing a plant, sharing its story and remembering its name, we hope to pass the knowledge of these treasures to you.

Table of Contents

Great Bulbs for
ALMOST ALL AREAS

36in 91.4cm

24in 61cm

.... 30.5cm

12in ....

AUTUMN   SUMMER

GROUP I
RED SPIDER LILY • CAMPERNELLE • GRAND PRIMO • SNOWFLAKE
GOLDEN DAWN • BYZANTINE GLADIOLA • HARDY AMARYLLIS
MRS. JAMES HENDRY • ARGENTINE RAIN LILY

AUTUMN   SUMMER

What makes a bulb a superstar?

My bulb hall of fame has some basic requirements. Even though you can expect to see listed some "special instructions," the requirements to be considered a superstar are simple:

If you are given a bulb, and it sits in your shed for about four months, and you throw it in the ground with reckless abandon, it will usually grow, bloom and thrive all on its own, with little or no care.

The superstar must *reliably*:
- come back year after year, barring cement or dense brush covering it, mowers scalping it, or varmints stealing it
- have a high probability of success with first time gardeners
- be low-maintenance, not requiring constant division or refrigeration
- bloom for an extended period, individual bulbs blooming at intervals
- have a showy or remarkable flower color, shape or bloom time

Lycoris radiata
red spider lily

The thing that always surprises me about the red spider lily is the color. It is now subconscious — the swing of my head, narrowing of the eyes, and foot on the brakes. Splashes of color, surreal exclamations back-dropped by a sea of brown, tucked in a tiny slice of city or spreading across a meadow, the tell-tale signs of where an old home once stood. When I passed by two weeks before, nothing was there. It was a weed-covered, empty lot, a task for somebody, a mowing job that had to be done every week. I always pray those mowers fall slack on their job with the heat of late August and September. Because, as quickly as the temperature changes with a Blue Norther, so the landscape will soon change. Abandoned lots are no longer chores. They become stories. The bulbs enchant me with their timing, their striking color, and their history: they are the alarm clock for the sleeping South. From June to August, it is so oppressively hot that people, plants and businesses all but shut down and fall asleep. Just when we think it will never end, a rain shower appears in the afternoon. Something — cooling temperatures; change in pressure; lightning induced, nitrogen charged, untreated water; shortening of days — who knows for sure what — causes all of the dormant, brown bulbs hidden under the earth to come alive. What appears is the first ring of the alarm clock, the harbinger of fall, our sign that summer is finally ending. Naked stalks shoot up out of the ground, red buds adorning their heads. These buds waste no time as they unfurl slender fingers that turn into the spider-shaped blooms that earn this Lycoris her name.

Some say the color is red. Others call it coral. Some go as far as to call the blooms orange. You decide for yourself. Maybe a color wheel next to a bloom would settle the dispute. But when I turn the corner on a lonely back-road and the vista suddenly opens into a field full of spider lilies, my brain sees red. The blooms tell me someone once lived in this place. A hopeful gardener planted a few bulbs here. Now a sweep of color, they speak of a forgotten time. Somehow, just a few inches below the surface of the soil, little brown reservoirs of life have survived. With no outside aid, they beat the odds against fifty, seventy-five, one hundred years of volatile Southern weather. Those few bulbs have now multiplied into an incredible display. Lines of the flowers stand in a row, guarding the crumbling foundation of a home long gone. Circles of blooms tell us where a massive shade tree once stood. Spotty masses mark the spot where a small garden bed enjoyed by a family has been scraped, tilled and plowed to make way for a new family. What a surprise when the flash of intense color springs from the earth, called to life despite last week's hot summer sun!

There is a problem with this alarm clock though. We need to hit the snooze button. A cool spell gets everyone excited, almost chipper. But the heat quickly returns and then lingers long past its welcome, into October or longer. You hear someone at the office, at a garden club meeting, or on the news say, "Can you believe it is still so hot?" They have already forgotten the brief respite. The appropriate response is: "No, I can't! Was it like this last year? This *is* unusual." This will make you sound civil, polite, and down to earth. So, if you are new to bulbs in the South, or warm climates, start looking for these beauties to make their annual appearance in the waning days of summer.

Perhaps the most moving display I have ever seen of *Lycoris radiata* was in Natchitoches, LA. Do you know how to pronounce Natchitoches? It is pronounced Naka-titch. When explaining this, I immediately follow with "It's where *Steel Magnolias* was filmed." The response is always the same: "Oh, I love that movie. It is a *charming* little town." If my listener is really Southern, it is a "chah-ming" little town. I was in Natchitoches for a presentation. While staying at the bed-and-breakfast downtown, I asked if they had a copy of the movie. "We sure do!" my host happily exclaimed as she pointed to the bookshelf. Four or more copies of the film were stacked, one to accommodate the whole house if each room simultaneously decided to watch it. I looked at the cover of the VHS and the dated fashions of the outfits struck a chord with me: my fondness for a movie with such dated styles told me that I was becoming older myself.

The next morning I picked up the paper and saw the town was sponsoring a *Steel Magnolias* movie tour. I looked at the map the newspaper showed, locations demarked by numbers. The numbers had corresponding descriptions at the bottom: Truby's hair salon, Easter in the park scene where the bunny rides away on a motorcycle, Truby's second hair shop, the cemetery scene where Sally Fields is comforted by an all star cast of actresses…. I stopped there. The cemetery was the reason I was in Natchitoches. I walked out of the bed and breakfast onto a meandering street, a street that no doubt followed a trail as old as 1772, when the first settlers came to the area. Under spreading oaks dripping with moss, the sidewalk snaked through Natchitoches. I passed historic homes, eventually arriving at the oldest part of town and the oldest cemetery in the South: the American Cemetery. I was there to speak at the Cemetery Preservation Workshop put on by the National Park Service. This cemetery was worth preserving.

Natchitoches is the third oldest town in America and the cemetery's roots date back to a French fort established there in 1714. Many different cultures are on display, contributing their unique influences to the site. A number of Revolutionary War soldiers found their final resting place there. It is a lovely, natural landscape. But as I approached the old wrought-iron fence, tree roots molding themselves around the iron bars, something surprising appeared: the cemetery was overrun with red spider lilies, marching everywhere. It brought to mind a name sometimes used for these feisty flowers: "British Soldiers." From under the cracks of cement barriers, between tombstones, under trees, brazenly growing directly over plots, the soldiers were marching everywhere. The number of red coats was a moving sight. This shady cemetery, full of old specimen oaks, camellias, and antique roses, comes alive every fall with the 1-2 foot tall splashes of red. I recognized again that Southerners have an emotional connection with spider lilies, a response that goes beyond the bulb's awesome display of beauty and is a living link to the past.

Lycoris radiata
red spider lily

Bloom

SIZE	4"–6" (10–14 cm)
COLOR	Coral red, more red to some, more orange-red to others
SHAPE	Spidery look with long filaments that leave the center of the bloom, dip a little, and come up again with distinctive anthers. Surrounded by modified petals
TIME	Mid September
FRAGRANCE	None

Foliage

EMERGE	October after September bloom
FADE	Late April
HEIGHT	7"–12" (20–30 cm)

Bulb

SIZE (CIRCUMFERENCE)	3"–5" (8–12 cm)
COLOR	Light brown to dark brown, skin sometimes peels to show next layer of white bulb, more mature bulbs have skin that peels and shows next layer of dark brown inflorescence
SHAPE	Teardrop that tapers into 1"–2" straight neck

Lycoris radiata

Care

SOIL	Any, but avoid standing water
LIGHT	Half-shade to full-sun
MOISTURE	Irrigation ok during dormant season, prefers well-drained soil but can handle wet feet
TEMPERATURE	Zone 7–10
PLANTING	Plant bulb from late spring to fall. Plant bulb at a depth that is equivalent to 2–3 times the height of bulb
DIVIDE/TRANSPLANT	April/May
VASE LIFE	1 week
FOLIAGE REMOVAL	April/May
NOTES	Sometimes will not bloom the first year or two. The bulbs do not like to dry out. When transplanting, keep roots moist or replant as soon as possible. *Lycoris radiata* is native to the U.S.

The American Cemetery
Natchitoches, Louisiana

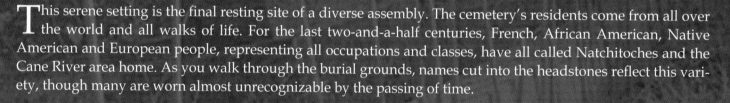

This serene setting is the final resting site of a diverse assembly. The cemetery's residents come from all over the world and all walks of life. For the last two-and-a-half centuries, French, African American, Native American and European people, representing all occupations and classes, have all called Natchitoches and the Cane River area home. As you walk through the burial grounds, names cut into the headstones reflect this variety, though many are worn almost unrecognizable by the passing of time.

The oldest monument shows a date of 1797, but historians believe many graves predate those markers. By the twentieth century, the cemetery was over-grown and neglected although still in use. Natchitoches women banded together in 1904, founding the American Cemetery Association so that funds could be raised to preserve it. Soon the town got behind the effort, and their endeavor continues to benefit Natchitoches today. A joint venture that includes The American Cemetery Association, the National Park Service and Northwestern State University of Louisiana's Heritage Resources degree program continues the legacy of Natchitoches' preservation pioneers. Each fall, the benefit of years of hard work is seen when hundreds of red spider lilies resurrect, carpeting the shade under the spreading great oaks of the property, testament to the cemetery's diverse residents and stewards.

Spider lilies in living art, page 162

Natchitoches folk artist Clementine
Hunter featured the spider lilies found
in graveyards and around slave quarters
in her paintings.

Narcissus x odorus
Campernelle

For those who have ties to small towns or farms in the South, Campernelles are steeped in nostalgia. Memories are released with their scent, a sweet fragrance a bit lighter than a jonquil that is not soon forgotten. Depending on location, the foliage emerges somewhere between November to December, the bloom coming late winter to early spring. Campernelles abound across the South, but they seem to prefer abandoned home sites.

One sunny February day, my dog Fischer and I dug at just such a place in East Texas. The old cinder-block house, half of it now removed and the other half falling down, was surrounded by abundant patches of the lemon yellow flower. I had spotted the site some time earlier and gotten permission to dig some of the bulbs for propagation. As I pushed my shovel into one of the clumps, Fischer, who was still a pup, jumped in and amongst the flowers, then hid around the house, trying to tempt me to play with him instead of working. Fischer always made my adventures a bit more adventurous when he was a puppy. His lack of coordination coupled with his exuberance for life was not normally a problem, as he would just run around empty pieces of land while I dug bulbs. But once he got going, it was hard for him to slow down, much less stop. In this instance he was getting too close to the nearby dirt road for my comfort. I stopped my digging and called him back closer. This happened time and time again and apparently became part of

the game. Against all logic, cars literally fly down old dirt roads sending a wake of dust behind them, so you usually see them before you hear them. But this time, I was concentrating on my task, and all of a sudden Fischer was across the road and into the pasture on the other side. I heard something coming, and it was moving fast. I called to my dog, but by the time he obeyed my call, his return across the road put him right in front of the oncoming truck. It slammed on its brakes, locking them and sliding on the dirt. It stopped short, just inches in front of Fischer's nose. Fischer shrank down and back, looking at the bumper, then looking up at me, horror registering in grayish blue eyes for the first time. He solemnly ran back to me and sat, shaking, next to me. I apologized to the guy then promptly tied Fischer to a fence post and continued digging. Another time, Fisher and I were not so lucky. But that comes later.

Narcissus x odorus
Campernelle

Bloom
SIZE	1"-2" (2-4 cm)
COLOR	Golden petals and golden cups
SHAPE	Star-shaped with long round cup
TIME	Late February
FRAGRANCE	Strong, sweet smell

Foliage
EMERGE	December
FADE	May
HEIGHT	8"-16" (20-40 cm)

Bulb
SIZE (CIRCUMFERENCE)	3"-4" (8-10 cm)
COLOR	Light brown to dark, slightly darker vertical stripes, golden brown when dried after harsh external layer pulled off
SHAPE	Teardrop shape without a long neck

Narcissus x odorus 'Campernelle'

Care
SOIL	Slightly acidic
LIGHT	Full-sun
MOISTURE	Irrigation ok during dormant season, prefers well-drained soil but can handle wet feet
TEMPERATURE	Zone 7-10
PLANTING	Plant from September to December. Plant bulb at a depth that is equivalent to 2-3 times the height of bulb
DIVIDE/TRANSPLANT	May
VASE LIFE	1 week
FOLIAGE REMOVAL	May
NOTES	Prefers slightly acidic soil but is surprising in its ability to adapt to numerous sites

Goodwood Museum and Gardens
Tallahassee, Florida

Goodwood was formerly a cotton plantation owned by Hardy Croom in the 1830s. Croom's interest in horticulture led him to a number of botanical discoveries, including a pitcher plant that was named for him. The property was chosen specifically because of its fertile soil, abundant moisture and climate. With Hardy Croom's sudden death, his brother was left to finish construction of the grand main house in the mid-1840s. By that time, the plantation had grown to 8,000 acres and required a staff of 250 to maintain it. After the Crooms left Goodwood, the gardens declined under new ownership, but in 1886 Elizabeth Arrowsmith came to the home's rescue. Her twenty-five years there brought a formal design to the gardens to mimic those of England, her original home. The purchase of Goodwood by Mrs. Fanny Tiers in 1911 saw tremendous expansion of the exterior living spaces because Goodwood was used as a winter house for family and friends from New Jersey. Mrs. Tiers planted bulbs, including many heirloom daffodils, whose blooming coincided with the family's visits to the home. In 1925, Senator William C. Hodges and his wife, Margaret, purchased the property. After the Senator's death, Margaret re-married but brought her new husband, Tom Hood, to Goodwood where she lived for fifty-three years. By establishing the practice of leaving the lawns unmown, the Hoods allowed the thousands of bulbs planted over the years to naturalize, making it the showplace it is today. In 1972 Goodwood was added to the National Register of Historic Places.

At Goodwood Museum and Gardens, look for *Narcissus x odorus* (Campernelle)

—31—

Narcissus 'Grand Primo Citroniére'
Grand Primo

My truck has warped rotors. I get them re-worked and I can brake just fine for a while. But not long after, when I put the brakes on, I feel the familiar wobble again. I really should talk to a professional to see if we can put an end to it. But I know where it started. I can trace the wobble back to a Grand Primo incident.

My dog Fischer and I were driving back to the farm from Houston. A few towns north of the city, I saw a piece of land covered with Grand Primo daffodils. In the yard there was a "For Sale By Owner" sign with a phone number on it, so I decided to see if the plants might be for sale, too. I gave the owner a call, and he said he had no problem with me digging up all the bulbs I wanted. The lot was now considered commercial property, and he didn't think anyone building a business on it would miss the plants. Then he warned me about the neighbor next door, the best watchdog he'd ever seen. Mr. Cedric, he said, might just take it on himself to come over and find out what I was doing on the land. Sure enough, as soon as I'd pulled up in front, the neighbor came over and asked if he could help me, which is Texan for "What business do you have here, son?" I greeted him by name and introduced myself. I told him the owner and I had spoken about digging the bulbs before the property sold. Mr. Cedric said it would be okay for me to drive my pick-up a little closer to the bulbs to make it easier to haul them. I had parked by the road for fear I'd get stuck. He assured me it would all work out just fine, then he wandered back over to his house.

After a long afternoon of digging, the sun was quickly heading down over the horizon and the warm late winter day wasn't so warm anymore. Fischer was pretty sure we had all of the bulbs we needed, so I knocked as much mud off my boots as I could and we collapsed into the truck. I put it into drive and the wheels started spinning, but there was no movement from the truck. Uh, oh. This was a problem on several different fronts. For one thing, I'd realized too late the bulbs were interspersed with poison ivy and I was already starting to itch. Another issue was that my dog and I were both muddy and tired and hungry, which is easier for one of us to deal with than for the other. And on top of it all, it was getting cold. Very cold. Suddenly, Mr. Cedric was peering through the driver side window shaking his head. Now, while I am thankful for considerate people, sometimes I'd rather no one know when I get myself into these predicaments. I can call AAA and leave with my pride somewhat intact. It was too late for that now.

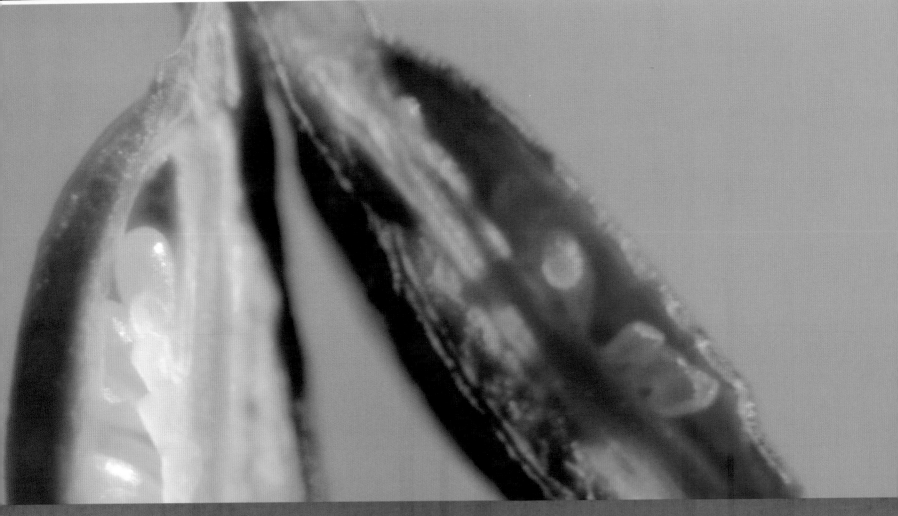

Mr. Cedric and I soon realized the more we worked on it, the deeper in the mud my back tires were sinking. The truck bed was heavy with the huge load of "free" plants along with a ton of dirt that clung to the bulbs. An hour and a half into the fiasco, Mr. Cedric and his buddy Butch—who had seen the action and wanted in on it—decided a chain was in order. Fischer was barking relentlessly, anxious to protect me from the untold number of people gathering to watch. His big paws were making mud pies on the windows of the truck, foggy breath and slobber adding to the dirt from the floorboards. "This cannot be good," I thought as I saw my axle being connected to another fellow's truck bumper. For some reason he thought it best to rev his motor to ramming speed before trying to jerk my truck out of the mucky trap. THUMP! Nothing happened. After thee more yanks, it worked. I feared my truck's frame would never be the same, but at least I could go home finally.

Fischer and I stopped at the town's gas station/grocery store to take care of a few things before heading home. Butch had beaten us there. I bought him a huge cup of coffee to match mine. I also picked up some cigars to replace the ones I'd seen Mr. Cedric polish off during our time together. His wife, in a wheel chair, answered the door when I stopped by, and she smiled a semi-toothless grin. "Oh, he's not here, young man. And you don't need to do anything to thank him. God bless you, and I'll give them to him."

The sun set and I drove north into a strong, cold wind. I later learned that wind brought with it one of the coldest nights on record. Fischer laid his head in my lap. In his sleep he wagged his tail a couple of times, and my truck wagged its tail, too.

Narcissus 'Grand Primo Citroniére'

Grand Primo

Bloom

SIZE	1" (2-3 cm)
COLOR	White with yellow cups
SHAPE	Cluster of small round blooms
TIME	Later Feb/Early March
FRAGRANCE	Strong, paperwhite smell but slightly sweeter

Foliage

EMERGE	November
FADE	May
HEIGHT	15"-22" (40-60 cm) Can grow much longer towards the end of the season

Bulb

SIZE (CIRCUMFERENCE)	8"-11" (20-28 cm)
COLOR	Light brown to dark, slightly darker vertical stripes, golden brown when dried after harsh external layer pulled off
SHAPE	Teardrop shape without a long neck

Narcissus
'Grand Primo citroniére'

Care

SOIL	Any
LIGHT	Full-sun
MOISTURE	Irrigation ok during dormant season, prefers well-drained soil but can handle wet feet
TEMPERATURE	Zone 7-10
PLANTING	Plant from September to December. Plant bulb at a depth that is equivalent to 2-3 times the height of bulb
DIVIDE/TRANSPLANT	May
VASE LIFE	1 week
FOLIAGE REMOVAL	May
NOTES	Grand Primo is probably the best *N. tazetta* for the South. Blooms from February to March. Foliage can grow even higher than listed when it begins to reach beyond competing plants for the sun in late spring

Stratford Hall Plantation
Stratford, Virginia

The Lee family of Virginia might be remembered primarily in American history for one of its sons, General Robert E. Lee. But he was actually the fourth generation of Lees to call the brick Georgian style Great House home. Thomas Lee, a successful land speculator and tobacco farmer and great-grandfather to Robert E. Lee, became acting Governor of Virginia while the area was still under British rule. At one time, the elder Lee owned over 16,000 acres in Virginia and neighboring Maryland. Two of his six sons were the only brothers to have signed the Declaration of Independence.

Robert E. Lee, born at Stratford Hall in 1807, was the last of his family born at the home to live into adulthood. He spent only his first four years of life at the plantation. In 1861, as an officer in the Army of Northern Virginia, Lee would write to his wife, Mary, that he wished he could buy back Stratford for his family. But he never would.

In 1929 the Lee family joined forces with a like-minded group of women to form the Robert E. Lee Memorial Association. The group raised funds to purchase and restore Stratford Hall. A year later, the Garden Club of Virginia began restoration of the gardens so that over 1600 acres along the Potomac River are now open to the public, including the West Garden which replicates an eighteenth century flower garden. Heirloom daffodils and roses, as well as other perennials and flowering bulbs that might have been grown at the height of the plantation's splendor show the variety of plant materials available to early American gentry. Guided tours of the home remind visitors of the part the Lee family played in America's independence as well as the hard choices they were forced to make when faced with war against fellow Virginians.

Leucojum aestivum
snowflake

T he white blooming snowflake brings me to a point about gardening that confuses some people: naturalizing *versus* perennial bulbs. Most gardeners want bulbs that are perennial, meaning they will return reliably from the original plant or bulb instead of having to be re-planted each year. Perennials are especially valuable in warmer climates where many bulbs are considered annuals, necessitating a yearly project of either digging and exposing the bulb to an artificial cool season (usually in the bottom bin of a refrigerator) or simply starting over each year with completely new bulbs to get a reliable bloom. Not all bulbs are perennial in all climates; but the snowflake bulb returns year after year from the Gulf Coast to Long Island. The other issue snowflakes bring up is whether or not a bulb will naturalize, spreading its progeny over a large area that increases annually. I love snowflakes because they not only return reliably each year, but they also multiply, populating a little geographic area or even a larger one if allowed. They propagate by both seed and division, filling in any holes until they become a dense sea of white bells nodding in the late winter/early spring breeze.

It is a memory of one of those oceans of snowflake blooms, one I wasn't expecting, that always makes me smile when I think of the flower. I often have the opportunity to speak to local garden clubs, and on a visit to speak to a group in the Old South, I was hosted by a lovely lady, Sweet Addie. Addie and the ladies asked if I'd go with them on a bulb hunt, so I got to town a bit early to visit several sites known to have heirloom bulbs in

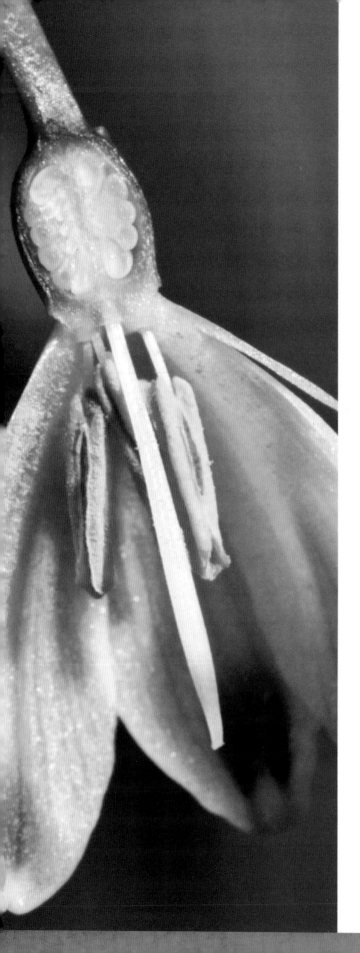

bloom. Sweet Addie was my driver. Each time she spied a stand of bulbs, she would slam on the brakes in the middle of the road. Large trucks were honking, swerving around us, or screeching to stop before they rear-ended our little troupe. She seemed absolutely oblivious to what was going on around us. We went on like this for some time, with my thoughts more on the inevitable whiplash I would soon be nursing than anything else. When we stopped to look at bulbs at the pet cemetery on our journey, I got some insight into how some of these beloved animals probably came to their final resting place, judging from my own automobile experience in the little town thus far.

Next, Sweet Addie decided it was time for me to visit her house, where she was preparing lunch for me. All of the sites so far had not been particularly exciting in a horticultural sense, although certainly memorable. We pulled down a dirt road bound for Sweet Addie's, turned off on to a more remote path and then onto a third, until I was totally turned around, happy after all that Sweet Addie had the wheel so I might actually find my way home.

Finally, we got to a fence out in the middle of a backcountry road and pulled on to her property, a plateau overlooking a ravine with a big river below us. What had to be at least a full acre of white snowflakes covered the level land before me. It was the most spectacular display of the little flowers I'd ever seen. The sight was almost good enough to make up for the fact that Thursdays at Sweet Addie's house is liver day and, what do you know, I landed at her house on Thursday. Although I am not a liver fan, I am a fan of the white snowflake and even more a fan of Sweet Addie for showing me the ones that had naturalized at her home. And by the way, the cake she made for my visit was spectacular. In the center was a bouquet of daffodils. I wondered if she knew daffodil bulbs are toxic to mammals? I figured if I hadn't keeled over from the liver, the daffodils probably wouldn't hurt me!

Leucojum spp.
snowflake

Bloom

SIZE	1"-2" (1-2 cm)
COLOR	White with little green dots at the tips of each petal
SHAPE	Cluster of small white bell-shaped flowers that dangle off of dainty flower stems
TIME	Late February/Early March
FRAGRANCE	None

Foliage

EMERGE	January
FADE	May
HEIGHT	11"-12" (30 cm)

Bulb

SIZE (CIRCUMFERENCE)	3"-5" (8-12 cm)
COLOR	Light brown to dark brown, skin does not peel easily
SHAPE	Teardrop with slightly curved neck

Leucojum aestivum

Care

SOIL	Any
LIGHT	Part-shade to full-sun
MOISTURE	Irrigation ok during dormant season, prefers well-drained soil but can handle wet feet
TEMPERATURE	Zone 7-10
PLANTING	Plant from September to December. Plant bulb at a depth that is equivalent to 2-3 times the height of bulb
DIVIDE/TRANSPLANT	May
VASE LIFE	1 week
FOLIAGE REMOVAL	May
NOTES	This will naturalize and is great for wetter, woodland conditions, although it blooms best in full-sun

Bayou Bend
Houston, Texas

Architect John F. Staub designed Bayou Bend in Houston, Texas, in 1927 for the three adult children of Governor Jim Hogg. Governor Hogg's daughter, Miss Ima, is known for her philanthropy in the Houston area. She also was a student and collector of early American decorative arts, and her former home has become one of the foremost museums dedicated to this field.

The gardens at Bayou Bend, an oasis in the midst of the fourth largest city in the United States, consist of connected garden rooms, including the White Garden and the Butterfly Garden, actually in the shape of a giant butterfly. Other garden rooms are named for impressive classical statues set in formal surroundings, such as the elegant Diana Garden. The flagstone paving the north terrace at the top of the Diana Garden boasts an early example of re-use. In 1927, the existing pink stone sidewalks in downtown Houston were removed to make way for a more modern material: concrete. The flagstones were taken to Bayou Bend to create the terrace floor.

Miss Ima generously donated Bayou Bend to the Museum of Fine Arts, Houston in 1957 for all to enjoy. This home is a tribute to her desire that "Bayou Bend may serve as a bridge to bring us closer to the heart of an American heritage which unites us."

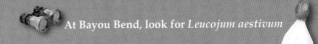

Snowflakes in living art, page 162

Narcissus 'Golden Dawn'
Golden Dawn

*T*he term "historic" is preferred over heirloom or antique by the American Daffodil Society and refers to plants introduced from 1576 – 1940. The early date comes from the beginning of Dutch experimentation with one of their favorite plants, Narcissus tazetta. Before the days of American or European football, plant hybridizing was considered a highly competitive sport, and no countries were more competitive than the English and the Dutch. Tulip bulbs are typically considered the primary game in this sport because of the "bulb bubble" that broke in the mid-1600s, causing economic ruin to some speculators who traded in the plants. But daffodils also played a part in the war of the bulbs between the two gardening countries. And as the Dutch concentrated their efforts more and more on tulips, English bulb farmers and horticulturists, as well as those in Ireland and Wales, created an ever-increasing list of daffodil hybrids for the public to consume. Just as in the earlier bulb fascination seen in Dutch Tulipamania, it became a symbol of leisure and wealth to own new hybrid daffodils that no one else in the neighborhood had. The Royal Horticultural Society, spurred along by Peter Barr, helped up the ante in the mid-to-late nineteenth century by promoting the plants grown by the Dutch with a catalog, an innovation that has been enticing home gardeners ever since.

When it comes to tolerating heat and humidity, bulbs closest to their original species seem happier than those highly hybridized half-breeds. Much like the downward spiral of animals that are "over-bred," plants often lose genetic disease- and insect-resistance the further they get from their initial state. In fact, a whole group of these hybrid daffodils were known as "Typhoid Mary" because of their susceptibility to rotting. The primary culprit was a white, trumpet daffodil named 'Madame de Graaff' that the Dutch de Graaff brothers hybridized in 1887. Interestingly, after moving to the United States, a member of this same family is responsible for one of the all-time favorite daffodils: 'Golden Dawn.' John Van Beck, a founder of the Florida Daffodil Society, deemed it a "must have" for modern Southern gardens.

Although 'Golden Dawn' is not technically a historic daffodil since its birth date is 1958, it can be considered an heirloom because it has naturalized around thousands of old homes for the last half century. The result of a marriage between tazetta and jonquil, its cups are large but with fewer blooms. Starting in mid March, for three weeks it will be covered with golden yellow flowers. They always remind me of spring, the same way the splashes of the bluegill and bass in the pond just outside my window at the little red cabin herald a new season of life.

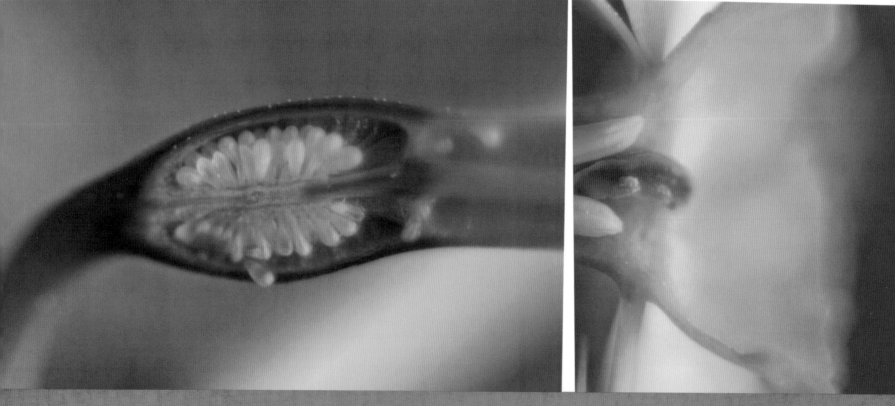

Narcissus 'Golden Dawn'
Golden Dawn

Bloom

SIZE	1"-2" (2-4 cm)
COLOR	Lemon yellow petals with gold cups
SHAPE	3-4 round blooms in a group
TIME	Mid March
FRAGRANCE	Sweet, thick smell

Foliage

EMERGE	November
FADE	May
HEIGHT	13"-18" (35-45 cm)

Bulb

SIZE (CIRCUMFERENCE)	4"-6" (10-16 cm)
COLOR	Light brown to dark, slightly darker vertical stripes, golden brown when dried after harsh external layer pulled off
SHAPE	Teardrop shape without a long neck

Narcissus 'Golden Dawn'

Care

SOIL	Any
LIGHT	Full-sun
MOISTURE	Irrigation ok during dormant season, prefers well-drained soil but can handle wet feet
TEMPERATURE	Zone 7-10
PLANTING	Plant from September to December. Plant bulb at a depth that is equivalent to 2-3 times the height of bulb
DIVIDE/TRANSPLANT	May
VASE LIFE	1 week
FOLIAGE REMOVAL	May
NOTES	Best yellow/golden combination for deeper South

Gladiolus byzantinus
Byzantine gladiola

Gladiolas are favorite old-timey plants, popular as long-lasting cut flowers. Most glads originated in Africa and thus enjoy the dry heat. The majority of glads not only prefer but require *well-drained soil, rotting when placed in a humid climate. One gladiola, however, does not mind heat or humidity because its roots are Mediterranean. The* Gladiolus byzantinus, *or Byzantine gladiola, is called "corn lily" or "cornflag" in that part of the world and has been noted since the seventeenth century growing alongside the grain in fields.*

My Byzantine glads came from several old home-sites, one of which was in northeast Texas. The lady offering them to me, I found out later, was only renting the house—so the plants were not technically hers to distribute. After letting me dig them, she told me she realized they were quite valuable. She did not give me a specific price for those I dug, but she obviously had one in mind, because when I handed her a generous amount of cash, she told me "you'll need to sharpen your pencil for these." Since I already had the plants in my hand, I pulled out a few more bills and made my retreat.

Once growing at the farm, the Byzantine glads quickly became a favorite of anyone seeing them in bloom. They are hard to resist, bright fuchsia funnel-shaped blooms alternating up the robust stalk. Strappy, clasping leaves alternate as well, possibly giving rise to the common name Jacob's ladder. Old House Gardens Nursery named it "Heirloom Bulb of the Year" in 2006, and complimented it by saying it has the look and resilience of a wildflower.

Each year these plants multiply with abandon. Not a true bulb, it is a "corm," a fleshy, swollen underground stem. Its corm is a well-designed water thermos,

extending the plant's viability when rain is scarce. Tiny new corms, called "cormels," emerge from the base of the old corm, providing for future plants from the dying one. It has been said that during the Second World War, the Dutch closely guarded the corms of gladiolas along with their tulip bulbs knowing they could be used as a last-resort food source when all else was gone. In my experience, the varmints of Northeast Texas also value them as a food source. I no longer store drying Byzantine gladiola corms in plastic trays in the field. Gophers and moles apparently view the trays as a lovely plate for their subterranean, Mediterranean evening meal.

Gladiolus byzantinus

Byzantine gladiola

Bloom

SIZE	Bloom spikes 15"-30" (40 to 60 cm) tall
COLOR	Brilliant magenta
SHAPE	linear, with larger individual funnel-shaped flowers on the bottom leading to smaller blooms at the top of the spike
TIME	Mid April
FRAGRANCE	None

Foliage

EMERGE	January
FADE	May
HEIGHT	17"-22" (45-60 cm)

Bulb

SIZE (CIRCUMFERENCE)	3"-5" (6-12 cm)
COLOR	Dark brown, rough textured husk. Sometimes peels off for more shiny area underneath; if no lower layer mottled white underneath of bulb appears
SHAPE	Flattened oval shape, officially a corm, not a bulb

Gladiolus byzantinus

Care

SOIL	Any
LIGHT	Full-sun
MOISTURE	Prefers well-drained soil, can handle irrigation
TEMPERATURE	Zone 7-10
PLANTING	Plant from September to December. Plant bulb at a depth that is equivalent to 2-3 times the height of bulb
DIVIDE/TRANSPLANT	May
VASE LIFE	2 weeks
FOLIAGE REMOVAL	May
NOTES	Gophers, moles, and voles may eat them within a day or two after the foliage emerges. Attracts many bumblebees and honey bees

Old City Cemetery
Lynchburg, Virginia

For more than two centuries, the Old City Cemetery in Lynchburg has been an ecumenical home to the community's dead. Although initially called a "Methodist cemetery," its first recorded resident in 1806 was actually a Presbyterian minister, James Tompkins. John Lynch, a founding father of the city, donated the land. Lynchburg's nickname "Tobacco Town" referred to the seventy tobacco-related businesses, which thrived because the town was the terminus of three different rail lines.

The cemetery is said to have more than 20,000 burial plots, three-quarters of which represent people of African descent. The largest influx of interments occurred in conjunction with the Civil War. Lynchburg, with a population of 6,000, tended up to 10,000 soldiers in its thirty makeshift hospitals at one time during the four years of the war, with estimates of 20,000 admissions. Three thousand of the patients are said to have died there. The Confederate Section of the cemetery is final resting place to more than 2,200 soldiers.

Stories of both the human and botanical residents are told at this National Register historic location. Jane Baber White, along with others who believed the legends and lore associated with the cemetery should not be lost, came together to document those stories with museums (five small ones on the property) and several publications that keep the traditions of Old City Cemetery alive. The plants that call the cemetery home are as diverse as its occupants. Family burial plots are often small private gardens. The property, known for its hundreds of antique roses, is listed as an official American Daffodil Society Display Garden. As director of the cemetery for twenty-seven years, a historian and an avid gardener, Jane traces both family and fauna and gives them life, using only plants that might have been found in eighteenth-century Virginia.

Antique roses at Old City Cemetery

Hippeastrum x johnsonii
hardy amaryllis, Johnson's amaryllis, St. Joseph's lily

According to Scott Ogden, in his book Garden Bulbs for the South *hardy amaryllis was not given the botanical name* Amaryllis *because of theft. Not that anyone stole the* plant, *but the* name *was taken from this heirloom and given instead to a South African plant family. So* Hippeastrum, *or "horse star," was collared on this plant, possibly because early botanists thought the flower's shape resembled a horse's head. You might see it, but it's a stretch as far as I'm concerned. We do know that it was named after an English watchmaker who gardened in Lancashire, a Mr. Johnson. Recorded at the turn of the nineteenth century, this earliest hybrid* Hippeastrum *is a cross between two South American plants,* H. reginae *from Peru and* H. vitatum *out of Brazil, that were gathered a hundred years before by explorers. The best of each of these two plants went to create the rich red prolific trumpets, the exterior white stripes that contrast so beautifully, and the black coating on the bulbs which, Ogden reminds us, keeps it from being vulnerable to what is the kiss of death for some bulbs: heavy clay soils.*

Hardy where other "amaryllis" might not be, *H. x johnsonii* tolerates cold well and can be found around old structures throughout Europe and North America. It is especially prevalent along fencerows and crumbling steps that lead to nowhere. The bulbs multiply on top of themselves, thirty to forty blooms in one clump. The hardy amaryllis prefers afternoon shade, tolerates poor soil and poor drainage, but doesn't like to dry out for long periods. Drought might not kill the plant immediately, but it will discontinue blooming. If more favorable conditions return quickly, it will resume blooming. It takes a couple of years to establish hardy amaryllis, but its

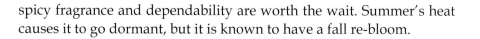

spicy fragrance and dependability are worth the wait. Summer's heat causes it to go dormant, but it is known to have a fall re-bloom.

There are new hybrids of amaryllis in Holland, the primary grower, and Israel is fast rising as a contender for hybridization of new and exciting flowers. Amaryllis bulbs have long been a popular Christmas gift, the red bloom a perfect seasonal favorite. Plant them in the garden after the chance of freeze is past for a gift that gives over and over. It might not *look* like a work-horse, but hardy amaryllis and its domesticated kin certainly *act* like one!

Hippeastrum x johnsonii

hardy amaryllis, Johnson's amaryllis,
St. Joseph's lily

Bloom

SIZE	2"-5" (7-12 cm)
COLOR	Red with white stripes
SHAPE	Robust long trumpet shape
TIME	Mid April
FRAGRANCE	Slight, almost spicy

Foliage

EMERGE	April
FADE	First freeze/November
HEIGHT	8"-12" (20-30 cm)

Hippeastrum x johnsonii

Bulb

SIZE (CIRCUMFERENCE)	7"-9" (18-22 cm)
COLOR	Brown
SHAPE	Round bulb that tapers into a thick flattened 1" long neck

Care

SOIL	Well-prepared, but also seen in standing water or in dry spots
LIGHT	Part-shade to full-sun
MOISTURE	Irrigation ok during dormant season, prefers well-drained soil but can handle wet feet
TEMPERATURE	Zone 7-10
PLANTING	Plant when there is no danger of hard freeze. Water if planting in the heat of summer. Plant bulb with a portion of the neck out of the ground and the bulb completely below the soil surface
DIVIDE/TRANSPLANT	In late winter early spring (protect from hard freezes)
VASE LIFE	1 week
FOLIAGE REMOVAL	After first frost or freeze
NOTES	This bulb actually goes through a summer dormancy as well as a winter dormancy. During the summer, the foliage begins to look pale. Shade from the hottest part of the day and irrigation can resolve this problem

Crinum

'Mrs. James Hendry'

*A*t first, I was scared to try to identify crinums. As a group, the strappy leaves of these bulbed beauties seem identical. Now, whether by the leaf margins, the size, the color, or by the bulb itself, I can at least put crinums into a specific family, if not identify the exact plant. Most make their homes in spots that are periodically soggy and aren't picky about the soil type. The bulbs and roots extend several feet into the earth, their scapes — or flower stalks — reaching just as high above the ground level. Our native crinum lily, C. americanum can be found in swampy areas from Georgia south to Florida and west to Texas.

Crinums are grown in gardens all over the United States, but few thrive outside the Southern states. Most species originated in Africa so they must be protected in areas where the ground regularly freezes. Historic garden crinums were introduced by plant collectors in the mid-nineteenth century. Sailors, traders or even African slaves could be responsible for crinums now found along the east coast of America. However, 'Mrs. James Hendry,' a hybrid from the early 1900s, was introduced in a German settlement in Florida by horticul-turist Henry Nehrling. It is a rare find. When I stumble on a display of the pink-tinged blooms, I recognize that the original gardener at the site knew his or her stuff. So when I came to a Victorian home near Brenham, Texas, and saw the mass of 'Mrs. James Hendry' crinums growing there, I appreciated their history. I requested permission to dig some of

the plants for production and went to work, careful to find the perimeter of the bulbs' roots so I didn't disturb them too much. Thankfully the crinums had been treated well and had fifteen years of good garden soil as their home. It was July in central Texas, 100-plus degrees in temperature and humidity. Unlike me, the fragrance and beauty of the blooms seemed undeterred by the oppressing heat. Once I isolated a large clump with a bulb as big as my boot, and I worked for almost twenty minutes just to loosen it. I felt like a real bulb hunter when I got that one out! It was worth every drop of perspiration. The delightful fragrance was my companion all night in my room. And since this crinum repeats blooming from spring until fall, I look forward to getting more of them into people's hands.

Another time, when I was digging crinums in central Texas, I was not quite so lucky. I was in Schulenburg with a buddy of mine for a presentation to a group. It is a great town, home of the Schulenburg Festival the first weekend in August. The festival hosts a rodeo and parade, a chili and barbeque cook-off, country music artists, cow chip toss, and golf and softball tournaments. Schulenburg is also known for its incredible "painted churches," wooden clapboard and steepled buildings built by the German and Czech immigrants in this part of Texas. Walking into these humble buildings does not prepare you for what's next: transportation to a European cathedral with intricate carvings and elegant trompe l'oeil effects that dare you to touch to see if they are real. Anyway, I saw a stand of crinums in the ditch right there in town, so I went to the city hall to ask if I could take a few. I have a tendency to get frustrated with people who are stand-offish, and since I was an outsider in this small community, I was getting that "hit the road, bud" vibe from the good folks at the city hall. I've found that if I can establish a common bond with people, they usually come around. So I started rattling off my newfound wealth of local information. They were not impressed. Then they noticed my college ring. Soon they were rattling off *their* information about Texas A&M, naming the family members and friends who attended school there. Ten minutes later I had the business card of one of the head guys at city hall with instructions to produce this as a free pass should anyone question my mission. I was off to the ditch to dig, with the card in my pocket and high hopes of retrieving a few of the crinums of Schulenburg.

My buddy and I dug. And dug. And dug some more. For forty-five minutes we worked in that awful clay, each on our own bulb, till we finally decided it best to join forces on a single one, determined to free

it for the greater good of humanity. And in that ditch, I learned a valuable lesson: No matter how much bulb you can see, there's most likely a lot left unseen.

I also learned something else that day: There are two main sounds that a bulb makes when being released from its earthly home. One sound is a few tiny *pop-pop-pops,* like little fireworks. Those are the little feeder roots letting go of their hold. Then there is another sound, one that no bulb hunter wants to hear. It is a single loud *thump,* followed by two more *thumps* as our behinds returned to the ground! As a survival technique, the plant's foliage will rip away, leaving the bulb to re-grow new leaves and continue on its merry way.

Crinum

'Mrs. James Hendry'

Bloom

SIZE	4" (10 cm by 10 cm)
COLOR	Blush
SHAPE	Large petals that split open and furl back exposing stamens and pistils
TIME	May to September
FRAGRANCE	Fresh soap, but a little more sharp and pleasant

Foliage

EMERGE	March
FADE	First freeze/November
HEIGHT	13"-20" (35-50 cm)

Bulb

SIZE (CIRCUMFERENCE)	10"-14" (25-35 cm)
COLOR	Brown with flaky skin
SHAPE	Round bulbs that taper into a long, sometimes highly curved neck. Bottom portion of bulb is flat, but this is not a large area and occurs below much of the curvature of the bulb

Crinum
'Mrs. James Hendry'

Care

SOIL	Any
LIGHT	Part shade to full sun
MOISTURE	Irrigation ok during dormant season, prefers well-drained but can handle wet feet
TEMPERATURE	Zone 7-10
PLANTING	Plant when no danger of hard freeze. Water if planting in the heat of summer. Plant bulb with a portion of the neck out of the ground and the bulb completely below the soil surface
DIVIDE/TRANSPLANT	In late winder early spring (protect from hard freezes)
VASE LIFE	1 week
FOLIAGE REMOVAL	After first frost or freeze
NOTES	Blooms proliferously in the spring, intermittently in the summer, and again in the fall. Large foliage, but the blooms tower above the foliage and are great for cut flowers

Habranthus robustus
Argentine rain lily

Sometimes the "Argentine" in this rain lily name also refers to another white rain lily (Zephryanthes candida) *that is found in South America. As I'll explain later,* Z. candida *has played a significant role in modern landscapes. I believe this bulb,* Habranthus robustus *will soon play just as significant a role, but that's not why I like it so much. This rain lily is a trooper. It came through for me on a humid, 100+ degree-day, and I'm confident it will do the same for home gardeners. The blooms are a cheerful response to a rainstorm, and these happy lilies also attract beneficial insects.*

They may appear in a solid massing clump, and also as individuals. Because the bulb propagates so easily from seed, little individual bulbs often start popping up all around the garden. They are very adaptable. *H. robustus* grows in both full-sun and in some shade. I have not seen the bulb blooming well in the full shade of evergreen canopy trees; but I have seen it under thickets of roses where very little light was coming in. It wasn't weak or leggy in this situation; in some cases, it seemed to prefer these areas to the full-sun spots.

The buds emerge a few days after a cooling rain. We first see little spots of color nestled deep in the foliage of the plant. Each day the bud grows taller and taller, and before you know it, the bud opens wide into a large white bloom with pink edging. Each bloom lasts for a few days. If you include the anticipation, bud stage, and bloom, you can have a week of enjoyment out of each flower. When gardeners

tell me this isn't long enough, I encourage them to remember this process can repeat four to six times, spring till fall. The many splashes of color during our hot summers excites everyone who happens upon this carefree rain lily.

After the bloom fades, there is still more to come. It doesn't take long—about two weeks—and a seed-pod will form where the bloom once was. These seed-pods break open to reveal hundreds of papery amaryllis seeds (*Habranthus robustus* is in the *Amaryllis* family). The seeds are very fertile, each maturing into an exact replica of the parent. To best ensure the continued propagation of your rain lily seedlings, collect the seed-pods, scratch the soil lightly, and spread the seeds around. Cover them with just a bit of soil so you cannot see the seed anymore, and then keep the area moist for several days. It is very easy to break the whole seed-pod off as you wander through the garden in the morning, shake the seeds directly from the pod where you want your new lilies to grow, and rake some dirt over the area with your boot. Soon you will have many of these happy rain lilies blooming all around your garden!

Habranthus robustus
Argentine rain lily

Bloom

SIZE	2"-3" (5-7cm)
COLOR	Blush
SHAPE	Trumpet
TIME	May to September
FRAGRANCE	None

Foliage

EMERGE	March
FADE	First freeze/November
HEIGHT	3"-8" (10-20 cm)

Bulb

SIZE (CIRCUMFERENCE)	2.5"-3.5" (6-9 cm)
COLOR	Brownish
SHAPE	Round with occasional long neck

Habranthus robustus

Care

SOIL	Well-prepared soil area
LIGHT	Part shade to full-sun
MOISTURE	Irrigation ok during dormant season, prefers well-drained soil but can handle wet feet
TEMPERATURE	Zones 7-10
PLANTING	Plant when there is no danger of hard freeze. Water if planting in the heat of summer. Plant bulb with a portion of the neck out of the ground and the bulb completely below the soil surface
DIVIDE/TRANSPLANT	Whenever desired, but protect from hard freezes and water well if dividing during hot, dry period
VASE LIFE	3 days
FOLIAGE REMOVAL	After first frost or freeze.
NOTES	Habranthus robustus is considered one the best rain lilies. Blooms quickly forming seed pods; blooming sized bulb can be grown from seed in one year. Trumpet-shaped flowers are often called lilies, even if they're not botanically in the Lilium family

Great Bulbs for
MANY AREAS

36in 91.4cm

24in 61cm

12in 30.5cm

AUTUMN   SUMMER

GROUP II

OXBLOOD LILY • CEMETERY WHITE IRIS • SPANISH BLUEBELL
PARROT GLADIOLA • PINK RAIN LILY • ELLEN BOSANQUET
WHITE SPIDER LILY • TIGER LILY • NAKED LADY

AUTUMN   SUMMER

This group is home to the most bulbs, since most bulbs are generally suited for most areas. In this group you will find bulbs that do well, but have a few extra requirements. Soil adaptability, irrigation needs, or sensitivity to extreme weather often play a factor. Some bulbs are grouped here because their blooms are not as big or as prolific. Take for example the oxblood lily (*Rhodophiala bifida*). For many reasons, we should include it in the first group of superstars. It is a highly adaptable bulb that produces striking red trumpet shaped blooms each fall. It multiplies freely, does not need to be refrigerated, and does not need to be divided to keep the blooms coming. But, critics contend each flower lasts only a few short days. In reality, this short bloom only happens if it blooms just before an onslaught of hot, dry, sunny weather. There are other powerful rebuttals to those who would so quickly cast off this treasure; but because of this strike against it, the plant goes into Group II. So remember, if you see plants included in this group, don't automatically discount them from your garden. Simply consider your particular landscaping desires, then match those with specific bulbs that meet both cultivation needs (environment) and aesthetic requirements. This systematic method will always yield the best results.

Rhodophiala bifida
oxblood lily, schoolhouse lily

Several firsts have occurred in my efforts to resurrect heirloom bulbs:
- *my first bulb experience, a red tulip*
- *the first bulb I found when I was writing my business plan, the double Roman*
- *and the first bulb I searched for specifically and rescued for propagation, the oxblood lily, also known as the surprise lily. (Who wouldn't go hunting for that?)*

That first rescue hunt took me to a little German community less than an hour away from Texas A&M, where I went to school. I'd heard this used to be the third largest town in Texas, but there wasn't much there anymore. In the early 1900s the area was littered with cotton plantations. The town's success rode on the back of the Southern Pacific rail line that hauled cotton to the East Coast. It was known for its beautiful Victorian homes built during the cotton era. Each fall, the crimson blooms of the oxblood lily, *Rhodophiala bifida,* emerged around the oak trees and next to those stately homes. When I began my search for the oxblood lily, also called the schoolhouse lily because of the timing of its bloom at the start of the school year, my mentor and friend, Dr. Bill Welch, who had done extensive research on the heirloom plants found in Texas, shared his knowledge with me. Although many people believe the oxblood lily to be native to Central Texas, it was actually an introduced plant from Argentina brought by colonist and German-born botanist/ farmer Peter Heinrich Oberwetter. Upon Oberwetter's arrival to Texas in the late

1840s, he started a collection of native rain lilies and began sending them to friends all over the world. When the Civil War broke out, he sided with the Union, probably because political upheaval had sent him packing from Germany in the first place. Like many other German colonists, Oberwetter fled to Mexico to escape persecution. Most likely in Mexico he first saw a version of the oxblood lily that became one of his passions. Returning to Texas after the war, he brought with him a number of different bulbs, but the oxblood lily is the plant most commonly associated with his legacy as a plantsman.

On my bulb hunt in this little German community I met the Parrot Lady. Since I knew the oxblood lily had been seen at sites in the town, I started asking around to find out specifically where it was growing. When I described the wide bladed, strappy foliage and blood-red blooms appearing in the late summer, a couple of locals pointed me in the direction of a home that had been abandoned for some time. They told me "an outsider" from Houston recently bought the neglected house and was planning to do major renovations, including landscaping. They felt sure she would share the plants on her property, if they were still there.

Well, the oxblood lily was there all right. But that house was scary, and I wasn't real excited about going to the door. The balcony in front was caving in, paint was peeling, and there was an awful screeching sound coming out of the house. It looked and sounded like a haunted house from a horror movie. The lady welcomed me at the door and graciously invited me in to an empty, dark hallway. The screeching sounds were deafening. There were parrots and cages everywhere. She told me she was commuting daily to her job in Houston almost two hours away, bound and determined to bring back the house to its former glory. And no, she did not mind sharing the lilies at all. So I dug a good start of the plant and headed back to College Station.

A few weeks later, I was at Dr. Welch's home and saw a painting I'd never noticed on the wall. It was a stately Victorian two-story with a balcony across the front, and a carriage and horses in the foreground that told me the scene was from the late 1800s. There on Dr. Welch's wall was the Parrot Lady's house. He explained that a friend of his had grown up in that little town and when he found the painting on a visit there, he just liked the look of the house. Seeing the house in its heyday, I pictured oxblood lilies along the front, their heads hanging in the heat of an early autumn day in Texas. And I hoped the Parrot Lady would follow through with her plan for the old home.

Rhodophiala bifida
oxblood lily, schoolhouse lily

Bloom

SIZE	1"-3" (4 to 6 cm)
COLOR	Dark red, vermillion
SHAPE	Skinny and pointed trumpet shapes with yellow anthers that protrude slightly from opening of bloom.
TIME	Mid September
FRAGRANCE	None

Foliage

EMERGE	October after September bloom
FADE	Late April
HEIGHT	7"-12" (20-30 cm)

Bulb

SIZE (CIRCUMFERENCE)	5"-8" (15-20 cm)
COLOR	Black, shiny black when mature. When too many layers are peeled, white bulb appears
SHAPE	Usually round or oval shaped; quickly tapers into a long neck that has distinctive curves

Rhodophiala bifida

Care

SOIL	Any
LIGHT	Part-shade to full-sun
MOISTURE	Irrigation ok during dormant season, prefers well-drained soil but can handle wet feet
TEMPERATURE	Zone 7-10
PLANTING	Plant bulb from late spring to fall. Plant bulb at a depth that is equivalent to 2-3 times the height of bulb. The top of the neck can stick out of the top of the soil
DIVIDE/TRANSPLANT	April/May
VASE LIFE	1 week
FOLIAGE REMOVAL	April/May
NOTES	Blooms will last much longer when not hit by a harsh week of late summer heat. They can bloom in full shade areas, if the location receives sun in the winter when the foliage needs it most

NARCISSUS:
A few favorite daffodils

N. 'Orange Phoenix' (Butter and Eggs)

N. jonquilla (jonquil)

N. pseudonarcissus (Lent lily)

N. bulbcodium (Hoop Petticoat)

N. x medioluteus (April Beauty, Twin sisters)

N. 'Telemonius Plenus' (Van Sion)

N. "Incomparabilis Group"

N. papyraceus (paper whites)

Belmont Estate
Fredericksburg, Virginia

Although the exact date this Georgian-style home was built is unknown, historians have narrowed the time-frame to somewhere between 1785 and the turn of the eighteenth century. When American born artist Julius Garibaldi Melchers and his wife Corrine bought the estate in 1916, the home had seen much change, both as a physical building and from its vantage point above the Rappahannock River. Five decades before, during the Civil War, the Union Army of the Potomac planned a crossing of the river near Belmont on five pontoon boats engineers constructed for the march south to Richmond. But the boats arrived late. General Lee and his Army of Northern Virginia were prepared, choosing this location to make their stand against the advancing troops. What ensued that December day of 1862 was a bloodbath for the Union Army and is now known as The Battle of Fredericksburg.

When the Melchers got to Belmont, it was in bad shape, although apparently from neglect, not war. The couple worked to make it a haven for family and friends, restoring the home and surrounding gardens. Corinne Melchers, an artist herself, established a small working farm and the beautiful gardens now found at Belmont. Triangular beds in the south lawn were filled with flowering bulbs and roses, a line of boxwood defining the

Daffodils in living art, page 162

Bartram's Garden

Philadelphia, Pennsylvania

America's oldest botanical garden, this farm was originally bought in 1728 by self-taught John Bartram who is considered to be America's first botanist. The Bartram family called the estate home for more than 125 years, each generation building on the legacy of Mr. Bartram and his desire to record all plants native to the New World. Bartram named several plants in honor of his friend and co-founder of the American Philosophical Society, Benjamin Franklin. One of these plants—a small tree called *Franklinia alatamaha* that may be seen at the garden today—was saved from extinction by Bartram on a botanical trip through Georgia in 1765. Another tree that calls the garden home is the oldest ginkgo tree in the United States.

The Bartram family is credited for bringing over 200 native American plants into cultivation, creating the first commercial plant nursery and subsequent catalog to advertise their innovation. Seeds and plants from the Bartrams went all over the world and, closer to home, even George Washington is recorded as ordering from Bartram's Garden for Mount Vernon.

A visit to the eighteenth-century stone house, a National Historic Landmark, includes the expansive gardens, wildflower meadow, wetlands area and a scenic trail that follows alongside the Schuylkill River. Guests get the rare opportunity to gain insight into the genius mind of Bartram, a man who made his life's goal one of conser-

At Bartram's Garden, look for *N.* 'Telemonius Plenus'

Franklinia alatamaha

Iris albicans
cemetery white iris, white flag

When heading into a town for the first time on a bulb hunt, I make it a point to start at the local cemetery. In my experience, whatever I find at the local cemetery will likely be found at old homesites throughout the town. By the same token, if the plots at the cemetery do not have bulbs, neither will the homes. When that's the case, I knock the dust off my boots and move on to the next town. Almost without exception, though, I find the bearded style cemetery white iris peeking out from behind headstones upon my arrival to an old cemetery. This plant is so prevalent in North America that some people believe it to be a native. It is actually from the sandy Arabian Peninsula. And while I'm not sure anyone remembers the real reason Iris albicans dots graveyards, there is a legend that the tradition began with Muslim soldiers. In their battles, it is said, they carried the rhizomes of this plant from their homeland in their pockets, marking the graves of their brothers as they fell in battle.

The tradition continued with the Spanish explorers, so much of Florida is covered with the fluttering ghosts each spring.

Unlike the bog-loving Louisiana iris, the lower growing cemetery whites don't mind drying out during the summer. This independence is probably the real reason we find white iris flagging graves. If additional watering is needed while the plants are in bloom, water the foliage only. A sprinkler may damage the paper-thin petals. Cemetery white irises herald springtime and are often seen side-by-side with a blue form called 'Madonna' iris that is closely related. Both of these bearded irises are recognized by the hairy yellow "beard" found on the lower three petals. Three upper petals curve to tent the interior of the bloom, which is mildly fragrant. The plants are sterile, meaning they do

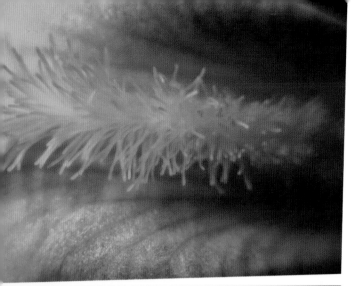

not have seeds capable of production. Although they can be divided any time of the year, it's best to divide them right after blooming or in the fall. They prefer to be left alone.

There are many native irises in America. The original Americans used the plant extensively. Threads from the leaves of the purple *Iris douglasiana,* indigenous to California and Oregon, were fashioned into "deer ropes." Webs made of the delicate ropes were woven as a net on deer trails, entangling antlers of the bucks as they passed along the path. The Pomo tribe called this method of hunting "Ba-dik." *Iris missouriensis,* native in much of the western U.S., was prized for its medicinal value. The Shoshone people created teas and poultices to treat everything from kidney disease to toothaches to venereal disease. Maybe if Europeans had known more about the native iris' healing qualities, there would have been fewer graves for the white cemetery iris to mark.

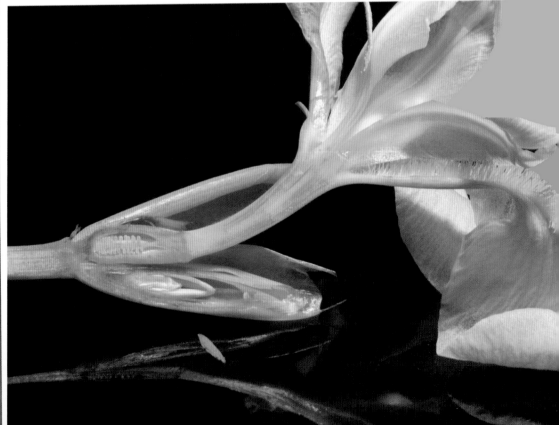

Iris albicans
cemetery white iris, white flag

Bloom

SIZE	3"-6" (8-14 cm)
COLOR	White, with yellow colored veins closer to the throat
SHAPE	Bearded iris appearance, outer petals lay out and furl down and inner petals curl up
TIME	Mid March
FRAGRANCE	None

Foliage

EMERGE	Year round
FADE	Slightly in the heat of summer
HEIGHT	7"-12" (20-30 cm)

Bulb

SIZE (CIRCUMFERENCE)	2"-4" (6-10 cm)
COLOR	Beige to dark brown
SHAPE	Long, cylindrical, lays flat

Iris albicans

Care

SOIL	Any
LIGHT	Part-shade to full-sun
MOISTURE	Prefers dry and or well-drained soil, but can handle irrigation
TEMPERATURE	Zone 7-10
PLANTING	Plant when there is no danger of hard freeze. Water if planting in the heat of summer. Plant bulb with a portion of the neck out of the ground and the bulb completely below the soil surface
DIVIDE/TRANSPLANT	Fall
VASE LIFE	1 week
FOLIAGE REMOVAL	Fall
NOTES	Called cemetery whites because they thrive in cemeteries with dry, cracked soil. They reliably bloom every spring

Melrose Estate

Natchez, Mississippi

In a strategic position above the Mississippi River, by the turn of the century Natchez had grown from a tiny French outpost at the end of the Natchez Trace to a town of 2,500 residents. An influx of immigrants from Europe and the northern U.S. poured in to take advantage of the burgeoning opportunities found there. With this increase in affluence and agriculture came another segment of population: hundreds of African slaves. The "Forks of the Road" market in Natchez grew into one of the largest slave markets in the South.

John T. McMurran, an attorney born in Pennsylvania, heard of Natchez from a friend and moved to the community in 1825. A few years later he married Mary Louisa Turner, the daughter of a Mississippi State Supreme Court justice. The couple began work on the Greek revival mansion, Melrose, in 1841. By that time, the McMurrans had two children and a prosperous law practice, were well-traveled and propertied, and owned five cotton plantations totaling over 9,600 acres. Three hundred and twenty-five slaves worked the properties.

A well-documented Cultural Landscape Report for the Natchez National Historical Park quotes personal family letters and tells us of the grounds at Melrose. The diary of architect Thomas K. Wharton speaks of the gardens "surpassing all....looking all the world like an English park..." with magnolias, camellias, cherry laurels, boxwoods, roses, tulips, hyacinths and jonquils.

Like most Southern plantations, Melrose was dealt both a personal and a financial blow by the Civil War. The Kellys, new owners in the early 1900s, worked to bring the glory back. Ethel Kelly added azaleas, hydrangeas, spireas and other blooming shrubs along with a vast array of perennials and blooming bulbs, restoring the graceful Southern garden that makes Melrose a real horticultural gem.

Hyacinthoides hispanica
Spanish bluebells, *syn. Endymion hispanicus*

On a garden tour to Europe, I had an experience that reminded me of the old adage "One man's trash is another man's treasure." My group had the privilege of visiting Les Vaux, private gardens developed over the past four decades by Lady Guthrie. They were the most incredible gardens I've ever seen. The house and gardens are on the Isle of Jersey, the most southern of the British Channel Islands. Because of the island's location one hundred miles from mainland England and less than twenty miles west of the French coastline, the climate is mild. The island was occupied by the Germans during World War II, so the residents annually celebrate their Liberation Day in May. Les Vaux plays a role in the tour offered to mark the holiday. Under Lady Guthrie's loving care, the gardens have evolved and now feature fine specimen trees from all over the world. On my visit, the tiny lady trekked with my companion and me across the Rozel Valley, up and down steep embankments as if they were flat as a tabletop. At the end of our garden tour, she asked if we'd like to see one of her favorite trees. She bragged on its ability to bloom constantly and reproduce prolifically. When she stopped in front of a mimosa, we tried to conceal our grins. This invasive Asian, known in the southern U.S. for its aggressive behavior, was her prized possession!

On leaving Lady Guthrie's home, we traveled to the Chelsea Flower Show. If you've not experienced this wonder, I urge you to plan on it, if at all possible. For a week each year since 1824, the annual show has incredible displays that demonstrate the beauty of nature harnessed by man. The flowers there are often the latest hybrids, cultivated

specifically to accomplish a desired trait, whether a certain color, a tight flower bud, or maybe a multi-layered bloom. But these flowers are not necessarily designed to survive in a garden setting. When we talk about low maintenance, hardy, heirloom bulbs, we should adopt a different aesthetic, a different definition of what we call beauty. The bulbs seen at Chelsea are not the ones found naturalizing down a fencerow. But in an open pasture, or along a forest's edge, heirloom bulbs make a display tough to beat. The hardiness of these bulbs gives them a different sort of attractiveness. It is this natural beauty that I saw in the fields of English bluebells, *H. non-scripta,* found throughout the landscape of Great Britain. While commonplace to Brits, we viewed the bulbs with awe, amazed at their natural beauty.

Although we rarely have the good fortune to grow English bluebells on this side of the pond, we do find success with their cousins, the Spanish bluebells. An heirloom bulb in the lily family, Spanish bluebells lack the perfume of the English ones. Another difference in the two can be found in the way they carry their blooms: the English have most of their flowers on one side of the stem, while the Spanish blooms dangle all the way around. Bluebells make themselves at home in a woodland setting where tightly clustered, modern, double-flowered annual hyacinths would appear gaudy and unnatural. The plants only get about 18" tall, and the bloom spike of azure-blue bells returns every spring. Their broad leaves go dormant in the summer's heat, but pairing them with a summer blooming perennial such as phlox, native salvia, or the purple-leafed oxalis covers seasonal bare spots. This type of companioning—what bulb growers Brent and Becky Heath of Virginia call adding "shoes and socks" plants to finish off the bed—not only extends bloom time of seasonal favorites, but adds texture, layers and richness to the landscape.

Most sources say Spanish bluebells hail from Spain, of course, as well as Portugal. Colonists are assumed to have tucked the tiny white bulbs into their belongings, bringing a piece of their homeland on their journey. However, the U.S. Department of Agriculture lists *Hyacinthoides hispanica* as a native in several places in North America, including Virginia, Delaware, Washington state, and parts of Canada. Could it be that when Spanish explorers came to the New World, they happened upon a meadow filled with nodding bluebells, kidnapped the little bulbs and promptly adopted them as their own? Another popular old saying tells us a prophet in his own land is not appreciated. Maybe a bluebell isn't either.

Hyacinthoides hispanica
Spanish bluebells, *syn. Endymion hispanicus*

Bloom

SIZE	3"–8" (15 to 20 cm)
COLOR	Blue
SHAPE	Bell-shaped with the end of the petals slightly curling up. Linear with larger bells on bottom of the stem, smaller toward the stop, and tight buds at the very top
TIME	April
FRAGRANCE	None

Foliage

EMERGE	November
FADE	May
HEIGHT	13"–18" (35–45 cm)

Bulb

SIZE (CIRCUMFERENCE)	3"–6" (10–14 cm)
COLOR	Yellowish, light brown bulbs
SHAPE	Almost completely round, slightly flattened

Hyacinthoides hispanica

Care

SOIL	Any
LIGHT	Part-shade to full-sun
MOISTURE	Irrigation ok during dormant season, prefers well-drained soil but can handle wet feet
TEMPERATURE	Zone 7–10
PLANTING	Plant from September to December. Plant bulb at a depth that is equivalent to 2-3 times the height of bulb
DIVIDE/TRANSPLANT	May
VASE LIFE	1 week
FOLIAGE REMOVAL	May
NOTES	Seen in England and all over the South, this bulb has sturdy blue bells. The foliage is attractive by itself and signals the coming spring

Eudora Welty House
Jackson, Mississippi

American author Eudora Welty called this Tudor Revival-style house her home from 1925 until she passed away at the age of ninety-two. Built by her father, the house was donated to the State of Mississippi at her death and is now designated as a National Historic Landmark. Welty's five decades of success in literature brought her acclaim as both a novelist and short story writer, and several of her works were also made into plays. Tales of Depression-era poverty in the South came to be her hallmark, but the gardens of her home paradoxically illustrate abundance. Welty's mother, Chestina, created the garden's plan. Eudora continued to refer to the landscape of her home as "my mother's garden" long after her mother was gone. The pair worked side-by-side, installing many bulbs, shrubs and other blooming plants that insured year-round color and interest.

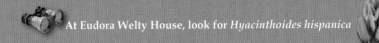

Gladiolus dalenii
parrot gladiola, Natal lily

Rescuing heirloom bulbs all over the country can be difficult. I often go hundreds of miles tracking down a tiny shred of hearsay with little sleep and even less success. But uncovering a plant all-but-extinct except as a picture or a scent in someone's childhood memory, getting it into commercial production and then back into gardens can be incredibly rewarding. The people and the stories I discover along the way make the rough parts worth it.

My first parrot gladiola bulbs came from Mary Anne Pickens of Industry, Texas. Past president of the Southern Garden History Society, Mary Anne is a fifth-generation Texan and still lives on her folks' property in Industry where her family ran a plant nursery. I assumed her gladiolas escaped from pots at the nursery, or were planted to show customers the glory of a mass of blooming parrot gladiolas. I questioned Mary Anne about those in her garden. They were relatively new, she said, a gift from her friend, Ann. But Mary Anne did recall a stand of parrot glads in New Ulm, Texas, near Industry. They filled the yard of an old house near her grandmother's place, she said. She didn't remember her grandmother having any parrot gladiolas, although there were other gladiolas in her garden. On my insistence, Mary Anne called her friend Ann. Maybe she'd share with us the trek the bulbs made before coming to live in Mary Anne's garden. Maybe Ann grew them after digging a bulb from her grandmother's garden? Or did they reach even further back?

Like most heirloom bulbs I've grown fond of in the last decade, the parrot gladiola has a lineage that did not take me in a straight line as I traced it. This hot orange bloomer, also called Natal lily, began its journey in Port Natal, South Africa. Records show it then traveled north to Ghent, Belgium. From there we know it went through

Holland and on to England. Accounts do not tell us specifically where it stopped along the way, but we have a number of clues, one of which may be seen in New York's Metropolitan Museum of Art. There, in Claude Monet's oil painting of his aunt's "Garden at Sainte-Adresse," we find parrot glads thriving on the shores of French Normandy in the mid 1800s. Although Monet's contemporaries deemed the plant's bright markings—and Monet's sensibilities—gauche, these parrot gladiolas demonstrate beautifully contrasting colors and reflected ambient light, characteristics seen in many of Monet's best-loved paintings.

As with many horticultural trends, there is a strong probability Europeans either influenced nineteenth-century Americans to add parrot gladiolas to their landscaping palette or brought them over themselves. The plants are easy to grow from seed. Each individual bloom is able to produce lots of seedlings, making it a prolific traveler. Like all gladiolas, this cousin of the iris has a strong family resemblance in the leaves of the plant. But the blooms put it in a class all its own. A hardy plant, parrot gladiola is believed to be the parent of all modern day gladiolas in commercial production for cut flowers. The happy colored bloom quickly became popular in southern gardens. Its South African heritage allowed it to thrive in the conditions presented by the Gulf Coast and other warm regions of America, unlike many other plants traditionally grown in Europe.

The path this native of Port Natal, South Africa took to arrive at a family farm in Texas is an example of what keeps me eternally on the hunt for both bulb and bulb story. When asked by Mary Anne if the parrot gladiola was a family treasure, Ann laughed.

"No. Afraid not. Got it at a garden center."

"Too bad!" says Mary Anne, our visions of the plants as precious hand-me-downs from generations past squelched. "I do enjoy picking them, though. And they surprise me every year when they come up. I'm glad I have them."

I'm glad you have them, too, Mary Anne.

Gladiolus dalenii
parrot gladiola, Natal lily

Bloom

SIZE	Bloom spikes 30"-40" (80 to 100 cm) tall
COLOR	Bright mixture of oranges and yellows
SHAPE	Linear, with larger individual funnel-shaped flowers on the bottom leading to smaller blooms at the top of the spike
TIME	May
FRAGRANCE	None

Foliage

EMERGE	November
FADE	July/August
HEIGHT	28"-31" (70-80 cm)

Bulb

SIZE (CIRCUMFERENCE)	3"-6" (9-16 cm)
COLOR	Dark brown, rough textured husk. Sometimes peels off for more shiny area underneath; if no lower layer mottled white underneath of bulb appears.
SHAPE	Flattened oval shape, officially a corm, not a bulb

Gladiolus dalenii

Care

SOIL	Any
LIGHT	Part-shade to full-sun
MOISTURE	Irrigation ok during dormant season, prefers well-drained soil but can handle wet feet
TEMPERATURE	Zone 7-10
PLANTING	Plant from February to May. Plant bulb at a depth that is equivalent to 2-3 times the height of bulb.
DIVIDE/TRANSPLANT	Mid-to-late-summer
VASE LIFE	2 weeks
FOLIAGE REMOVAL	Mid-to-late-summer
NOTES	Formerly named Gladiolus natalensis, this plant is believed to be the parent of all modern large gladiolas used for cut flowers. Will seed around garden and form into blooming sized bulbs

Zephyranthes grandiflora

pink rain lily, zephyr lily

I was taking a new acquaintance on a bulb hunt on the back-roads of northeast Texas, when I began to get a bit nervous that our hunt would be a dud. Then I spied five clear pink blooms between the diamonds of a metal chain-link fence, also known as a "hurricane" fence, pronounced either her-*eh*-kane or her-*uh*-kun, depending on where you live along the Gulf Coast.

This tropical rain lily, *Zephranthes grandiflora,* has naturalized throughout the Southern U.S. The tiny bulbs are remarkably hardy in the colder climes if they are given a bit of mulch. The ones we spotted that day were blooming their heads off in the partial shade among trash trees and brown weeds, the only green on the abandoned lot. The throat joining the tropical rain lily's six or eight petals is a contrasting bright white, and orangey yellow anthers extend out from the center. The Latin name, *zephranthes*, refers to Zephyros or Zephyr, god of the west wind. I can't help but think they were named when a warm breeze made them wave in an open field somewhere, because it is a remarkable sight indeed.

Since the plants commonly known as rain lilies are grouped into two different genera, it becomes rather confusing. The flowers of *Zephyranthes* and *Habranthus* are very similar, but there are a few distinctions. The blooms of the *Habranthus* are slightly irregular, tilt

to the side, and have different size stamens. The *Zephyranthes* blooms point straight up, typically in a star shape with six equal stamens in the center: three tall and three shorter. This pink rain lily is one of the most prolific bloomers, coming in just behind *Habranthus robustus.* Both plants are poisonous if ingested by humans, but butterflies and other insects love them.

Zephyranthes grandiflora
pink rain lily, zephyr lily

Bloom

SIZE	2"-3" (5-7cm)
COLOR	Pink
SHAPE	Petals separate, furl open and face out or up
TIME	May to July
FRAGRANCE	None

Foliage

EMERGE	March
FADE	First freeze/November
HEIGHT	3"-5" (10-20 cm)

Bulb

SIZE (CIRCUMFERENCE)	2"-4" (6-9 cm)
COLOR	Brown to light brown skin when dry
SHAPE	Round with occasional long neck

Zephyranthes grandfilora

Care

SOIL	Well-prepared
LIGHT	Part-shade to full-sun
MOISTURE	Irrigation ok during dormant season, prefers well-drained soil but can handle wet feet
TEMPERATURE	Zone 7-10
PLANTING	Plant when there is no danger of hard freeze. Water if planting in the heat of summer. Plant bulb a couple inches below the soil
DIVIDE/TRANSPLANT	In late winter or early spring. Protect from hard freezes
VASE LIFE	3 days
FOLIAGE REMOVAL	After first frost or freeze
NOTES	A traditional and favorite rain lily. It happily opens wide with solid pink petaled blooms. Benefits from irrigation and a little fertilization

Crinum
'Ellen Bosanquet'

A grower once shared with me his trick for making crinum customers happy: he tells them it might take five years before a newly planted crinum blooms. It is most certainly sooner than that, but with the mindset that it will take a while, folks are quite happy with him when theirs — obviously a special one — blooms in just two or three years. One of my customers let me know of her 'Ellen Bosanquet' and its special bloom.

Her friends Daryl and Joan moved to Texas from California after fostering over 200 children in a thirty-year period. They loved to share their photo albums, naming each child who had come through their home and telling a little something about him or her. Often they would tell where the child currently was, and how many children that foster child had. Sometimes they had school photos of this new generation right next to the parents' school photos that were yellowed with age.

One day Daryl started losing weight. It wasn't that he didn't need to take off a few pounds around the middle, but it kept dropping, and they became worried. The doctor told them it was cancer, get your things in order and call in your family. Within a few weeks, Daryl was bed-ridden, and within a month, he'd passed away. The day my customer got the call about Daryl's death, she was outside in her garden. Just after she hung up the phone, a brilliant scarlet color caught her eye. It was a color she didn't

remember seeing there by the entry. When she got closer, she realized it was the 'Ellen Bosanquet' crinum she'd planted just the year before. It wasn't supposed to bloom for a couple more years, she thought. A singular flower stood alone on a lanky stalk. She picked the flower and took it inside. Even though she'd never known Joan to be much of a plant person, for some reason she felt Joan would like this bloom. She dried the flower, wrote a simple verse on a piece of paper and glued the bloom and stem to the paper. Then she put a frame around it and marked the back with day she had picked it.

A few days after Daryl's funeral, when all of the family had returned to California, my customer went over to deliver the framed crinum to her friend. She told Joan the 'Ellen Bosanquet' had bloomed when it really wasn't yet time. She explained how she'd felt compelled to press it and give it to her. Joan began to cry. After being transferred to Texas, she said, they missed having family close by and the liveliness of a house filled with children. Daryl told Joan he also missed something very strange: the rambling bougainvillea that climbed and clung to anything it could, including the fence outside their dining room. Daryl was amazed how the plant not only bloomed, but seemed to thrive on neglect. It did not care that all of his attention went instead to the different children that sat around that dining table. Joan said that the photo albums and frequent phone calls helped with their loneliness for family. But although Daryl bought baskets and buckets of bougainvilleas year after year, the heat and humidity of East Texas relentlessly battled against him. Where the plant grew effortlessly at their California home, he had never been able to repeat the bright cherry pink blooms reliably since they'd left. That same happy color now was before her, albeit on a very different plant. It reminded her of home. It reminded her of him.

Crinum
'Ellen Bosanquet'

Bloom

SIZE	3"–5" (8–12 cm)
COLOR	Burgundy
SHAPE	Long trumpet-shaped
TIME	May to July
FRAGRANCE	None

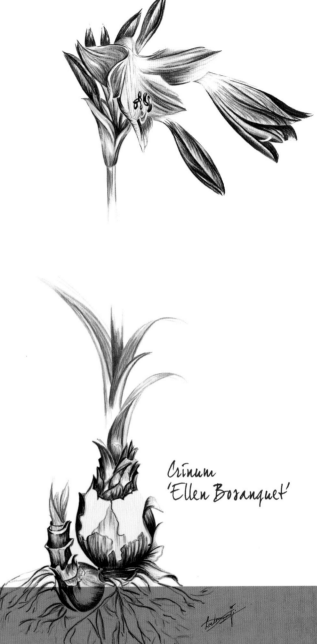

Crinum
'Ellen Bosanquet'

Foliage

EMERGE	March
FADE	First freeze/November
HEIGHT	13"–20" (35–50 cm)

Bulb

SIZE (CIRCUMFERENCE)	10"–16" (25–40 cm)
COLOR	Brown with flaky skin
SHAPE	Rounder than most crinum bulbs. Tapers into a long, sometimes highly curved neck. Bottom portion of bulb is flat, but this is not a large area and occurs below much of the curvature of the bulb

Care

SOIL	Any
LIGHT	Full-sun
MOISTURE	Irrigation ok during dormant season, prefers well-drained soil but can handle wet feet
TEMPERATURE	Zone 7–10
PLANTING	Plant when no danger of hard freeze remains. Water if planting in the heat of summer. Plant bulb with a portion of the neck out of the ground and the bulb completely below the soil surface
DIVIDE/TRANSPLANT	In late winter/early spring (protect from hard freezes)
VASE LIFE	1 week
FOLIAGE REMOVAL	After first frost or freeze
NOTES	Best crinum for sturdy, dark pink flowers in the middle of summer. Great for cut flowers, foundation plantings, or border or backdrop

CRINUM:
Some crinums, old and older

C. 'Carroll Abbott'

C. x hebertii (milk and wine lily)

C. 'Summer Nocturne'

C. 'Bradley'

C. 'Stars and Stripes'

Hymenocallis liriosme
white spider lily

Hymenocallis 'Tropical Giant' – a cultivated variety of our native white spider lily – grows so well in the southern U.S. that many people assume it's native. But from the southern states down to Mexico and Central America, no less than seventeen strains of native spider lilies can be found. Growing in low or swampy spots, our native spider lilies include the spectacular Cahaba lily of Georgia.

In the early to mid-1800s, explorer Jean Louis Berlandier, a Swiss-French botanist, charted the plants of Mexico, an area that included sections of present-day Texas. In his journal he describes a scene when his party found itself surrounded by knee-high lilies. This type of display is not a thing of the past, however. Drive into the country in late spring, and you could find yourself in the middle of the spectacular beauties, the white spider lilies.

It has been my privilege to hire people close to me to work for The Southern Bulb Company. It can be dangerous for friends and family to work together, and it does come with its share of tense moments. But for two summers in a row I hired Grant Cox, a young man a couple of years younger than I and who was in the Corp of Cadets with me at Texas A&M. Our first summer he helped me dig bulbs, and the second summer he helped me sell bulbs. We got to do a tour across Texas. Grant's brother joined in the fun as we went from festival to festival, spreading the word about this new heirloom bulb company located in Texas and selling flower bulbs to fairgoers around the state. It was a lot of fun: Luling Watermelon Festival, the Lampasas Spring-Ho where the queen of the festival is the "Lampasas Ho," the Clute Mosquito Festival, and of course the Rabbit Fest in Copperas Cove

where we had a "hoppin good time!" The Schulenburg Festival was probably one of the best ones, and we also went to one in Waxahachie. The list goes on and on and on.

But that first summer with Grant was mostly hunting trips, digging bulbs all over the place. Late July we heard reports of the white spider lily, *Hymenocallis* 'Tropical Giant' blooming freely in Grant's one time home, Crockett, Texas. So Grant and I went there, going up and down every single road in town. We were starting to get a little discouraged when all of a sudden we turned the corner and found a really long row of the pure white lilies blooming along the curb. It was an area that was half shaded, the other half was in full sun, and both were blooming equally well. We marked our location on the GPS to come back and get them when they had stopped blooming. Well, we never made it back. So if you are in Crockett, Texas, and you see a stand of the white spider lily, ask if you can take a few for me.

Hymenocallis liriosme
white spider lily

Bloom

SIZE	3"-4" (8 to 10 cm)
COLOR	White with contrasting orange anthers on the protruding stamens
SHAPE	Center white cup with elongated, skinny white petals that come from underneath the cup, continue out-wards for 8 to 12 cm and trail down. Strong stamens originate between the petals and the cups and hold vertical orange anthers in the middle of the open flower
TIME	April
FRAGRANCE	Slight fragrance

Foliage

EMERGE	Spring
FADE	Summer
HEIGHT	13"-18" (35-45 cm)

Bulb

SIZE (CIRCUMFERENCE)	6"-10" (16-25 cm)
COLOR	Light brown to dark brown with flaky skin
SHAPE	Round with flat bottom and top slightly tapers in thick neck, some-times neck and bulb appear as one

Hymenocallis liriosme

Care

SOIL	Usually seen in clay or muddy areas, but does well in almost all environments
LIGHT	Part-shade to full-sun
MOISTURE	Irrigation ok during dormant season. Often seen in swampy conditions
TEMPERATURE	Zone 7-10
PLANTING	Plant when no danger of hard freeze remains. Water if planting in the heat of summer. Plant with neck at the soil surface
DIVIDE/TRANSPLANT	In late winter or early spring (protect from hard freezes)
VASE LIFE	1 week
FOLIAGE REMOVAL	Naturally over summer
NOTES	A true native that is mentioned in descriptions early French expeditions across Texas. Often seen in swamps, it thrives in a multitude of conditions

Lilium lancifolium
tiger lily

*L*ilies. *Even people who are not gardeners recognize this faithful bulb. Egyptian tombs are marked with carvings of them, hence their association with death. The Bible is filled with references to lilies. The name "lily" actually comes from the Greek word* lirion, *referring to the beautiful white* L. candidum, *or Madonna lily. The Madonna lily is said to be the first plant cultivated for garden use, originating in the Middle East, possibly Israel. In the language of flowers, the lily symbolizes purity and innocence.*

But exactly what *are* lilies? Since a number of plants have common names that include "lily," such as daylily or spider lily, it can be confusing. A true lily is in the *Lilium* genus, a family characterized by edible bulbs with overlapping scales rather than a papery covering. Their leaves look like narrow ribbon curls up and down a rigid stem which is topped by a showy fragrant bloom.

There are a number of beautiful lilies native to North America, but most heirloom garden lilies originated in Asia. One of those, the tiger lily, can be found all over the southern U.S. There is some dispute as to how it came to North America from its home in Japan, Korea and China, where the bulbs are apparently used as food. However they arrived, the spotted orange blooms have been popular for decades with American gardeners. Like our native spotted lilies, they prefer a woodland setting with acidic soil and afternoon shade during their summer blooming season. I've seen incredible stands of the tiger lily from Texas to Louisiana and Georgia.

The ones I grow at the farm came from a house in northeast Texas that I drove by one day. Tiger lilies surrounded every tree at this old home. I knocked on the door and a stooped older lady and her physically fit,

Tiger lilies in living art, page 162

middle-aged son answered. The son said he would gladly share the black bulbils, which are tiny bulbs from which the seedlings of the tiger lily come. The gentleman, who told me he'd served our country in the Army's Special Forces, walked around with me and explained his unsuccessful experience in trying to save the bulbils. Apparently, he found, they do not like to be stacked and left in a coffee can in the garage. "You can't treat them like seeds," he told me. "They'll rot on ya!" I promised him I'd plant them right away. So I thanked him, both for his military service and for his horticultural service.

Another lily commonly found in older gardens is the Philippine or Formosa lily, *L. formosanum* (see photo on page 122). It is one of the easiest of all lilies to grow, well adapted to heat and humidity because its native environment is Taiwan and further south on the Philippine Islands. There is a lot of variability in the Philippine lily, including a dwarf variety that stays under 4' tall. The standard often reaches upwards of 6' with its white bloom. Unlike most lilies, the dwarf Philippine lily produces true from its seed. This is a highly desirable trait, because it allows gardeners to get a big crop of them very quickly. It is also the only lily able to go from seed to blooming-sized bulb in one year. Each July, trumpet shaped flowers of the Philippine lily sway like ghosts under the full moon. Afterwards, the seedpods dry and turn brown, pointing skyward like giant candelabras.

The first time I saw the dwarf Philippine lily in full bloom was next to skyscrapers in Houston. I was in love and knew I wanted to grow it for my customers. A little research led me to Heidi Sheesley, owner of a wholesale nursery called Tree Search Farms. Heidi focuses on hard to find plants and is always generous with me, sharing seeds from rare species. In most cases, the seed from the Philippine, or Formasa lily, comes "true to type." That means I can put seed from a lily into the ground and expect the resulting plant to look like its parent. That is not always the case. There can be a wide degree of variability when planting from seed.

Tony Avent of Plant Delights Nursery in Raleigh, North Carolina travels on bulb hunting expeditions around the world. While in Taiwan, he noted incredible variation in size, coloration, and form of lilies based on the elevation it grows in the wild, from 1 foot tall while above the tree-line, up to 7 feet further down into the lowlands. Seeing lilies thrive in higher elevations reminds us again that gardeners in cooler parts of the country might have success with these typically warm-season naturalizing bulbs, but they could also see some variability from the expected form.

Lilium lancifolium
tiger lily

Bloom

SIZE	3"-6" (10 to 15 cm) long trumpets
COLOR	Orange with black dots
SHAPE	Furled open trumpets
TIME	July
FRAGRANCE	None

Foliage

EMERGE	April
FADE	First freeze/November
HEIGHT	34"-55" (90-140 cm)

Bulb

SIZE (CIRCUMFERENCE)	5"-8" (14-20 cm)
COLOR	White bulblets
SHAPE	Numerous lily scales form together to make one teardrop shaped bulb

Lilium lancifolium

Care

SOIL	Neutral to slightly acidic
LIGHT	Part-shade to full-sun
MOISTURE	Irrigation ok during dormant season, prefers well-drained soil but can handle wet feet
TEMPERATURE	Zone 7-10
PLANTING	Plant in late winter or early spring. Plant bulb at a depth that is equivalent to 2-3 times the height of bulb
DIVIDE/TRANSPLANT	In late winter or early spring (protect from hard freezes)
VASE LIFE	2 weeks
FOLIAGE REMOVAL	After first frost or freeze
NOTES	The "vase life" of the flower can be greatly extended with the use of the dried flowers—once dry they turn up and make a candelabra of former blooms

LILIUM:
Lilies to remember

L. longiflorum (Easter lily)

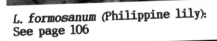

L. formosanum (Philippine lily):
See page 106

St. Andrew's Episcopal Church

The Heights, Houston, Texas

The Houston Heights area is recognized for its lovely Victorian houses and Craftsman style bungalows, boasting over one hundred properties listed on the National Register of Historic Places. Soon after its inception as a planned community in 1896, the Heights—so named for its location several feet above the city of Houston—became home to St. Andrew's Episcopal Church, then known as St. Paul's Mission. After meeting in homes, schools, meeting halls and two other sanctuaries for more than fifty years, St. Andrew's moved into its current location on Heights Boulevard. The building had no major changes until 1993 when the resurgence of families to the city from the suburbs swelled the community, increasing the congregation enough to warrant expansion.

St. Andrew's beautiful display of Easter lilies (*Lilium longiflorum*) has been around for many years in some form or another, multiplying like the loaves and fishes in Christ's parable. The congregation, led by Mrs. Addie Smith, traditionally plant the donated Easter lilies in the week following the Holy Day services. This Japanese import is recorded to have entered the U.S. in 1919 by way of the southern coast of Oregon as a souvenir in the suitcase of returning World War I soldier Louis Houghton. Since that time, the Oregon/California coast has become the largest producer of potted Easter lilies in the world.

Easter lilies in living art, page 162

St. Andrew's Episcopal - Heights. 1947

Lycoris squamigera
naked lady, magic lily, surprise lily

*O*ne of the questions I get asked most frequently is "what is your favorite bulb?" I do have favorites, and one of them is a naked lady. It is not because of the common name, I promise you. In fact, when I go to speak to a room full of knowledgeable heirloom plant gardeners, I still get embarrassed when an elderly woman stands and, in a booming voice that contradicts her stature, yells out "Tell me about the naked ladies!" She most often beams mischief, looking around at the other gardeners, some with hands over their mouths in horror. There are always others in the room with the same devilish grin and twinkling eyes, although theirs are just a little downcast because they didn't get to ask the question that made my face turn red first.

A lady called me one day about jonquils her mother had on a piece of property not far from the farm. The old house was on a slight hill and in some disrepair. A male voice said "just a moment" through the closed door, and I introduced myself to a frail, older lady who answered the door. Her husband nodded in a nearby chair as she answered any question I directed towards him. She explained that his diabetes prevented him from walking much. He also wore gloves, I guess to keep his hands warm, even though it didn't seem especially cold to me in their home. It is overwhelming what a high percentage of people I meet out on my digs who have a diabetic parent or spouse needing constant care. I had no idea this insidious disease was so prevalent. I'm not sure if it's because the age of the gardeners matches the age of the old plants I'm about to rescue, or if it's due to the economic condition of the places where heirlooms have been allowed to flourish undisturbed.

Anyway, the woman and I went out into their yard and began to dig some of the naturalized patches of jonquil bulbs that she no longer wanted. I noticed nearby a row of the distinctive flat, gray foliage of *Lycoris squamigera*. It blooms in late summer, but the foliage emerges in the wintertime; in *Garden Bulbs for*

the South, Scott Ogden describes it as being in concert with the daffodil season. So from February to April, only the foliage is noticed. It then dies back, and in the middle of summer the bloom suddenly appears. My hostess told me she had seen the bloom for forty years, but she'd never put together this wintertime "weed" in her law with the beautiful blooms shooting out to cool a hot summer day. This disconnect is common with many bulbs. As heirloom bulbs naturalize, the original gardener might be long since gone, and the new caretaker is not aware of the cycle of these perennial wonders.

Blooming for me in late July, and one of the most-cold hardy *lycoris,* the bare 2-3′ stalks end in pink, trumpet-shaped flowers that burst into bloom simultaneously. Each petal is stained with contrasting blueish-purple at the very tip. The term "naked ladies" actually applies to a number of different flowers that bloom before any foliage appears, having "naked" stalks with no foliage on them. They tend to be late summer or fall bloomers. Out in California, you have Cape belladonna, *Amaryllis belladonna* from South Africa, that is the show of summer. But in the southeastern regions of the United States, Cape belladonna is prone to bulb rot from too much summer rain, so *Lycoris squamigera* is a better choice. You can't get much better than the naked lady, I promise. Scott Ogden calls it a "mule" of the garden. This plant originated in Asia, and in Chinese, its common name means, "stone garlic." It doesn't get the name because of its taste (it is inedible), but because it is tough as a rock and the bulb resembles that of the garlic. Asian scientists are discovering that, like garlic, *Lycoris squamigera* has medicinal value as well as aesthetic. Research is now going on in this country, too, and an extract made from the greens and bulb of the naked lady is being tested as a remedy for bird flu.

Lycoris squamigera

naked lady, magic lily, surprise lily

Bloom

SIZE	3"-4" (8 -10 cm)
COLOR	Pink with almost blue-tipped petals
SHAPE	Pink trumpet shapes that furl open.
TIME	Late summer, fall
FRAGRANCE	None

Foliage

EMERGE	January
FADE	April
HEIGHT	7"-12" (20-30 cm)

Bulb

SIZE (CIRCUMFERENCE)	7"-9" (18-23 cm)
COLOR	Light brown to dark brown, skin sometimes peels to show next layer of white bulb, more mature bulbs have skin that peels and shows next layer of dark brown inflorescence
SHAPE	Round, tapering off into a skinny neck

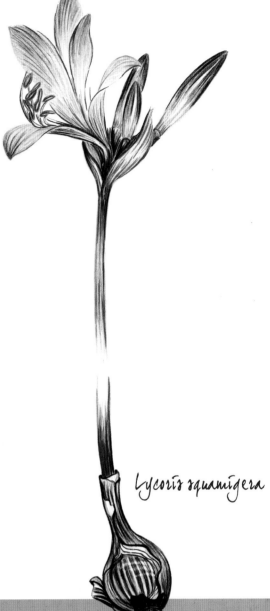

Lycoris squamigera

Care

SOIL	Any
LIGHT	Part-shade to full-sun
MOISTURE	Irrigation ok during dormant season, prefers well-drained soil but can handle wet feet
TEMPERATURE	Zone 6-8
PLANTING	Plant bulb from late spring to fall. Plant bulb with a portion of the neck out of the ground and the bulb completely below the soil surface
DIVIDE/TRANSPLANT	April/May
VASE LIFE	1 week
FOLIAGE REMOVAL	April/May
NOTES	Struggles in the warmest areas, but color is unmatched in summer gardens. Don't mistake the foliage for another plant when it comes up in the spring, even though the bulb blooms in July

Lockerly Arboretum
Milledgeville, Georgia

Along the banks of the Oconee River lies the former capital of the state of Georgia, Milledgeville. The edge of the frontier at the time, the land was home to the Creek Indian tribe who ceded it to the white traders in 1802 to cover debts. Its founders designed the city in a grid pattern much like our nation's capital.

A near perfect locale for cotton farming, Milledgeville grew prosperous and plantations popped up all over the area. Architects found the community eager for elegant houses, and soon a style deemed "Milledgeville Federal" became the rage. Each resident was anxious to outdo his neighbor with homes built primarily by African craftsmen, both slave and free. One of the mansions built in this era was "Rose Hill," constructed by Richard J. Nichols just south of the city and named for the Cherokee roses that grew there.

The Civil War brought incredible destruction to the Milledgeville area. But in 1927, R.W. Hatcher bought the plantation and re-named it "Lockerly Hall" in honor of a British castle. Under Hatcher's watch, Lockerly's landscape was restored, and camellias, azaleas and other blooming shrubs were added to the perennial gardens. Because of its location above a fall line, the plantation's climate is diverse, making its plant life diverse as well. It is equally home to the alpine fauna of the Piedmont and the coastal vegetation of the Oconee River Basin.

In 1965, mining tycoon Edward Grassman purchased Lockerly as a guesthouse for his company, and he designated much of the property surrounding the mansion as an arboretum for the people of Milledgeville. His desire to make it a horticultural laboratory as well as preserve its natural beauty gave rise to the Lockerly Arboretum Foundation. The foundation continues to oversee the hiking trails and gardens of Lockerly, including an additional 193 acres donated in 1999 by the Oliver Worley family.

LYCORIS:
More lycoris to love

L. albiflora

L. aurea

L. incarnata

Great Bulbs for
LIMITED AREAS

24in · 61cm

12in · 30.5cm

AUTUMN   SUMMER

GROUP III
AUTUMN CROCUS • ROMAN HYACINTH
TEXAS TULIP • GRAPE HYACINTH
WHITE RAIN LILY

AUTUMN   SUMMER

In my extensive travels, I still have not seen it all, but I have seen some things that get me very excited as a horticulturist. However, like a child whose hand is slapped when he grabs for another cookie, I have tempered my enthusiasm for some of these bulbs. When I was younger and met a person I was fond of, I put my full faith and confidence in that person. But as I grew older, I realized that sometimes a little more caution is in order. The same can be said of a bulb I discover successfully growing in a certain area. There is often more to that success than meets the eye, and I have learned to doubt first then, gladly be proven wrong.

My hardest lesson was that gorgeous red Texas tulip, *Tulipa praecox that I mentioned in the introduction and will tell you more about here.* It enchanted me from first sight. So, in my excitement, I encouraged everyone to share in its splendor, and I offered it to *all* of our customers. But, when I asked my customers how the bulb was doing for them, I realized my mistake.

The Texas tulip is a perfect example of a bulb with very specific requirements. As long as those requirements are met, the bulb will bloom and spread and awe everyone who sees it, making it appear carefree in nature. What I know now is that it is a great bulb, for *limited areas.* Here are some thrilling bulbs that, even in my enthusiasm for them, I have to admit, do best in certain areas.

Sternbergia lutea
autumn crocus, winter daffodil

*I*n 2009, I had the rare privilege of addressing the North American Flower Bulb Wholesalers Association. It was a bit intimidating. After all, these are the experts, coming in from all over the world, and I was going to talk to them about their bulbs. I decided the best approach was to tell them my personal story in the same way I do for other groups that invite me to speak, weaving botanical information I've learned as a grower of warm climate bulbs with a mix of anecdotes and beautiful flower photos. When I speak to garden clubs, civic groups and landscaping professionals, I get a consistent response, so I have come to rely on this approach. But this group did not respond with the enthusiasm I had grown to expect. In fact, the Dutch bulb experts were completely somber. Not only did they not laugh at my jokes, they didn't even smile. I decided by the end of my speech that I had been a flop. Afterwards, however, the audience inundated me, coming up to say how much they enjoyed my talk. Guess that's a Dutch thing. While I was showing the Mediterranean bulb Sternbergia lutea, a discussion started in another part of the room where a contingency of Israeli growers was sitting. A gentleman from

that group called out to me, "We know that bulb. We have that bulb in our country. This is the plant your Bible speaks of when you see 'lily of the valley.'" The man approached me after my talk, excited to tell me more about a plant few contemporary American gardeners recognize. He told me Sternbergia lutea is a true heirloom bulb, one the Babylonians are known to have traded in twentieth century B.C. I couldn't argue with that. This plant is, in every regard, an heirloom. He then invited me to visit Israel to go bulb hunting. I haven't gotten to go yet, but I look forward to that exciting trip.

Each fall the happy yellow blooms of the fall crocus can be found naturalized across prairie black land as well as in some clay soils throughout the South. I've found stands from North Carolina to north Texas, growing with abandon beside abandoned cars in an open field. Scott Ogden tells of the rumor that Thomas Jefferson brought the first *Sternbergias* to this country for his gardens at Monticello. The plants — a smaller blooming version — are now scattered across the Virginia countryside, backing up the validity of this claim. *S. lutea*'s bloom is so large it resembles a spring daffodil. It amazes me such a huge bloom comes out of such a tiny bulb. After the bloom, the foliage remains thoughout the winter and then goes dormant with summer heat. One thing I've learned about this hardy plant is not to leave the bulbs unplanted for too long. They are so anxious to show off, they will bloom in their crates!

Sternbergia lutea
autumn crocus, winter daffodil

Bloom

SIZE	2"-4" (5-10 cm)
COLOR	Bright yellow
SHAPE	Large upward facing cup, hence the common name "butter cups"
TIME	September
FRAGRANCE	None

Foliage

EMERGE	October after September bloom
FADE	May
HEIGHT	3"-8" (10-20 cm)

Bulb

SIZE (CIRCUMFERENCE)	3"-5" (10-12 cm)
COLOR	Brown
SHAPE	Round and tapers into skinny neck

Sternbergia lutea

Care

SOIL	Blackland clay that dries in the summer
LIGHT	Part-shade to full-sun
TEMPERATURE	Zone 6-8
PLANTING	Plant bulb from late spring to fall. Plant bulb at a depth that is equivalent to 2-3 times the height of bulb
DIVIDE/TRANSPLANT	April/May
VASE LIFE	1 week
FOLIAGE REMOVAL	April/May
NOTES	A delight to find in the South, but limited to areas with particular soil types in the middle and deeper South. Their blooms almost seem like fall blooming daffodils or a yellow crocus, but they are in the genus Sternbergia. Natives of Israel

Hyacinthus orientalis

Roman hyacinth

One January, I made a visit to the JC Raulston Arboretum in North Carolina. As I was walking around, I got a whiff of something just delightful. Thinking it must have been a tree blooming, I looked up. Finding none, my view went a little lower, looking for winter-blooming shrubs as the source of scent. Again I found nothing. Finally, my eyes drifted down to the corner of a rock wall. A tiny patch of Roman hyacinths peeked out from the stones. They looked completely at home in this setting, naturalized in the crevices and cracks of the rock wall, content with their surroundings and in full bloom, filling the whole garden with their fragrance.

This is exactly the type of setting where you might find them in their native Mediterranean home. They are called "Roman" hyacinth because they thrive along the famous old Roman roads. The roads for the Roman Empire were built up in layers, using rectangular or polygonal blocks for the final road topping. Curbing alongside the roads was made of squared rocks called "umbones." The roads gently curved down to the curb on each side for better drainage. This low spot between the curb and the road quickly filled with dirt and became a perfect environment for tiny seeds, or bulbs, to germinate. The hyacinths can be found there still today, pushing their way from the remains of the crumbling rocks, filling the air with their fragrance.

Even before the Romans, however, we know the Greeks spoke of the hyacinth. The Greek poet Homer tells of the first bloom emerging when the young warrior Hyakinthos' blood spilled on the ground after Apollo accidentally killed him. All modern-day hyacinths are bred from this parent plant and are known for their distinctive, spicy fragrance. Both the modern and heirloom versions retain this qual-

ity, although arguably the old one is more pure. The heirloom variety might not be quite as full-blooming and individually showy as the new breeds, but it offer more blooms per bulb than the modern hyacinth. The species hyacinth may be found naturally occurring in blue, white, and less frequently, pink. But breeders have been able to isolate the colors to create all sorts of mixes with these, including purples and even a soft gray.

After I got a tip about some Roman hyacinths naturalized near a historic little German town in central Texas, my buddy Chad Jones and I went looking for them. It was a gorgeous, sunny late-December day. I knew it might be too early for them to be in full bloom just yet. But Chad was an experienced bulb hunter who had weathered a previous crinum incident with me. We trekked up and down every single road in the area, not that there were that many roads to choose from, anyway. But when we passed by a culvert and turned down one little stretch, we came upon an old house with hoop wire fencing. Chad looked down and saw a tiny blue bloom. It was right next to the dirt road in front of this old house. I knocked on the door but no one was home, so we went back into town and stopped at a store to ask who lived there. The lady at the store happened to be the mother of the homeowner. She told us when to expect her son to return, and so we went out to wait for him. When we explained why we were there, he seemed a little surprised at first. But he said, "Sure, no problem. You wanna come in for a beer?" Chad and I looked at each other, shrugged, and followed the guy into a side room on the house, a lean-to he'd turned into a game room of sorts. There was a little tap coming out of the wall. He poured a couple of beers for us and shared some about his life. He'd recently been through a divorce and was trying to sort things out. He was a really nice guy and I could tell he was just glad for the company. And I was glad he shared his story and his hyacinths. That afternoon confirmed my belief that all plants come with their own story, in some form or another.

Hyacinthus orientalis
Roman hyacinth

Bloom

SIZE	4"-6" (12-15 cm)
COLOR	Roman hyacinths are most often seen in white and blue forms; however, pink Roman hyacinths exist, as well as shades in between these three colors
SHAPE	Cylindrical cluster of smaller flowers that have long tubular bodies that split at the stops creating a wide star-shaped appearance
TIME	January to February
FRAGRANCE	Strong, unique smell

Foliage

EMERGE	December
FADE	April
HEIGHT	4"-6" (12-15 cm)

Bulb

SIZE (CIRCUMFERENCE)	2"-5" (7-12 cm)
COLOR	Pink and purple. Sometimes skin appears as a tight gradient of smaller purple dots on bulb
SHAPE	Teardrop shape without a long neck, flat bottom

Hyacinthus orientalis

Care

SOIL	Performs well in most soils, but benefits from soil preparation
LIGHT	Full-sun
MOISTURE	Prefers well-drained soil and likes to dry in the summer
TEMPERATURE	Zones 8 and colder
PLANTING	Plant from September to December. Plant bulb at a depth that is equivalent to 2-3 times the height of bulb
DIVIDE/TRANSPLANT	May
VASE LIFE	1 week
FOLIAGE REMOVAL	May
NOTES	Rare, but worth finding. Nothing in the garden will give the January color and fragrance like a Roman hyacinth. One bulb can send up 2-3 flower stalks causing it to stay in bloom for almost a month

Tulipa praecox
Texas tulip

When you say bulbs, *people think tulips. In fact, anytime I tell someone that I grow bulbs, they automatically turn to their friend and say, "He grows tulips!" Why? I don't know. Possibly it is because the Dutch have done such a great job at getting the word out about their primary export. Perhaps a photo of a field overflowing with red tulips says romance to the hardest of hearts, and strikes an internal chord even more than roses do. But whatever the reason, my brother convinced me that until I offered easy-to-grow tulips from The Southern Bulb Company, success would remain out of my grasp.*

There were rumors of a tulip that did well in the Gulf Coast region. More specifically, I'd heard of a red tulip that was perennial in Texas. Was it possible? I started my quest with a bit of suspicion. I found information that pointed to the fact there were indeed some hardy "breeding bulbs" brought to America. They were originally grown in Europe to parent tulips that withstood harsh conditions. But the Europeans looked down on this tulip as too plain, preferring more dramatic blooms to the simplicity of the little red tulip. Colonists in the 1700s recognized the flower's reliability, bringing the bulb with them to the New World.

I quizzed my friend Greg Grant, ornamental horticulture instructor at Stephen F. Austin University in Nacogdoches, Texas, and co-author with Dr. Bill Welch of *Southern Heirloom Gardens*. Greg pointed to some plants with wavy grayish foliage growing in his garden. He mentioned there might be stands of this bulb he called the Texas—or fire—tulip in north central Texas. He suggested I ask Jimmy Turner, Director of Gardens at the Dallas Arboretum and Botanical Garden, what he knew about the plant. So I went to Dallas to ask

Jimmy about this elusive plant. Not only did he know about them, he gave me two hairy little bulbs from his own garden. His plants originated from his mother's Lone Oak, Texas, landscape. In this area of Texas, the bulb had been thriving for decades.

But it didn't make sense. Why wouldn't every gardener in Texas already be growing the *Texas* tulip? I planted my puny little bulbs and kept up the quest, gathering more and more information, taking the rumors and using them as clues for my hunt.

Some of my bulb hunting buddies and I decided to try one more time to find the Texas tulip along Interstate 35. We set out on a mid-March day, four of us crammed into the cab of the truck. Over and over, one road after another, with no sign of the elusive bulb's bloom, we finally promised each other we were done after this last back road. Just as I started to U-turn, Ben—one of my hunting buddies—convinced me to take one more right turn. When I did, we spied a twenty-by-twenty-foot sea of red massed on an abandoned lot. Close by was an old white frame house. Wisteria bloomed all over it, and it was surrounded by more of the foot-high stalks topped with deep red blooms, then jet black insides lined with honeybee yellow. It was spectacular! The blue-

purple of the wisteria in combination with the red was breathtaking. We knew we'd stumbled on a treasure, *Tulipa praecox*, the legendary Texas tulip. "*Praecox*" means " to ripen early," hinting that it is an early blooming tulip, probably the reason we'd not found it before now.

What I learned, a little too late, is that there is a pattern in the reports of naturalized stands of these tulips: soil type. Applying a soil profile map confirmed my suspicions. These bulbs fingered through the Blackland Prairies of Texas, an ecoregion that is actually part of a larger prairie extending from Kansas to San Antonio. Forests and cities jutting in and out of it, these prairie islands of tallgrass—which originally went from Canada to Mexico—were home to bison herds that numbered in the millions. Later, settlers claimed it for farming and cattle, diminishing the prairie to less than half of one percent of its original size and making it "the most-endangered large ecosystem in North America" according to The Nature Conservancy.

While I have to say thanks to Greg and Jimmy for encouraging me, even when I was ready to give up on finding naturalized stands of the Texas tulip, I do *not* thank the gophers, or the voles, or the moles or whatever small, toothy mammal devoured well over half my crop at the farm. Or the ones that ate through the black plastic crates holding hundreds of harvested bulbs soon to be on their way to my customers. And, I don't thank the humidity along the Gulf Coast or in sandy loam soils where the abundant moisture rots the tulip bulbs. In places like Jackson, Mississippi, you can plant them. But you must be aware of their special requirements. They thrive on neglect. No summer irrigation, no disturbance, and none of the constraints that improve growing conditions for most plants. Although I learned the Texas tulip's limitations the hard way, it taught me valuable lessons that led me to a number of other tulips for warm climates. But that's another story.

Tulipa praecox
Texas tulip

Bloom

SIZE	1"-2" height (3-5 cm)
COLOR	Bright red
	Outside cup pinkish at base transferring into bright red petals. Inside of cup jet black at base outlined by honey bee yellow band transferring into bright red petal
SHAPE	Cup-shaped
TIME	Mid-to-late-March
FRAGRANCE	None

Foliage

EMERGE	December
FADE	Mid-to-late-April
HEIGHT	6" high (15 cm)

Bulb

SIZE (CIRCUMFERENCE)	2.5"-3.5" (6-9.5 cm)
COLOR	Mottled light brown to brown. White where outer layers of skin have been peeled back. Vertical darker brown lines seen at times in well dried but healthy bulb
SHAPE	Oblong, almost tear-drop shape depending on growth habit and location

Tulipa praecox

Care

SOIL	Prefers soil to dry out during summer. Clay to sandy loam
LIGHT	Full winter sun
MOISTURE	Natural rainfall or irrigation, dry during summer
TEMPERATURE	Zones 5-8
PLANTING	August to November
DIVIDE/TRANSPLANT	Late April to July
VASE LIFE	3-4 days
FOLIAGE REMOVAL	May 1st at the earliest

TULIPA:
Tulips you'll want to try

T. clusiana var. chrysantha

T. 'Lady Jane'

T. 'Tinka'

T. saxatilis (bakeri) 'Lilac Wonder'

T. 'Tubergen's Gem'

DeGolyer House and Gardens
Dallas, Texas

One of two restored homes on the grounds of the Dallas Arboretum, the DeGolyer House and Gardens were added to The National Register of Historic Places in 1978. The Spanish Colonial Revival style home rests amid incredible gardens on a bluff above White Rock Lake. The Dallas skyline is visible across the lake to the north. The mansion was built in 1939 by Everette DeGoyler, one of the founders of the American Association of Petroleum Geologists. The estate was called "Rancho Encinal" to honor the property's grand oak trees. Mr. DeGoyler spent a portion of his career in Mexico and is credited for locating two of the largest oil fields in the world—Potrero del LLano No. 4 and Las Naranjas. His book collection of both Mexican history and oil and gas law are an integral part of the DeGolyer Library of Southern Methodist University in Dallas.

Whatever influence Mr. DeGoyler may have had on the design of the 21,000 square-foot stucco and red tile house, it was his wife, Nell DeGolyer, who influenced the gardens at Rancho Encinal. The forty-four-acre property now forms the major part of the Dallas Arboretum, including "A Woman's Garden," an outdoor room with a tiered fountain, and "Nancy's Garden," named in memory of Nancy Dillard Lyon, a young mother who died tragically. The centerpiece of the garden is a statue of her two daughters.

The transition of the private home and landscape to public garden was a natural one. Although the DeGolyer estate is enjoyable all year, springtime is especially memorable. "Dallas Blooms" brings in thousands of visitors every March and April when the Arboretum displays its half-million blooming bulbs. Tulips, daffodils and azaleas explode into masses of glorious color for the largest event of its kind in the South.

Tulips in living art, page 162

Muscari neglectum
grape hyacinth, blue bottle

A friend gave me an article from the British version of House and Garden. In it were dozens of selections of a striking flower called grape hyacinth. From the close-up photos in the article, it was hard to believe the flowers grow only 3-6 inches tall. I flipped though the article with amazement. There were taller selections and smaller selections, bigger bulbs and smaller bulbs, white varieties, grey varieties, and purple varieties. I wondered if these would do well for us, because here in the states, I only know of one variety, the blue-purple flower I find blooming with abandon each spring on old homesites: Muscari neglectum.

It is a powerful flower. I usually see the bloom emerge in mid March, a carpet of purples and blues that catches my eye. As I drive down the back country highways, I enjoy sweeping sections of landscapes dotted with this small flower, massed with its brethren to form a purplish blue oneness. *Muscari* are a precursor to the Texas bluebonnets that bloom in April. Smaller, and of a species completely unrelated to bluebonnets, grape hyacinths add their cool color in similar ways to Texas' state flower and create beautiful landscapes across the South.

As individuals, grape hyacinths are delicate and intricate flowers. I have taken many photos of them, laying on my stomach and pulling blades of grass out of the camera lens' path to get a clear shot. Only at that moment can I fully appreciate the gradient between the colors, the richness of each bloom, and the unique bells that gather so tightly together forming the whole story of this flower's beauty.

I often find grape hyacinth naturalized in the black gumbo clays that stretch across the central part of Texas. Other bulbs that thrive in this region are *Sternbergia lutea*, *Rhodophiala bifida*, and *Tulipa praecox*. It is easiest to find the grape hyacinth bulbs when the plant is in bloom. If I

gather them blooming, it is best for the bulbs if I leave them in a clump. I only have to stick my shovel four to six inches deep in the black clay to get below the bulbs.

Assuming I'm not on a rescue mission saving a flower from an impending bull-dozer or new road, I like to leave some behind when I hunt bulbs. I use my shovel to break the soil loose around the hole and fill in the empty spot. Then I'll separate a section of the clump and place a few bulbs back to ensure there will be more flowers for years to come and the landscape will not be significantly altered.

When I need to break out bulbs individually, I mark blooming *Muscari* sites with a surveyor flag, stake, or with a technique my friend Zac Coventry invented during his brief tenure at The Southern Bulb Company: popsicle sticks. At the end of the growing season, I come back and dig the bulbs. There I'll find small whitish round bulbs with numerous tiny bulbs attached at the base. These can be broken off and replanted. Since they are small and have the potential to dry out if they are left out of the ground for too long, I replant them quickly.

The grape hyacinths at the bulb farm prosper in a sandy loam soil now, but I will never forget the relentless hours Brad Gaultney and I spent digging them up in a terrible heat, bulb by bulb out of the black gumbo clay, to get them in the first place. Fischer was with us and — still a pup — hadn't learned to stay by me. So Brad and I babysat my dog, dug bulbs, and made the memories that I know can only be made once in a lifetime. Every time the grape hyacinths are blooming, their deep blue bells bring that hot, happy day back to me.

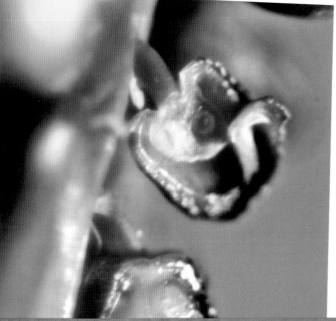

Muscari neglectum
grape hyacinth, blue bottle

Bloom

SIZE	2"-3" (6-8 cm)
COLOR	Mixture of purples and blues
SHAPE	Loose cylinder of egg-shaped flowers on top of a single stem
TIME	Mid March
FRAGRANCE	None

Foliage

EMERGE	December
FADE	May
HEIGHT	2"-4" (7-10 cm)

Muscari neglectum

Bulb

SIZE (CIRCUMFERENCE)	1"-3" (3-6 cm)
COLOR	Light mottled brown appearance
SHAPE	Small teardrop-shaped bulbs

Care

SOIL	Blackland clay that dries in the summer, but performs well in sandy loam as well
LIGHT	Part-shade to full-sun
TEMPERATURE	Zones 6-8
PLANTING	Plant from September to December. Plant bulb at a depth that is equivalent to 2-3 times the height of bulb
DIVIDE/TRANSPLANT	May
VASE LIFE	1 week
FOLIAGE REMOVAL	May
NOTES	Can carpet areas with a deep blue and proceeds the blues of the bluebonnet wild flowers. Gulf Coast regions can have difficulty with this flower

Zephyranthes candida
white rain lily

For several years I tried unsuccessfully to grow white rain lilies commercially at the farm. How could these naturalized wildflowers from South America thrive in ditches all over the place and yet flail under my loving care? Then, on a trip to Longwood Gardens for a Garden Writers Association meeting, I made a discovery. After dinner in the incredible Conservatory ended, I walked out into a lovely, fall night in the Pennsylvania countryside. There they were, sparkling silver in the darkness, hundreds of white rain lilies! As I examined them more closely the next day, I had an epiphany: the rain lilies' roots were submerged in water. I thought back to each location where I'd seen the plant in the wild: bogs, culverts, and stream banks throughout the southern U.S. I promptly removed the bulbs at my farm from the mounded soil row and sunk them in crates I lined along the pond. The lilies began to come alive, multiplying with abandon, a treasure-trove of glittering white blooms marking the beginning of autumn.

Spaniard Juan Diaz de Solis docked off the eastern coastline of South American in 1516, leading an expedition charged with discovering a shipping passage between the Atlantic and Pacific Oceans. It is said that the expedition came upon a stand of shining white rain lilies that went on for miles. Rio de la Plata, or "River of Silver," is the widest river in the world, separating present day Argentina from neighboring Uruguay and ending at the Atlantic Ocean. Inhabitants of the area killed Solis' entire party, except for one fourteen-year-old cabin boy, Francisco del Puerto. A number of years later when another expedition came to the area looking for treasure, they found the boy, now a warrior of the Charrua tribe. The Spaniards took Francisco back to his

homeland. Although his descriptions of the failed Solis expedition were helpful for further expeditions, he was not able to re-adjust to European ways. He returned to Uruguay where he spent the rest of his life, it is believed, upon the banks of the Rio de la Plata.

In the late sixteenth century, Sir Francis Drake wrote in his expedition journal about the "Plate River" he came upon in his circumnavigation of the world. It was assumed the adjective "plate" was a mistranslation of the Spanish name for the river. But Early Modern English vernacular, the same used by translators of the King James Bible, utilized the term "plate" to refer to silver or gold. And while some insist this speaks to the legends of ore thought to be upstream of the river, the fabled Sierra de la Plata, I can't help but think of the night I came upon the white rain lily in the cool autumn night. They are a treasured discovery for each generation, reminding us summer is over and harvest is here.

Zephyranthes candida
white rain lily

Bloom

SIZE	1"-3" (3-6 cm)
COLOR	*Zephyranthes candida* is white, but other rain lilies can be seen in shades of pink and white, however yellow, gold, orange and salmon
SHAPE	Star shaped, with petals separated, opened. Some rain lilies are more open and flat, while others remain pointed but open
TIME	May to October
FRAGRANCE	None

Foliage

EMERGE	March
FADE	Depends on rain lily
HEIGHT	3"-8" (10-20 cm)

Bulb

SIZE (CIRCUMFERENCE)	1"-4" (4-9 cm)
COLOR	Brown, *Z. candida* can appear white when pulled from wet conditions
SHAPE	Round with occasional long neck

Zephyranthes candida

Care

SOIL	Well-prepared soil area
LIGHT	Part-shade to full-sun
MOISTURE	Irrigation ok during dormant season, prefers well-drained soil but can handle wet feet. *Z. candida* prefers wet conditions and can be grown with the bulbs under the water
TEMPERATURE	Zones 7-10
PLANTING	Plant when no danger of hard freeze remains. Water if planting in the heat of summer. Plant bulbs 2"-3" below the surface of the soil
DIVIDE/TRANSPLANT	In late winter early spring (protect from hard freezes)
VASE LIFE	3 days
FOLIAGE REMOVAL	After first frost or freeze. For winter growing rain lilies, leave foliage on through winter
NOTES	This entire genus is worthy of planting. Spruce up any summer garden with a myriad of colors. Called rain lilies because they normally bloom 2-3 days after a good summer thundershower

ZEPHYRANTHES:
Rain lilies for every garden

Z. atamasca (Atamasco lily)

Z. 'Labufarosea'

Z. 'Grandjax'

Z. drummondii (evening rain lily)

Any Bulb,
ANYWHERE

So you've fallen in love with a bulb—or two or ten.

But when you look at the environment it needs to flourish, you find your garden is not the proper home for it. It's too hot, or too cold or too small. It's too bad.

Or is it?

If a plant won't "naturalize"—return year after year—in your garden, it can be used in other ways: in a traditional landscape as annual color, as a potted plant or in a floral arrangement that is then recycled into the landscape. Bulbs also make thoughtful, living gifts. Every bulb has horticultural and aesthetic importance. If you have tried one of the heirloom bulbs here unsuccessfully or you just know that you can't provide it with the environment it needs, you can still enjoy it. Forcing bulbs, creating living art and container gardening are ways to get Mother Nature to be a little more flexible.

Don't discount your favorite bulbs or think they are "bad" because their cultural needs differ from your home's landscape, or because your garden is a balcony in the middle of a city or a fluorescent-lit office space. Now that you know the conditions each bulb prefers, you can create the perfect home for almost any plant. Whether you are in a warm climate and you admire a cool climate bulb, or you live north of the Mason-Dixon line and are salivating for one of the Southern beauties, don't despair. A stunning red amaryllis bloom at Christmastime or a unique container filled with spring blooming beauties has the ability to transport the garden into any space, joy-in-a-pot. Look for the bulb that best fits both your taste and your purpose. Then mimic its optimum climate, and grow away.

No bulb is out of reach for *anyone*.

BLOOMS ON DEMAND

One of the most common questions bulb growers receive is how to make a bulb bloom for a certain event. Timing bulbs to grow and bloom at the desired moment is called "forcing." Some favorite bulbs to force in the U.S. include paperwhites, amaryllis, tulips, Easter lilies and daffodils. But don't limit yourself: all bulbs can be forced. Here is one example of how to force bulbs. If you check in the Resources section, you'll find websites with detailed information on forcing specific bulbs and varieties that respond best. The most important thing to remember is to pay close attention to the specific plant's requirements.

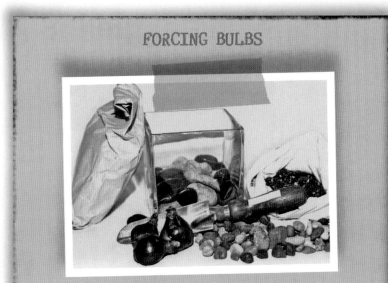

FORCING BULBS

STEP 1. Select a healthy bulb that is not dried out or mushy.

STEP 2. (Skip to Step 3 if your bulb has been pre-chilled.) Put bulbs into a well-ventilated area that is kept between 40-45 degrees, such as a refrigerator, for 8-12 weeks. Bulbs and fruits do not mix well, so you'll need to keep your fruit somewhere else as your bulbs chill. Off-gas ethylene from ripening fruits can damage bulbs.

STEP 3. Plant bulbs 3"-5" below the surface of soil, either in the landscape or in a container with a well-drained soil mix. As a general rule, bulbs should be planted at a depth twice their height. They may be placed densely together, for particularly striking results. You might even throw in another type of bulb that likes similar conditions for a pinch of extra flavor!

STEP 4. Sit back and enjoy the show. Before you know it, you will be basking in your new garden!

WHY CHILL BULBS?

Some bulbs bloom best in cool climates, while others prefer warm. These preferences are described as "chilling hours," and they must be met for the plant to bloom. A chilling hour is any hour, day or night, that the temperature is 32 to 45 degrees. Chilling hours are also pertinent to other plants, like some fruit trees.

TULIP ENVY

One of the most prevalent forced bulbs is a cold climate plant that Southern folks envy and Northern gardeners treasure: the tulip. Most tulips need about 2,000 chilling hours to bloom, roughly equivalent to twelve weeks. Warm climate areas usually receive less than 1000 hours of chilling. Obviously, this discrepancy must be addressed if you live in a warm climate and want to grow tulips. You will need to choose a warm climate bulb, move to New York, or give the bulb the necessary cooling to cause it to bloom. Using your refrigerator is the easiest solution. This great gardening tool is found in almost every home in America.

Using Bulbs in
LIVING ART

If you find cut flowers somewhat bittersweet because their beauty is so fleeting, you have an interest in conservation, or you just want to find other ways to incorporate the beauty of flowers into your home, try creating living art. Incorporating bulbs into arrangements allows you to experience the bulbs in entirely new ways. Artist Loela Barry has created arrangements with a wide variety of forms and functions out of some of my favorite heirlooms. She enjoys pulling elements from her surroundings into her art, so along with bits of driftwood, moss, and even eggshells you'll see everyday objects such as teacups and table settings, too. As you learn the basics of how she envisions her arrangements and the ways she utilizes different bulbs, you can begin to use your bulbs in entirely new ways. And if the bulb you have used in your living arrangement is one that will naturalize in your area, you can replant it when you are done. You'll be able to feel the peace of the garden anywhere in your home.

Spider Lily Twist (p. 25)

What you need:
- A few flowering *Lycoris radiata* bulbs (red spider lily)
- *Cyperus alternifolius* (umbrella sedge)
- Driftwood
- Oasis®, floral tape, wire, moss,
- Water solution containing plant nutrients
- Tools: scissors, knife and cutting board

How to do it:
1. Insert a small piece of soaked Oasis® into a pocket or suitable cavity on the driftwood
2. Fold the umbrella sedge leaves back for a free-flowing accent to be used in the design. Almost any kind of greenery will work
3. Carefully tuck the spider lilies, complete with bulbs, into the driftwood pocket
4. Accent the wooden lines with a horizontal placement of one spider lily laid across the piece
5. Shelter the bulbs with moist moss and spray with water solution

Bayou Drift (p. 45)

What you need:

- A few bunches of flowering *Leucojum spp.* (snowflake) bulbs
- A bunch of red *Nandina domestica* (heavenly bamboo) berries
- About 10 *Aspidistra eliator* (cast iron) leaves
- Driftwood
- Twine
- Light gauge wire
- Water solution with plant nutrients
- Tools: scissors, knife, pliers

How to do it:

1. First, soften the main veins of the *Aspidistra* leaves so you can bend them without breaking. Do this by squeezing vein at middle of leaf and pulling it through fingers towards stem
2. Fold them double and tie with small piece of wire. Then stick them into the cavities of the driftwood to create pockets for flowers and to provide greenery. You can also use the *Aspidistra* leaves to create pockets in parts of the driftwood that do not have natural pockets
3. Tie bundles of snowflakes together with the twine and position them in appropriate spots, following the shape of the driftwood
4. Bulbs are not hidden but used as prominent part of the arrangement
5. Add red berries to provide some accent color
6. Wrap some *Aspidistra* leaves around the leg to give attractive footing
7. Finally, put a few snowflakes in smaller pockets and drape some twine in the center to compliment the bulbs

Asian Branch (p. 109)

What you need:

- 4-6 *Lilium asiatica* (Asian lilies) or *Lilium lancifolium* (tiger lilies)
- A tree root with wild arms
- Leaves from *Narcissus* or other bulbs that have already bloomed
- *Aspidistra eliator* (cast iron) leaves
- A pedestal
- Shiny wire
- Tools: garden-shears; scissors; pliers

How to do it:

1. Wrap some of the tree root arms with the leaves and wire. Start from the base and work outward until you reach the tip. End by letting the last point of the leaf stand upright as an accent
2. End the wire wrapping similarly with a short spiral accent
3. Lay the lily plants horizontally on the root with the flowers on the front end. Lay them on top of each other, but take care that the flowers are spread well so they are not damaged. Use the wire spiral ends to support them as needed
4. Cover the bulbs with one or two *Aspidistra* leaves and add wet moss to keep them moist
5. With these kind of floral sculptures it is important to make sure it looks attractive, 360 degrees around
6. The stamens of these lilies can easily stain. If you use the arrangement outdoors it is no problem, but if it is intended to go indoors, it is wise to remove the stamens

Rise and Shine (p. 119)

What you need:
- 5–10 flowering bulbs of *Lilium longiflorum* (Easter lilies)
- A large glass vase
- A glass topped table
- Black Japanese stones or similar stones
- A wooden cross
- Wood shavings
- Egg shells
- Florist wire
- Tools: hand planer, hammer and nails

How to do it:
1. Place the cross in the vase and fill half way with stones to keep it upright
2. Place the lilies around the cross so that their flowers are more or less on the height of the cross beam
3. Lightly tie them around the cross with the wire to keep them in position
4. Drape shavings on the edge of the vase as well as on the tabletop. Add a few washed egg shells to the shavings
5. Take full advantage of the reflections in the glass in your placement

Myrtle Dance (p. 117)

What you need:
- Several bunches of flowering *Narcissus*
- A piece of driftwood for the base—preferably a branch split in half
- A few pine twigs with catkins
- Tools: scissors, knife, pliers, drill

How to do it:
1. Trim the driftwood base so that it is stable enough to support the arrangement
2. Drill a hole towards one end to hold the pine twig
3. Remove all needles and most catkins from the twig-leave one catkin on each twig end
4. Position the twig in the hole
5. Now lay one or two *Narcissus* plants with the bulb away from the twig and the flowers at its foot
6. Position another one or two *Narcissus* with the bulbs in the same area, but hang the flowers over one of the twig arms
7. Fill the base with loose catkins. On each end, set a small twig with catkins and attached needles to create a trimming effect

A Spot of Tea-lip (p. 143)

What you need:
- Flowering *Tulipa spp.* (Tulip) bulbs
- A bucket full of *Pinus spp.* (Pine) needles
- Newspaper
- Twine
- Light gauge wire
- Chicken wire (optional, to increase strength of newspaper pot)
- Tea set
- Water solution with plant nutrients
- Tools: scissors, knife, pliers

How to do it:
1. Cut newspaper to fit the table and moisten the paper
2. String pine needles together with wire, putting 20-30 needles in a bundle, adding the next group of needles till it is long enough to go all the way around the edge of your table
3. Lay the pine needles on top, leaving the center open for your tea-pot and tulip pot
4. Make another STRING of pine needles in the same fashion as before, but just long enough to go around the pot containing the tulips so that it makes a "skirt", with the wire at the bottom and the loose needles extending up
5. Bundle 3-7 tulips, including the bulbs; tie together with twine and put in the pot in the center of the table
6. OPT: Mold chicken wire into a plate and line with newspaper, then ball up a piece of moist newspaper and place in the center and place more blooming tulip bulbs on the moist paper; top with more needles
7. Finish off with a lovely teapot, cup and saucer (this one courtesy of Anthropologie)

AFTER YOU WATER

*A flower bulb is a living, breathing, growing miracle,
full of promise and hope.*

Just as we do, plants have intimate ties to their environments. Should we question their preferences? Flowers, even the fleeting pleasure of a solitary bloom, are well worth any of their peculiar demands. Putting up with these quirks might seem anathema to those who desire only easy plants that bloom constantly. But seasons are known best not by a date on the calendar. Certain feelings well up within us with the onset of autumn, with winter, with spring, with summer; a recognition and comfort that comes with predictable, inevitable change in the environment, a change that bulbs have responded to for eons.

My intent is not to discourage anyone from becoming a bulb gardener. I want to encourage everyone to become a *smart* bulb gardener, and to recognize plants are tied as inextricably to their environments as we are to ours. By creating a relationship with your environment, knowing a plant's needs and preferences and how they intersect with your lifestyle, you *and* your plant will not only grow, you will flourish.

Let me tell you a final bulb story. One Thanksgiving I spotted narcissuses blooming at the farm: my Chinese Sacred lilies and double Roman bulbs. Normally, these bulbs bloom in January, not November. Their sweet fragrance and crisp blooms and foliage were a wonderful surprise. I began to ponder what had happened. The summer before had been long and dry. Suddenly, the weather switched to cool and rainy, consistently wet, but not too wet. As a result, the narcissus bulbs went from a dormant state to a growing stage with no

breaks. It was the "perfect storm" needed for a well shaped, healthy looking bloom at Thanksgiving. Since the bulbs were suited to the environment, they certainly would return the next year, probably at a more normal time. But the unexpected blooms of the bulbs were spectacular. The thrill I got from them reminded me of my little red tulip from so long ago. But these narcissus bulbs would return to bloom again, unlike my tulip.

Looking back, I see that my tulip was not without value. It gave me great joy to see the gorgeous red bloom appear because of something I had done. It also caused my child's eyes to be opened to the beauty of flower bulbs, a vision that eventually expanded to include a career. My young mind made a connection between the brown "rock" my mom bought for me and the beautiful red bloom. Somewhere in the world, re-blooming in subsequent years is a natural occurrence for a tulip. In my environment—Bakersfield, California —a little more work was required.

Your relationship with each bulb is specific. I hope by sharing my experiences, you will see ways you can develop this connection; a little time, a little priming, a little patience might be all you need to get your garden in order, bringing new friends into the fold. Remember that heirlooms were not always considered old-fashioned. Long ago, someone was introduced to a new friend. This new bulb proved itself loyal and—with the passing of time and the making of memories—grew into an heirloom.

RESOURCES

BOOKS

Bender, Steve and Rushing, Felder. *Passalong Plants*. Chapel Hill, North Carolina: University of North Carolina Press, 2002.

Bender, Steve. *The Southern Living Garden Book*. Birmingham, Alabama: Oxmoor House, Inc., 1998.

DeHertogh, August and LeNard, Marcel. *The Physiology of Flower Bulbs*. Amsterdam, The Netherlands: Elsevier Science Publishers, 1993.

Heath, Brent and Becky. *Daffodils for North American Gardens*. Houston, Texas: Bright Sky Press, 2001.

Howard, Thad M. *Bulbs for Warm Climates*. Austin, Texas: University of Texas Press, 2001.

Murphy, Edith Van Allen. *Indian Uses of Native Plants*. Glenwood, Illinois: Meyerbooks, 1990.

Ogden, Scott. *Garden Bulbs for the South*. Portland, Oregon: Timber Press, Inc., 2007.

Squire, Sally McQueen. *A Gardener's Guide to Growing Bulbs on the Gulf Coast*. Houston, Texas: River Bend Publishing Company, 1998.

Van Beck, Linda M., Sara L. *Daffodils in Florida, A Field Guide to the Coastal South*. Florida: Van Beck, 2004.

Welch, William C. *PERENNIAL GARDEN COLOR*. Dallas, Texas: Taylor Publishing Company, 1988.

Welch, William C. *The Southern Heirloom Garden*. Dallas, Texas: Taylor Publishing Company, 1995.

White, Jane Baber. *Once Upon a Time…A Cemetery Story*. Old City Cemetery. Lynchburg, Virginia.

White, Jane Baber. *The Book of Attributes for the Living Horticultural Collections of the Old City Cemetery Museums and Arboretum*. Lynchburg, Virginia.

ONLINE (BULBS)

www.aggiehort.tamu.edu (includes "The Southern Garden" by Dr. William C. Welch, and Earth-Kind™ – Texas AgriLife Extension Service information)

www.bayoucityheirloombulbs.com

www.bulbsociety.org

www.easterlily.org

www.onlineplantguide.com

www.pacificbulbsociety.org

www.southernbulbs.com

www.plants.usda.gov

The following sites include information on forced bulbs:

www.brentandbeckysbulbs.com

www.bulb.com

www.daffodilusa.org

www.davesgarden.com

www.extension.iastate.edu

www.marthastewart.com

www.oldhousegardens.com

ONLINE (HISTORIC SITES)

AMERICAN CEMETERY, Natchitoches, LA: www.nps.gov/history/nr/travel/caneriver/ame.htm

BARTRAM'S GARDEN: www.BartramsGarden.org

BAYOU BEND: www.mfah.org/bayoubend

BELMONT: www.umw.edu/belm/

DeGOYLER HOUSE: www.dallasarboretum.org/Gardens/DeGolyer_Gardens.htm

EUDORA WELTY HOUSE: http://mdah.state.ms.us/welty/garden.html

GOODWOOD PLANTATION: www.goodwoodmuseum.org/gardens.php

LOCKERLY HALL and ARBORETUM: www.lockerly.org

MELROSE PLANTATION, Natchez, MS: www.nps.gov/natc/historyculture/places.htm

OLD CITY CEMETERY, Lynchburg, VA: www.gravegarden.org

ST. ANDREW'S EPISCOPAL CHURCH, Houston, TX: www.saintandrewsepiscopal.org

STRATFORD HALL: www.stratfordhall.org

PHOTO CREDITS

Unless otherwise noted, all photographs taken by the authors and artists of *Heirloom Bulbs for Today*.

COVER:
Courtesy of *Southern Living Magazine* (©2008 Southern Living, Inc., Reprinted with permission); photo by Ralph Anderson

FOREWORDS:
Page 5 – Susan Northrup Eldredge
Page 9 & 159 – Gerda Barry, from her gardens in the Drakensberg Mountains, South Africa

GROUP I:
Page 25 – Hunter, Clementine. "A Bouquet of Three Spider Lilies", courtesy Thomas N. Whitehead Collection; special thanks to Ben Collins and Kathy Whitehead for their knowledge of Ms. Hunter's work
Page 28 – John Wiesinger
Page 30 – Goodwood Museum and Gardens, Amanda C. Hammerli
Page 38 & 39 – Stratford Hall and Ken McFarland
Page 44 – Bayou Bend, Museum of Fine Arts - Houston
Page 54 & 55 – Jane Baber White
Page 74 – Ben Arcuni

GROUP II:
Page 77 & 81 (N. 'Telemonius Plenus') – J. Drew Mc Farland
Page 78 & 79 – Belmont Estate and Beate' Jensen
Page 80 & 81 ©John Bartram Association, Bartram's Garden, Philadelphia, PA
Page 81 (*Franklinia alatamaha*) – Jeff McMillian, www.almostedenplants.com
Page 86 & 87 – Melrose Estate, Natchez National Historical Park
Page 92 & 93 – Eudora Welty House by Charles H. Byrd, Jackson, MS
Page 95 & 96 – Abe Vermaak, Drakensberg Mountains, South Africa
Page 96 - Monet, Claude (1840-1926). Garden at Sainte-Adresse. 1867. Oil on canvas, 38 5/8 x 51 1/8 in (98.1 x 129.9 cm). Purchase, special contributions and funds given or bequeathed by friends of the Museum, 1967 (67.241), The Metropolitan Museum of Art, New York, NY, U.S.A. Image copyright © The Metropolitan Museum of Art/Art Resource, NY
Page 119 (St. Andrew's Episcopal Church) – courtesy of Cheryl D. Duffin and www.saintandrewsepiscopal.org
Page 124 – Lockerly Arboretum and James M. Garner

GROUP III:
Page 146 – Dallas Arboretum and Jimmy Turner
Page 143 & 165 – Ceramic tea set, courtesy of Anthropologie (www.anthropologie.com)
Page 156 – (*Zephyranthes drummondii*) - Jason McKenzie

INDEX

RED CABIN PLAN

*S*ince I spend so much time either at the bulb farm or on the road, I've been unable to "put down roots" here at the cabin. But now I'm at a new phase in my life. When Cherie brought Loela and Johan to visit me in Golden, we had the opportunity to spend time outside under the huge post oaks, envisioning a new garden for my home.

In order to design a sustainable landscape at this location, several issues had to be addressed. Between the cows browsing, the sink draining, the grasshoppers chomping and my hectic schedule, it seemed I should just leave well enough alone. But Cherie and Loela convinced me I could have the best of all worlds, including a garden plan that fit into the natural environment. Here is the plan Cherie designed and Loela drew up for the red cabin. In the next few pages you'll visit me in each season of the year and see how the garden changes. You'll also see Cherie's notes about what to expect and why she chose certain plants and features for my new landscape.

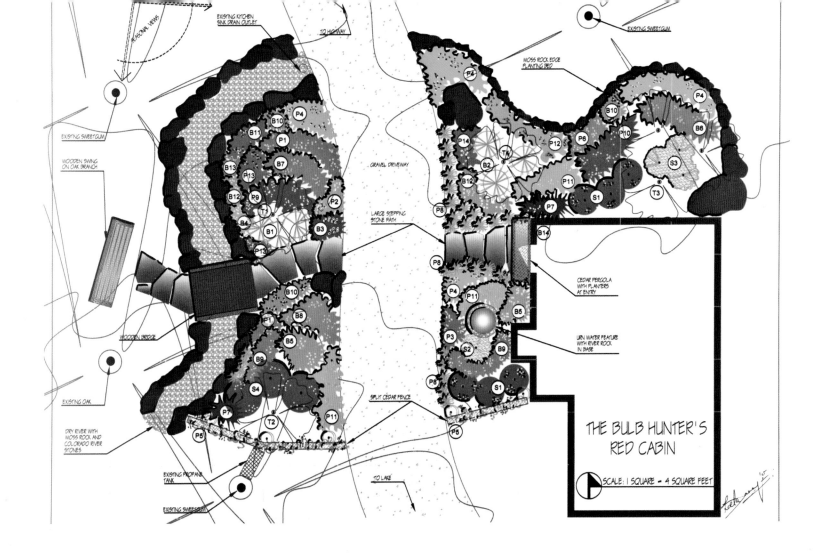

THE BULB HUNTER'S RED CABIN

SCALE: 1 SQUARE = 4 SQUARE FEET

PLAN KEY	BULBS	BLOOMING SEASON
B1	*Crinum* 'Ellen Bosanquet'	Summer
B2	*Crinum* 'Mrs. James Hendry'	Spring
B3	*Gladiolus communis* subsp. *byzantinus* (hardy gladiola)	Spring
B4	*Habranthus robustus* (Argentine rain lily)	Spring
B5	*Iris albicans* (cemetery white iris)	Spring
B6	*Narcissus* 'Golden Dawn'	Spring
B7	*Narcissus x odorus* Campernelle	Winter
B8	*Leucojum aestivum* 'Gravetye Giant' (snowflake)	Winter
B9	*Lilium longiflorum* (Easter lily)	Spring
B10	*Lycoris radiata* (red spider lily) / *Lycoris squamigera* (Magic Lily)	Autumn
B11	*Muscari neglectum* (grape hyacinth)	Winter
B12	*Zephyranthes candida* (rain lily)	Spring
B13	*Sternbergia Lutea* (Autumn Crocus)	Autumn
B14	Forced bulbs in planter boxes of arbor	

PLAN KEY	BULBS
P1	*Achillea* 'Moonshine' (Greek yarrow)
P2	*Ajuga reptans* 'Rosea'
P3	*Dianthus caryophyllus* 'Juliet'
P4	*Glandularia Canadensis* 'Blue Princess' (verbena)
P5	*Lonicera sempervirens* (coral honeysuckle)
P6	*Lysimachia nummularia* 'Aurea' (creeping jenny)
P7	*Muhlenbergia rigida/Miscanthus sinensis* (muhly grass/Japanese silver grass)
P8	*Ophiopogon japonicus* 'Nana' (dwarf mondo grass)
P9	*Phlox divaricata* (blue phlox)
P10	*Phlox paniculata* (fall phlox)
P11	*Rudbeckia hirta* 'Goldsturm' (black-eyed susan)
P12	*Salvia farinacea/Lavendula angustifolia* (blue sage/lavender)
P13	*Hylotelephium* 'Autumn Delight'

PLAN KEY	BULBS
S1	*Buddlia davidii* 'Black Knight' (butterfly bush)
T1	*Cercis canadensis* (redbud tree)
T2	*Chionanthus virginicus* (fringe tree)
T3	*Lagerstroemia indica* 'Natchez' (white crape myrtle tree)
S2	*Philadelphus* (mock orange)
S3	*Spiraea prunifolia* 'Plena' (bridalwreath spiraea)
S4	*Viburnum rufidulum* (rusty blackhaw)
T4	*Vitex agnus-castus* (vitex, chaste tree)

AUTUMN

Fall at the Red Cabin brings cooling rains and a color palette of reds and yellows. Tree leaves turn shades of red and yellow too, including hot red on the 'Natchez' crape myrtles and vibrant yellow on the fringe tree. Yellow autumn crocus and red spider lily repeat the favor on either side of the cabin.

WINTER

Wooden structures bring color of their own to the garden in winter, as well as keep the cattle from munching tender plants. Visitors to the cabin are welcomed by forced bulbs in the new entry arbor planters. Although much of the garden sleeps, yellow buds begin to emerge as countless daffodils proclaim spring is ahead.

SPRING

Daily, new blooms emerge with every color now abounding throughout the garden. Masses of single plants or similarly colored blooms are powerful, so neighbors driving by can appreciate the garden from afar. The dry river allowing for run-off of gray water from the kitchen sink also catches heavy rains from the sloping drive, causing rain lilies to burst into bloom.

SUMMER

Butterflies and hummingbirds have found a new home at the cabin, thankful for the habitat created for them. Vines ambling up the entry arbor give relief from the heat. Collected rainwater bubbles up from the olive jar fountain near the door. Soon the garden will rest again. But for now, it is alive with color and sound. Across the footbridge, the swing hanging from the oak tree provides a place to pause and enjoy the garden.

ACKNOWLEDGEMENTS

Cherie has diligently worked to get information and anecdotes out of me. Loela's detailed portraits of profiled plants show each element with beautiful accuracy, and her designs for creating living arrangements with the bulbs showcase a unique way to let bulbs brighten our lives. Johan's intimate botanical photography captures details rarely seen. Without the creative gifts of these three, the stories these magnificent bulbs have to tell would still be bumping around in my truck with me. I am grateful to them for making this book a reality, and to Bright Sky Press for understanding how important it was for me to share this information with you.

My thanks also go to my mentor and friend, Dr. Bill Welch, for his continued advice throughout this bulb project of mine, now going into its seventh year. Sally Ferguson and the International Flower Bulb Center were incredibly generous with their time. Brent Heath, Linda and Sara Van Beck, and Jason Delaney provided great assistance on nomenclature and history.

My heartfelt gratitude to you all.

Soil Ecoregions – Continental US

This map is based on the Level III Ecoregions of the Continental United States map, revised 2007,
National Health and Environmental Effects Research Laboratory, U.S. Environmental Protection Agency

1. Coast Range
2. Puget Lowland
3. Willamette Valley
4. Cascades
5. Sierra Nevada
6. Southern and Central California Chaparral and Oak Woodlands
7. Central California Valley
8. Southern California Mountains
9. Eastern Cascades Slopes and Foothills
10. Columbia Plateau
11. Blue Mountains
12. Snake River Plain
13. Central Basin and Range
14. Mojave Basin and Range
15. Northern Rockies
16. Idaho Batholith
17. Middle Rockies
18. Wyoming Basin
19. Wasatch and Uinta Mountains
20. Colorado Plateaus
21. Southern Rockies

22. Arizona/New Mexico Plateau
23. Arizona/New Mexico Mountains
24. Chihuahuan Deserts
25. High Plains
26. Southwestern Tablelands
27. Central Great Plains
28. Flint Hills
29. Cross Timbers
30. Edwards Plateau
31. Southern Texas Plains
32. Texas Blackland Prairies
33. East Central Texas Plains
34. Western Gulf Coastal Plain
35. South Central Plains
36. Ouachita Mountains
37. Arkansas Valley
38. Boston Mountains
39. Ozark Highlands
40. Central Irregular Plains
41. Canadian Rockies
42. Northwestern Glaciated Plains
43. Northwestern Great Plains

44. Nebraska Sand Hills
45. Piedmont
46. Northern Glaciated Plains
47. Western Corn Belt Plains
48. Lake Agassiz Plain
49. Northern Minnesota Wetlands
50. Northern Lakes and Forests
51. North Central Hardwood Forests
52. Driftless Area
53. Southeastern Wisconsin Till Plains
54. Central Corn Belt Plains
55. Eastern Corn Belt Plains
56. Southern Michigan/ Northern Indiana Drift Plains
57. Huron/Erie Lake Plains
58. Northeastern Highlands
59. Northeastern Coastal Zone
60. Northern Appalachian Plateau and Uplands
61. Erie Drift Plain
62. North Central Appalachians
63. Middle Atlantic Coastal Plain
64. Northern Piedmont

65. Southeastern Plains
66. Blue Ridge
67. Ridge and Valley
68. Southwestern Appalachians
69. Central Appalachians
70. Western Allegheny Plateau
71. Interior Plateau
72. Interior River Valleys and Hills
73. Mississippi Alluvial Plain
74. Mississippi Valley Loess Plains
75. Southern Coastal Plain
76. Southern Florida Coastal Plain
77. North Cascades
78. Klamath Mountains
79. Madrean Archipelago
80. Northern Basin and Range
81. Sonoran Basin and Range
82. Laurentian Plains and Hills
83. Eastern Great Lakes and Hudson Lowlands
84. Atlantic Coastal Pine Barrens

Plant Cold Hardiness Zones – Continental US

This map is based on the USDA Plant Hardiness Zone Map, Agricultural Research Service, USDA

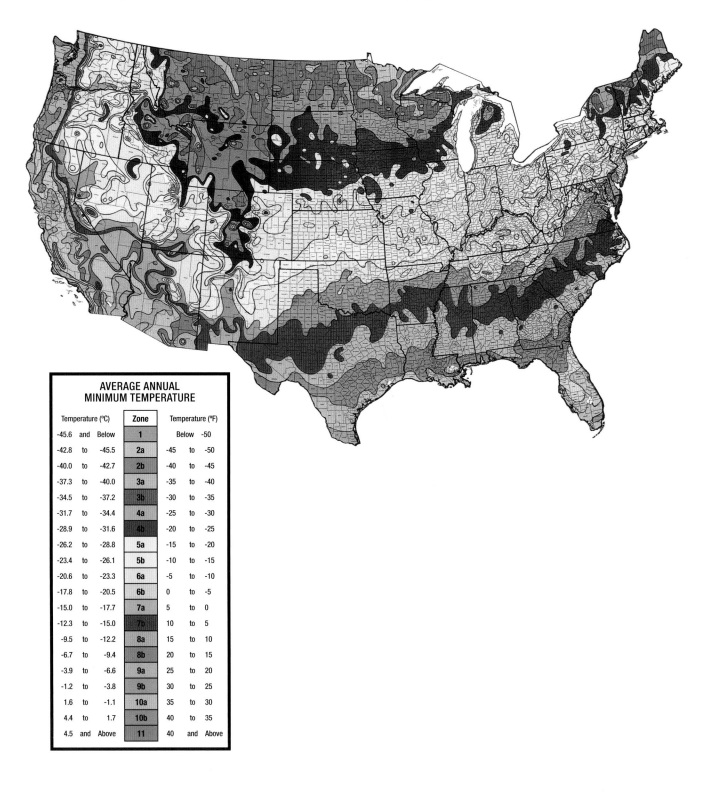

AVERAGE ANNUAL MINIMUM TEMPERATURE

Temperature (°C)			Zone	Temperature (°F)		
-45.6	and	Below	1	Below		-50
-42.8	to	-45.5	2a	-45	to	-50
-40.0	to	-42.7	2b	-40	to	-45
-37.3	to	-40.0	3a	-35	to	-40
-34.5	to	-37.2	3b	-30	to	-35
-31.7	to	-34.4	4a	-25	to	-30
-28.9	to	-31.6	4b	-20	to	-25
-26.2	to	-28.8	5a	-15	to	-20
-23.4	to	-26.1	5b	-10	to	-15
-20.6	to	-23.3	6a	-5	to	-10
-17.8	to	-20.5	6b	0	to	-5
-15.0	to	-17.7	7a	5	to	0
-12.3	to	-15.0	7b	10	to	5
-9.5	to	-12.2	8a	15	to	10
-6.7	to	-9.4	8b	20	to	15
-3.9	to	-6.6	9a	25	to	20
-1.2	to	-3.8	9b	30	to	25
1.6	to	-1.1	10a	35	to	30
4.4	to	1.7	10b	40	to	35
4.5	and	Above	11	40	and	Above